Competition Law and Economic Regulation

Competition Law and Economic Regulation

Addressing Market Power in Southern Africa

Edited by **Jonathan Klaaren**
Simon Roberts
Imraan Valodia

WITS UNIVERSITY PRESS

Published in South Africa by:

Wits University Press
1 Jan Smuts Avenue
Johannesburg, 2001
www.witspress.co.za

978-1-77614-090-9 (print)
978-1-77614-091-6 (PDF)
978-1-77614-168-5 (EPUB North & South America, China)
978-1-77614-169-2 (Rest of World)
978-1-77614-200-2 (Open Access web PDF)

Project managed by Inga Norenius
Edited by Lee Smith
Proofread by Inga Norenius
Index by Tessa Botha
Cover design by Hothouse South Africa
Typeset by MPS Ltd

Contents

Part Four: Conclusion

Tables, figures and boxes

Acknowledgements

This book comprises contributions from active academics and practitioners in the field and we wish to thank each of them for their efforts. We are grateful for their diligent and timely submission of drafts and edits. We are also grateful to all the participants in the African Competition and Economic Regulation conference held in Victoria Falls, Zimbabwe, in March 2015, some of whom presented valuable work that could not be included here. Thanks are also due to our partner in this event, the Competition and Tariff Commission of Zimbabwe. In addition, we wish to thank the Research Project on Employment, Income Distribution and Inclusive Growth (REDI3x3) for supporting the work published in Chapter 8. We are grateful to Zapiro for permission to reproduce the cartoon in Chapter 3, as well as the National Research Foundation for funding the rights to the cartoon. The University of Johannesburg's Research Committee and the National Research Foundation supported the publication of the book as a whole. Finally, we appreciate and wish to acknowledge the careful and professional work of the Wits University Press team.

Jonathan Klaaren
Simon Roberts
Imraan Valodia

Acronyms and abbreviations

ACER	Annual Competition and Economic Regulation
BLNS	Botswana, Lesotho, Namibia, Swaziland
CAC	Competition Appeal Court
CCC	Complaints and Compliance Committee
CCRED	Centre for Competition, Regulation and Economic Development
CCSA	Competition Commission of South Africa
CLP	Corporate Leniency Policy
Comesa	Common Market for Eastern and Southern Africa
CSP	concentrated solar power
DoE	Department of Energy
DPE	Department of Public Enterprises
dti	Department of Trade and Industry
EC	European Commission
ERP	effective rate of protection
ESI	electricity supply industry
EU	European Union
FRA	Food Reserve Agency
GM	genetically modified
GTAZ	Grain Traders' Association of Zambia
Icasa	Independent Communications Authority of South Africa
IPP	independent power producer
ISMO	Independent Systems and Market Operator
LLU	local loop unbundling
LRCE	long-run competitive equilibrium
MFN	most favoured nation
MMT	mobile money transfer
MNO	mobile network operator
MYPD	Multi-Year Price Determination
MW	megawatt
Nersa	National Energy Regulator of South Africa
NPA	National Ports Authority
Potraz	Postal and Telecommunications Regulatory Authority of Zimbabwe
PPA	power purchase agreement
R&D	research and development
RAS	Regulatory Accounting System
RBZ	Reserve Bank of Zimbabwe
REFIT	Renewable Energy Feed-In Tariff
REIPPPP	Renewable Energy Independent Power Producers Procurement Programme
RIA	regional integration agreement
SACU	Southern African Customs Union

SADC	Southern African Development Community
SCI	Sasol Chemical Industries
SOE	state-owned enterprise
TNPA	Transnet National Ports Authority
UNCTAD	United Nations Conference on Trade and Development
USSD	Unstructured Supplementary Service Data
ZCTC	Zimbabwe Competition and Tariff Commission

Introduction: The development of competition and regulation in southern Africa

Jonathan Klaaren, Simon Roberts and Imraan Valodia

Introduction

In March 2015, South Africa's Centre for Competition, Regulation and Economic Development (CCRED) partnered with the Zimbabwe Competition and Tariff Commission to host the inaugural Annual Competition and Economic Regulation (ACER) week at Victoria Falls in Zimbabwe. Much of the success of the week was in combining rigorous training led by regional and global experts with a conference programme that was designed with inputs from authorities in the region to make sure it was topical and directly relevant. The discussions were especially vibrant and the subject matter of particular relevance to solving the challenges of enforcement and growth for agencies in the southern African region and beyond. The papers in this volume were selected from those presented at the ACER conference, following a rigorous refereeing process.

The period since the early 1990s has seen the emergence and consolidation of competition and regulation authorities in a number of countries across the continent. This volume aims to play a role in critically analysing key competition issues and in considering the interface of competition and a range of economic policy questions. The papers we collected and edited for presentation in this volume fit into three clusters: cartel law enforcement, issues in competition and regulation, and competition and regulation in reshaping African markets. The conclusion, a substantive chapter in its own right, addresses competition and regional integration as part of an inclusive growth agenda for Africa.

The areas covered here show that there are complex and interesting developments in the competition and regulation space within the region. There is thus a clear need for an overall assessment and for measures to foster the development of a body of knowledge and literature that originates from the experiences of countries in the region, rather than relying exclusively on international precedent and learnings. One example of this is Thula Kaira's discussion in chapter 3 of the poor translation of cartel findings in South Africa into follow-on investigations and prosecution in neighbouring countries in the Southern African Customs Union and the Southern African Development Community (SADC), and ultimately into damage claims based on an assessment of the overcharge to consumers across borders.

The emphasis of this volume, and of what we hope will be similar research going forward, is thus on developing African case studies to contribute to the international literature in this area, for training and knowledge-sharing purposes. These issues are of interest from both an academic and a practitioner perspective. They are particularly relevant in terms of regional economic development where countries in the region often face the same challenges of small, concentrated markets with barriers to entry that are especially high and where the resources to enforce measures against anticompetitive conduct are limited.

Where do competition law, economics and policy fit within new development strategies for Africa?

It is worthwhile to identify and interact with some of the broader literature within which the chapters in this volume should be viewed. We are particularly interested in what might be termed the competition–economic development interface. Our departure point here is the envisioning work of Eleanor Fox (2003). The questions we ask are: How do competition law, economics and policy fit within new development strategies for Africa and what strategies, in the competition and regulation space, are needed to improve the efficacy of these policies to generate improved economic development outcomes? A number of the chapters in this volume delve into this issue, especially so in the concluding piece by Simon Roberts, Thando Vilakazi and Witness Simbanegavi ('Competition, regional integration and inclusive growth in Africa: A research agenda').

There has been a welcome trend in recent years towards analysis and thinking about African development in an evidence-based, critical and globally informed yet Africa-located fashion. One example is the volume titled *Good Growth and Governance in Africa: Rethinking Development Strategies* (Noman, Botchwey, Stein and Stiglitz, 2012). Analysis in this new vein is based upon economic evidence and thinking but is nonetheless capacious enough to attend to the institutional and political aspects of economic growth and development strategies in Africa that are in our experience both impossible to avoid and necessary to understand.

Institutions of economic governance are central to addressing the factors affecting and holding back the growth of African economies, including the distorting effects of the apartheid-era management of the growth of the South African economy. There are tools, practices and resources from which to work. And, there are a set of governance agencies – a number of them prominent among the institutions present at the ACER conference – which are dedicated to the inclusive growth of the economies in the region. Indeed, the assumption of ACER is that these agencies are capable of playing a more active role in promoting development, within their institutional and political constraints.

Mushtaq Khan (2012a, b) has framed these debates in a way that seems relevant for the southern African region. His contribution starts with an appropriate attention to methodological detail, treating one of the most influential contributions of the market-enhancing economists, the work of Daron Acemoglu, Simon Johnson and James Robinson (2001). Their work has particular relevance for southern Africa due to its attention to the economic consequences and development prospects and pathways of settler and non-settler societies. Acemoglu, Johnson and Robinson's work focuses on property rights and other institutions as determinants of growth and is particularly distinctive for its methodological innovations, such as the use of mortality rates. Khan argues that their methodological innovations do not justify their assertion that stable property rights causally explain the relatively better economic development 100 years after the arrival of white settlers. Instead, as he puts it, 'the transitions here were not periods of stable property rights but the absolute reverse. They were periods of systematic, widespread and violent destruction of almost all pre-existing rights because these rights did not serve the interests of settlers who were setting up capitalist economies in their own interest' (Khan, 2012b, p. 71). Instead of a clamour for immediate (and expensive) stable property rights, Khan argues in favour of 'governance capabilities to manage property rights over many valuable resources that will remain weakly defined during early stages of development' as well as 'complementary governance capabilities on the part of the state to manage incentives and opportunities for technological catching up, while creating compulsions for entrepreneurs not to waste resources' (Khan, 2012b, pp. 74–75). The mining camp that was Johannesburg of the nineteenth century did not become Johannesburg aspiring to world-class status in the twenty-first century through strict adherence to good governance practices.

These particular prescriptions may be put within a more general analysis of two contrasting (and competing) approaches to the place of governance within development and development strategies (Khan, 2012a). One is the market-enhancing approach and one is the growth-promoting approach. Those espousing the market-enhancing approach argue that 'the lack of democratic accountability and the presence of patron-client politics, extensive corruption and a weak rule of law had a lot to do with Africa's relatively poor performance' (Khan, 2012a, p. 115). The alternative growth-promoting approach at times calls for ambitious growth-promoting strategies such as those associated with East Asian economies like South Korea (Khan, 2012a).

While the centre of gravity is certainly on the growth-promoting side of this divide, the call is itself nuanced – '[t]o take account of the limited reform capabilities in real contexts, a targeted approach to developing governance capabilities makes sense' (Khan, 2012a, p. 115). Khan's argument is for incremental approaches to governance reform. Specifically, this means paying attention to addressing market failures affecting investment in new sectors and technologies, to enhancing and upgrading labour skills and training, and to identifying specific land bottlenecks and developing moderately efficient agencies to address land-use problems.

We see our steering comments in this chapter and the particular empirical studies of our contributors in the chapters that follow as responding to Khan's call for specific determinations of what the pathways, agencies and sectors are that will allow for dynamic (and as yet unforeseen) economic growth paths. In a nutshell, one could call these new-generation strategies of industrial policy.

This discussion leaves us with the issue of where competition law and policy fit within the active role for the state envisioned thus far. To explore the competition law and policy interface with industrial policy and to do so in a regional context, we begin with the work of Eleanor Fox. In general, Fox's work challenges competition practitioners and researchers to move beyond a narrow conception of competition enforcement in terms of the investigation and litigation of cases. Such work should instead be contextualised within the bigger picture of making markets work as tools for giving the poorest people in the world access to fundamental needs and granting people the dignity of participating and sharing in the economy (CCRED, 2015). As would of course be the case with a number of analysts, Fox's work might be appropriated in service of a market-enhancing as well as a growth-promoting approach to governance. We are drawn to her pragmatism and her capacity to accept that the ideal institutional arrangements, perhaps of best fit with what she terms 'pure competition', are not necessarily what is appropriate for limited-capacity states in Africa. In this sense, her work complements that of Khan.

Fox's work talks to the chapters in this volume in understanding how institutional choices are made and the way they impact on the development of the regime of competition and economic regulation within, and across, countries. For example, penalising and deterring cartels involves taking on large vested interests. While high penalties may be required, it is difficult to impose these too early in the life of a young competition regime. It first has to establish its credibility. Regulation may also be required to nurture effective rivalry and support investment, or it might protect incumbents.

The challenges of competition law enforcement globally are outlined by Fox (2003) as a set of futures of international competition law in her article 'International Antitrust and the DOHA Dome'. These futures are particularly relevant to the southern African region. Indeed, this region itself has connections in particular with the East African Community and is part of the tripartite free trade area now in the process of being established.

Fox begins her analysis with economics, detailing four categories of problems for developing countries with the default institution of nation-by-nation enforcement of competition regimes. These problems are:

(1) Developing countries cannot protect themselves from world cartels, and those harms spill over to the rest of the world. (2) Discovery and information problems abound; information needed for enforcement is beyond reach. While industrialized countries can ease the problems by bilateral agreements, developing countries do not have the clout to obtain such cooperation. (3) Exploitative and protectionist national industrial policies trump antitrust. State action slips through the cracks of the WTO

[World Trade Organization]; states 'privatize protection.' (4) Nations do not have enforcement incentives commensurate with world welfare; indeed, nation-to-nation reciprocity can lead to world-welfare reducing solutions. (Fox, 2003, pp. 927–928)

Hers is indeed a big-picture view, albeit one aware of its own place in that big picture and alive to the need for collective feasible action.

In that spirit, Fox looks into the feasibility and desirability of adopting some form of global competition governance, noting the strong support for such a measure. In her view, there are three distinct possibilities:

First, the strong form would establish a complete antitrust [e.g., competition] regime for matters significantly affecting world commerce, possibly even encompassing a world antitrust enforcement system and court. This regime might or might not be integrated with trade; it might be 'antitrust on its own bottom.' A second model would envision a framework measure sensitive to the trade-and-competition context. A third approach is a minimal form of the second model combined with certain 'on the ground' tasks such as technical assistance and peer review. (Fox, 2003, p. 926)

Putting the identified problems together with the available solutions, Fox displays vision and pragmatism, recognising that the time of the first model has not yet arrived, that the second model is her preferred due to its addressing the most pressing underlying economic issue, and ultimately opting for the third as within the capabilities of states such as those in Africa. Her preference for the second model of a European Union-style framework measure at a global level is based on its ability to 'utilize the trade law concepts that discipline government action in restraint of trade [and how it would then] focus on the most critical problems of private and public/private transnational restraints that cannot be solved horizontally because of nationalistic impulses' (Fox, 2003, p. 926). The working cutting edge in the details of these analyses – Khan's and Fox's – perhaps lies in the identification of which industrial policy measures are 'exploitative and nationalistic' and which are feasible and facilitative for economies to play catch-up in a globalised and competitive economy.

Even if there are not such precise prescriptions given, we see evidence, in the chapters presented here and elsewhere, of a clear common thread in the thinking of practitioners and researchers in terms of leveraging the enforcement muscle, reputation and scope of competition regimes to contribute to reversing patterns of stagnant economic growth and high barriers to participation that have left so many in Africa in a state of dire poverty. In this sense, the research covered here aims to respect and fulfil the socioeconomic rights, among other fundamental needs of individuals, which are enshrined in the constitutions of South Africa and many other countries in southern and eastern Africa.

Overview of chapters and their relationship to the theme question

Below we provide some of the direct linkages between the general points we have explored in the previous section and the specific arguments and research provided in the next 11 chapters of this volume.

Cartel law enforcement

The first cluster of chapters investigates the efficacy of the South African competition authority to counter the harmful effects of cartels, which respect no boundaries.

In this vein, chapter 1 by Tapera Muzata, Simon Roberts and Thando Vilakazi, 'Penalties and settlements for South African cartels: An economic review', examines the notable success of the corporate leniency policy in uncovering cartel conduct in South Africa. They focus on the importance of high-powered incentives for colluding firms to break ranks as well as the ongoing extent of collusive activity. The chapter sets out how cartel penalties can be understood in terms of the basic economic theory relating to deterrence and incentives and reviews how the Competition Commission has approached penalties, which have mainly been in the form of settlements.

Chapter 2 by Ratshidaho Maphwanya, 'Cartel likelihood, duration and deterrence in South Africa', studies factors in deterrence through a survey of law firms. The analysis factors in durability and duration of cartels from a set of uncovered cartels. In each area, Maphwanya replicates international studies, enabling comparisons of South Africa with international experience. The ability to conduct such comparisons allows for both measuring and improving the enforcement capability that African competition regimes possess.

Chapter 3 by Thula Kaira, 'Cartel enforcement in the southern African neighbourhood', reviews cartels uncovered in South Africa with apparent regional scope. Significantly, Kaira assesses enforcement in other SADC countries, noting that for the most part these countries did not investigate or uncover the collusion. Mostly, the authorities did not investigate the same markets. As Kaira points out, this begs the important question of why not. Various lessons are drawn, including the value of countries within SADC having a leniency policy as well as robust powers of search and seizure. The chapter demonstrates the significant yet limited capabilities of African competition authorities.

Issues in competition and regulation

Chapter 4 by Reena das Nair and Pamela Mondliwa, 'Excessive pricing under the spotlight: What is a competitive price?', considers the contentious *Mittal* and *SCI* excessive pricing cases. The chapter 'test drives' the Competition Appeal Court decision in *Mittal* on the *SCI* case, presenting a thorough analysis. It asks the key question of whether the price bore a reasonable relationship or constituted abuse of dominance. The significance of dealing appropriately with large, powerful, state-owned incumbent firms is heightened in a regional context where, as noted in the conclusion, the effects of the lack of competition may be significant.

Chapter 5 by Reena das Nair and Simon Roberts, 'Competition and regulation interface in energy, telecommunications and transport in South Africa', analyses the relationship between competition and regulation through a critical assessment of the work of economic regulators and the competition authorities in South Africa in the core areas of energy, telecommunications and transport. The authors draw on working papers done as part of an in-depth review of economic regulation coordinated by CCRED for national government during 2014. The chapter argues that economic regulators should take into account the dynamic gains from greater competitive rivalry when setting rules and making decisions. It concludes that regulation that is conducive to creating 'synthetic competition' by ensuring the participation of several competitors has shown positive outcomes in terms of the dynamic gains from rivalry in the renewable energy subsector of energy and in the ports subsector of transport. The chapter thus continues to explore the productive overlap of competition law and policy with economic development.

Competition and regulation in reshaping African markets

Chapter 6 by Nicholas Sitko and Brian Chisanga, 'How multinational investments in grain trading are reshaping Zambia's market', reviews the trend and implications of multinational corporations in Zambia in grain trading in terms of effects on independent wholesalers, margins and farmers. The chapter finds that these investments have proved beneficial, resulting in declining wholesale market margins, increased trustworthiness and professionalism in the sector, and enhanced advocacy for predictable agricultural policies. However, there are competition aspects to these trade and investment flows that must be taken into account in an economic development perspective. If poorly managed, these developments could spark industry consolidation and a reversal of these positive gains.

Chapter 7 by Anthea Paelo, Genna Robb and Thando Vilakazi, 'Competition and incumbency in South Africa's liquid fuel value chain', analyses competition issues in the liquid fuels industry, especially with respect to the wholesale and retail level, in relationship to the oil majors. The authors draw on a recent study based on interviews with market participants and on publicly available sources to assess the nature and extent of barriers to entry and expansion of firms in the wholesale of liquid fuels. Their analysis focuses on access to supply, to customers and to key infrastructure, as well as policy and regulatory challenges rather than the known shortage of skills and finance in the sector. They suggest a set of short- and long-term remedies for increasing access and competition in transportation and storage, as well as wholesaling infrastructure, thus promoting inclusive growth.

Chapter 8 by Gaylor Montmasson-Clair and Reena das Nair, 'South Africa's renewable energy experience: Inclusive growth lessons', investigates the interplay between economic regulation, competition policy and inclusive growth in South Africa, using a case study on South Africa's utility-scale renewable energy sector. Through South Africa's Renewable Energy Independent Power Producer Procurement Programme, the South African government is procuring utility-scale renewable energy-based electricity generation capacity from independent power producers. The scheme was specifically crafted (through economic regulation) to promote competitive outcomes and foster inclusive growth and the chapter assesses outcomes in the sector through both an economic regulation and an inclusive growth lens. The early attention to competition concerns in the regulation of this sector should serve as a model for other sectors within and among SADC member states.

Chapter 9 by Genna Robb, Isaac Tausha and Thando Vilakazi, 'Competition and regulation in Zimbabwe's emerging mobile payments markets', argues that mobile money transfer in Zimbabwe has given rise to greater financial inclusion but also to potential competition problems. With a 65% market share in the mobile network operator market and a market share of over 90% in the mobile payments market, the dominant firm is in a strong position to exploit network externalities. The situation is similar in other SADC countries. The chapter thus concludes by noting the worth of a cooperative approach among Zimbabwe regulators. This market is a prime example of one where attention to inclusive growth and to dynamic competition can dovetail with efficient market policy.

Chapter 10 by Tatenda Zengeni, 'Evaluating the competitiveness of Zimbabwe's poultry industry', also looks at trade and competitiveness issues in Zimbabwe. It provides a detailed account of the poultry industry, which is a significant one to the Zimbabwean economy. The factors affecting competitiveness in this industry include stiff competition from cheap imports, rising input costs of maize and soya meal and illegal imports being sold at subeconomic prices. Complementing the grain trade focus of the Zambian case study, the chapter evaluates these factors and the impact of changing trade protection in Zimbabwe.

Chapter 11 by Simon Roberts, Thando Vilakazi and Witness Simbanegavi, 'Competition, regional integration and inclusive growth in Africa: A research agenda', focuses on the interface of competition, inclusive growth and regional integration. It considers recent developments in competition economics alongside the record of competition enforcement and political economy factors, drawing on research on key sectors. Moving beyond the level of detail in this introduction, the authors explore and emphasise the regional dimensions of anticompetitive arrangements stretching across countries, in oligopolistic industries often dominated by the same large multinational firms. This points to the critical need for cross-country research and collaboration to understand the arrangements as part of an agenda to promote market outcomes for more inclusive growth.

References

Acemoglu D, S Johnson and JA Robinson. 2001. The colonial origins of comparative development: An empirical investigation. *American Economic Review* 91: 1369–1401.

CCRED (Centre for Competition, Regulation and Economic Development). 2015. 'Exclusionary practices: Is marginalisation easier than the law "thinks" it is?' Public lecture by Eleanor Fox, Johannesburg, 23 July.

Fox EM. 2003. International antitrust and the Doha dome. *Virginia Journal of International Law* 43: 911–932.

Khan MH. 2012a. Governance and growth challenges for Africa. In A Noman, K Botchwey, H Stein and J Stiglitz (eds), *Good Growth and Governance in Africa: Rethinking Development Strategies*, pp. 114–139. Oxford: Oxford University Press.

Khan MH. 2012b. Governance and growth: History, ideology and methods of proof. In A Noman, K Botchwey, H Stein and J Stiglitz (eds), *Good Growth and Governance in Africa: Rethinking Development Strategies*, pp. 51–79. Oxford: Oxford University Press.

Noman A, K Botchwey, H Stein and JE Stiglitz (eds). 2012. *Good Growth and Governance in Africa: Rethinking Development Strategies*. Oxford: Oxford University Press.

Part One

Cartel law enforcement

1 Penalties and settlements for South African cartels: An economic review

Tapera Muzata, Simon Roberts and Thando Vilakazi

Introduction

The South African competition authorities have developed a fairly extensive track record in penalising cartels. While the Competition Act (No. 89 of 1998) came into force in September 1999, in practice cartels really started being uncovered only after the Competition Commission of South Africa's (CCSA) adoption of a corporate leniency programme in 2004 and the programme's amendment in 2008 (Lavoie, 2010; Makhaya, Mkwananzi and Roberts, 2012). Since then there have been a large number of cases (see also World Bank and ACF, 2016), and the experience provides interesting insight into the challenges faced in making decisions regarding the appropriate penalties. In 2011 and 2012, the Competition Tribunal and the Competition Appeal Court (CAC) made a series of decisions around the issues and relevant principles for determining penalties for collusion. And, from 2012 to 2014, the CCSA undertook an extensive 'fast-track settlement' process for collusion by construction companies involving lower penalties in exchange for an 'all-in' settlement of bid-rigging conduct (Roberts, 2014). With criminal sanctions for collusive conduct coming into force in 2016, it is also a good point to assess the penalties under the administrative regime up until that point.

The Corporate Leniency Policy's (CLP) notable success in uncovering cartel conduct in South Africa has highlighted both the importance of high-powered incentives for colluding firms to break ranks and come forward, as well as the ongoing extent of collusive activity. The latter suggests that the combined effect of the penalties and the probability of getting caught were previously too low to achieve the necessary deterrent effect. In chapter 2 of this volume, Ratshidaho Maphwanya addresses leniency and other factors underlying the durability of cartels.

We consider the decisions of the Tribunal and CAC through the lens of economic principles and the implications for evolving standards for penalties, and set out how cartel penalties can be understood in terms of the basic economic theory relating to deterrence and incentives. We then review how the CCSA has approached penalties, which have mainly been in the form of settlements.

Settlement implies a lower penalty in exchange for cooperation and early resolution. Our review includes a brief discussion of the construction settlements.
We then critically assess the record on determining penalties in settlements and
contested cases, taking into account evidence on the size of cartel mark-ups in
South African cases. The concluding section reflects on the evolution that has
taken place and the guidelines issued by the CCSA in 2015.

Overview of Tribunal and CAC decisions

The first penalty was imposed by the Tribunal for anticompetitive conduct on the
part of *Federal Mogul*.[1] This was followed by *South African Airways*[2] (SAA), where
the Tribunal set out its approach to applying the factors under section 59(3) of
the Act for determining financial penalties together with the weightings for each
factor. Parties thereafter commonly referred to the 'SAA tests' when presenting
arguments in the determination of penalties, even though the Tribunal noted
the need to draw distinctions between various types of contravention in terms
of the factors under section 59(3). In particular, 59(3) indicates that the nature,
duration, gravity and extent of conduct are relevant considerations, implying
that different types of conduct can be distinguished for the purpose of penalty.

It seems obvious that prohibited resale price maintenance (as in *Federal
Mogul*), failure to notify a merger, cartel conduct and various abuses of dominance (as in *SAA*) are all different in nature and therefore a single 'ruler' for
determining penalties need not apply for all. Reinforcing this observation is the
fact that the Act does not provide for financial penalties for some contraventions, even where an effect has to be proven, such as in sections 4(1)(a) and 8(c).
In other words, notwithstanding anticompetitive effects, a form of safe haven
from financial penalties is provided for the catch-all categories of conduct not
separately defined but where the conduct *is* found to be harmful. By comparison, the 4(1)(b) prohibitions on horizontal restrictive practices, where a financial
penalty is applicable – price fixing, market division or collusive tendering – are
per se prohibitions without the requirement to demonstrate harm. They are simply presumed to be harmful.

Internationally, several considerations applying to cartel conduct are now
widely recognised (Connor, 2001; Motta, 2008; Werden, 2009; Wils, 2006). First,
there are good grounds for a presumption that the conduct is harmful. Second,
it is impossible to determine the size of the anticompetitive harm to consumers and to the economy, without extensive data analysis and generally after a
substantial time has passed following the end of the cartel. Even then, such estimates are likely to be within a wide range, depending on the assumptions made.
The analysis of harm may be required for damages claims that are brought by
customers after cartel findings by competition authorities. The assessments are
also an important area of academic inquiry, generally a substantial period after
the conduct. Third, the harm includes non-price factors such as collusion undermining the beneficial effects of competition in spurring better service and quality. Fourth, the primary importance of penalties is for deterrence and hence they

ought to be self-evidently greater than the expected gain to a firm considering a cartel. Fifth, the deterrence effect must take into account that the probability of the cartel being uncovered is much less than one.

The *Pioneer Foods* decision in the bread cartel case was the first penalty imposed by the Tribunal in a contested cartel case.[3] Pioneer contested its participation in a cartel (specifically, cartel arrangements nationally and in the Western Cape) despite being implicated by the other major producers. Premier Foods was granted conditional leniency, and Tiger Brands and Foodcorp reached settlements of R99 million (5.7% of bread turnover) and R45 million (6.7% of bread turnover), respectively. Pioneer also argued that such arrangements as there were had no effect on the bread price. The Tribunal found that there had been collusive conduct in 2006 in the Western Cape, and across the country from 1999 to 2006. Penalties of R46 million were imposed (9.5% of bread turnover in the Western Cape) and of R150 million (10% of bread turnover nationally, excluding the Western Cape).

Section 59(2) of the Act stipulates that an administrative penalty may not exceed 10% of the firm's turnover in, and its exports from, the Republic in the preceding financial year. In determining Pioneer's penalties, the Tribunal found that the 'maximum' penalty percentage of 10% (confusingly termed the 'threshold' by the Tribunal) was appropriate for the national cartel, with a small discount for the Western Cape where the conduct was shorter in duration. However, the Tribunal limited the turnover on which the percentages were applied to the 'infringing line of business'.[4] The Tribunal's reasoning was that the penalty should go beyond 10% of this turnover only if there was evidence that the anticompetitive conduct in one product market was extended or 'leveraged' into other markets.

In appealing the Tribunal decision, the CCSA argued that it confused determining the penalty, which under the Act is not in any way restricted to, or based on, fractions of 10% of the turnover of the infringing line of business (also termed the 'affected turnover', as in the Tribunal's decision in *Aveng & others*),[5] and the precautionary cap on the penalty which is explicitly set at 10% of *total turnover including exports* from the Republic.[6] A cartel mark-up (the additional profit margin from the collusive conduct) can easily be more than 10% in a single year, meaning it was impossible, with cartels typically existing for many years, for a penalty capped at 10% of the turnover of the particular line of business for a single year to be an adequate deterrent. For meaningful deterrence, the size of the penalties needs to be considered relative to the likely gains being made rather than merely making observations that penalties appear 'large' in rand terms.[7] The appeal was withdrawn pursuant to the settlement reached between the CCSA and Pioneer on the wheat flour and maize meal cartels.

The Tribunal acknowledged the importance of deterrence in its determination of the penalties in the next cartel case, *Southern Pipeline Contractors* (SPC), regarding cast concrete pipes and culverts.[8] This cartel, which had run for more than 30 years, was uncovered in 2007 following the leniency application of Rocla (a subsidiary of Murray & Roberts). The Tribunal set out an approach which followed international practice, including that of the European Commission (EC), which takes deterrence as the starting point. This approach uses the turnover of the products cartelised but contemplates a starting percentage higher than 10% and multiplies by the number of years of the conduct, taking both mitigating and aggravating factors into account. The 10% measure is only applied as the cap on the total penalty arrived at (as per section 59(2)), as a proportion of the *total* turnover of the firm and not only the infringing line of business.

The CAC, while agreeing with the emphasis on deterrence, found in *SPC* that the harm in terms of the mark-up from the cartel conduct needed to be assessed.[9] The CAC reduced the penalty for SPC to one-half of that determined by the Tribunal. In the penalty computation the CAC took only one year into account, although it is not clear why, as the CAC recognised the cartel had continued over many years. The CAC's reasons for reducing the fine on SPC included that the conduct had been limited to a specific product line and that there was no evidence of increases in profit margins, including reference to the fact that when costs had increased SPC had not passed on the full increase.[10] These reasons proved flawed. After the cartel ended, companies entered other product and geographic markets, illustrating the impact of the market-division arrangements (Khumalo, Mashiane and Roberts, 2014). In addition, a cartel which is effective will set prices at or close to the monopoly price. At this price a cost increase will *not* be fully passed through precisely because the price is so high already that consumers' willingness to pay has been exploited relative to their income and imperfect alternatives. These two observations demonstrate why the cartel was indeed one of the most egregious contraventions, although the CAC had drawn the opposite inferences. It is notable that the cartel was of such long duration that there was no readily available pre-cartel benchmark to use and it is wrong to assume that immediately after the ending of explicit coordination, pricing will simply shift to be competitive (meaning the immediate post-cartel period should not be used). There are substantial challenges in measuring cartel mark-ups, especially in a case such as this (Khumalo, Mashiane and Roberts, 2014).

The Tribunal's decision in the wire mesh cartel (*Aveng & others*) followed *SPC* and further developed the approach it took. Of the four wire mesh producers against which the CCSA referred, BRC obtained conditional leniency and Aveng (Africa) Limited, trading as 'Steeledale', admitted the conduct and settled with the CCSA. Reinforcing Mesh Solutions (RMS) admitted the conduct but contested its extent and the appropriate penalty, while Vulcania Reinforcing denied it was part of the cartel although it admitted to attending several meetings with its competitors in the cartel.

The Tribunal set out its approach in six steps:

- Step one: determine the affected turnover (based on the sales of the products or services affected by the conduct which reflects the 'effect of the cartel as a whole') in the relevant year of assessment based on the last financial year of the period for which there is evidence that the cartel existed.
- Step two: calculate the 'base amount' for the penalty determination. This percentage of the affected turnover will be between 0 and 30% (following

the EC) and will be influenced by several factors under section 59(3) of the Act, specifically under 59(3)(a), (b) and (d): nature, gravity and extent of the contravention; loss or damage suffered; and market circumstances.

- Step three: where the contravention exceeds one year, multiply the amount obtained in step two by the number of years (duration) of the contravention.
- Step four: round off the figure achieved in step three if it exceeds the section 59(2) cap of 10% of total turnover.
- Step five: adjust the outcome of step four on the basis of mitigating and aggravating factors specific to the firm's conduct (under sections 59(3)(c), (e), (f) and (g)), including its behaviour, extent of cooperation with the CCSA, level of profit derived and whether the respondent had previously been found guilty of a contravention of the Act.[11]
- Step six: round off the amount derived in step five if it exceeds the cap provided for in section 59(2) of the Act.[12]

These steps follow the European approach, cited approvingly by the CAC in *SPC*, while also taking into account the factors in the Act.

The Tribunal applied the steps, deciding on a base penalty in the case of each firm, multiplying by the years, which meant the cap was binding in the case of RMS, and then applying a reduction of 40% in the case of each firm reflecting mitigating factors, such as that they were not instigators and at times disrupted the cartel arrangements. It is not clear why the cap applies at both steps four and six.

Notably, in *Aveng & others* the Tribunal accepted the arguments of both RMS and Vulcania that they had profited little from the cartel, in the absence of evidence from the CCSA on this factor. It appears that the Tribunal understands that the CCSA should obtain such information in its investigation and should have led it in the hearing. This is a complex task. Determining the competitive counterfactual is very difficult. In addition, a cartel may shield an inefficient firm from the rigours of competition and thus keep that firm in the market when it would have exited absent the cartel. The latter scenario may be harmful to consumer welfare even while the inefficient firm does not appear to be making excess profits.[13]

The Tribunal then applied the six steps again in determining penalties in the plastic pipes cartel (*DPI & others*).[14] For MacNeil, Amitech and Petzetakis, the Tribunal again determined a base amount of 15%, which was multiplied by the number of years of participation in the cartel. After applying the 10% cap of total turnover, the Tribunal discounted the penalty by 20, 40 and 80% respectively, taking into account mitigating and aggravating factors. In the case of Petzetakis, the Tribunal's 80% reduction in the penalty was due to the managing director, Michelle Harding, having unilaterally exited the arrangement following attendance at a conference on business ethics. Harding had informed the group chief executive (based in Greece) about her intention, which was endorsed as long as it did not compromise 'the bottom line'.[15] Harding was subsequently fired although no link can apparently be drawn between this and her decision to leave the cartel. Petzetakis had been a ringleader in the cartel.[16] However, the owners of the firm obtained a substantial reduction in the penalty because of Harding's decision (a benefit apparently not shared with Harding!). Ultimately, the penalty of R9.92 million was just 1.6% of one year of Petzetakis' affected turnover, for a cartel in which they had participated for six years (since acquiring the company).

The Tribunal also applied the six-step approach in the case involving an alleged cartel between four firms that manufacture mining roof bolts (*RSC & others*).[17] Of these firms, RSC (a subsidiary of Murray & Roberts at the time) filed for corporate leniency and Aveng (Duraset) subsequently agreed to a settlement with the CCSA where the administrative penalty levied was 5% of Duraset's total turnover. The remaining firms, Dywidag-Systems International (DSI) and Videx Wire Products, admitted many of the contraventions, including collusive tendering. However, they argued that the practices had ceased more than three years before the initiation of the complaint and that, in relation to one of the contraventions that allegedly fell within the three years, the CCSA's case was not explicitly brought against them in the referral but rather against the two other respondents.

In its ruling, the Tribunal found only one contravention in relation to an Anglo Platinum tender and thus considered this as the affected turnover. In the second and third steps, the Tribunal determined a base amount of 18% of this turnover for one year for what it considered to be the most 'aggravating' form of cartel contravention (bid rigging). The Tribunal considered mitigating factors to be the fact that the primary purpose of the bid rigging was not achieved and the conduct related to only a single tender for a single customer. However, the Tribunal also took into account the fact that senior management was involved in the conduct, and that the firms admitted to several contraventions that were not considered (in the turnover) only due to prescription, and thus increased the base amount by 10%. DSI received a penalty of R1.8 million, and Videx a penalty of R4.7 million.

The preceding discussion shows that the Tribunal's approach to determining penalties in contested cartel cases has evolved over time in a manner that seeks to account more explicitly (and predictably) for the factors under section 59(3). It has seen potentially more severe penalties, imposing percentage amounts of up to 30% of affected turnover (reflecting an understanding of collusive mark-ups) and taking into account the duration of cartels. This is an important step in so far as firms will be better able to evaluate the likely penalty if they lose a contested case, and weigh this against the penalty they are likely to be able to agree if they approach the CCSA to settle the matter (discussed below). These aspects have important implications for the effectiveness of deterrence and the incentives of firms.

Deterrence and incentives in determining penalties and settlements

The principle of deterrence

Penalties play two roles: punishment and deterrence, with the latter being more important (Niels, Jenkins and Kavanagh, 2011; OECD, 2009). To achieve deterrence, the likelihood of cartel detection and the resulting penalty (which together give the expected penalty) must be sufficiently high when set against the illicit gain from the conduct.[18] Very high penalties have little deterrent effect if there is no realistic possibility of detection. The size of the expected penalty should also be weighed against the harm to society to ensure deterrence of the conduct. However, estimating the probability of detection, societal harm and illicit gains is not an easy task.

The probability of detection could be estimated as the proportion of cartels that are uncovered relative to the total universe of cartels that exist. However, due to the secret nature of cartels it is difficult to accurately ascertain the extent of this universe and, as such, the probability of detection is difficult to establish. Of course, the probability of detection is always less than one (and likely to be substantially so given that secret cartels are designed to remain hidden), which implies that achieving deterrence requires imposing a significantly higher penalty than the cartel gain. There is effectively a trade-off between the probability of detection and the level of the penalty – a lower probability of detection implies that higher penalties are required. Estimates of the probability of detection at substantially below one have been given as one explanation for the significant increase in penalties in the European Union (EU) in recent years (Ascione and Motta, 2008).

While harm to society will differ from the cartel gains and may be lower than these gains, in practice optimal deterrence is best achieved if penalties directly reflect the benefits that accrue to firms engaging in cartel conduct (Motta, 2008; Wils, 2006). This is reflected in the EC's fining guidelines[19] where fines are set based on the value of sales in the relevant market and the duration of the infringement. Value of affected sales and duration are considered a proxy for the economic importance of the infringement, where economic importance can be interpreted as the importance to either the economy or to the firms involved in the cartel conduct. Accounting for duration of infringement seems to acknowledge that the gains from cartel conduct are earned in each period of involvement in the cartel. Jurisdictions such as the EU, Switzerland, the Czech Republic, Hungary, Italy and Norway use duration as a multiplier, while the US, Germany, Russia and the Netherlands account for duration through the turnover or volume of affected commerce considered in the calculation of the basic penalty (ICN, 2008). The duration of a cartel, while reflecting past harm, is also indicative of cartel durability (and hence expected future cartel returns, absent detection).

The EC guidelines indicate that the basic fine is taken as a proportion (up to 30%)[20] of the sales in the relevant market, reflecting an approximation of the illicit cartel gains and harm to the economy. The number of years of duration is then used as a multiplier.

Some concerns have been raised that large penalties could lead firms into bankruptcy and to increased consumer prices as firms attempt to recoup losses from penalties (Van Cayseele, Camesasca and Hugmark, 2008). Most jurisdictions, including South Africa, have caps on penalties and some make provisions for the presentation of objective evidence demonstrating that the penalty would irretrievably jeopardise a firm's economic viability and cause its assets to lose all value.[21] In other words, a firm should demonstrate that the penalty leads to insolvency, which, in general, is likely to occur if the penalty is larger than the market value of the firm/shareholders' equity (Niels, Jenkins and Kavanagh, 2011). The CCSA's (2015) guidelines on determining administrative penalties also reflect these considerations. At competitive prices, there may be inefficient firms that are not sustainable while efficient firms make healthy returns. Inefficient firms could be seen as potentially prone to bankruptcy as a result of high penalties. Firms that are too inefficient to compete outside the shelter of the cartel would be eliminated by the competitive process even in the absence of the penalty (Motta, 2008). To the extent that penalties would lead some firms into bankruptcy, it could be argued that competition is lessened because of the reduction in the number of firms. It must, however, be noted that competition is not simply a function of the number of firms but of how they behave. It would be perverse to not adequately penalise a cartel on grounds of sustaining a larger number of firms in the market because this could undermine deterrence.

In addition, penalties represent a sunk cost which does not affect the pricing and supply decisions of firms. These decisions are essentially about weighing up the increased sales from a discounted price against the cost of supplying the additional volumes demanded. Increased competition post-cartel also means that individual firms cannot profitably raise prices without losing sales to competitors. Leniency programmes which exempt the whistleblower from paying a penalty, lower penalties from differential settlements among those firms that cooperate with competition authorities, and the higher penalties imposed on firms that elect to litigate put firms in asymmetric positions regarding the need to raise prices to recoup penalties (Buccirossi and Spagnolo, 2006). Consequently, it is unlikely that firms would raise prices to recoup penalties under competitive conditions.

Settlements and deterrence

Settlements generally award benefits to a firm (such as a lower penalty or less burdensome remedy) in exchange for its admission to the conduct, acceptance of penalties and/or remedies and cooperation regarding prosecution of remaining parties (Wils, 2008). Firms have greater incentives to settle when they face a high probability of an adverse finding in court, resulting in a penalty larger than that on offer in settlement. Firms may also consider the saving in terms of litigation costs. Similarly, competition authorities have greater incentives to settle when they face litigation costs, resource constraints and continued consumer harm (due to continued anticompetitive conduct) that exceed the cost of settling (lower fines and diminished deterrence). In the EU, firms earn automatic discounts of 10% if they elect to settle cases with the EC. In France, this discount ranges between 10 and 30% (Lasserre and Zivy, 2008). However, firms are unlikely to settle if they believe that the courts will provide larger fine reductions than the authority's settlement procedure (discussed later in relation to the South African context).

Settlement is separate from a leniency programme in which a firm is granted a reduced or zero penalty for providing information and evidence of an infringement. Settlements free up resources which are then diverted to screening and other investigations, thereby increasing the probability of uncovering more cartels (Adelstein, 1978; Landes, 1971; Lasserre and Zivy, 2008; Motta, 2008). This is achieved through the early settlement of cases. As such, a successful settlement procedure reduces the time between case inception and final decision. Competition authorities should therefore be open to settle with, and extend larger benefits to, firms that come forward earlier on in the investigation. In the EU, there has been some debate on the time limit within which settlement can be explored, with the EC notice limiting this to around the time it issues a Statement of Objections (Lasserre and Zivy, 2008).

Counterbalancing the benefits of early settlements is the diminished deterrence associated with lower penalties (Miceli, 1996). If, due to a settlement procedure, the amount of the penalty is likely to be significantly reduced, then the cartel profits are more likely to outweigh a possible penalty. Relatively low expected penalties under settlements also reduce the attractiveness of leniency. Underdeterrence in settlements can be avoided by having harsher overall sentencing, enabling discounts while still having meaningful penalties (LaCasse and Payne, 1999).

A review of the CCSA's approach to settlements

In this section we critically assess the CCSA's approach to settlements for cartel conduct through the lens of economic principles. Section 59(3) of the Act provides no guidance as to the relative importance of each listed factor for determining penalties or how they should be considered, whether by the Tribunal in imposing a penalty or in confirming a settlement reached between a respondent and the CCSA.

Firms will try to weigh up the penalty that they think the CCSA is likely to agree in settlement against the fine that they expect the Tribunal (or higher courts) to impose. There is thus a critical interrelationship between the process that the Tribunal follows for fine determination and the approach of the CCSA in settling matters. If administrative penalties required by the CCSA for settlements are high relative to the expected penalties from the Tribunal then firms would look to contest the matter, as in *SPC*. Certainly the evidence of cartel mark-ups (discussed below) indicates that penalties in general should be higher. With regard to settlements, we examine whether the CCSA should adopt the same approach (applying the factors in the same way) as the Tribunal in determining a penalty in a contested case, or whether it should maintain its current approach based on a case-by-case treatment of settlement.

In the early years, before the inception of the CLP in 2004, the CCSA prosecuted mostly 'non-secret' cartels and, typically, the penalties for participants were nominal. The arrangements generally did not concern a concealed attempt to coordinate market conduct. We therefore draw a distinction between this early period and after 2004, where the focus shifted to detecting, penalising and hence deterring secret cartels. The post-2004 experience also reveals the effect that the CLP had on firms' incentives to come forward and settle with the CCSA. There has been a discernible evolution in the way the CCSA has approached settlement from 2004 to date, towards achieving greater deterrence.

Following the introduction of the CLP, the CCSA saw a marked increase in the initiation and prosecution of 'hard-core' cartel cases (Lavoie, 2010). In this early period there was a high degree of uncertainty regarding the level of penalties that the Tribunal would impose in a contested hearing. The uncertainty and risk could be addressed through settlement, providing a way out for cartelists. The CCSA used settlements as a way to induce firms to 'clean up' while avoiding litigation of a large number of cases (Makhaya, Mkwananzi and Roberts, 2012). The settlements thus provide an indication of the firms' and the CCSA's expectations of penalties in contested cases – penalties imposed by the Tribunal would be significantly higher. An interesting feature of the South African experience is that there were a large number of settlements before the basis on which cartel penalties should be determined had been clarified through decided cases, and later through the CCSA's settlement guidelines. This was a result of the large number of cartel cases which were uncovered from 2007 to 2009 (and the incentives to reach settlements) against the time taken for cases to be heard and decided by the Tribunal and the CAC, with the CAC's *SPC* decision being finalised only later, in 2011.

In the years following the introduction of the CLP, the CCSA's approach evolved as it gained experience in handling the new leniency process and faced an increasing number of cases to prosecute, together with firms wishing to settle. There were some apparent inconsistencies in the CCSA's approach during this early period, perhaps consistent with the actions of an authority getting to grips with a new leniency regime and with setting penalties at consistent and appropriate levels. For example, in the bread cartel case, there was apparently overlapping leniency for two firms, as Tiger Brands provided information on more widespread conduct than the initial CLP applicant, Premier Foods. Thus, Tiger Brands received leniency for some conduct and received a penalty of only 5.7% of their national bread turnover for the multi-case settlement. This penalty could be viewed as being both relatively low for a multi-case settlement and inconsistent with the CCSA's approach, subsequent to 2007, of consistently granting immunity to only one applicant in each matter.

As the CCSA followed through on leniency applications, there were increased settlements, peaking in terms of number in 2013 (figure 1.1). The CCSA's prioritisation and investigation strategy led to the uncovering of far-reaching bid-rigging conduct in construction. The CCSA adopted a fast-track settlement process (see box 1.1) which led to 15 settlements in 2013 alone, just for this matter, along with a number of other construction-related matters. There were further settlements in 2014 and 2015.

Two further matters led to large numbers of settlements in 2014 and 2015. Cycling suppliers and retailers were found to have attempted to coordinate around pricing in a number of meetings and through an online forum. It was not clear to what extent this had been implemented and the penalties in the 17 settlements were relatively small, nominal amounts, and not disclosed in the confirmatory orders. The CCSA also uncovered an extensive cartel rigging bids for furniture removal, which led to 11 settlements, most in the 7–9% of turnover range.

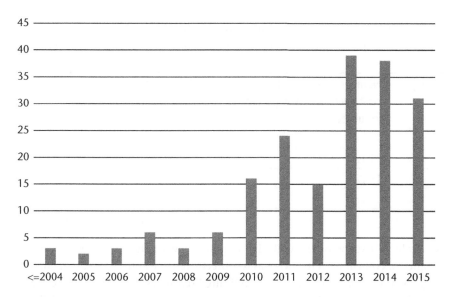

Figure 1.1 Number of cartel settlements confirmed by the Tribunal, 2004–2015

Source: CCSA and www.comptrib.co.za

Box 1.1 The CCSA approach to dealing with collusion in construction: The 'fast-track' settlement

In September 2009, the CCSA initiated wide-ranging investigations into collusion in the construction sector following leniency applications on specific projects and an earlier initiation related to the construction of soccer World Cup stadia. The CCSA invited construction firms to come forward and settle contraventions of the Competition Act in respect of collusive tendering. The invitation also called for full disclosure by a specified date (15 April 2011) in exchange for a low, 'all-in' penalty (see Roberts, 2014).

Firms that were first to notify the CCSA of particular instances of collusion were still eligible for leniency and would enjoy immunity from penalties for those instances. Firms that did not opt for settlement risked prosecution and penalties for each instance of collusion they were involved in, and for which evidence was provided by other cartel members who cooperated with the CCSA. Twenty-one firms applied for fast-track settlement, and 300 incidents of bid rigging, including the soccer stadiums and major road-construction projects, were uncovered.

Given the number of incidents of collusion and that the fast-track settlement offered an 'all-in' lower penalty across contraventions that cut across different categories of work, as well as potentially multiple instances of collusion by the same firms, there was a need to standardise penalties relative to the number of contraventions. Penalties were determined in ranges based on category or class of construction project as set out by the Construction

continued

Industry Development Board regulations. Penalties were then calculated as a percentage of the firm's turnover in each category or class, as follows:

Category	Number of non-prescribed contraventions by applicant in subsector	Penalty: percentage of turnover of applicant in subsector
A	1–4	1–4
B	5–12	4–7
C	13–22	7–10
D	23+	10–12

Source: CCSA (2011, p. 7)

The scale and scope of the collusive practices meant that prosecuting each instance of collusion on its own was resource-intensive and a procedural challenge for a competition authority with limited resources. There were therefore mutual benefits to settlement for both the competition authorities and the firms involved ('all-in' lower penalties). In June 2013, the CCSA concluded settlements with 15 firms, amounting to R1.46 billion (± US$150 million) in penalties. There were further settlements in 2014 and 2015, totalling 29 settlements in all, under the fast-track programme (table A1.1).

In terms of the penalties agreed with firms through 186 individual settlements across more than 50 cartels since the inception of the CCSA, table A1.1 in the Appendix indicates that penalties can be grouped in four ranges: less than 3%, 3–4.9%, 5–6.9% and 7+%. The percentages are of a single year's turnover of the entity involved in the conduct. The following broad observations can be made.

Turnover

In settlements, the CCSA has generally expressed penalties as a percentage of the total annual turnover of the relevant business entity. At times, a narrower turnover has been used, or specific product lines have been excluded from the turnover (see table A1.1). The CCSA has not focused on the affected turnover, on which there may be some dispute and on which evidence led in the Tribunal hearing may have bearing. Instead, it has generally taken the total turnover of the relevant entity, whether a firm, division, unit or subsidiary 'which controls its decision-making process' (Lavoie, 2010, p. 144).[22] For more recent settlements, following the decisions of the Tribunal specifying affected turnover and a multiple relating to the years of conduct, the CCSA has used affected turnover in some cases and higher percentage penalties have been imposed (table A1.1).

When the CCSA used the turnover of the entity or division in earlier years, it allowed for the subtraction of lines of business from the turnover of the entity where it could be demonstrated that it was not part of the cartelised products. For example, in the cartel of cast concrete products manufacturers (of items such as pipes and culverts), turnover from a major unrelated project was excluded. This in effect reduces the turnover used to an amount closer to the affected turnover.

Notwithstanding the possibility of using a base percentage of up to 30% of affected turnover, in settlements the CCSA has generally worked off a base of 10% of the turnover derived in this way, with most (where the percentage is specified) being between 3 and 7% (table A1.1). Indeed, aside from the furniture removals cartel settlements, there have been just 12 settlements in the range above 7%. This implies low penalties, especially for those cartels where the conduct related to the main business of the entity and ran for a number of years.

While the CCSA has argued for higher penalties, the settlement penalties appeared high when considered against the Tribunal's decisions in the contested case of *Pioneer*, where the Tribunal imposed a penalty of only 10% of affected turnover on the firm with no multiplier for duration, and this penalty was obviously only imposed after the time taken for the case to be heard. For settlements to be attractive to the firm, they have to be lower than the penalty the firm expects will be imposed. A firm settling would take into account the prevailing interest rate in likely paying the penalty several years earlier than if it were imposed by the Tribunal following a contested hearing and probably on a wider turnover than the affected turnover used by the Tribunal. The considerable number of settlements reflected the views of respondents that higher penalties were going to be imposed.

Size of penalties

Generally, the firms that received penalties of less than 3% were those involved in non-secret arrangements, including where the contravention arose from provisions of contractual agreements. A large number was reached in 2007 or earlier. This group includes the collective arrangements of the Board of Healthcare Funders, SA Medical Association and Hospital Association of South Africa in negotiating private healthcare pricing, which was deemed to contravene the Act (settled in 2004/2005). From 2013 to 2015 there were also a number of construction settlements which fell outside of the formal fast track but were still concluded on advantageous terms.

Seventeen of the 35 settlements between 3 and 4.9% related to price fixing of grain silo storage fees – arrangements which were prevalent throughout the industry as part of the regulatory hangover. There were also a number of notable settlements in this range where there was significant and material cooperation (discussed below), such as Keystone Milling, Afrisam and Apollo Tyres. Most settlements in the two lower ranges were also prior to referral.

The 51 settlements with penalties of 5% or more were the more traditional hard-core cartels; all but one were after 2007 and the majority were settlements post-referral.[23] Aside from the furniture removal cartel noted above, these settlements were largely accounted for by the bread and milling, scrap metal, concrete pipes, plastic pipes and bitumen cartels – the types of products in which cartels are found around the world (Connor and Helmers, 2006).

A subset can be identified of the highest penalties agreed in settlement, of between 7 and 9%. Three of these were settlements of more than one contravention, and, if considered on a per-contravention basis, would fall in a lower category.[24] The other settlements included cartel ringleaders and settlements which were very late and where firms did not cooperate with the CCSA. For example, in the case of Aveng (Infraset), representatives of the firm sought to mislead the CCSA in the concrete pipes cartel investigation.[25] Nonetheless, firms in this category still received an implied discount for settling.

Cooperation and firm behaviour

The obvious benefit of a clear leniency policy and creating incentives for cartelists to come forward is that the applicant provides the authority with valuable information that helps to reduce the cost of investigation and successful prosecution, while the firm benefits from a zero penalty. In cases where there is little or no documentary evidence, there is much value in a second firm admitting to the conduct and providing useful information when settling. In countries such as South Korea this is recognised through an automatic penalty discount for the second firm to settle.

The CCSA has favoured and rewarded early and substantial cooperation by firms, particularly those that have provided new and relevant information for the case, in some instances information exceeding what a CLP applicant can provide, such as Tiger Brands in the bread and milling cartels.[26]

Firms have also been rewarded for making 'exceptional' efforts to conduct internal investigations regarding anticompetitive conduct. The point is that material cooperation is about actions taken and not only expressions of cooperation amounting in effect simply to meeting the requirements of the investigation. The penalties for Sasol Chemical Industries[27] (SCI) in fertiliser, and Tiger Brands[28] and later New Reclamation[29] as a ringleader in the scrap metal case, were mitigated by their efforts to conduct internal investigations to uncover cartel conduct within their businesses. However, the SCI penalty was also increased to reflect the fact that senior management had withheld information. In the cement matter, AfriSam received a lower fine than Lafarge, reflecting early cooperation and the provision of extensive information, including witness statements obtained through an internal investigation at the firm.[30]

In instances where respondents failed to cooperate with the CCSA, sought to frustrate the investigation or misled the authority, the relevant fine was adjusted upwards.[31]

Duration and extent

Throughout the cases reviewed, the duration and extent of the conduct affected the severity of the fine, although to a relatively limited extent and certainly not by setting the penalty proportional to the duration. There are several reasons for this. First, at the settlement phase, without all the evidence being led, there is likely to be some uncertainty about the duration, especially when the managers involved at an earlier stage of the cartel are no longer employed by the settling firm.

Second, there have been long-running cartels where coordination was essentially part of the norms of business, and the CCSA had an incentive to uncover all of this conduct through the assistance of the settling firms. There are perhaps two main reasons for the extent of collusive conduct. There was extensive regulation of markets, often by or on behalf of producer groups, under apartheid (Makhaya and Roberts, 2013). In areas such as agriculture and cement, it is now evident that deregulation simply led to the producers continuing with secret cartel arrangements in a range of markets. There are also very tight-knit industries in South Africa, with multi-market contacts between firms that facilitate collusion. This appears to have been the case with construction products such as cast concrete pipes, reinforcing steel and wire mesh, in which the same main construction firms have subsidiaries, as well as in construction tenders (das Nair, Khumalo and Roberts, 2012). It appears that the CCSA sought to use settlements to incentivise firms to examine conduct across different markets and make a step-wise change. This is evident first in the baking and milling matters, where the initial discovery of a cartel in bread sales in the Western Cape (and leniency granted to Premier Foods) led to extensive collusion being uncovered at a national level in bread, wheat flour milling and maize milling, especially through the cooperation of Tiger Brands as part of its settlement. It is also reflected in the leniency applications and settlements following the cast concrete products cartel, where Aveng and Murray & Roberts, in particular, reviewed their operations across different markets (Makhaya, Mkwananzi and Roberts, 2012).

Third, at the time, firms in the very long-running cartels (such as the three-decade-long concrete pipes cartel) may not in any case have been penalised by the Tribunal above a cap of 10% of the turnover of these products (affected turnover). This reflected a probable alternative which the CCSA had to consider in setting the penalties in settlements.

In summary, while in terms of duration the CCSA's approach has generally been that the longer a firm has been involved in the conduct the larger the penalty, this has not been approached in terms of a multiplier to increase the penalty proportional to the duration. Having addressed a legacy of collusive conduct in many markets in areas such as construction products and agriculture, and with a much wider awareness in business of what constitutes a cartel, it could be argued that it is now appropriate to take a harder line on duration, as reflected in the approach of the Tribunal in *Aveng & others* and in the CCSA's guidelines.

Other considerations

As might be expected, smaller players in a cartel in terms of influence have been penalised less than the ringleader(s). Examples of firms that received larger penalties include New Reclamation, which was influential in the scrap metal cartel, and Aveng Steeledale,[32] a founding member in the mesh and rebar cartels.

Other things being equal, firms such as Pioneer[33] and SCI[34] received higher penalties for multi-case settlements, although the penalties were favourable if one were to consider all the contraventions separately. There has thus been an incentive to settle several cases at once with the CCSA, reflecting cooperation on the part of the firm in seeking to identify and settle all the contraventions (including those not yet referred), compared to a piecemeal approach.

Profitability and harm

The CCSA has not focused on calculating cartel mark-ups (the increased profit margin from the cartel) but has rather taken it as given that cartel conduct is profitable for cartelists for the purposes of settlement. Indeed, as discussed below, estimating the level of cartel overcharge at the time of investigation is particularly onerous and tantamount to pursuing a full excessive pricing case in terms of the evidentiary burden, a process which would seem to contradict the recognised resource and time savings associated with settling a matter. Only recently has the CAC implicitly acknowledged the complexity of using profit figures to estimate the effects and profitability of cartel conduct.[35]

Evaluation

As noted, if the administrative penalties which the CCSA is likely to agree in settlements are believed to be high, then firms are more likely to contest cases at the Tribunal. However, when settlement penalties are considered low there is likely to be underdeterrence. Firms may also choose to settle partly to avoid the extensive costs and duration of litigation, although this is difficult to assess from the Tribunal consent orders given that firms may not state this publicly. This may in fact lead firms to settle even where there is only a limited discount on offer for doing so, although in general it is understood that legal costs are significantly smaller than fines (Motta, 2008).

Generally, the CCSA has agreed higher penalties with ringleaders and long-standing cartel members (except in multi-case settlements) and lower penalties in cases where cartel arrangements may have been a legacy of apartheid government policy. Within specific cartels, there are differences in the final settlement amounts, reflective of the CCSA having effectively applied the section 59(3) factors to each individual firm. This is consistent with step five of the Tribunal's approach in *Aveng & others*, where mitigating and aggravating factors are considered. It is more difficult to compare the CCSA's approach across cartels, given differences in the nature of the cartel, duration, measurements of turnover and extent of the conduct.

The Tribunal's approach to penalty determination was initially not in line with the CCSA's approach to settlements in that the Tribunal did not impose much higher penalties, as a percentage of affected turnover and accounting for duration, than those agreed in settlements by the CCSA. It is only in recent decisions that the Tribunal has adopted a basis for determining penalties that acknowledges the importance of deterrence, provides greater certainty for firms, and allows the methodology of the CCSA to align with that of the Tribunal in terms of the actual penalties determined through settlement and/or a contested case in the Tribunal.

Review of penalty determinations in light of evidence of mark-ups in South Africa

Estimates of cartel mark-ups serve as both an indicator of the extent of profitability of cartel conduct for member firms as well as the potential harm to consumers over the period of the cartel. The overcharge is effectively the difference between the price charged during the cartel period and the prices that would have been charged in a competitive market absent the conduct. In addition, higher prices have the distortionary effect of reducing demand. Of course, the primary difficulty with this exercise is determining the appropriate counterfactual period, and the price and likely volumes sold against which to compare the observed cartel prices. In the case of long-standing cartels, such as in concrete pipes, defining this counterfactual for the analysis is challenging as there is no 'before cartel' competitive period. And, prices will not necessarily adjust to the competitive level for a considerable time after the explicit cartel ends (Khumalo, Mashiane and Roberts, 2014).

International studies have typically found that cartel mark-ups are approximately 15–25% of the cartel price (Khumalo, Mashiane and Roberts, 2014, p. 4). Assessments of the impact of the CCSA's interventions on cartel conduct in several sectors suggest comparable mark-ups. Given this evidence of high mark-ups for contraventions in South Africa, there is scope to increase both administrative penalties in settlements and those penalties issued by the Tribunal. We summarise these findings below.

Precast concrete products
Members of the concrete pipes cartel agreed market shares in the three main geographic areas, fixed prices and agreed not to compete in the remaining areas. The findings in this particular study, in which different counterfactuals were defined for the main areas of trade, were that: overcharge in the Gauteng (Johannesburg) region was in the range of 16.5–28%; overcharge in the KwaZulu-Natal (Durban) region was in the range of 51–57% (Khumalo, Mashiane and Roberts, 2014, p. 636). The estimated overcharge for the KwaZulu-Natal region was very high when compared to the international studies, but it should be noted that demand is inelastic and the market was very concentrated, while in Gauteng there were also fringe firms present that were not part of the explicit cartel.

Wheat flour
The CCSA made several interventions in the milling industry, including uncovering a cartel in wheat milling in late 2006. Members of this long-standing cartel (many of which were vertically integrated into several levels of the 'wheat-to-bread' value chain) attended numerous meetings in which they agreed to fix the price of milled wheat products; create uniform price lists for wholesale, retail and general trade customers; fix the timing and implementation of price increases; and allocate customers. One study estimated an average overcharge of approximately 25% on both white and brown flour prices to independent bakeries and an average overcharge on cake flour sold in the wholesale channel of approximately 7% (Grimbeek

and Lekezwa, 2013). Another assessment found that in the Western Cape the over-charges on white bread flour and cake flour were 42 and 32%, respectively, while in Gauteng they were approximately 24 and 33%, respectively (Mncube, 2014).

Review of Tribunal and CAC decisions on determining penalties

As part of the debate on appropriate standards for fines and settlement penalties, such as would be embodied in guidelines, we revisit the decisions of the Tribunal and the CAC in light of the economic framework, incentives and evidence on mark-ups.

An appropriate framework for determining penalties creates disincentives for engaging in cartel conduct while encouraging firms to come forward. This begins with the level of turnover that the firm believes can be affected by either a settlement with the CCSA or a penalty determined by the Tribunal. The CCSA's approach has been to focus on the turnover of the relevant business unit within which decision making regarding the cartel conduct lies. This is in contrast to the Tribunal's approach in the mesh case (*Aveng & others*) of assessing the turnover from products affected by the contravention. Notably, in either approach the turnover considered and the base percentage are interrelated.

The Tribunal in its decisions on concrete pipes, wire mesh, plastic pipes and mining roof bolts started with a base for the penalty of 10–30% of turnover. This is appropriate given the preference for using the affected turnover. An approach that takes the affected turnover but is restricted to a maximum of 10% of this turnover will clearly not deter, given that mark-ups are typically higher than this and firms earn supra-competitive returns in each year of the cartel. On the other hand, an approach that takes the affected turnover but where a high base per cent is set (close to 30%), and where this is multiplied by the duration of conduct, can still be a deterrent. We emphasise that for deterrence the penalty has to be substantially higher than the return earned, given that the probability of getting detected is far less than one, and the penalty is paid sometime in the future while the cartel returns are earned today. The risk of high legal costs and reputational damage can reinforce the effect of a high penalty in some cases, particularly where legal costs are high relative to the size of the penalty and where firms have high visibility in terms of media coverage and publicity (Aguzzoni, Langus and Motta, 2013; Günster and Van Dijk, 2011).

The incentive to settle is also enhanced if the penalty likely from a contested hearing clearly outweighs the returns from cartel conduct rather than simply seeking to balance them. This is so as it provides scope for the CCSA to substantially discount the likely penalty without running the risk that it will benefit a firm to collude and then to settle when found out because of the low level of penalties under such settlements.

While ideally firms should know with a reasonable degree of accuracy the discount for settling, in reality there will always be uncertainty given the range of factors to be taken into account and the different views of them taken by the Tribunal and the CAC. This implies that, while there may be some convergence in the penalty framework of the CCSA, the Tribunal and the CAC, there are cases where it may still make sense for the CCSA to base the settlement penalty on the (wider) turnover of the entity. Such cases will include where there is a high degree of uncertainty about the affected turnover and duration of the conduct. This is therefore an alternative approach which can be taken, depending on such uncertainties.

Two further considerations undermine deterrence. First, the 10% total turnover cap applicable under section 59(2) may be too low, especially in the case of single-product firms. Second, the practice of the Tribunal in recent decisions of awarding discounts in steps four and six (see above) may be too expansive. These two steps effectively allow a firm whose conduct may warrant a high penalty to have its penalty discounted at both stages.[36] In *RMS & others* (wire mesh cartel) the CAC seems to agree that there are concerns regarding the Tribunal's approach of discounting at both steps four and six.[37] Furthermore, the practice of discounting after the cap has been applied means that a single-product firm can contemplate a penalty substantially below 10% of one year's turnover – a penalty likely to be much lower than the rewards from collusion.

This in turn affects the settlement processes of the CCSA. Firms involved in the most egregious of contraventions that would otherwise receive high penalties from the CCSA have an incentive to take their chances at arguing for very narrow turnover to be used by the Tribunal and for additional discounting. This undermines the CCSA's ability to settle and to obtain useful evidence from settling parties that may assist in prosecuting other cartelists.

A further concern that arises from the Tribunal's decision in *Aveng & others* is the suggestion that in motivating for a particular penalty in settlement, evidence should have been led by the CCSA on the loss or damage suffered, including through examining the change in prices after the cartel was exposed. While this may be a fair requirement in the context of a full hearing, it seems unduly onerous at the level of settlements with the CCSA. Such evidence is particularly difficult to compile in the absence of an economically reasonable counterfactual. It also reduces the benefits from settling matters at an early stage of investigation for the CCSA and for the firm concerned, which may avoid the testing of evidence at the Tribunal that demonstrates significant losses suffered by consumers, evidence which could motivate for an even higher penalty being levied by the Tribunal.

The evidentiary burden should be different at the settlement stage and the wider turnover of the entity should be considered, particularly where there is uncertainty about the turnover to be considered and the duration of the conduct. In those cases where firms wish to motivate that specific turnover be excluded from the calculation of a settlement penalty, the onus should be on the firm to clearly demonstrate that the specific turnover should be exempt or to refute the presumption in the Act that the cartel was profitable. At the settlement stage, the CCSA has relied on being able to presume the harm and profitability of the conduct, although firms are required to provide sufficient evidence about the workings of the cartel to motivate for their own settlement and to assist in the prosecution of others. Importantly, the CCSA has considered the weight of additional evidence provided by each firm in assessing the level of penalty to be agreed in settlement, as described above.

Greater predictability will improve the incentives of firms to settle with the CCSA, particularly if there is also an understanding that the penalties likely to be imposed in a contested hearing at the Tribunal are high. In other jurisdictions a stated policy of partial leniency for the second and subsequent informants is used to enhance the incentives to come forward. In South Korea, under Article 35(1)(iii) of the Enforcement Decree, a 'second reporter' who reports to the Korea Fair Trade Commission and cooperates before or after the investigation commences can qualify for a 50% discount on the penalty and partial exemption from corrective orders, subject to several conditions (Jung et al., 2010). The EU leniency process also sets out conditions for granting a discount on penalties for the second and third applicants. In South Africa there may be benefit in exploring such an approach.

As noted, an appropriate framework for determining penalties creates disincentives for engaging in cartel conduct. It also provides sufficient incentive for firms to come forward for leniency or to settle cases. Firms should believe that contesting a cartel case at the Tribunal is likely to result in a high penalty, while at the same time they should be aware that settling is not an 'easy way out'. Together, these aspects, and the increasing probability of being caught, create deterrence. The threat of high penalties and the concomitant legal and reputational costs also increase the level of deterrence. Our review reveals how the competition authorities have moved towards an appropriate framework on a case-by-case basis. This started from the *SAA* approach being adopted to per se cartel conduct. The much larger number of cartel cases than expected then saw the CCSA evolve an approach to settlement, as well as appreciate the importance of deterrence to alter the risk and reward calculus of firms considering colluding with their competitors. This is in line with international experience that has seen a move towards higher penalties. The most recent decisions of the Tribunal and the CAC in this regard suggest an increasing recognition that the level of penalties (through settlement and contested cases) is critical to deterring future violations of the Act.

Conclusions

The framework for penalties for cartel conduct ought to be fundamentally premised on deterrence. In this regard, it is important to remember the straightforward gains to firms from colluding, which underlies why the conduct is a per se contravention requiring no assessment of effects. In addition, the harm to the economy extends beyond simply the collusive price mark-ups and includes the negative effects on quality, service and effort. The low probability of secret collusive arrangements being detected must also be taken into account.

The very large number of cartels uncovered from 2007 naturally led the CCSA to appreciate the benefits of settlements. Settlements that reward cooperation reveal more information about the conduct and can greatly assist in prosecuting the remaining cartel members, especially where there is little documentary evidence of the conduct. Moreover, incentivising settlement also led to other cartels being uncovered as part of settling firms' commitments to cooperation. The CCSA's approach evolved pragmatically according to these priorities and not along the lines of the tests that had been set down by the Tribunal for penalties in *SAA*.

The reasons for settlements being made at different penalty levels were explained by the CCSA on a case-by-case basis in the Tribunal hearings motivating their confirmation. Discounting of settlement penalties to below 6% has reflected meaningful cooperation, including proactive early settlement. These cartels had all generally run for several years at least and were of relatively tight-knit groups of firms for whom this had become a norm in the way of doing business. Assessing what the competitive counterfactual would have been was nigh impossible. The pragmatic approach reflected considerable uncertainty about the penalties that would be imposed by the Tribunal and higher courts for this conduct. At the same time there was a need to deal with the far-reaching collusive conduct, apparently almost a norm in many sectors such as construction products.

After the Tribunal and CAC decisions in *Pioneer* and *SPC*, the decisions of the Tribunal in the wire mesh, plastic pipes and mining roof bolts cases have set out a coherent approach that, while taking the narrower affected turnover, applies a high base percentage and multiplier for duration to this. While the guidelines issued are an important step towards increasing certainty for firms, the CCSA's approach to settlement could provide clear expectations as to the discounts off the expected penalties, with substantial discounts to incentivise early cooperation that assists in the prosecution of the remaining members (along the same lines as leniency). Importantly, there should be a progression towards higher penalties through the settlement process, given a move by the Tribunal towards harsher penalties as well. A misalignment in the approaches of the CCSA and the Tribunal will undermine deterrence.

Lastly, we note also that there are coordinated arrangements which do not fit clearly into the characterisation of secret cartel agreements while nevertheless falling foul of section 4(1)(b). Several of these arrangements are a legacy of extensively regulated markets. This warrants a somewhat different approach, which has been reflected in lower percentage penalties.

Notes

1   *Competition Commission v Federal Mogul Aftermarket Southern Africa (Pty) Ltd & others*, case no. 08/CR/Mar01.

2   *Competition Commission v South African Airways (Pty) Ltd*, case no. 18/CR/Mar01.

3   *Competition Commission v Pioneer Foods*, case no. 15/CR/Feb07 and 15/CR/May08.

4   *Pioneer Foods*, paras. 141–142.

5   *Competition Commission vs. Aveng & others*, case no. 84/CR/Dec09.

6   Notice of Appeal by Competition Commission to Competition Appeal Court of Competition Tribunal decision in cases 15/CR/Feb07 and 50/CR/May08, 24 February 2010.

7   The apparently large penalties have led both the CAC and the Supreme Court of Appeal to observe that the administrative penalties bear a close resemblance to criminal penalties. Supreme Court of Appeal, *Woodlands Dairy v Competition Commission* 2010 (6) SA 108 (SCA). The decision related to what standards to hold the CCSA to in exercising its powers in conducting an investigation. The CAC in its decision on *SPC* and *Conrite Walls* noted that 'a penalty which is of a criminal nature should be

proportional in severity to the degree of blameworthiness of the offending party, the nature of the offence and its effect on the South African economy in general and consumers in particular' (para. 9). The Constitutional Court in *Senwes* questioned the Supreme Court's position on this, case no. CCT 61/11 [2012] ZACC 6, para. 65.

8 *Competition Commission v Southern Pipeline Contractors and Conrite Walls (Pty) Ltd*, case no. 23/CR/Feb09.

9 *Southern Pipeline Contractors and Conrite Walls vs. Competition Commission*, case no. 105/CAC/Dec10.

10 The CAC noted (para. 56) that the participation of SPC in the cartel activities had been limited to Gauteng and to the specific sale of concrete pipes (and not culverts or manholes); that there was little evidence on the record to suggest significant consumer losses or the extent of the increased profit that flowed to SPC from the cartel; and that SPC had indicated that the increase in costs from 2002–2007 had been higher than the increase in return (revenue) over that period. With regard to profits, the CAC indicated that the increase in profit could have been determined by a ratio analysis based on figures provided in the financial statements. The CAC also found that the evidence available could not sustain the Tribunal's conclusion that this was the most egregious kind of cartel behaviour envisaged in the Act (para. 57). However, the CAC did acknowledge (para. 58) that penalties should be sufficiently onerous to act as a deterrent.

11 This is in contrast to step two where the Tribunal considers the effects of the cartel as a whole (which should generally be the same for all respondents) and not the circumstances of an individual firm as in step five.

12 *Aveng & others,* paras. 133–154.

13 See *MacNeil Agencies and the Competition Commission*, case no. 121/CACJul12, para. 35. In this recent judgment involving MacNeil Agencies (implicated in the plastic pipes cartel), the CAC notes that collusive firms may operate inefficiently and the harm that consumers feel is not related to the collusive firms' profits but to the amount that consumers spend on their products or services.

14 *Competition Commission v DPI Plastics & others*, case no. 15/CR/Feb09.

15 Para. 219. Petzetakis did not apply for leniency as Harding claimed not to be aware of the possibility.

16 It had interestingly also been a subsidiary of Murray & Roberts (as Main Industries), which had a ringleader in the concrete pipes cartel, Rocla.

17 *Competition Commission v RSC Ekusasa Mining & others*, case no. 65/CR/Sep09.

18 Firms may also consider the negative reputation effect of entering a cartel which is likely to be uncovered at some point. This depends on the likelihood of detection and, as all substantial firms are normally involved in a cartel, does not mean any individual firm will necessarily suffer from a poorer reputation than another.

19 European Commission, 'Guidelines on the Method of Setting Fines Pursuant to Article 23(2)(a) of Regulation No 1/2003' [2003] OJ C210/02 (2006).

20 Versus 20% in the US.

21 European Commission 'Guidelines'. The South African competition authorities have also allowed for extended payment terms.

22 See *Adcock Ingram*, where the operating entity was fined, although it was part of Tiger Brands. The turnover was much wider than the affected turnover of the conduct,

which was on intravenous drips. In the case of Aveng Duraset's settlement of the mining roof bolts cartel, the fine was levied on Duraset's turnover. Duraset had five divisions reporting to the same managing director, who was actively involved in cartel meetings (case no. 65/CR/Sep09). In settlements of the concrete pipes and culverts cartel, only World Cup 2010 joint venture turnover was excluded in the case of two firms, and the turnover was thus that of all cast concrete products, not only the sales of products subject to the cartel arrangements.

23 The only one in 2007 is Tiger Brands, which was in fact settling more than one contravention.

24 These are the SCI Sasol Nitro, Aveng (Steeledale) and Pioneer Foods settlements.

25 *Competition Commission and Concrete Units (Pty) Ltd*, case no. 23/CR/Feb09, hearing transcript 31 March 2010.

26 *Competition Commission and Tiger Consumer Brands (Pty) Ltd*, case no. 15/CR/Feb07, hearing transcript 28 November 2007. In its submissions the CCSA stated that Premier Foods and Tiger Consumer Brands were both granted leniency partly because the CLP was a new policy and the CCSA was more inclined to grant leniency to parties that cooperate than to deny it.

27 *Competition Commission and Sasol Chemical Industries Ltd*, case no. 31/CR/May05.

28 Foodcorp was implicated in the same cartel but received a larger penalty, at least partly because they waited until the matter was referred before coming forward.

29 *Competition Commission and The New Reclamation Group Ltd*, case no. 37/CR/Apr08.

30 *Competition Commission and Lafarge Industries South Africa (Pty) Ltd*, case no. 23/CR/Mar12, hearing transcript 28 March 2012 at 11.

31 See *Competition Commission & others and American Natural Soda Ash Corporation & others*, case no. 49/CR/Apr00; *Competition Commission and Adcock Ingram Critical Care (Pty) Ltd*, case no. 20/CR/Apr08; and *Competition Commission and Aveng (Africa) Ltd*, case no. 24/CR/Feb09.

32 *Competition Commission and Aveng (Africa) Ltd t/a Steeledale*, case no. 84/CR/Dec10.

33 *Competition Commission and Pioneer Foods (Pty) Ltd*, case no. 10/CR/Mar10 and 15/CR/Mar10.

34 *Sasol Chemical Industries.*

35 *MacNeil Agencies*, para. 86.

36 In *RSC & others* the Tribunal took a strong position in terms of a high base percentage applied at step two. The base amount applied to DSI and Videx was 18%. This was increased by 10% at step five due to significant aggravating factors. Despite this, because the affected turnover was defined narrowly, the penalty amount constituted less than 1% of DSI's and less than 2% of Videx's annual turnover.

37 *RMS & others*, case no. 119/120/CAC/May2013, para. 63.

References

Adelstein R. 1978. The plea bargain in theory: A behavioural model of the negotiated guilty plea. *Southern Economic Journal* 44: 488–503.

Aguzzoni L, G Langus and M Motta. 2013. The effect of EU antitrust investigations and fines on a firm's valuation. *The Journal of Industrial Economics* 61: 290–338.

Ascione A and M Motta. 2008. Settlements in cartel cases. In C-D Ehlermann and M Marquis (eds), *European Competition Law Annual 2008: Antitrust Settlements under EC Competition Law*, pp. 67–83. Oxford: Hart Publishing.

Buccirossi P and G Spagnolo. 2006. *Optimal Fines in the Era of Whistle-Blowers*. Centre for Economic Policy Research Discussion Paper No. 5465. http://www.cepr.org/pubs/dps/DP5465.asp.

CCSA (Competition Commission South Africa). 2011. 'Invitation to Firms in the Construction Industry to Engage in Settlement of Contraventions of the Competition Act' (online document).

CCSA. 2015. 'Guidelines for the Determination of Administrative Penalties for Prohibited Practices' (online document).

Connor JM. 2001. *Global Price Fixing: Our Customers Are the Enemy*. Norwell, MA: Kluwer Academic Publishers.

Connor JM and CG Helmers. 2006. *Statistics on Modern Private International Cartels: 1990–2005*. Department of Agricultural Economics, Purdue University Working Paper No. 06-11.

das Nair R, J Khumalo and S Roberts. 2012. Corporate conduct and competition policy in intermediate industrial products. *New Agenda*, Quarter 1: 16–21.

Grimbeek S and B Lekezwa. 2013. *The Emergence of More Vigorous Competition and the Importance Of Entry – Comparative Insights from Flour and Poultry*. CCRED Working Paper 2013/1.

Günster A and MA van Dijk. 2011. 'The Impact of European Antitrust Policy: Evidence from the Stock Market' (online document).

ICN (International Competition Network). 2008. 'Setting of fines for cartels in ICN jurisdictions'. ICN Cartel Working Group Report to 7th ICN Annual Conference, Kyoto, April.

Jung K, H Park, M Yu, Kim and Chang. 2010. 'Leniency Regimes: Jurisdictional Comparisons: South Korea'. In *The European Lawyer Reference Series* (3rd edition) (online document).

Khumalo J, J Mashiane and S Roberts. 2014. Harm and overcharge in the South African precast concrete products cartel. *Journal of Competition Law and Economics* 10: 621–646.

LaCasse C and A Payne. 1999. Federal sentencing guidelines and mandatory minimum sentences: Do defendants bargain in the shadow of the judge? *Journal of Law and Economics* 42: 245–269.

Landes W. 1971. An economic analysis of the courts. *Journal of Law and Economics* 14: 61–107.

Lasserre B and F Zivy. 2008. A principled approach to settlements: A few open issues. In C-D Ehlermann and M Marquis (eds), *European Competition Law Annual 2008: Antitrust Settlements under EC Competition Law*, pp. 143–169. Oxford: Hart Publishing

Lavoie C. 2010. South Africa's corporate leniency policy: A five-year review. *World Competition* 33: 141–162.

Makhaya G, W Mkwananzi and S Roberts. 2012. How should young institutions approach competition enforcement? Reflections on South Africa's experience. *South African Journal of International Affairs* 19: 43–64.

Makhaya G and S Roberts. 2013. Expectations and outcomes: Considering competition and corporate power in South Africa under democracy. *Review of African Political Economy* 138: 556–571.

Miceli T. 1996. Plea bargaining and deterrence: An institutional approach. *European Journal of Law and Economics* 3: 249–264.

Mncube L. 2014. The South African wheat flour cartel: Overcharges at the mill. *Journal of Industry, Competition and Trade* 14: 487–509.

Motta M. 2008. On cartel deterrence and fines in the European Union. *European Competition Law Review* 29: 209–220.

Niels G, H Jenkins and J Kavanagh. 2011. *Economics for Competition Lawyers*. New York: Oxford University Press.

OECD (Organisation for Economic Cooperation and Development). 2009. 'Determination and Application of Administrative Fines for Environmental Offences: Guidance for Environmental Enforcement Authorities in EECCA Countries' (online document).

Roberts S. 2014. Establishing new institutions: A note on the role of strategy and economic analysis in uncovering collusion in the South African construction sector. In N Charbit and E Ramundo (eds), *William E. Kovacic: An Antitrust Tribute – Liber Amicorum – Volume II*. New York: Institute of Competition Law.

Van Cayseele P, PD Camesasca and K Hugmark. 2008. The EC Commission's 2006 fine guidelines reviewed from an economic perspective: Risking over-deterrence. *The Antitrust Bulletin* 53: 1083–1126.

Werden G. 2009. Sanctioning cartel activity: Let the punishment fit the crime. *European Competition Journal* 5: 19–36.

Wils W. 2006. Optimal antitrust fines: Theory and practice. *World Competition* 29: 183–208.

Wils W. 2008. The use of settlements in public antitrust enforcement: Objectives and principles. *World Competition* 31: 335–352.

World Bank and ACF (African Competition Forum). 2016. 'Boosting competition in African markets'. Conference edition.

Appendix

Table A1.1 Profile of CCSA settlements, 1999–2015

Cartel	Firm	Factors	Special turnover	Date	CLP?
Penalty 0<3%					
medical	Mediclinic	prior referral, no admission of guilt, no payment of penalty	not specified	2015	no
construction (2)	Western Granite Bricks	prior referral, full cooperation	total turnover	2015	no
construction (2)	Dura Soltanche Bachy	full cooperation, prior referral, implicated in multiple projects	total RSA turnover	2015	yes
electric cables	Malesela Taihan	prior referral, full cooperation	total turnover	2015	yes
construction (2)	WBHO Construction	post-referral, full cooperation	civil engineering division	2014	yes
construction (2)	Giuricich Coastal Projects	post-referral, full cooperation	total turnover	2014	yes
bullet proofs	Fields Wear CC	post-referral, full cooperation	total turnover	2014	no
fishing	Premier Fishing SA	prior referral, late but full cooperation	total turnover	2014	no
fishing	Saldanha Foods	prior referral, late but full cooperation	total turnover	2014	no
construction (2)	Hochtief Construction AG	ringleader, single conduct, agrees to full cooperation, prior referral	civil engineering	2013	yes
gas (1)	Air Products South Africa	big player, ringleader	LIN and LAR only	2013	yes
animal feed	Wes Enterprises	predominant nature of the conduct is vertical, small player	retail sales	2013	no
animal feed	MGK Operating Company	predominant nature of the conduct is vertical, bigger player	retail sales	2013	no
construction (2)	MVA Bricks	post-referral, full cooperation	affected turnover	2013	yes
construction (2)	Cast Industries	post-referral, change of ownership	affected turnover	2013	yes
sheep breeding	DSBS Society	prior referral, full cooperation, industry association	total sales	2013	no

continued

Cartel	Firm	Factors	Special turnover	Date	CLP?
steel (1)	Trident Steel	full cooperation, prior referral	affected turnover	2012	yes
property	Erf 179 Bedfordview	post-referral, smaller player, late cooperation	total turnover	2012	yes
construction (2)	Bosun Brick Midrand	full cooperation, 1st runner for CLP, prior referral	affected turnover	2012	yes
airlines	SAA	early cooperation	inbound and outbound route revenue	2012	no
bitumen	SABITA	industry association	annual sponsor/membership fees	2011	yes
polymers	Safripol	agreement from competition board compliance, smaller player		2010	no
milk	Lancewood	small player, factual and legal position different, financial position		2009	yes
health	UDIPA	non-secret		2007	no
health	SAOPA	unique circumstances		2007	no
boilers	Zip Heaters	distribution agreement terms		2007	no
fasteners	CBC Fasteners	sale agreement terms		2007	no
fasteners	Nedschroef	sale agreement terms		2007	no
airlines	SAA & SA Express	conduct ceased after initiation	joint turnover	2006	yes
airlines	SAA	cooperation, conduct had ceased		2006	no
airlines	Deutsche Lufthansa	cooperation, conduct had ceased	SA turnover	2006	no
health	BHF	non-secret		2005	no
export	USA Citrus Alliance	efficiency benefits, export cartel, effects in the US		2005	no
health	SAMA	non-secret		2004	no
health	HASA	non-secret		2004	no
property	IEASA	non-secret, cooperation		2004	no
Summary	non-secret, cooperation, unique circumstances, very few conducts				

continued

Cartel	Firm	Factors	Special turnover	Date	CLP?
Penalty 3<5%					
furniture removal	Key Moves	prior referral, full but late cooperation, very few conducts	total turnover	2016	yes
gas (3)	African Oxygen	prior referral	affected turnover	2015	yes
logistics	BLG Leads Logistics	prior referral	total turnover	2015	yes
logistics	NYK	prior referral	total turnover	2015	yes
furniture removal	Oppertune Trading	prior referral, full but late cooperation, very few conducts	total turnover	2015	yes
furniture removal	A & B Movers	prior referral, full but late cooperation, very few conducts	total turnover	2015	yes
furniture removal	H and M Removals	prior referral, full but late cooperation, very few conducts	local and long distance	2015	yes
furniture removal	Reliable Removals	prior referral, full but late cooperation, very few conducts	total turnover	2014	yes
glass	Mccoy's Glass	full cooperation, voluntarily left the cartel	affected turnover	2013	yes
animal feed	Astral Operations	post-referral, full cooperation, voluntary assistance with investigations	affected division	2013	yes
gas (2)	Springlights Gas	small player, established by the ringleader	total turnover	2013	yes
medical	Shekinah	post-referral, agrees to full cooperation	affected turnover	2013	no
airlines	Primkop	prior referral, ringleader, single conduct	total turnover	2013	yes
cement	AfriSam SA	prior referral, cooperation	all cement turnover in SACU	2011	yes
grain storage (2)	Rand Merchant Bank	prior referral, cooperation	grain affected by agreement	2011	no
grain storage (2)	NWK Limited	prior referral, cooperation	grain affected by agreement	2011	no
grain storage	Grain Silo Industry	industry association	membership fees	2011	no

continued →

Cartel	Firm	Factors	Special turnover	Date	CLP?
grain storage	GWK Limited	not wholly secret	grain silo storage turnover	2011	no
grain storage	MGK Bedryfsmaatskappy	not wholly secret	grain silo storage turnover	2011	no
grain storage	Moorreeburgse Koringboere	not wholly secret	wheat daily storage tariff silo turnover	2011	no
grain storage	NTK Limpopo Agric Beperk	not wholly secret	grain silo storage turnover	2011	no
grain storage	NWK Limited	not wholly secret	grain silo storage turnover	2011	no
grain storage	Overberg Agri Bedrywe	not wholly secret	wheat daily storage tariff silo turnover	2011	no
grain storage	OVK Operations Limited	not wholly secret	grain silo storage turnover	2011	no
grain storage	Sentraal-Suid Co-operative	not wholly secret	wheat daily storage tariff silo turnover	2011	no
grain storage	Senwes Limited	not wholly secret	grain silo storage turnover	2011	no
grain storage	Suidwes Agriculture	not wholly secret	grain silo storage turnover	2011	no
grain storage	Vrystaat Kooperasie Beperk	not wholly secret	grain silo storage turnover	2011	no
tyres (1)	Apollo Tyres SA	post-referral, cooperation – change of ownership, financial position	affected turnover	2011	yes
property	Liberty Group	contravention in contractual agreement	property portfolio revenue	2011	yes
polymers	SCI Polymers	contravention from merger remedy w/ comp. board, cooperation, leader	polymers turnover	2011	no
grain storage	Afgri Operations	not wholly secret	grain silo storage turnover	2011	no
grain storage	Kaap Agri Bedryf	not wholly secret	grain silo storage turnover	2011	no
grain storage	Tuinroete Agri	not wholly secret	grain silo storage turnover	2011	no
milling	Keystone Milling	small player, short duration, cooperation	total turnover	2010	yes
Summary	not wholly secret, cooperation, very few conducts, contravention through contractual arrangement				

continued

Cartel	Firm	Factors	Special turnover	Date	CLP?
Penalty 5<7%					
furniture removal	Del Transport	prior referral, full but late cooperation, fewer conducts	total turnover	2015	yes
scrap metal	SA Metal Group	post-referral	ferrous and non-ferrous	2015	yes
electric cables	ATC (Pty) Ltd	prior referral, full cooperation	total turnover	2014	yes
furniture removal	Joel Transport	prior referral, full but late cooperation, few conducts	total turnover	2014	yes
furniture removal	De Wet Human	prior referral, full but late cooperation, few conducts	total turnover	2014	yes
medical	Hosanna	post-referral, agrees to full cooperation	total turnover	2013	no
fish	Oceana Group (& Brands)	prior referral, cooperation	pelagic fish operations in SA	2012	yes
freight service	Schenker SA	prior referral, cooperation, conduct mainly by international holding company	turnover from affected routes	2012	yes
freight service	Kuehne + Nagel	prior referral, conduct mainly by international holding company	turnover from affected routes	2012	yes
bitumen	Engen Petroleum	post-referral	bitumen	2012	yes
bitumen	Shell South Africa Marketing	post-referral, cooperation	bitumen	2012	yes
cement	Lafarge Industries SA	prior referral, cooperation (less information than AfriSam)	all cement turnover in SACU	2012	yes
tyres (2)	Maxiprest	post-referral, cooperation	specific product lines in Gauteng	2012	yes
milling	Carolina Rollermeule	post-referral, small player, cooperation but no new info	total turnover	2011	yes
scrap metal	National Scrap Metals	post-referral, consistency with other fines, late cooperation, limited involvement	total turnover	2010	no
scrap metal	Power Metal Recyclers	post-referral, consistency with other fines	total turnover	2010	no
scrap metal	Universal Recycling	post-referral, consistency with other fines	URC and SteelCo	2010	no
scrap metal	Abeddac Metals	post-referral, consistency with other fines	total non-ferrous	2010	no

continued

Cartel	Firm	Factors	Special turnover	Date	CLP?
scrap metal	Amalgamated Metals	post-referral, consistency with other fines	total non-ferrous	2010	no
plastic pipe	Marley Pipe Systems	post-referral, limited duration	turnover less unaffected products	2010	yes
plastic pipe	Flotek Pipes Irrigation	post-referral, consistency with other fines, limited duration, poor cooperation	total turnover	2010	yes
plastic pipe	Swan Plastics CC	post-referral, consistency with other fines, late cooperation	total turnover	2010	yes
concrete pipe	Cobro Concrete	post-referral, unique circumstances, cooperation		2010	yes
bitumen	Masana Petroleum	prior referral	black fuels	2010	yes
roof bolts	Aveng (Africa) - Duraset	prior referral, duration of cartel, withdrew themselves from cartel	only Duraset	2010	yes
medical	Thusanong Healthcare	post-referral, short duration, unique circumstances	all operations	2009	yes
medical	Dismed Criticare	post-referral, longer duration, smaller player	all operations	2009	yes
bread	Foodcorp	post-referral, cooperation, multi-case, late settlement	baking operations	2009	no
scrap metal	New Reclamation Group	prior referral, ringleader, cooperation	affected market turnover	2008	no
bread, milling	Tiger Consumer Brands	prior referral, multi-case settlement, cooperation, long duration, extent of conduct	national bread turnover	2007	yes
Summary		post-referral, consistency with other fines, duration, unique circumstances			
Penalty >7%					
furniture removal	Execu Move	prior referral, full but late cooperation, many conducts	domestic turnover	2015	yes
steel (2)	Amsteele Systems	prior referral, full cooperation	affected turnover	2015	yes
furniture removal	Transfreight	prior referral, full but late cooperation, many conducts	total turnover	2014	yes
furniture removal	Crown Relocations	prior referral, full but late cooperation, many conducts	total turnover	2014	yes
furniture removal	Matthee Furniture	prior referral, full but late cooperation, many conducts	total turnover	2014	yes

continued ➞

Cartel	Firm	Factors	Special turnover	Date	CLP?
furniture removal	Superdoc Thirteen	prior referral, full but late cooperation, many conducts	total turnover	2014	yes
furniture removal	JH Retief Transport	prior referral, full but late cooperation, countless conducts	total turnover	2014	yes
furniture removal	Patrick Removals	prior referral, late but full cooperation, countless conducts	total turnover	2014	yes
furniture removal	Cape Express Removals	prior referral, full but late cooperation, countless conducts	total turnover	2014	yes
furniture removal	Propack Removals	prior referral, full but late cooperation, countless conducts	total turnover	2014	yes
scrap metal	Columbus Stainless	post-referral, full cooperation	affected turnover	2014	yes
airlines	Singapore Airlines	cooperation, duration	passenger turnover booked in SA	2012	yes
milling	Foodcorp	post-referral, full cooperation	affected, milling division	2012	yes
mesh, rebar	Aveng (Africa) – Steeledale	post-referral, repeat contravention by Aveng, ringleader, multi-case	only Steeledale not Aveng	2011	yes
concrete pipe	Concrete Units	post-referral, late cooperation, smaller player	turnover excl. WC2010 JV project	2010	yes
concrete pipe	Cape Concrete Works	post-referral, late cooperation, smaller player	turnover excl. WC2010 JV project	2010	yes
milling	Pioneer Foods	post-referral, multi-case settlement	Sasko grain excl. baking & Africa	2010	yes
fertiliser	SCI Sasol Nitro	post-referral, multi-case settlement, late cooperation	SCI Nitro excl. unaffected products	2009	no
concrete pipe	Aveng (Africa) - Infraset	post-referral, ringleader, lack of cooperation	turnover excl. paving products	2009	yes
soda ash	ANSAC	post-referral, non-secret, lack of cooperation, very late settlement	soda ash turnover in SA	2008	no
medical	Adcock Ingram (Tiger Brands)	post-referral, lack of cooperation, extent of conduct	only Adcock operations	2008	yes
Summary	poor cooperation, ringleader, multi-case, extent of conduct				
Unstated penalties					
logistics	NYK Logistics	prior referral	not specified	2015	yes
car rental	ACSA	prior referral	total turnover	2015	no

continued

Cartel	Firm	Factors	Special turnover	Date	CLP?
logistics	Wallenius Wilhelmsen	prior referral, multiple conducts	total turnover	2015	no
petroleum	Tosaco	prior referral	total turnover	2015	yes
logistics	NYK	prior referral, full cooperation	total turnover	2015	yes
plumbing tubes	Copper Tubing	post-referral	total turnover	2015	yes
logistics	CSAV	prior referral, multiple conducts	total turnover	2015	no
cycling	Mailot Jaune Trading	post-referral	not specified	2015	no
cycling	Melody Street Trading	post-referral	not specified	2015	no
cycling	Albatros	post-referral	not specified	2015	no
cycling	Pedal-On-Marketing	post-referral	not specified	2015	no
airlines	British Airways	prior referral, full cooperation	turnover in SA	2014	no
veterinary	SAVC	prior referral, industry association	not specified	2014	no
processed fruit	Rhodes Food Group	prior referral, full but late cooperation	total turnover	2014	no
construction (2)	Inca Concrete Products	multiple conducts, full cooperation, prior referral	total turnover	2014	yes
airlines	Cargolux International	post-referral, full cooperation	total turnover	2014	no
cycling	Summit Cycles	post-referral	not specified	2014	no
cycling	Dynamic Choices	post-referral	not specified	2014	no
cycling	Saloojee Cycles	post-referral	not specified	2014	no
cycling	Moneymine	post-referral	not specified	2014	no
cycling	Tridirect	post-referral	not specified	2014	no
cycling	Johnson Cycle Works	post-referral	not specified	2014	no
cycling	Le Peloton	post-referral	not specified	2014	no

continued

Cartel	Firm	Factors	Special turnover	Date	CLP?
cycling	DBS Distributing	post-referral	not specified	2013	no
cycling	West Rand Cycles	post-referral	not specified	2013	no
cycling	New Just Fun	post-referral	not specified	2013	no
cycling	Pedaling Dynamics	post-referral	not specified	2013	no
cycling	Cytek Cycle Distributors	post-referral	not specified	2013	no
cycling	Bowman Cycles	post-referral	not specified	2013	no
glass	National Glass Distributors	full cooperation, conduct only in Gauteng	not specified	2013	yes
test equipment	Aztec Components	post-referral	not specified	2013	no
test equipment	Lamda Test Equipment	post-referral	not specified	2013	no
airlines	Martinair Vargo	post-referral	total turnover in SA	2013	no
gas (4)	Egoli Gas	not ringleader, buys gas from Sasol and competes with Sasol at the same time	business customers	2013	yes
airlines	Air France Cargo	not ringleader, unilaterally drop fuel surcharge between Dec. 2001 and April 2002	not specified	2012	no
airlines	British Airways	full cooperation	BAWC (a division of BA)	2012	yes
Summary	prior referral, small player, common circumstances, full cooperation, few conducts				
Construction fast track					
construction (1)	Murray and Roberts	big player, multiple practices, did not disclose all	not specified	2015	yes
construction (1)	Basil Read Holdings	full cooperation, prior referral, conditional immunity	none	2015	yes
construction (1)	Stefanutti	full cooperation, prior referral, conditional immunity	none	2015	yes

continued →

Cartel	Firm	Factors	Special turnover	Date	CLP?
construction (1)	Haw & Inglis	full cooperation, prior referral, conditional immunity	none	2015	yes
construction (1)	JT Ross	full cooperation, prior referral, conditional immunity	none	2015	yes
construction (1)	Pele Kaofela	did not respond to invitation, implicated in single project	total turnover	2015	yes
construction (1)	G Liviero and Son	full cooperation, prior referral, conditional immunity	none	2014	yes
construction (1)	Giuricich Bros	full cooperation, prior referral, conditional immunity	none	2014	yes
construction (1)	Vlaming	full cooperation, prior referral, conditional immunity	none	2014	yes
construction (1)	Civcon Construction	late application, implicated in single project	total turnover	2014	yes
construction (1)	Harding Allison	did not respond to invitation, implicated	total turnover	2014	yes
construction (1)	B & E International	did not respond to invitation, implicated	total turnover	2014	yes
construction (1)	Cycad Pipelines	did not respond to invitation, implicated	total turnover	2014	yes
construction (1)	N17 Toll Operators	did not respond to invitation, implicated in single project	total turnover	2014	yes
construction (1)	Esorfranki	full cooperation, prior referral, only implicated in 1 project	not specified	2013	yes
construction (1)	Narvo construction	full cooperation, prior referral, disclosed and settled one conduct	not specified	2013	yes
construction (1)	Hochtief Construction	late application, liable for 1 conduct, not implicated in any other	not specified	2013	yes
construction (1)	G Liviero & Son	implicated in projects which it did not initially disclose, liable for 2	not specified	2013	yes
construction (1)	Tabular Technical	disclosed two conducts, liable to settle one	not specified	2013	yes
construction (1)	Vlaming	disclosed five conducts but implicated in one more, got CLP for three, liable for three	not specified	2013	yes
construction (1)	Guiricich Bros	implicated in multiple conducts, disclosed some, got CLP for eight, liable to settle one	not specified	2013	yes
construction (1)	Ramdel Construction	late application disclosed and settled three conducts, not implicated in any other	not specified	2013	yes

continued

Cartel	Firm	Factors	Special turnover	Date	CLP?
construction (1)	Haw & Inglis	big player, engaged in multiple practices, settled six conducts, got CLP for three	not specified	2013	yes
construction (1)	Reubex	big player, multiple conducts, disclosed and settled nine conducts	not specified	2013	yes
construction (1)	Basil Read Holdings	big player, multiple conducts, did not disclose all, got CLP for two, liable to settle seven	not specified	2013	yes
construction (1)	Aveng (Africa)	big player, multiple conducts, did not disclose all, got CLP for 26, liable for 17	not specified	2013	yes
construction (1)	Stefanutti	big player, multiple practices, disclosed some, implicated in others, liable for 21	not specified	2013	yes
construction (1)	Murray & Roberts	big player, late application, multiple practices, did not disclose all, liable for 17, got CLP for some	not specified	2013	yes
construction (1)	WBHO Construction	big player, late application, multiple practices, did not disclose all, did not agree to settle some	not specified	2013	yes

Sources: CCSA and www.comptrib.co.za

2 Cartel likelihood, duration and deterrence in South Africa

Ratshidaho Maphwanya[1]

Introduction

One of the preoccupations of competition authorities around the world is the investigation and prosecution of hard-core cartels. Cartels form when firms in a horizontal relationship (one between competitors) cooperate instead of compete. Saved from the burden of rivalry, firms have market power to charge higher prices and can collectively constrain supply, which would not be possible under conditions of competition. This has a negative impact on the cartel's customers and ultimately on consumers. Cartel conduct is therefore considered the most deplorable of all anticompetitive conduct engaged in by firms, reflected in the manner in which competition authorities around the world deal with this conduct. South African competition law is no different in that cartel conduct is outlawed in the Competition Act (No. 89 of 1998, as amended).

Enforcing anti-cartel laws forms the backbone of competition policy worldwide. A competition authority must put in place measures aimed not only at prosecuting cartels, but also at deterring future cartel conduct. Enforcing these laws must always be twofold. First, enforcement means detecting and prosecuting existing cartels. Second, the authority must deter future cartels either by the same firms (specific deterrence) or by other firms (general deterrence). There are several studies dedicated to revealing the immediate impact of prosecuting cartels (e.g., Connor, 2014; Khumalo, Mashiane and Roberts, 2014; Mncube, 2013). This study focuses primarily on deterring future cartels.

In studying cartel deterrence, this chapter relies on the cartel decision-making equation which shows that firms will be deterred from engaging in cartel conduct only if the expected penalty is more than the additional profits and other benefits derived from collusion. The expected penalty is the product of the actual penalty imposed after successful prosecution and the probability of detection, taking into account the appropriate discount rate. For a particular penalty amount, as the probability of detection increases from zero to one, the expected penalty approaches the actual penalty. The value of the penalty and the probability of detection can be influenced by various factors, some of which can in turn be influenced by the competition authorities. Some are straightforward, such as merely being seen to be enforcing the available anti-cartel laws, but others require a more concerted effort by the authorities for the desired effect. This study seeks to determine whether the competition authorities are using the tools at their disposal as efficiently as possible to deter firms from colluding.

Two approaches were employed in achieving this objective. The first was to survey competition attorneys. Competition attorneys advise firms on their conduct, on whether the conduct constitutes collusion, and on the pros and cons of revealing the conduct by applying for leniency to the Competition Commission of South Africa (CCSA). The survey provides indicators of firms' actions and perceptions regarding the different components of deterrence associated with competition enforcement in South Africa. This approach is similar to other surveys conducted globally and locally on issues related to cartel deterrence.

The second approach was to compile and analyse a database of discovered South African cartels, including data on the duration of each cartel. The database contains the characteristics of these cartels that influence cartel stability, deterrence and durability, such as the presence of homogeneous products, the number of firms in the cartel, the presence of industry associations as well as the tool instrumental in their detection. This replicates international studies and allows comparisons to be drawn between the experience in South Africa and that of other countries.

From here, the chapter proceeds as follows: I start by presenting a brief literature review on cartel deterrence and the cartel decision-making equation before discussing important aspects of the chapter's methodology. I then present the survey results and the results of the cartel data analysis before concluding.

The economics of cartel deterrence

The objectives of competition enforcement concerning cartels must be twofold – the detection and prosecution of existing cartels, and, ultimately, the deterrence of future cartel formation (Agisilaou, 2013). It is necessary to distinguish between general and specific deterrence. General deterrence refers to the deterrence of contraventions *ex ante* by threatening violators with heavy enough sanctions to deter contravention in the first place (Buccirossi et al., 2009). Specific deterrence refers to the deterrence of a violator *ex post* by imposing a heavy enough penalty so that they do not contravene again (Smith and Gartin, 1989).

The primary objective of a competition policy regime must be general deterrence as it allows for the targeting of many more contraventions before they have even happened. This allows for significant savings in resources. Nevertheless, several jurisdictions, including South Africa, have put in place measures aimed at improving specific deterrence. These include consideration of repeat contraventions in calculating penalties. The concept of marginal deterrence must also be kept in mind. This refers to ensuring that the sanction is proportional to the severity of the conduct so that violators get harsher sanctions for more severe violations (Shavell, 1992).

A successful cartel deterrence framework must ensure that the costs associated with detection and prosecution outweigh the benefits of collusion (Motta, 2008).

A firm will only be deterred from colluding if the costs of colluding expressed as the severity of the sanction multiplied by the probability of detection exceed the additional profits derived from colluding. The formula in figure 2.1 is a useful representation of this.

$$\Delta\prod < (p*F)$$

Figure 2.1 Criminal decision-making equation

Source: Motta (2008)

Where $\Delta\prod$ is the additional profits derived from colluding, p is the probability of detection and F is the penalty imposed upon detection and prosecution. A firm will only be deterred from colluding if (p*F) exceeds $\Delta\prod$. The product (p*F) can be described as the expected penalty. For a given penalty, as the probability of detection increases (from 0 to 1), the expected penalty also increases and deterrence is strengthened. Below I consider the make-up of this equation. The idea is to show from the literature how these variables change and how, to a certain extent, they can be influenced by competition authorities. The research presented in this chapter focuses mostly on the two variables that make up the expected penalty – the probability of detection and sanctions.

The probability of detection

The probability of detection is the centrepiece of a deterrence strategy. It would be useless for a competition regime to put in place harsh sanctions if they are not accompanied by a competent detection plan. The expected sanction equals the actual value of the sanction times the probability of detection (Landes, 1983). As the probability of detection increases, the expected value of the fine for the cartelists equally increases and this leads to a higher level of deterrence. Bryant and Eckard (1991) were until recently the only economists to attempt to estimate the probability of detection for firms in a cartel by using data from a sample of 184 cartel conspiracies detected by competition authorities in the US between 1961 and 1998. They ran a statistical model that relied mostly on the duration of cartels detected during that period. The results of the model showed that the probability of a cartel being detected in any given year was between 13 and 17%. Bryant and Eckard noted that these were likely to be upper bounds given that they had relied only on data from cartels that *had* been detected.

In a more recent study, Combe, Monnier and Legal (2008) relied on the model developed by Bryant and Eckard to replicate this research for the European Union (EU). They estimated the probability of detection for cartels in the EU to be between 12.9 and 13.3% in any given year. It is important to put these numbers into context: a probability of detection of 15% in a given year equates to approximately 1/7. If we input this fraction into the cartel deterrence equation above, it tells us that for deterrence to be achieved given a probability of detection of around 15%, the level of sanctions must equal approximately seven times the gains from collusion.

The methodology employed by these economists is of great value to this research. Nevertheless, due to differences in the stage of development of the South African competition authorities it cannot be directly transferred to this research. The research in this line of inquiry relied on a statistical birth and death model that describes the onset and duration of cartels. The authors then use the maximum likelihood method to estimate the model's parameters. The parameters estimated are the number of cartels (active but ultimately caught) and the probability of being caught. This methodology is based on a very specific set of assumptions, including the stage of development of the competition regime. The model parameters can only be estimated when T is large, being tantamount to when the competition regime has reached a steady state. This would be an unsustainable assumption for the South African competition regime.

Notwithstanding the difficulty in applying these models in South Africa, there is still value to be gained from their inclusion. Both studies include (as part of their broader research) information on the average duration of cartels in their respective jurisdictions. This measure is useful in that it indicates the likely survival of a cartel in a particular jurisdiction. This can be considered as an imperfect proxy for the probability of detection. The length of time a cartel will be able to survive is influenced by a number of things, such as the efficiency of the cartel, but, importantly, also the efficiency of the competition authority. Bryant and Eckard (1991) calculated the average duration for cartels in the US to be 6.25 years. Combe, Monnier and Legal (2008) calculated this average for cartels in the EU to be 7.6 years. There are a few other studies that have also calculated the average duration of cartels without necessarily calculating the probability of detection. Zimmerman and Connor (2005) use a sample of 167 modern international cartels detected between 1990 and 2004 to calculate the average duration of about 6.3 years. Levenstein and Suslow (2006) use a sample of 72 cartels detected in either the US or the EU between 1990 and 2006 to calculate an average duration of about 7.5 years.

There are two key points to be noted. Firstly, the research presents results of the probability that a cartel ultimately detected would have been detected in any given year. This research provides little insight into the 'global' probability of detection for cartels. Secondly, because competition authorities (but more importantly, firms themselves) do not know this 'global' probability of detection, they rely on inferences from signals they receive from the competition environment and from the competition authorities in particular.

These perceptions of probability are based on a collection of information gathered from observing the market and the competition authorities. Most potential criminals are not well versed in the actual efficiency of the justice system and hence rely on any signals given out (Cook, 1980). This is important, as competition authorities can influence the signal sent out and increase cartel deterrence. The most effective signal that competition authorities can send out is through enforcing competition law, as firms will respond to this observable signal (Besanko and Spulber, 1989). If firms can see the competition authorities prosecuting anticompetitive conduct, it is likely that fewer firms will engage in such behaviour out of fear of prosecution.

A tool employed by competition authorities that increases not only the global probability of detection but also the perceived probability of detection is a leniency policy. Leniency policies allow for firms that participated in cartels to confess their contraventions in exchange for immunity from (or leniency in) prosecution (Aubert, Rey and Kovacic, 2006). This 'deal' is generally done in exchange for information that will assist the competition authority in prosecuting the other firms in the cartel. Leniency policies are successful because they turn collusion into a prisoner's-dilemma-type game where each firm in the cartel constantly has to consider whether fellow cartelists are going to apply for leniency and whether it should beat them to the door (Harrington, 2008).

Inasmuch as they increase the probability of detection, leniency programmes can only work if they are accompanied by a probability of detection greater than zero (Harrington, 2008). As firms perceive the probability of detection to be increasing, it becomes more likely that they will apply for amnesty. Facing imminent detection by a competition authority, applying for and receiving immunity becomes a much more attractive option. Firms are less likely to apply if they believe they will not get caught. This is the reason why competition authorities may be tempted to exaggerate their effectiveness at detecting cartels, as this creates the impression of a probability of detection approaching one (Miller, 2009). Events such as high-profile cartel busts and dawn raids may increase the perception that cartel conduct is likely to be detected.

Sanctions

A large enough sanction, coupled with a high probability of detection, will increase cartel deterrence (Bishop and Walker, 2002). Fines should be high enough to cover the harm that accrues to all the economic actors affected by the conduct (Page, 1990). Unless the fines are high enough to make collusion unprofitable, they will not achieve their deterrence objective (Cyrenne, 1999). The optimal penalty for a cartel should be equal to the sum of the deadweight loss and the wealth transfer that occurred from consumers/customers to the cartel (Page, 1990). This can be explained as the penalty being equal to the net harm imposed by the cartel on everyone except the cartel members (Landes, 1983).

Certain jurisdictions, South Africa included, apply a cap on the financial penalty that can be imposed on firms that contravene competition laws, primarily due to legality concerns. This means that it is not inconceivable that there may be instances where the optimal penalty to deter cartels is not within a competition authority's reach. A study conducted on a sample of 191 cartels in the EU shows that in 37% of the cases, the cartel overcharge exceeded the maximum possible fine (Smuda, 2012). In these cases, the optimal penalty to achieve deterrence was not within the reach of the competition authorities. This suggests that a successful deterrence strategy may have to include other tools, above and beyond financial penalties.

Firms found guilty of collusion may be subject to civil claims beyond the fines assessed. Allowance for civil claims by third parties increases the severity of the punishment imposed on cartel members and hence increases deterrence (Frazer, 1995). In the US, firms found guilty of cartel conduct are subject to treble damages in civil suits. This substantially increases the cost of being in a cartel and therefore increases deterrence. Civil claims are not included in the granting of amnesty as part of leniency applications in the US, meaning that the threat of treble damages is likely to be a strong deterrent (Levenstein and Suslow, 2011). This may, however, discourage leniency applications, as firms fear the imposition of civil damages even after being granted immunity from prosecution by competition authorities. The issue is complex and South Africa is no exception.

In certain jurisdictions, executives/employees who are found to have engaged in cartel activity on behalf of their firms can be prosecuted in criminal or civil proceedings (Kolasky, 2004). Unlike other sanctions, personal liability links competition contraventions to the personal well-being of the people involved in these activities. By threatening people with possible jail time or heavy personal fines, competition authorities restrict the ability of company executives to divorce themselves from the actions of their firms. This seemingly heavy-handed approach is premised on getting at the managers of firms and on the belief that explicit cartel conduct is a very serious economic crime (Lipsky, 1991).

In addition to the financial (administrative fines and civil claims) and the criminal penalties imposed, the fact and the threat of reputational damage may also influence the behaviour of firms. As the sinister nature of cartel conduct becomes better known by customers, suppliers, competitors and members of the public, it becomes more likely that firms that are prosecuted for cartel conduct will suffer reputational damage (Buccirossi et al., 2009). This damage can be considered an additional monetary sanction if some of the firm's customers or suppliers are unwilling to continue doing business with a firm that has been found guilty of being in a cartel.

The administrative penalties, civil damages and, where applicable, criminal sanctions make up the combination of factors that firms must weigh against additional profits when making a decision on whether or not to form or join a cartel. Competition authorities must therefore ensure that this combination of tools is set at a level high enough to discourage anticompetitive conduct.

Methodologies

This research assesses the state of the cartel decision-making equation for South Africa. I have used a few proxies to make findings on certain aspects of the equation, and, when the results are considered in their entirety, it becomes possible to make findings on the state of cartel deterrence in the country. This research does not seek to find definitive values for the variables in the equation – it is doubtful that any research could do that. However, there is still value in probing their likely behaviour as this gives insight into deterrence.

I employed two distinct methodologies in trying to answer my set of research questions. Firstly, I conducted a survey of competition lawyers. Surveys have been used in the past to get insight into questions around cartel deterrence (see the survey by the Office of Fair Trading [OFT, 2007] and also by the CCSA and the Competition Tribunal [2009]).[2] I surveyed competition lawyers as proxies for the firms in the market, and used the survey to examine the behaviour of firms in response to the competition authorities and the competition regime in general.

The rationale for choosing to survey attorneys was that, as key intermediaries, they have insight into how their clients generally respond to various competition-related issues. The survey was conducted with the top competition law firms in the country[3] and asked questions related to cartel deterrence, the Corporate Leniency Policy (CLP) and criminal prosecution of individuals for cartel conduct. Surveying competition lawyers as a proxy for their client firms is not unprecedented. A similar methodology was employed by Feinberg (1985), Benckenstein and Gabel (1982) and the OFT (2007). The survey was conducted using questionnaires that were sent to respondents via email and a few preliminary interviews.

The survey generally had a low response rate. However, the responses were reflective of views from all the major law firms in the country, which in itself is a very small population size. Other research done in this field has also suffered from a low response rate, likely due to issues of confidentiality. My survey had a response rate of about 18%.[4] A survey by Feinberg (1985) on a similar subject had a responses rate of 18%. The survey by Benckenstein and Gabel (1982) had a response rate of 29.8%.

The second methodology employed was a statistical analysis of a database compiled using information on cartels prosecuted in South Africa. The database includes information on hard-core cartels that have been detected by the CCSA in the years since the introduction of the Competition Act in 1999, as well as information about the duration of each cartel and how each cartel was detected. I use this database to make certain findings on the state of cartel deterrence in the country.

The main aspect of this study is the duration analysis, in which I studied data on the duration of South African cartels and calculated an average duration. My intention was to compare my results to the results of studies such as those by Bryant and Eckard (1991), Combe, Monnier and Legal (2008), Zimmerman and Connor (2005) and also Levenstein and Suslow (2006), all of which include estimates of the average duration of cartels in various jurisdictions. This can be used to draw inferences on the effectiveness of the South African competition enforcement regime by comparing it to other, more developed competition jurisdictions.

The thinking is that if a competition authority is effective at detecting cartels that are active within its jurisdiction then it is likely that cartels will be active for a relatively shorter duration. With this in mind, it is also likely that firms will know this (as they observe cartels in the economy with a short lifespan) and be relatively less inclined to participate in collusion. Although imperfect, this analysis can still be used as a fair proxy for cartel deterrence in South Africa. Most of the data required for the database were collected from the website of the Competition Tribunal,[5] where decisions on all completed competition cases are published. The analysis was conducted for the period from 1999 to 2012.

Further, the study considers those aspects of South African cartels that may be conducive to cartel conduct. I study the extent to which South African cartels have included homogeneous products, whether they were concentrated as well as the presence of industry organisations. The impact of these factors on cartel deterrence is then considered.

Both of these methodologies – the lawyers' survey and the duration database – although different in application, present key information on the state of cartel deterrence in South Africa. It is important to keep in mind that cartel deterrence cannot be measured with certainty as there is no unit of measurement. What can be presented, however, is an analysis of the various factors that influence deterrence. This kind of analysis provides insight into whether firms in the country are likely to be sufficiently deterred or not. It also allows recommendations to be made on aspects of South Africa's cartel enforcement that can be improved. In the next section I present the main findings of the survey.

Analysis of survey results

Response to competition enforcement

The first group of questions in the lawyers' survey asked how firms respond to competition enforcement. The main question asked the attorneys to estimate the proportion of their clients that apply for leniency once given information that they may have contravened the Act. While leniency is a complex matter, the basic model underlying this question is as follows: prior to seeking external legal advice, firms may be uncertain about whether their conduct contravenes the Act. After obtaining advice from attorneys, uncertainty no longer exists. Firms now know that their conduct violates the Act and they have to decide how to proceed, knowing that detection by the CCSA is likely to lead to sanctions. A firm that considers its cartel decision-making equation at this point and is deterred will probably apply for leniency as this saves it from the likely sanction. A firm not deterred may choose not to apply for leniency. The survey responses are set out in table 2.1.

Table 2.1 Overall average percentage responses for survey question 2

Range (%)	Responses (%)
0–50	32
50–60	31
60–70	3
70–80	0
80–90	0
90–100	35
Total	100*

Source: Own survey and analysis

Note: * Percentages do not add up to 100 due to rounding.

More than 60% of the respondents submit that, of their clients who received legal advice that they may have contravened section 4 of the Act, fewer than 60% applied for leniency. The balance did not apply for the CLP. In fact, only 35% of the attorneys responded that more than 90% of their clients applied for leniency after they had been informed that their conduct contravened the Act. The results can be analysed further, using the multiplication rule of probabilities[6] (Ash, 2008) to produce probabilities that firms will apply for leniency. This reveals a 60% probability that a firm that receives legal advice that it has contravened the Act will apply for leniency. The high number of firms (40%) not applying for leniency even though they know they have contravened the Act has particularly negative implications for the competition authorities. Practically, it implies that a substantial number of firms either consider the probability of detection to be low enough to make collusion worth the risk, or, alternatively, the sanctions that are imposed by the competition authorities, and by society in general, are low enough to make collusion worth it. There are undoubtedly also other reasons for not applying for leniency.

Factors driving leniency applications

This section considers the drivers of CLP applications. These are the features of the jurisdiction that lead to firms applying for leniency. The respondents were given a list of ten factors that may influence CLP applications and were asked to rank each factor's importance on a scale of one (not important) to five (most important). I used the responses to compute average scores for each factor, presented in figure 2.2.

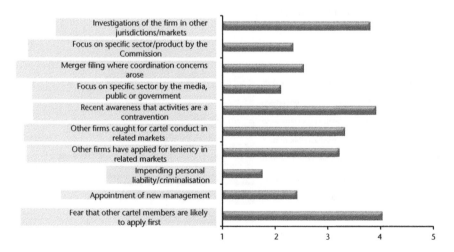

Figure 2.2 Drivers of leniency applications

Source: Own survey and analysis

According to respondents, the factor contributing most to firms applying for leniency is the fear that other firms in the cartel will apply first. This is obvious vindication for the CLP, as it means that the prisoner's dilemma effect mentioned above has a notable impact on firms' decision making and hence on deterrence. Another factor considered important is recent awareness that the conduct is a contravention. It is surprising, however, that there are firms still finding out that certain conduct is a contravention of the Act, given that it has been in place for approximately 15 years.

The presence of a competition investigation of the firm in other jurisdictions or markets also appears to be important to firms when applying for leniency. This is not surprising, as a firm is likely to consider that a competition authority investigation in one market or jurisdiction means the probability of detection has increased for all the contraventions the firm is involved in. The fourth most important factor is when other firms are caught for cartel conduct in related markets. When the CCSA investigates a firm (or other firms) in a related market, it is likely that the firm will interpret this as an increase in the probability that it will be detected.

An unexpected factor is the little weight respondents gave to focus on a sector by the CCSA or by the public, media or government. It appears that firms do not consider this to increase the probability of detection and hence it does not prompt them to apply for leniency. Firms respond to the CCSA detecting other cartels but not to the fact that the CCSA has prioritised a sector or industry. The respondents submit that impending personal liability or criminalisation has minimal impact on firms applying for leniency. It may be that the delayed implementation has led firms to question whether it will ever be implemented. It would not be unforeseen to see an influx of leniency applications when the date for implementing personal liability is announced and the prospect becomes a reality. Figure 2.3 compares these results to the results of the 2009 survey done by the CCSA for the ten-year review.

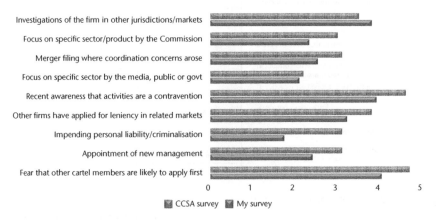

Figure 2.3 CCSA survey and my survey comparison

Sources: CCSA and Competition Tribunal (2009) and own survey

Note: The factor 'Existing Investigation by the Commission' was not listed in my survey, but appeared in the CCSA survey.

The factor considered most important by respondents to both surveys is the fear that other cartel members are going to apply for leniency first. As noted, this shows that the CLP acts as a deterrent through the prisoner's dilemma effect. The rank of the importance of the different factors remained broadly the same across the two surveys, although the relative importance (average score) placed on specific factors by the respondents decreased in my survey. However, whether the respondents considered the fear that other firms will apply for leniency as 'very important' as opposed to 'important' is less significant than what factors drive CLP applications relative to one another.[7]

Drivers of deterrence

The respondents were asked to rank the importance of a range of factors which influence cartel deterrence. Similar to the question above, the respondents were given a list of ten factors that may influence cartel deterrence and asked to rank each factor's importance on a scale of one (not important) to five (very important). The results are presented in figure 2.4.

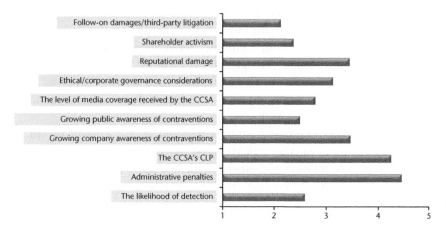

Figure 2.4 Drivers of cartel deterrence

Source: Own survey and analysis

According to the respondents, the factor that is most important for cartel deterrence is administrative penalties. This is unsurprising as profit-maximising firms are more likely to respond to sanctions that affect their bottom line. There is a question around whether administrative penalties are high enough to actually deter firms from colluding; the empirical studies cited above suggest they are. However, the 10% cap on administrative penalties is likely to further limit deterrence. Smuda (2012) shows that in most instances, the penalty that would be sufficient to deter firms from colluding is usually not available to the competition authorities due to the cap (in section 59(2) of the Act in the case of South Africa).

Another factor considered important in driving deterrence is the CLP. This is to be expected; the literature is clear about the likely impact of a leniency policy on cartel deterrence. Other factors that the respondents consider important are the growing awareness by companies that their conduct is a contravention and the reputational damage associated with being found to be in a cartel. These two factors are interesting as they speak to an increased appreciation of competition law by stakeholders in the economy. Reputational damage must be considered as forming part of the group of sanctions imposed on firms when they are detected.

What is surprising is the low importance attached to the growing public awareness that cartel conduct is a contravention, given the high importance attached to reputational damage. It may be that firms are more worried about reputational damage from the perspective of other firms or the state, as opposed to from members of the public

Criminalisation and strengthened deterrence

The attorneys were asked whether the introduction of criminal prosecution for individuals involved in cartel conduct on behalf of their firms was likely to improve deterrence. More than half (56%) believe it will increase cartel deterrence. This is consistent with most economic literature on the deterrence effect of criminal prosecutions. Some respondents gave qualified responses, mostly citing aspects that may influence its success or failure, such as the CCSA being able to operationalise criminal prosecutions as a strong tool through cooperation with the National Prosecuting Authority.

Twenty-two per cent of respondents indicated that since the debate on criminalisation was introduced, their clients have asked about it and some have requested compliance training and other internal measures to ensure that they are compliant with competition laws. This suggests that the impending introduction of criminalisation is already having a deterrent effect.

The attorneys were asked to identify impediments to the CLP and ways in which cartel deterrence can be improved in South Africa. On the first question, more than half of the responses (56%) cited the lack of protection for leniency applicants against follow-on damages as a factor that may dissuade firms from applying for leniency. Some respondents noted that this may have more of an impact when criminal prosecution is introduced. The risk of further liability outside of the competition framework may harm the CLP.

There was very little consistency in the responses on how cartel deterrence can be improved. However, an issue that was brought up several times was protecting leniency applicants from prosecution or follow-on damages. Other suggestions were improved efficiency in dealing with cartel cases by the CCSA and also more predictability in how firms will be prosecuted, especially when criminalisation is introduced. Unsurprisingly, none of the attorneys suggested an increase in penalties as a way of improving deterrence.

Analysis of the database of South African cartels

Duration of South African cartels

Using data from decisions and consent agreements published by the Tribunal, I created a database showing the duration of each cartel prosecuted by the CCSA. In the period from the introduction of the Competition Act in 1999 until 2012, the CCSA completed (i.e., finalised in the Tribunal either through settlement or prosecution) 99 cases involving aspects of section 4 prohibited conduct. Of these, 28 were instances of hard-core collusion. The substantial disparity is because several of the cases, although not instances of hard-core collusion, involved other prohibited horizontal arrangements. There is also a lot of duplication in that firms that form part of the same cartel may be prosecuted through different proceedings. Table 2.2 presents the main findings of this study.

Table 2.2 Basic statistics on cartel duration

	Results
Cartels	28
Mean	6.7 years (6 years 8 months)
Median	7.3 years (7 years 4 months)
Min.	0.1 years (1 month)
Max.	11.3 years (11 years 4 months)

Source: Own survey and analysis

The mean duration for a cartel – how long it survived on average – before being detected and prosecuted by the CCSA is 6.7 years or six years and eight months. The median duration is 7.3 years or seven years and four months. The cartel that lasted the shortest duration of all the cartels detected by the CCSA was the price-fixing arrangement between South African Airways, SA Airlink and Comair.[8] These firms colluded to fix the introduction of a fuel surcharge on the price of tickets for domestic and international flights in May 2004. The CCSA detected this collusion in the same month and it hence lasted for less than one month.

Determining which cartel was active the longest is not a straightforward exercise, the main reason being the existence of several cartels prior to introducing the Act in 1999. The cement cartel is one example. Before 1996, the cement industry was a legal cartel through an exemption dating as far back as the 1940s. However, when the exemption was withdrawn in 1995, the industry continued to operate in the same manner.[9] The precast concrete products cartel had been active since the 1970s.[10] Several of the cartels in agricultural products stemmed from the marketing boards that were set up through the Marketing Act of 1937 as part of the government's broader interventions in the agricultural sector (Roberts, 2009). When the marketing boards were disbanded in 1996, firms in the different markets simply carried on as (now) illegal cartels. It is difficult to measure the duration of these cartels with precision. The Act coming into place in 1999 suggests there may not be much value in doing so in any event.

Two of the longest-running cartels in the post-Competition Act era are the polymers cartel involving Sasol Polymers and Safripol[11] and the pelagic fishing cartel.[12] Both preceded the introduction of the Act and were detected only in 2010. Other long-running cartels that preceded these two were detected sooner, once the Act was in place.

Table 2.3 compares my results to those of other studies that have covered the same ground with regards to other jurisdictions. I pay closer attention to the studies by Zimmerman and Connor (2005) and Levenstein and Suslow (2006) as they were conducted over a similar time frame to mine, and also consider cartels from a similar 'generation'.

Table 2.3 Comparison of various studies' results

	Cartels	Period	Mean	Median	Jurisdiction
My results	28	1999–2012	6.7 years	7.3 years	South Africa
Bryant and Eckard (1991)*	184	1961–1988	6.25 years	4.7 years	US
Combe et al. (2008)*	86	1969–2008[†]	7.6 years	5.7 years	Europe
Zimmerman and Connor (2005)	167	1990–2004	6.3 years	4.4 years	US and Europe
Levenstein and Suslow (2006)	72	1990–2006[†]	7.5 years	6.0 years	US and Europe

Sources: *Own survey; Bryant & Eckard (1991); Combe et al. (2008); Zimmerman & Connor (2005); Levenstein & Suslow (2006)*

Notes: * An average of the results from the two measures of duration applied was used to compute one mean and median result for both duration measures. These authors used two estimates of duration due to imprecise data.
[†] The authors did not indicate the cut-off date for their study. Combe et al. noted they had considered cartels from 1969 to the 'present day' (the paper was published in 2008). Levenstein and Suslow noted they had considered cartels from 1990 onwards (the paper was published in 2006).

It is remarkable how similar the results of all the studies are. Despite the differences in the time periods considered and the jurisdictions within which the cartels operated, the average duration for cartels that are eventually detected in each of the studies is around six to eight years; that is, a cartel will last, on average, between six and eight years before it is detected by the competition authorities. This suggests that a cartel that will eventually be detected by the CCSA is likely to survive on average for more or less the same duration in South Africa as cartels in Europe and the US. These results are fairly positive for the South African competition regime, if only because it means the CCSA and the Tribunal are in good company.

Drivers of detection

I also considered the factors that contribute the most to the CCSA's enforcement efforts, in other words, those that have led to the detection of cartels in South Africa. The results are shown in figure 2.5.

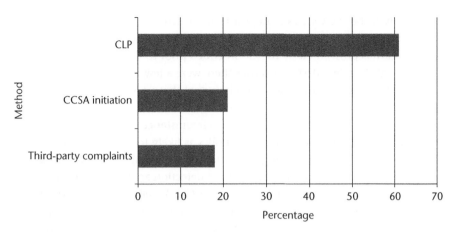

Figure 2.5 Method of detection frequency

Source: Own data

Figure 2.5 shows the factors that have led to cartel detections, as reported mainly in Tribunal decisions. The factor that has contributed the most to cartel detection in South Africa is the CLP – 61% of the cartels prosecuted by the CCSA. This accords with the results of the survey discussed above and with economic theory (see Motta and Polo, 2003). The other two factors that have contributed to cartel detection are the CCSA's own complaint initiations (21%) and third-party complaints (18%), including complaints by rivals, customers, members of the public and the government. Figure 2.6 shows a time series of cartel detections, highlighting the enforcement tool responsible.

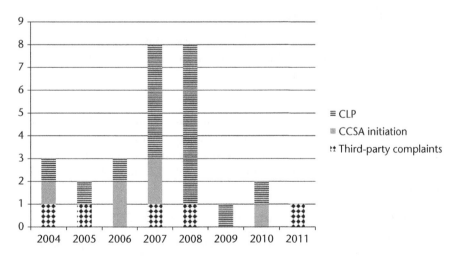

Figure 2.6 Enforcement tools leading to cartel detection

Source: Own analysis

A majority of the cartels prosecuted by the CCSA through the CLP between 1999 and 2012 involved conduct detected in 2007 and 2008.[13] Moreover, a closer look at the dates when these cartels were detected supports the finding that the

CLP is likely to be the CCSA's strongest tool for detecting cartels. The CLP was initially introduced in February 2004[14] and amended in May 2008.[15] None of the hard-core cartels prosecuted by the CCSA ended prior to the introduction of the CLP. Although Lavoie (2010) notes that there were a few cartel complaints prior to introducing the CLP, this study's results reveal that none of these complaints led to any kind of finding in the Tribunal.

It is also important to keep in mind the circumstances that may have served to support the CLP. As noted, a leniency policy is likely to work if it is accompanied by a probability of detection greater than zero (Harrington, 2008). Activities perceived to have increased the probability of detection are likely to lead to more firms applying for leniency. For instance, the CCSA undertook a prioritisation strategy in 2006/2007 that included a focus on the following sectors: food, agroprocessing and forestry; financial services; infrastructure and construction; and intermediate industrial products (CCSA, 2007). In 2007, the CCSA received leniency applications for cartels in bread and precast concrete products in its identified priority sectors (Makhaya, Mkhwananzi and Roberts, 2012).

This prioritisation of certain sectors (and cartels in general) created a credible threat of detection that probably increased the effectiveness of the CLP. The CCSA additionally adopted a more proactive approach to cartel enforcement involving screening techniques for identifying markets likely to be cartelised (Makhaya, Mkhwananzi and Roberts, 2012). In addition, the amendment to the CLP in 2008 is likely to have improved deterrence. However, it appears that the majority of the CLP applications that led to prosecutions preceded implementation of the amendment.

Cartel stability in South Africa

In this section, I consider the characteristics of the various cartels detected by the CCSA and assess the extent to which South African cartels possess the characteristics that could influence cartel stability.

Number of firms in the cartel

It is more likely that firms will reach and maintain an agreement if there are fewer firms involved. This does not mean, though, that a cartel cannot form when there are numerous firms – cartels can always find ways around the challenges posed by having numerous members. Table 2.4 shows the number of firms involved in the cartels the CCSA prosecuted.

Table 2.4 Number of firms in cartels prosecuted by the CCSA

Number of firms in cartel	Number of cartels	Percentage of cartels
2–5	15	54
6–10	6	21
11+	7	25
Total	28	100

Source: Own analysis

More than half of the cartels prosecuted by the CCSA involved five firms or fewer. Only 25% of the cartels prosecuted by the CCSA involved over ten firms. Table 2.5 lists the relationship between the number of firms in a cartel and the duration of the cartel.

Table 2.5 Number of firms in and duration of cartels

Firms involved in cartel	Average duration (years)
2–5	6.0
6–10	7.7
11+	7.3

Source: Own analysis

The results do not show the expected negative relation between the number of firms in a cartel and the duration of the cartel. Moreover, the cartels with the fewest number of member firms (two to five) have the shortest average duration. One of the longest-running cartels post-1999 was a two-firm cartel involving Sasol and Safripol, but this does not appear to be the trend.

Industry association

The presence of an industry association can help to solve problems of monitoring for a cartel, which makes it easier for the firms involved to maintain the collusive agreement (Porter, 2005). If firms are required to submit their market information to an industry association, this may make it easier and quicker for the cartel to detect when firms are not adhering to the cartel agreement. Table 2.6 shows the proportion of the cartels detected by the CCSA that involved an industry association in some capacity.

Table 2.6 Industry association involvement

Industry association	Percentage
Yes	61
No	39
Total	100

Source: Own analysis

More than half of the cartels detected by the CCSA involved the participation of an industry association. Participation may be passive or active. It is likely that the presence of an industry association may be more empowering for a cartel with a large number of members. Table 2.7 indicates the link between the number of firms in a cartel and the presence of an industry association.

The results reveal a positive relationship between the number of firms in a cartel and the involvement of an industry association. All the cartels that involved over ten firms also involved the participation of an industry association. As the number of firms in a cartel increases, it becomes more of a challenge to monitor

Table 2.7 Number of firms in cartels with industry association

Number of firms in cartel	Percentage involving industry association
2–5	40
6–10	67
11+	100

Source: Own analysis

all the firms in the cartel; the presence of an industry association serves to mitigate this challenge. This is likely to increase cartel stability, further increasing the size of the expected penalty necessary to achieve deterrence.

Product homogeneity

Product homogeneity[16] is considered to increase the likelihood of collusion. It is easier for firms with homogeneous products to reach agreement on the terms of collusion and this will improve cartel stability. Table 2.8 shows the extent to which South African cartels involved homogeneous products.

Table 2.8 Product homogeneity in South African cartels

Product homogeneity	Percentage
Yes	61
No	39
Total	100

Source: Own analysis

Over 60% of the cartels prosecuted by the CCSA involved homogeneous products. Table 2.9 shows the relationship between product homogeneity and cartel duration.

Table 2.9 Product homogeneity and cartel duration

Product homogeneity	Average duration (years)
Yes	7.7
No	5.1

Source: Own analysis

The results of the study appear to support a positive link between product homogeneity and cartel duration and stability. Cartels that involve homogeneous products have on average endured for over two-and-a-half years longer than cartels that do not involve homogeneous products.

Conclusions

The results paint a positive picture of cartel deterrence in South Africa, a jurisdiction still very much in its infancy. The CCSA's efforts in detecting cartels have yielded results across several markets. The work is ongoing, however, as it appears firms may still perceive the expected penalty to be low. It is hard to say if this is due to a low probability of detection or to insufficient sanctions. In any case, collusion is not only ongoing but there are also firms that risk detection even after being informed by attorneys that their conduct is a contravention.

The CCSA's CLP has had great success despite certain challenges. It is difficult to argue with the number of cases that have been closed through leniency applications. However, it is of concern that there are still a large number of clients that choose not to apply for leniency after being informed that their conduct is likely to be a contravention of the Act. Assuming that the clients accept their attorney's legal advice as accurate, these firms have not been successfully deterred.

The results of the analysis of cartel duration, however, appear to paint a positive picture of the South African competition regime. On average, a cartel that is eventually detected by the CCSA survives for 6.6 years or 6 years and 7 months. Given the harm caused by hard-core cartels, this number will without a doubt concern policy makers and consumers alike. However, South Africa is in line with international jurisdictions which are much more developed. Given the resources that the CCSA has continuously dedicated to the fight against collusion, it is likely that this average may reduce over time as the CCSA becomes more efficient and members of the public and the business community become more informed about competition law.

Worryingly, the study also shows that South African cartels exhibit characteristics that are likely to improve cartel stability and hence make deterrence more challenging. More than half of the cartels detected by the CCSA involved a small number of firms (less than five) and homogeneous products. The cartels with a large number of firms appear to rely on industry association. This notwithstanding, the CCSA appears to have done fairly well in detecting these cartels. Improvement can certainly be made, such as higher penalties which are likely to increase deterrence, all things being equal. The introduction of personal liability is likely to also be a positive step in the fight against cartels in South Africa.

Notes

1   Ratshidaho Maphwanya is a senior merger analyst in the mergers and acquisitions division of the Competition Commission of South Africa. The views expressed in this chapter are his views and do not necessarily reflect the views of the Commission.

2   This is mainly because secondary data on firm behaviour when it comes to this aspect are by definition not available.

3   This is based on reviews released by the Global Competition Review, http://global competitionreview.com/surveys/article/37416/south-africa (subscription required).

4   Bowman Gilfillan indicated a preference to send one response for the firm, which means the response rate is actually about 21%.

5   See www.comptrib.co.za.

6   The proportions of the firms that will apply for leniency are multiplied with the mid-point of the range and then summed to generate a probability that a firm will apply after receiving legal advice.

7   Whether something is 'important' or 'very important' is a subjective consideration; what matters most is which factors are more important than others.

8   Competition Tribunal, case no. 20/CR/Mar05.

9   Competition Tribunal, case no. 93/CR/Nov11.

10   Competition Tribunal, case no. 23/CR/Feb09.

11   Competition Tribunal, case no. 48/CR/Aug10.

12   Competition Tribunal, case no. 50/CR/May12.

13   These numbers are not necessarily reflective of the total number of leniency applications received by the Commission in this period; in fact, they underestimate the overall total. The disparity is due to the fact that the study only considers completed cases and hence would not include cases that are still ongoing or leniency applications that have been denied.

14   Notice 195 of 2004, Government Gazette No. 25963 of 6 February 2004.

15   Notice 628 of 2008, Government Gazette No. 31064 of 23 May 2008.

16   According to OECD (1993), 'products are considered to be homogenous when they are perfect substitutes and buyers perceive no actual or real differences between the products offered by different firms'. In addition to the conventional product homogeneity described above, homogeneity within product segments has also been considered. For instance, if a product includes variations by quality but there is homogeneity within the different quality segments then the product(s) cartelised are considered homogeneous. Petrol is an example of this. There is differentiation within the broader petrol market (93 octane petrol is different from 95 octane petrol though 93 octane petrol is the same across the different manufacturers and the same applies to 95 octane petrol). Products with these kinds of characteristics are considered homogeneous in this study.

References

Agisilaou P. 2013. *Collusion in Industrial Economics and Optimally Designed Leniency Programmes: A Survey*. Centre for Competition Policy, University of East Anglia, Working Paper 13-3.

Ash RB. 2008. *Basic Probability Theory*. Mineola, NY: Dover Publications.

Aubert C, P Rey and WE Kovacic. 2006. The impact of leniency and whistleblowing programs on cartels. *International Journal of Industrial Organization* 24: 1241–1266.

Benckenstein, AR and HL Gabel. 1982. Antitrust compliance: Results of a survey of legal opinion. *Antitrust Law Journal* 51: 459–516.

Besanko D and DF Spulber. 1989. Antitrust enforcement under asymmetric information. *The Economic Journal* 99: 408–425.

Bishop S and JM Walker. 2002. *The Economics of EC Competition Law: Concepts, Application and Measurement*. London: Sweet & Maxwell.

Bryant PG and EW Eckard. 1991. Price fixing: The probability of getting caught. *The Review of Economics and Statistics* 73: 531–536.

Buccirossi P, L Ciari, T Duso, G Spagnolo and C Vitale C. 2009. *Deterrence in Competition Law*. Governance and the Efficiency of Economic Systems Discussion Paper No. 285.

CCSA (Competition Commission South Africa). 2007. 'Annual Report 2006/07' (online document).

CCSA and Competition Tribunal. 2009. 'Unleashing Rivalry: Ten Years of Enforcement by the South African Competition Authorities' (online document).

Combe E, C Monnier and R Legal. 2008. *Cartels: The Probability of Getting Caught in the European Union*. Bruges European Economic Research Paper No. 12.

Connor, JM. 2014. *Price-Fixing Overcharges: Revised 3rd Edition*. SSRN Working Paper No. 2400780.

Cook PJ. 1980. Research in criminal deterrence: Laying the groundwork for the second decade. *Crime and Justice* 2: 211–268.

Cyrenne P. 1999. On antitrust enforcement and the deterrence of collusive behaviour. *Review of Industrial Organization* 14: 257–272.

Feinberg R. 1985. The enforcement and effects of European antitrust policy: A survey of legal opinion. *Journal of Common Market Studies* 23: 373–384.

Frazer T. 1995. Monopoly, prohibition and deterrence. *The Modern Law Review* 58: 846–859.

Harrington Jr, JE. 2008. Optimal corporate leniency programs. *The Journal of Industrial Economics* 56: 215–246.

Khumalo J, J Mashiane and S Roberts. 2014. Harm and overcharge in the South African precast concrete products cartel. *Journal of Competition Law and Economics* 10: 621–646.

Kolasky W. 2004. Criminalising cartel activity: Lessons from the US experience. *Competition and Consumer Law Journal* 12: 207–223.

Landes WM. 1983. Optimal sanctions for antitrust violations. *The University of Chicago Law Review* 50: 652–678.

Lavoie C. 2010. South Africa's Corporate Leniency Policy: A five-year review. *World Competition* 33: 141–162.

Levenstein MC and VY Suslow. 2006. What determines cartel success? *Journal of Economic Literature* 44: 43–95.

Levenstein MC and VY Suslow. 2011. Breaking up is hard to do: Determinants of cartel duration. *Journal of Law and Economics* 54: 455–492.

Lipsky Jr, AB. 1991. Deterring cartel behavior: Harmonies and disharmonies, problems and solutions. *Antitrust Law Journal* 60: 563–569.

Makhaya G, W Mkhwananzi and S Roberts. 2012. How should young institutions approach competition enforcement? Reflections on South Africa's experience. *South African Journal of International Affairs* 19: 43–64.

Miller NH. 2009. Strategic leniency and cartel enforcement. *The American Economic Review* 99: 750–768.

Mncube, L. 2013. The South African wheat flour cartel: Overcharges at the mill. *Journal of Industry, Competition and Trade* 13: 1–23.

Motta M. 2008. On cartel deterrence and fines in the European Union. *European Competition Law Review* 29: 209–220.

Motta M and M Polo. 2003. Leniency programs and cartel prosecution. *International Journal of Industrial Organisation* 21: 347–379.

OECD (Organisation for Economic Cooperation and Development). 1993. 'Glossary of Industrial Organisation Economics and Competition Law' (online document).

OFT (Office of Fair Trading). 2007. *The Deterrent Effect of Competition Enforcement by the OFT*. OFT Discussion Document 962. http://webarchive.nationalarchives.gov.uk/20140402141250/http:/www.oft.gov.uk/shared_oft/reports/Evaluating-OFTs-work/oft962.pdf

Page W. 1990. Optimal antitrust penalties and competitors' injury. *Michigan Law Review* 88: 2151–2166.

Porter RH. 2005. Detecting collusion. *Review of Industrial Organization* 26: 147–167.

Roberts S. 2009. 'Food Production in South Africa: Corporate Conduct and Economic Policy'. Draft paper for Initiative for Policy Dialogue Task Force on Africa Meeting, Pretoria, 9–10 July (online document).

Shavell S. 1992. A note on marginal deterrence. *International Review of Law and Economics* 12: 345–355.

Smith AD and PR Gartin. 1989. Specifying specific deterrence: The influence of arrest on future criminal activity. *American Sociological Review* 54: 94–106.

Smuda F. 2012. *Cartel Overcharges and the Deterrent Effect of EU Competition Law*. Centre of European Economic Research Discussion Paper No. 12-050.

Zimmerman J and JM Connor. 2005. *Determinants of Cartel Duration: A Cross-Sectional Study of Modern Private International Cartels*. Department of Agricultural Economics Working Paper, Purdue University.

3 Cartel enforcement in the southern African neighbourhood

Thula Kaira

Introduction

South Africa began to implement its modern competition law in 1998 after a series of reforms following the 1994 political transformation. Its successful enforcement against cartels is yet to be replicated in other economically interconnected countries in the Southern African Customs Union (SACU) and the Southern African Development Community (SADC). Of the BLNS (Botswana, Lesotho, Namibia, Swaziland) countries within the SACU community, only Lesotho does not have a competition law or enforcement system. The SADC operates on a larger scale and has 14 member states: Angola, Botswana, Democratic Republic of the Congo, Lesotho, Madagascar, Mauritius, Mozambique, Namibia, Seychelles, South Africa, Swaziland, Tanzania, Zambia and Zimbabwe. All the SACU countries are members of the SADC as well. For the purposes of this chapter, all countries that are members of the SADC and/or SACU are neighbouring countries to South Africa.

Sectors such as mining, petroleum and agricultural products have been a subject of anticompetitive interest in South Africa, notably in relation to cartel activity. Despite the high number of cartels that have been unearthed in South Africa, there does not seem to be equivalent success in the neighbouring countries. This chapter deals with this issue by reviewing selected cartels that have been unearthed in South Africa, with possible links to other SACU/SADC member states. It also references a survey on selected SACU/SADC member states in relation to their cartel enforcement and sectors that have been a subject of cartel investigation in South Africa. The chapter ends with an attempt to highlight lessons that other competition authorities in the SACU/SADC can learn from the success story of the Competition Commission of South Africa (CCSA) in cartel enforcement.

Why neighbours must be worried about cartels unearthed in South Africa

South Africa is a key source of direct and indirect investment in sectors such as mining, retail and, to an extent, manufacturing. SACU's BLNS countries' import bill from South Africa has been dominated by petroleum and related products (including bitumen), cement, motor vehicles, iron ore and concentrates. By 2012, Botswana was the fourth-largest destination for South African exports, at 5.1% of the exports, which accounted for 91.4% of total intra-SACU imports (see SACU, 2012). As for the SADC, the main intra-SADC trade export items include petroleum, agricultural products, electricity and clothing and textile products (SADC, n.d.).

Competition policy and law in SACU/SADC countries is increasingly emphasising job creation, poverty reduction and citizen or small and medium enterprise (SME) empowerment. The International Competition Network has recognised that these alternative objectives of competition policy go mostly hand in hand with the traditional ones (ICN, 2002). The fact is that even the very alternative objectives will not be achieved where there are cartels. This is partly why cartel enforcement has become an important part of competition policy in many countries. Cartel activity has the propensity to stage-manage competition and provide a facade of competition when in actual fact there is collusion and a reduction in consumer surplus.

Where cartels thrive, there are a number of adverse effects. Business opportunities will remain controlled by cartels. Penetrating markets with cartels becomes difficult as cartelists will lower prices when they detect prospective entry, making inward investment costly and causing the exit of struggling firms. This in turn concentrates job creation in a sector among the cartel members. Cartels affect the objectives of regional trade integration and free movement of goods (e.g., customer and market allocation), as cartel members may create barriers to entry and frustrate the entry and growth of competitors. Cartels do not grow markets; they stagnate market growth.

Cartel enforcement in South Africa

Some cartels in South Africa involve markets historically characterised by legal cartels. These legal cartels were outlawed in the 1990s, but long-standing market relationships appear to have prolonged coordinated conduct in many of these markets (Roberts, 2004). An example given by Boshoff (2015) is the bitumen cartel. This market is one originally characterised by a legal cartel exempted from competition policy until 2000. Subsequently, information exchange continued among market participants, allegedly for the purpose of continuing to calculate a reference price requested by government and industry (Boshoff, 2015).

In 1999, the then minister of trade and industry, Alec Erwin, emphasised the pivotal role that the competition authorities were to play in transforming 'an economy inherited in 1994 that was rigid, protected, locked up in inefficient institutions, highly monopolised and concentrated' (CCSA and CTSA, 2009, p. 1).

There is no doubt that the CCSA has demonstrated a tough stance towards cartels, not only by word of mouth, but by clear actions that have removed any doubt of the CCSA's capacity to investigate, get and secure admissible evidence and prosecute successfully. The capacity of the Competition Tribunal of South Africa to handle referrals has also been demonstrated. However, despite record fines and assured vigorous enforcement, there is little indication that cartels are in decline in South Africa (see Planting, 2013). This has led to recent proposed amendments to criminalise certain hard-core cartels, including price fixing and market allocation. Kelly (2010) notes that the introduction of criminal sanctions is based partly on recognition of how important competitive markets are in capitalist economies for maximising consumer welfare, and partly on the apparent inability of administrative fines to serve as an effective deterrent to cartelisation.

In a landmark report, the World Bank (2016, p. viii) noted that products that have been found to be affected by cartels in Africa include fertilisers, food (including wheat, maize and bread), pharmaceuticals, construction materials (including cement) and construction services.[1] Table 3.1 highlights some key cartels with possible overspill into SACU/SADC countries.

Cartel enforcement in neighbouring countries

Cartel enforcement in neighbouring countries has not been as successful as that in South Africa. Reasons for this are many, ranging from capacity to lack of sufficient understanding of competition law by enforcers as much as by adjudicators/courts. Of 14 SACU/SADC countries, 9 have functional competition laws and institutional arrangements to deal with the enforcement thereof. A sample of six of the nine countries was considered reasonable for purposes of the survey that was carried out to review their cartel enforcement activities.

Considering the cartels unearthed in South Africa and the trends in trade and investment between SACU/SADC and South Africa, the chances are high that a cartel in South Africa is most likely also taking place or has taken place in other SACU/SADC countries. In a worst-case but likely scenario, companies may discontinue cartels in South Africa but continue in other SACU/SADC countries where enforcement is weak or non-existent. It is clear from the survey that SACU/SADC countries with functional competition authorities have not investigated, or have investigated but not been successful in gathering the required evidence, or the case has been dismissed on appeal in the same cartels that were successfully investigated and prosecuted in South Africa.

Table 3.2 summarises the survey results. It shows the cartel legal provisions as well as enforcement activities of the six countries in sectors where cartels have been unearthed in South Africa. These sectors include bread, flour, construction, cement, fertiliser, wheat and petroleum.

Except for South Africa, only Botswana and Zambia have busted cartels using dawn raids (none has been through cartel leniency). While no fines have been recorded due to appeal challenges on procedural errors, Botswana unearthed five cartels in five years: supply of food rations to government; car panel beating (Car World & Other); supply of sugar beans to government; and supply of infant formula to government. Three attempted bid-rigging cases were thwarted: supply of communication equipment to the Botswana Police Service; stationery to the Botswana government's Central Transport Organisation; and supply of security

Table 3.1 Cartels uncovered in South Africa, 2003–2010

Name of cartel	Brief facts	End result	Enforcement in SACU/SADC country
Fertiliser cartel	In 2003,[1] the CCSA raided the premises of the suspected cartel members, following which Sasol filed a marker application for leniency for fixing prices of various fertiliser products.	Sasol eventually settled for R250 million (Bonakele, 2009; see also Seria, 2010).	Only Zambia investigated a case in the fertiliser sector (although the case is yet to be determined on appeal).
Cement cartel	The CCSA initiated investigations on 2 June 2008 against four main cement producers: Pretoria Portland Cement Company Limited (PPC), Lafarge Industries South Africa, AfriSam Consortium (Pty) Ltd and Natal Portland Cement Cimpor (Pty) Ltd (CTSA, n.d.).[2]	The CCSA raided the premises of the four cement producers on 24 June 2009. Subsequently, PPC applied for leniency. Lafarge and AfriSam settled with the CCSA and agreed to pay penalties of 6 and 3%, respectively, of their yearly turnover for cement sales in the SACU region in 2010.	Of the SACU/SADC countries, Namibia, Tanzania and Zimbabwe submitted to have investigated similar cartels but did not uncover any cartel. No leniency applications were made to authorities in Botswana, Namibia and Swaziland by the respondent companies that had subsidiaries in these other countries.
Mining-supply cartel	The CCSA uncovered a mining-supply cartel in 2009 (Creamer, 2009).[3] The four companies involved were Aveng Africa's Duraset, RSC Ekusasa Mining, Dywidag-Systems International and Videx Wire Products.	ARSC, a subsidiary of Murray & Roberts Steel, was the first to admit it had colluded with its competitors, and submitted a leniency application on 26 September 2008. The members had agreements to allocate customers and products and also to collude on tenders.	None of the SACU/SADC countries investigated similar cartels. Botswana, Namibia, Zambia and Zimbabwe have mining and related industries, which import mining-related components from or through South African agents.
Construction cartel	In 2009, a probe by the CCSA showed that top construction companies had fixed state and other contracts worth billions of rands (Sapa, 2013).	In July 2013, the CCSA settled with 15 out of 18 construction firms that participated in the Construction Settlement Project (CSP) (see Gedye, 2013). The total combined administrative penalty imposed by the Tribunal for the 15 firms amounted to R1.4 billion (see CCSA, 2014, p. 11).	None of the SACU/SADC countries are reported to have investigated similar or related cartels in their countries.

continued

Name of cartel	Brief facts	End result	Enforcement in SACU/SADC country
Steel cartel	The CCSA unearthed the cartel after a raid of Cape Town Iron and Steel Works/Murray & Roberts, Highveld Steel & Vanadium and the South African Iron and Steel Institute offices, which were used as cartel secretariat. The cartel was at the peak of the construction works for the 2010 Football World Cup (Le Roux, 2008).	Following the raid, the CCSA received an application for leniency from one of the companies under its Corporate Leniency Policy (CLP).	None of the SACU/SADC countries are reported to have investigated similar or related cartels in their countries.
Bread/flour/ wheat milling cartel	In March 2010, the CCSA, subsequent to its investigation into collusion in the wheat milling market, referred its findings to the Tribunal against Pioneer Foods Ltd, Foodcorp Ltd trading as Ruto Mills, Godrich Milling Ltd, Premier Foods Ltd and Tiger Brands Ltd (CCSA, 2010).[4] The flour cartel fixed the price of flour and allocated customers from 1999 to 2007 (see Mncube, 2014).	Penalties were meted out against the cartel members.	Zambia and Zimbabwe investigated cartels in bread but did not uncover any cartel. Zimbabwe investigated a cartel in flour and Zambia in wheat, without success. Most SADC countries import wheat from South Africa.
Bitumen cartel	In 2010/2011 the CCSA initiated a price-fixing complaint in respect of bitumen against the six oil companies operating in South Africa: Total, BP, Shell, Chevron, Engen and Sasol.[5]	Engen agreed to pay R28.8 million and Shell agreed to pay R26.2 million.	None of the SACU/SADC countries are reported to have investigated similar or related cartels in their countries. Botswana, Lesotho, Mauritius, Swaziland and Zimbabwe are net importers of bitumen and bituminous products from South Africa.

Source: Compiled by the author

Notes: [1] In November 2003, Nutri-Flo, a small fertiliser blender and distributor (a customer of Sasol), lodged a complaint with the CCSA alleging that three large fertiliser suppliers in South Africa (Sasol, Kynoch and Omnia) were engaged in abuse of market power involving various fertiliser products. However, in the cause of articulating this conduct, the complainant alluded to the fact that there was collusion between the three suppliers. The Competition Appeal Court (CAC) of South Africa held that the complainant did not intend to complain about the cartel conduct and that the CCSA should have initiated a separate investigation for this conduct. See CAC case no. 93/CAC/Mar10; CT case no. 31/CR/May05.
[2] At least 11 affidavits were made by executives from Stefanutti Stocks, one of the country's biggest construction firms, to the Hawks and the National Prosecuting Authority. The statements were also handed to the CCSA for its probe into construction industry tender rigging, thought to involve contracts worth at least R30 billion. Suspected bid riggers were Wilson Bayly Holmes Ovcon, Stocks & Stocks civil engineering, Murray & Roberts, Group Five, Concor and Aveng.
[3] De Beers, Gold Fields, Harmony, Anglo Platinum, Lonmin and Sasol Mining were among the mining houses that bought roof bolts from the companies.
[4] The case was initiated following revelations by Premier Foods during the bread cartel investigation that the cartel, which involved largely the same companies, also covered their milling operations.
[5] Bitumen and bituminous products are used in road construction and rehabilitation. All the oil companies are members of the South African Bitumen and Tar Association (Sabita). The CCSA submitted that Sabita was a platform to share price-sensitive information among horizontal competitors, and to jointly determine a wholesale list price (and a price index) for bitumen.

Table 3.2 Cartel legal provisions and enforcement activities of selected countries in southern Africa

Questions	Botswana		Namibia		Swaziland		Tanzania		Zambia		Zimbabwe	
	Yes	No	Yes	No	Yes	No	Yes	No	Yes	No	Yes	No
Does your competition agency (agency) deal with cartels?	X		X		X		X		X		X	
Are cartels in your jurisdiction 'per se' offences?	X		X		X		X		X		X	
Are cartels in your jurisdiction a 'rule of reason'?	X			X		X		X	X			X
Has your agency investigated any cartel in the following sectors:												
Bread		X	X		X		X		X		X	
Flour		X	X			X	X			X	X	
Construction		X	X			X	X		X			X
Cement	X			X		X		X	X			X
Fertiliser		X	X			X		X	X		X	
Stock feed		X	X			X		X		X	X	
Plastic pipes		X	X			X		X		X	X	
Retail supply		X	X			X		X		X	X	
Edible oil		X	X			X		X		X	X	
Wheat		X	X			X		X		X	X	

continued →

Questions	Botswana		Namibia		Swaziland		Tanzania		Zambia		Zimbabwe	
	Yes	No	Yes	No	Yes	No	Yes	No	Yes	No	Yes	No
Steel		■		■		■		■		■		■
Petroleum		■		■		■	■		■		■	
Air passenger		■		■		■		■		■		■
Does your agency have a leniency programme?	■		■		■		■		■			■
Does your agency have whistleblower protection in cartels?	■		■		■		■		■			■
Have you successfully 'busted' any cartel using the leniency programme?		■		■		■		■	■			■
Have you 'busted' a cartel using 'dawn raids'?	■			■	■		■		■			■
Have any appeals against your agency's cartel busting been upheld by a higher organ/court?	■		n/a		n/a		■		n/a		n/a	
Do you consider your agency as reasonably capacitated to investigate a cartel?	■		■		■		■		■			■

continued →

Questions	Botswana	Namibia	Swaziland	Tanzania	Zambia	Zimbabwe
Indicate which cartels are 'per se', if any.	Price fixing, bid rigging, market/customer/geographical allocation, sales/production quotas, concerted practice, concerted refusal to join an arrangement crucial to competition	None	None	None	All cartels are per se offences	All cartels are per se offences
Indicate which cartels are 'rule of reason', if any.	Joint ventures	All cartels	All cartels	All cartels, including price fixing between competitors, a collective boycott by competitors or collusive bidding or tendering.	n/a	n/a
What is the minimum (if any) and maximum penalty (if any) in your jurisdiction?	Max. 10% up to three years during the currency of the cartel	Max. 10% of global turnover	Fine not exceeding E250 000 (R250 000) or imprisonment to a term not exceeding five years or both.	5–10% of last audited accounts based on global turnover	Max. of 10% based on latest turnover	Max. imprisonment

Source: Compiled by the author

services to the Companies and Intellectual Property Agency. Attempted bid rigging is not provided for in the Competition Act.

Except for South Africa, Zambia is the only country that has processed a fine. This was a case[2] in which 15 car panel-beating garages conspired to collectively charge a fixed amount for issuance of quotations to insurance companies. The tip-off to the case came after an advocacy workshop the competition authority had conducted for insurance companies. Top Gear Zambia, the ringleader, was fined 2% of its turnover while the others were fined 1%. A landmark case on a cartel in the fertiliser industry involving Omnia Zambia and Nyiombo Investments,[3] where they were fined 5% of their turnover, has been in the appeal process and is yet to be concluded by the Supreme Court of Zambia.

Except for Namibia and Zimbabwe, all the countries indicated that they are sufficiently capacitated to deal with cartel enforcement. Namibia and Zimbabwe have had their competition law implementation systems peer-reviewed under the auspices of the Competition and Consumer Policies Branch of the United Nations Conference on Trade and Development (UNCTAD). Recommendations to foster enforcement machinery are under implementation, which for Zimbabwe include an overhaul of the whole competition law as well as finalisation of a national competition policy.

Lessons from South Africa for other SACU/SADC countries

South Africa's aggressive investigation and enforcement against cartel conduct is unparalleled in any of the SACU/SADC countries. The World Bank (2016) has noted that cartels are the most harmful anticompetitive practice, but anti-cartel enforcement remains relatively weak in Africa. The Bank noted that between 2013 and 2014, 42 horizontal agreement cases were completed by 9 authorities; of those, 50% were investigated by the CCSA (World Bank, 2016, pp. viii, 15–16). While the experiences of South Africa may be unique and not necessarily applicable to or replicable in other countries, competition authorities in SACU/SADC countries can derive some lessons for a successful cartel enforcement regime by reviewing certain fundamentals that lie behind the enforcement machinery and success of the CCSA. These are discussed below.

Corporate leniency and use of settlement agreements

It has been widely held that the CLP has been the single most decisive factor in facilitating a successful cartel enforcement regime in South Africa. The CLP was introduced in 2004 but the first application was received in 2007. In December 2006, the CCSA initiated investigations against Premier, Tiger Brands, Foodcorp and Pioneer Foods, all of whom allegedly had been involved in the bread cartel (Bonakele and Mncube, 2012). After contested proceedings, the Tribunal ruled that Pioneer Foods had engaged in fixing the price of bread products in the Western Cape province and nationally, imposing on Pioneer Foods a fine of R196 million. Following this, Pioneer Foods approached the CCSA with the intention of settling all the other cases that had been referred to the Tribunal for adjudication or that were currently under investigation by the CCSA in which it was a respondent.[4]

From the first leniency application, the initial fine of R196 million showed the respondents that the CCSA was serious. Following this, Pioneer Foods settled all the other cases that were under investigation. UNCTAD (2010) has observed that CLPs are effective only if cartelists not seeking leniency perceive significant punishment to be sufficiently likely. These programmes involve a commitment to a pattern of penalties designed to increase incentives for cartelists to self-report to the competition law enforcer.[5] The UNCTAD report highlights the following as necessary conditions for an effective leniency programme:

- Anti-cartel enforcement must be sufficiently active for cartel members to believe that there is a significant risk of being detected and punished if they do *not* apply for leniency;
- Penalties imposed on cartelists who do not apply for leniency must be significant and predictable to a degree. The penalty imposed on the first applicant is much less than that imposed on later applicants;
- The leniency programme must be sufficiently transparent and predictable to enable potential applicants to predict how they would be treated; and
- To attract international cartelists, the leniency programme must protect information sufficiently for the applicant to be no more exposed than non-applicants to proceedings elsewhere.

The CLP in South Africa was revised in 2008 and was intended to be a policy designed to encourage disclosure by offering immunity from penalisation for cartel conduct in terms of the Competition Act. It was intended, as leniency programmes generally are, to undermine cartel stability by creating a 'prisoner's dilemma' – where none is sure whether the other will reveal the cartel and thus benefit from reduced fines. It does so by modifying the incentives of cartel members and amending the interactions of the system in which they participate. Its success has been largely due to the immunity afforded to the whistleblower from prosecution and the administrative fine that may be imposed by the Tribunal. Lopes, Seth and Gauntlett (2013) posit that at the core of any successful cartel enforcement programme is the effective management of incentives.

Cartels are notoriously difficult to expose due to the fact that they are by their very nature secretive and, to varying degrees, incentivised by secured levels of profit. To this end, an effective enforcement policy must be able to remove or greatly diminish the incentive for parties to collude by imposing penalties that have real and serious implications for those firms involved, while concomitantly creating an adequate incentive for firms and individuals to disclose their involvement in cartel conduct to the competition authorities. Typically, the trade-off made by competition authorities in this regard is to offer some form of immunity to those firms or individuals that disclose and cooperate in the exposure of cartel conduct (Lopes, Seth and Gauntlett, 2013).

Dawn raids ignite leniency applications

Dawn raids that pre-emptively assist to obtain relevant evidence go hand in hand with any CLP.[6] In South Africa, a good number of leniency applications were received from firms after they were dawn-raided, and credible circumstantial or other evidence collected by the CCSA, notably in the construction sector. Competition authorities thus not only need a leniency programme, but must demonstrate that:

- They have the power to raid;
- They actually carry out raids in a legally enshrined manner (i.e., according to the rules of procedure and/or the respective legislation). Where a raid has not been carried out according to the legislation and/or rules of procedure, the respondent parties will ensure that the case does not see the light of day on the merits or substance of the case. Cases will thus be lost on 'technical grounds' – but technical grounds are and should be considered to be part of 'the law';
- When they raid, they can collect information that is relevant, that is, they have the capacity to obtain credible records (physical or electronic) which will address the issues raised in the charge sheet or search warrant;
- When they raid, they will not get cold feet as various influential forces launch media or other covert attacks on the institution, its staff and processes, resulting in a case being abandoned and/or mysteriously 'frozen' in its tracks; and
- When a leniency application is actually made, the staff dealing with it know exactly what they are supposed to do to ensure that leniency processing details are followed to the letter.

Transition period of learning and growth

The South Africa Competition Act was promulgated in 1998, following which it underwent some teething problems. Its effective implementation was systematically assisted by increased investment in staff training and exposure at both the CCSA and the Tribunal. Learning from established competition authorities such as the Federal Trade Commission of the US and those under the Organisation for Economic Cooperation and Development assisted the South African competition authority to move out of the transition phase with a clear focus and a clear enforcement priority scheme.

The cliché 'enforcement is the best advocacy' has proved true for the South African competition authorities. While some authorities in the southern African region have claimed that they are not ready for enforcement because they are concentrating on advocacy, a late entry into enforcement leads to lack of experience in dealing with cases such as cartels. Additionally, procedural mistakes are better committed early on, in the establishment years. Table 3.3 shows fines meted out by the Tribunal only three years after the establishment of the CCSA in 1999.

Early enforcement warning shots are important to raise public awareness about what the competition authority can actually do, as opposed to what it says it can do. Thus, by the time the CLP was introduced in 2004, the CCSA had

Table 3.3 Fines meted out by the Tribunal

Reporting year ending 31 March	Respondent	Penalty	Contravention
2002/2003	Federal Mogul	R3 million	Section 5(2)
	Hibiscus Coast Municipality	No penalty	Section 5(1)
	Patensie Sitrus Beherend Beperk	No penalty	Section 8(d)(i)
2003/2004	The Association of Pretoria Attorneys	R223 000	Section 4(1)(b)(i)

Source: CCSA and CTSA (2009, p. 42)

already demonstrated its capability with the cases involving Federal Mogul and the Association of Pretoria Attorneys.

Managing risk of mistakes and emotionalism

It is important not to dwell on mistakes made and also to ensure that those mistakes are not institutionalised. Team leaders and their members may make tactical and operational errors when dealing with their first cases. This is because initial training in cartel investigations is often undertaken by foreign experts using their laws and rules of procedure, which the novice investigating officers in a developing competition authority may take as applicable in their jurisdictions as well. This is a natural mistake but a lesson for new and developing competition authorities is to ensure that they follow the investigating process indicated in their laws and/or rules of procedure. The rules of procedure must equally be alive to constitutional provisions and precedents set in court decisions. Each country has certain rules of procedure that must be adhered to if the merits of a case are to be entertained by the adjudicating bodies or the courts.

Emotionalism in case selection, investigation, prosecution and adjudication can be fatal to a case, no matter how well trained and exposed the officers may be. This needs to be checked and managed within the relevant processes. Declarations of interest must be a part of the process. However, administrative bodies such as competition authorities should not see themselves as ordinary civil litigants. Unlike ordinary litigants, competition authorities should not care about winning at all costs but rather about obtaining the best possible outcome for the economy. In this regard, they should remain independent, impartial and open-minded throughout their processes.

Overall, a systematic risk-monitoring and review framework must be in place. CCSA key risk-management areas and mitigations are indicated in table 3.4.

An early case that made the CCSA reflect on its procedures was the PPC case, where a search and seizure summons was quashed by the High Court primarily because the CCSA alerted the media before the summons was executed. In another case, the CCSA's haste to publicise a cartel prosecution led to the unwarranted disclosure of confidential information relating to the defendant, Reclaim. However, the CCSA did not relent in its pursuit of cartels but ensured that a similar mistake was not made in other cases.[7]

Table 3.4 CCSA risk management and mitigation

Disaster recovery	The loss of data, unauthorised access and use of information and corruption of the network. An IT security audit took place in the 2013/2014 financial year. The findings from this audit were addressed during the course of the 2013/2014 financial year.
Adverse decisions from courts on powers and procedures	Court decisions on appeal, which were handed down during the period under review, have impacted negatively on the Commission's ability to initiate and investigate complaints submitted to it by third parties. The Commission's response to this has been to improve its internal procedures.
Reputational harm	The reputation of the organisation might be damaged if the Commission executes its legislative mandate, powers and duties inappropriately. This risk is being managed by taking due consideration of public interest concerns, stakeholder perceptions and policy expectations.
Independence undermined	The Commission may be subject to external influences in executing its legislative duties. The Commission manages this risk by ensuring transparency in decision making and justifying its decisions on merit within the parameters of the Competition Act. It also engages in continuous advocacy with its stakeholders.
Unmanageable caseload	The current caseload has placed the Commission's structure and resources under severe pressure and has a negative impact on the quality of service delivered. The Commission manages this situation by focusing its resources on priority cases and sectors, as well as the effective screening of cases. The issue of space constraints has been escalated to the minister of economic development in order to address the organisation's inability to hire much-needed staff, given the current premises.

Source: CCSA (2014, p. 80)

Collaboration with other agencies

When the CCSA investigated the construction cartel case, other local enforcement agencies were involved as well, due to the multiplicity of legal issues that were at play. In this case, the Hawks and the National Prosecuting Authority and its Specialised Commercial Crimes Unit were involved. In Botswana, the Competition Authority has collaborated successfully with the Directorate on Corruption and Economic Crime as well as the Public Procurement and Asset Disposal Board in dawn raids. Zambia launched joint dawn raids with the Anti-Corruption Commission in the fertiliser cartel investigations. It is also possible to have bilateral cooperation where there are cross-border effects. According to Bachmann and Afrika (2011), the benefits of bilateral agreements regarding international cartels are clear. They afford the exchange of information and assist counterpart agencies that may not have sufficient capacity to deal with complex cartels (Bachmann and Afrika, 2011).

It is worth noting that while competition authorities may not readily share confidential information secured through a leniency application, this could be overcome by obtaining waivers from leniency applicants or those cartel participants who are willing to settle. A competition authority will have to engage a counterpart agency formally to have access to such information. The SADC's *Heads of State Declaration on Regional Cooperation in Competition and Consumer Policies and Laws* states that:

- Cooperation shall be enhanced by establishing a transparent framework that contains appropriate safeguards to protect the confidential information of the parties and appropriate national judicial review;
- Member States shall have regard to comity principles, including positive comity, as an instrument of regional and bilateral cooperation within the region, including informal positive comity referrals among competition enforcement authorities;
- Member States shall review those provisions in their laws that stand in the way of these cooperative efforts and explore areas where they are prepared to enter into binding agreements.[8]

Competence and knowledge management

Competition authorities must invest in sustainable training of their staff in their own substantive competition legislation, rules of evidence collection and handling, rules of procedure for summoning witnesses, interviewing techniques and referral. While such training is indispensable, there should be a knowledge-application monitoring system in the organisation to ensure that those who are trained in a specific area actually apply the knowledge and do not continue to seek further training. Practical application and demonstration of knowledge in a case is important, develops confidence and achieves the requisite enforcement objectives of the competition legislation. The CCSA has invested in an elaborate knowledge-management (KM) system through a range of strategies and practices that allow it to identify, create, represent, distribute and facilitate the adoption of peer learning and the experience of insights and expertise.

By 2014, the KM system at the CCSA had evolved from primarily a document-management system to a far more integrated one, where users actively utilise its workflow capabilities and process automation to further enhance the quality of their cases. All cases lodged with the CCSA now go through an automated process and supporting documents can be shared with users.[9] The CCSA is working on KM systems being integrated with the existing information technology infrastructure, the organisational culture and procedures and the human resources policy. The CCSA (2014) has recognised that culture and user behaviours are the key drivers and inhibitors of internal information sharing, and are strategising on ways to stimulate people to use and contribute to KM systems.

The KM is assisted greatly by workplace skills plans and annual training reports, which other competition authorities, such as that in Botswana, have also been producing since 2012.

Use of temporary and external staff

The engagement and requisite training of temporary and/or external staff (investigators, inspectors, analysts, etc.) may assist greatly in cases where existing staff are overwhelmed with work, or where the need to remain focused on investigation, analysis and prosecution is beyond the capacity and scope of existing staff numbers, skills levels and funding. It may also be necessary to devise effective ways to dispose of cases while achieving the key enforcement objectives. During 2013/2014, the CCSA completed settlements under the Construction Settlement Project (CSP), a special dispensation for uncovering bid rigging and settling the cases. The process uncovered more than 300 private- and public-sector rigged projects, including major infrastructure developments in South Africa such as the 2010 Fifa Soccer World Cup stadia, dams, business/residential buildings, the Gauteng Freeway Improvement Project and other national roads (see CCSA, 2014). In addition to this case, the CCSA had about 30 other cartel investigations going on.

Where funds permit, it may be necessary to employ specialised legal and economic consultants to assist with such a workload. Internal counsel may be knowledgeable about a case but other administrative work within the authority may divide their time. In cases where internal staff fall prey to high emotionalism, which may affect their ability to see the details and could result in derailing the case, the use of external counsel may provide the necessary accountability, leaving internal counsel to devote time to reviewing external counsel submissions and providing policy guidance.

Political will and support

In various countries and at various times, competition policy has had a number of other legitimate objectives, ranging from industrial policy and economic development goals to economic freedom. But even when it only seeks to enhance economic welfare, it has been posited that effective competition policy is inherently deeply political, since it entails the use of political power to constrain or even redistribute economic power (Büthe, 2015). Political awareness and commitment to a cause matter a lot, especially in developing countries.

There is clear political will and support in South Africa to see the CCSA being as successful as it can be. The minister for economic development in South Africa, Ebrahim Patel, has noted that competition policy is particularly important for South Africa because of the relatively high levels of market concentration across the economy. He has highlighted the fact that the exclusive nature of apartheid led to dominance by a limited number of companies in many industries (CCSA, 2014).

The relatively small, closed economy and the privatisation of major state manufacturing companies in the 1980s added to securing an environment replete with monopoly power. In this environment, collusion and rent seeking continued as an entrenched culture in even some of the most important and productive companies (CCSA, 2014). Patel indicated that competition policy must be used to combat cartels and abuse of market dominance, and that this must become a greater focus of the authorities in the period ahead.

Such well-informed political support has, however, not been given on a silver platter – it has been earned over the years by the CCSA. It is the duty of the competition authority to demonstrate its relevance to the political establishment by ensuring that its outcomes feed into the national development vision and expected deliverables in terms of jobs, poverty, narrowing socioeconomic gaps, fighting corruption/cartels and supporting SME growth and sustenance. Political will and support should be expressed in the following overt features:

- Publicly promulgated, clear and consistent political support for the very existence of a competition authority;
- Publicly declared autonomy in the operations and processes of the competition authority as it investigates high-profile cases;[10]
- Reasonable funding of the operations of the competition authority in relation to government's expectations of its deliverables;
- A clear political message to special interest groups of government's commitment to the rule of law in commerce and trade, which competition policy is envisaged to bring about; and
- National consensus on the understanding of the egregious nature of cartels.

Arising from the above, political will and commitment can be used as a channel to bring to the fore the destructive nature of cartel conduct. Public understanding of the nature of cartels and the damage they bring about, not only to competition but to society at large, is important. Not only the competition authorities but all those involved in business at policy, leadership, entrepreneurial, advisory or operational levels should understand this. This extends to those involved in authorising cartel investigations, those who undertake the investigations, those who analyse the findings, those who adjudicate and those who deal with appeals. Where a system is inherently divided and/or at any level considers cartels not to be a serious form of anticompetitive activity, business will be quick to recognise this and will not undertake to stop their cartel activity. CLP will equally not yield much in terms of confessions, as has been the case in other SACU/SADC countries.

The right case for the right moment

Finding the right case for the right moment is very important to bring credence to cartel enforcement. The bread cartel case, for instance, brought instant recognition of the work of the CCSA to ordinary South Africans. While the case neither guaranteed nor brought about lower bread prices following the busting of the cartel, it provided a good platform to launch the CCSA's cartel enforcement programme and to link it to consumers. The steel and construction cases were linked to the World Cup, which event was on the lips of every South African. Busting cartels for the sake of it should not be an end in itself, but must be seen to have some form of impact in society. A caution here is that competition authorities should not lose sight of their role as watchdogs of all sectors in the economy while pursuing cases which could earn them more publicity.

Demonstrate benefit of cartel enforcement to government and consumers

The news that a number of South African construction firms were guilty of tender rigging and price fixing to the tune of R30 billion was surely welcomed by the Treasury. In 2012, companies paid administrative fines of about R934 million for violations of the Competition Act. Most of these fines (R482 million) were paid by companies that engaged in price fixing, market allocation and collusive tendering in a cartel. Tembinkosi Bonakele (CCSA, 2014) indicated in his statement in the annual report that the CCSA had undertaken a study of the impact of uncovering the construction cartel. Using estimates of overcharges as a result of the cartel, the study found that consumer saving as a result of the cartel being uncovered ranged between approximately R4.5 billion and R5.8 billion for the period 2010 to 2013. In addition, there was a noticeable change and dynamism in the market, with firms entering territories they had previously not traded in (CCSA, 2014). Carrying out such impact studies is an important advocacy tool that enhances a competition authority's value to society.

In the Pioneer Foods white maize meal and milled wheat products cartel cases, the benefits arising from the fine included the following (see Bonakele and Mncube, 2012):

- Pioneer Foods had to pay a fine of R500 million to the National Revenue Fund; and
- The CCSA, National Treasury and the Economic Development Department separately agreed that the Department would submit a budgetary proposal and business case motivating for the creation of an Agro-Processing Competitiveness Fund of R250 million, drawn from the penalty, to be administered by the Industrial Development Corporation.

Fines and penalties must be punitive

One school of thought posits that fines and penalties in legislation must be punitive enough to merit the effort of uncovering a cartel. Another is of the view that even if the fines and penalties are low, the point is to name and shame – the bad publicity and reputational damage (if any) that a company suffers may provide some form of deterrence and discipline market behaviour. However, the effectiveness of this will depend on the levels of competition culture in a particular economy and on the society's norms.

In South Africa, penalties are up to 10% of the previous year's gross turnover. Tanzania has the highest fine and can fine from a minimum of 5% up to 10% of global turnover of the companies involved. Namibia has a maximum of 10% based on global turnover.[11] Botswana has a maximum fine of 10% (domestic market turnover) for each year during the currency of a cartel, up to a maximum of three years. Zambia has a maximum fine of 10% based on domestic turnover, while Zimbabwe has the lowest fine at US$5 000. Apart from South Africa, Mauritius and Zambia, none of the SACU/SADC countries have successfully meted out any cartel-related fines (see World Bank, 2016).

A fine balance is needed between cartel enforcement in terms of high fines and discounting penalties to those who cooperate during investigations. Senona (2013), a legal counsel at the CCSA, acknowledges the need to discount a penalty when determining the appropriate penalty against a cooperating firm. Bonakele and Mncube (2012) hail penalty discounting as a remedial tool to take centre stage as a competition law remedy.

Attract public attention: Media, legal and academic discourse

The level of public interest, particularly in the media, legal and academic fraternity, has brought competition law, in particular cartel enforcement, to the fore. Almost all leading legal firms in South Africa have a division solely devoted to competition law. Universities have students writing dissertations on competition law and enforcement. This development is arguably unprecedented in any part of Africa. In 2007, a renowned cartoonist captured the nation's anti-cartel sentiments (figure 3.1).

Figure 3.1 Zapiro, *Mail & Guardian*, 15 November 2007

Develop legal clarity and precedents through Tribunal and court decisions

Through the initial years of trial and error, the South African competition authorities and the judiciary provided legal clarity and precedents, with internationally quotable Tribunal and court decisions. Oxenham (2015) notes that within a space of 18 months, South Africa witnessed significant developments in the investigation and prosecution of cartel conduct. One of the key developments was the Supreme Court of Appeal's confirmation that leniency applications submitted to the CCSA by a leniency applicant are subject to legal privilege unless the CCSA makes reference to the application in a complaint referral to the Tribunal[12] – in which case it will be taken to have waived privilege. Another court held that the Tribunal may make a declaration that it has found the conduct of an applicant for immunity to be a prohibited practice, even if the applicant is not cited as a respondent, provided that natural justice is followed and there is a proper factual basis.[13]

Such jurisprudence is necessary to develop the law and to streamline legal processes accordingly. It also helps to give clearer meaning to the law and provides for greater consistency and certainty in future case direction for both the CCSA and the respondents.

Efficient and capacitated institutional arrangement

South Africa has an efficient institutional arrangement comprising the CCSA, the Competition Tribunal and the CAC. A number of countries, such as Botswana, Swaziland, Tanzania and Zambia, have in recent years experienced direct or indirect attacks against their institutional arrangements. The South African system provides a clear separation between the investigatory, adjudication and appeal functions. This system avoids a situation where case success is frustrated by the conflict of roles played by any organ in the enforcement chain. However, this does not lessen the fact that operating effectively in all three stages – detection, prosecution and penalisation by the CCSA – is crucial to disrupting existing cartels and deterring new ones from forming (see Harrington, 2007, in CCSA and CTSA, 2009). Most importantly, it appears that the implementing institutions (the CCSA, the Tribunal, CAC and the Supreme Court of Appeal) are well capacitated to deal with their respective mandates.

Strong code of ethics and incorruptible staff, adjudicators and courts

An institution may have the best system, funds and political support, but if there are unethical and corruptible staff and adjudicators, the system will struggle to achieve the desired enforcement goals and objectives, especially in cartels. Cartel profits are in the hundreds of millions of US dollars and, often enough, it does not take much to corrupt a public official. Codes of conduct have been adopted by most competition authorities.

Enduring long and costly investigation and litigation processes

Cartel investigations may take years from the initiation of the investigation to settlement. A competition authority must brace itself for protracted legal battles, interlocutory or points *in limine* (preliminary points of law) before the substantive merits of the case are heard. The soda ash cartel investigation in South Africa was opened in 1999 and took nine years to reach settlement in 2008. The CCSA's investigations revealed a contravention of the Competition Act and the complaint was referred to the Tribunal on 14 April 2000. The American Natural Soda Ash Corporation (Ansac) opposed the referral on the grounds that the agreement was not a contravention of the Act, but, rather, was integral to the operation of a legitimate and transparent corporate joint venture, which existed for the promotion of export sales, generated significant logistics efficiencies and impacted pro-competitively on the South African market. Between February 2000 and July 2008, the case was held up by extended litigation involving points *in limine* and appeals. In May 2005, the Supreme Court of Appeal decided that the matter be heard before the Tribunal. The Tribunal hearings into the merits of the case began in mid-2008, and Ansac closed its case within a month. In September 2008, Ansac and its fellow respondent and South African agent, CHC Global, approached the CCSA to discuss a settlement. This case took nine years to reach settlement. With the threat of staff turnover and loss of institutional memory, a competition authority will need to ensure that there is a system of continuity in such cases, in the context of both human resources (proper and easily traceable records) and financial resources, in order to effectively sustain them.

Leadership

There is a need for anti-cartel leadership that is seen to be not only knowledgeable but also well inclined to undertake sustained action against cartels. Such leadership should prioritise resources accordingly and ensure that maximum impact is gained from the prioritisation. Leadership will also be expected to engage in impactful debates that create awareness of a competition authority's unflinching stance against cartels. This kind of leadership should show examples of visible enforcement achievements and not merely play public relations. Such leadership should equally ignite the right national debate and interest in the work of a competition authority. Leadership must project a visionary dedication to the rule of law, transparency and fairness in investigations and prosecutions. For instance, Spicer (2009, in CCSA and CTSA, 2009, p. 34) remarked about David Lewis, former chairperson of the Tribunal: 'What has particularly struck me about Lewis is the combination of toughness, independent-mindedness, but ultimately the fairness of his approach. Business can expect no favours, but it can generally be confident that the law will be fairly applied.'

Conclusion

Cartel leniency confessions and settlements in South Africa have not resulted in similar confessions in SACU/SADC countries where there are functional competition authorities. It is unlikely that such confessions will ever be received in the absence of the competition authorities actually demonstrating that they have the capacity and resolve to detect and punish cartel offences. As useful as it is, a CLP is merely a document and in and of itself will not invite confessions from cartel participants. Life has to be breathed into CLPs by competition authorities going out into the marketplace and getting admissible evidence that can attract punitive penalties. To do this, competition authorities must invest not only in systems, but also in developing the staff involved in advocacy, cartel investigations, analysis, prosecution and adjudication to understand investigation procedures, rules of evidence, collection and handling.

It is also worth noting that a number of competition authorities in the SADC have been undertaking market studies/inquiries into specific sectors to understand the nature of such sectors and their competition dynamics. This has been done by individual competition authorities at the national level as well as in the regional collaborative context under the SADC and the African Competition Forum in sectors that include transport, sugar, cement and poultry. Such investment is timely and will assist the authorities to better understand particular sectors and how the cross-regional corporate strategies and linkages can be monitored to ensure that cartels are detected timeously. It will also facilitate the necessary cooperation among competition authorities.

Notes

1   The World Bank (2016, p. 61) reports, for instance, that cement prices in Africa were 183% higher on average than the world price of cement at the end of 2014.

2   Case no. CCPC/RBP/009 of 2011.

3   Case no. CCPC/RBP/052 of 2012.

4   See case no. 15/CR/Mar10, *Competition Commission vs. Pioneer Foods (Pty) Ltd*, 30 November 2010.

5   'The Use of Leniency Programmes as a Tool for the Enforcement of Competition Law against Hardcore Cartels in Developing Countries', Geneva, 26 August 2010, TD/RBP/CONF.7/4.

6   Utilising powers of search and seizure and market inquiries, the CCSA has demonstrated a far more proactive and robust enforcement of the cartel provisions in the Act. Accordingly, given the more proactive approach adopted by the CCSA, companies operating in South Africa need to ensure that internal compliance programmes are regularly updated.

7   See commentary by Paul PJ Coetser, head of Competition Department, Werksmans Attorneys, then chairman, Competition Law Committee of the Law Society of South Africa, in CCSA and CTSA (2009, p. 34).

8   Paras. 1 (e)–(h).

9   The Swaziland Competition Commission has adopted a similar system.

10 The ICN (2002) has noted that autonomy is generally considered essential to the effectiveness of advocacy work. However, a distinction should be made between formal and factual independence. In some countries a high degree of formal independence goes together with a certain isolation of the competition authority from the executive branch of government, which does not favour the advocacy activities of the agency. In other jurisdictions, competition agencies with a low degree of autonomy, forming a directorate of a ministry subject to ministerial oversight, claim that their decisions are generally respected in an environment of transparency and accountability. That is to say, formal independence need not coincide with factual independence and it is factual independence that really matters.

11 Excessive fines which take into account turnover not generated in the country where the contravention occurred may lack credibility and may be subject to legal challenges, especially when the turnover generated in the fining country is insignificant when compared to the company's global turnover.

12 *Competition Commission v Arcelormittal SA Ltd & Others* (680/12) [2013] ZASCA 84, para. 50.

13 *Premier Foods v Manoim NO* (20147/2014) [2015] ZASCA 159; 2016 (1) SA 445 (SCA); [2016] 1 All SA 40 (SCA) (4 November 2015).

References

Bachmann, S-D and SS Afrika. 2011. Cartel regulation in three emerging BRICS economies: Cartel and competition policies in South Africa, Brazil and India – A comparative overview. *SSRN Electronic Journal* May, DOI: 10.2139/ssrn.1869963.

Bonakele T. 2009. 'The unraveling of a fertiliser cartel as Sasol settles with the Commission on a record fine', *Competition News*, Edition 32, June, www.compcom.co.za/wp-content/uploads/2014/09/June-09-Newsletter-32.pdf .

Bonakele T and L Mncube. 2012. *Designing Appropriate Remedies for Competition Law Enforcement: The Pioneer Foods Settlement Agreement.* CCRED Working Paper 1/2012.

Boshoff WH. 2015. Illegal cartel overcharges in markets with a legal cartel history: Bitumen prices in South Africa. *South African Journal of Economics* 83: 220–239.

Büthe T. 2015. The politics of market competition: Trade and antitrust in a global economy. In L Martin (ed.), *The Oxford Handbook of the Political Economy of International Trade*, pp. 213–232. Oxford: Oxford University Press.

CCSA (Competition Commission South Africa). 2010. Media release, 15 March.

CCSA. 2014. 'Annual Report 2013/14' (online document).

CCSA and CTSA (Competition Tribunal South Africa). 2009. 'Unleashing Rivalry: Ten Years of Enforcement by the South African Competition Authorities, 1999–2009' (online document).

Creamer M. 2009. 'South Africa's Competition Commission uncovers cartel activity', *Mining Weekly*, 30 September, http://www.miningweekly.com/article/south-africas-competition-commission-uncovers-mining-cartel-activity-2009-09-30/rep_id:3650.

CTSA (Competition Tribunal South Africa). n.d. 'Consent Orders' (online document).

Gedye L. 2013. 'Construction: Collusion may be the industry's fatal flaw', *Mail & Guardian*, 8 February.

Harrington J. 2007. Behavioral screening and the detection of cartels. In C-D Ehlermann and I Atanasiu (eds), *European Competition Law Annual 2006: Enforcement of Prohibition of Cartels*, pp. 51–68. Portland, OR: Hart Publishing.

ICN (International Competition Network). 2002. *Advocacy and Competition Policy*. Report prepared by the Advocacy Working Group, ICN Conference, Naples, Italy 28–29 September.

Kelly L. 2010. The introduction of a 'cartel offence' into South African law. *Stellenbosch Law Review* 21: 321–333.

Le Roux M. 2008. 'Cartel exposed in South Africa's steel industry', *Resource Investor*, 18 July, http://www.resourceinvestor.com/2008/07/17/cartel-exposed-south-africas-steel-industry.

Lopes N, J Seth and E Gauntlett. 2013. 'Cartel Enforcement, the CLP and Criminal Liability: Are Competition Regulators Hamstrung By the Competition Act from Co-Operating with the NPA, and Is This a Problem for Competition Law Enforcement?' Paper presented at the Seventh Annual Competition Commission, Competition Tribunal and Mandela Institute Conference on Competition Law, Economics and Policy in South Africa, 5–6 September (online document).

Mncube L. 2014. The South African wheat flour cartel: Overcharges at the mill. *Journal of Industry, Competition and Trade* 14: 487–509.

Oxenham J. 2015. 'South Africa: Developments in Cartel Enforcement'. In GCR (Global Competition Review), *The African and Middle Eastern Antitrust Review 2015* (online document).

Planting S. 2013. 'Cartels persist despite record fines, tighter legislation', *Moneyweb*, 5 February.

Roberts S. 2004. The role for competition policy in economic development: The South African experience. *Development Southern Africa* 21: 1–17.

SACU (Southern African Customs Union). 2012. 'Merchandise Trade Statistics 2012' (online document).

SADC (Southern African Development Community). n.d. 'SADC Facts & Figures' (online document).

Sapa (South African Press Association). 2013. 'Competition Commission probes R30bn construction "cartel"', *Moneyweb*, 4 February.

Senona L. 2013. 'Enforcement against Cartels: A Fresh Approach to Determining Penalties in South Africa – for Better or for Worse?' (online document).

Seria N. 2010. 'South Africa targets Sasol, Arcelor in cartel push', *Bloomberg*, 29 September.

Spicer M. 2009. A personal reflection from organised business. In 'Unleashing Rivalry: Ten Years of Enforcement by the South African Competition Authorities, 1999–2009' (online document).

UNCTAD (United Nations Conference on Trade and Development). 2010. 'The Use of Leniency Programmes as a Tool for the Enforcement of Competition Law against Hardcore Cartels in Developing Countries', UN Doc. TD/RBP/CONF.7/4, Geneva, 26 August (online document).

World Bank. 2016. *Breaking down Barriers: Unlocking Africa's Potential through Vigorous Competition Policy*. Washington, DC: World Bank.

Part Two

Issues in competition and regulation

4 Excessive pricing under the spotlight: What is a competitive price?

Reena das Nair and Pamela Mondliwa[1]

Introduction

Excessive pricing is arguably the most contentious area of competition enforcement in many jurisdictions. There are diverse views on the need for intervention by competition authorities in dominant firms' pricing of products and services (Evans and Padilla, 2005b; Ezrachi and Gilo, 2009; Motta and de Streel, 2006; Roberts, 2008). Those arguing against intervention are of the view that it is generally unnecessary as prices significantly above a competitive level will ordinarily attract new entry, resulting in competition which will in turn drive prices down (Calcagno and Walker, 2010; O'Donoghue and Padilla, 2006). Other grounds that are often cited for limited or non-intervention are the difficulties in calculating the counterfactual or 'competitive' price for determining excessiveness and that enforcement of excessive prices may deter or chill investment (Ezrachi and Gilo, 2010; O'Donoghue and Padilla, 2013). The validity of the non-interventionist approach has, however, been questioned, with analyses showing that the self-correction argument may not hold in certain situations, particularly in small economies with highly concentrated markets and high barriers to entry (Ezrachi and Gilo, 2010). The difficulties of the assessment are not unique to excessive pricing. Other pricing contraventions, such as predatory pricing and margin squeeze assessments, are also highly complex, with the former requiring the determination of an appropriate measure of cost.

These diverse views have resulted in varying approaches by different jurisdictions. For example, the US has no provision in its antitrust policy that prohibits excessive prices and it is generally accepted that monopoly prices may be part of the dynamic competitive process. The view is that markets can 'self-correct' by attracting new entry.[2] The European Commission (EC) has also adopted a limited intervention approach towards excessive pricing and there is a legitimate reluctance to act as price regulators who decide on what the right price should be. However, there are instances in which the EC will intervene (discussed below) (European Commission, 2016). Several member states' competition authorities are more active than the EC in pursuing such cases.

The Competition Commission of South Africa has taken on a few excessive pricing cases under section 8(a) of the Competition Act of 1998. Under this provision, an excessive price is defined as a price for a good or service which bears no reasonable relation to the economic value of that good or service, and is higher than the value. The Act, however, does not define economic value and this is a key area of debate in the South African case law. There have been at least six cases dealing with excessive pricing in South Africa over the past decade in a range of industries, including pharmaceuticals (antiretroviral drugs), telecommunications, steel, petrochemicals and fertilisers. The first key case in the steel industry, *Harmony Gold v Mittal Steel SA* (the *Mittal* case), was the subject of Competition Tribunal and Competition Appeal Court (CAC) rulings, and has been written about extensively (Calcagno and Walker, 2010; das Nair, 2008; Davis, 2011; Ezrachi and Gilo, 2009; Lewis, 2009; Roberts, 2008). The other cases were settled prior to being heard and therefore the authorities have not made findings on the determination of economic value that can be debated (see Roberts, 2012, for descriptions), or findings were only made based on other contraventions, for example in the Telkom case in the telecommunications sector.

Excessive pricing and the assessment thereof has again come under the spotlight in South Africa with the release of the Competition Tribunal decision in June 2014, followed by the CAC's decision in June 2015, in the case against Sasol Chemical Industries (SCI). The case referred by the Commission to the Tribunal alleged that SCI charged excessive prices for the sale of petrochemical products – purified propylene and polypropylene – which are main inputs in the plastics sector. The Tribunal found in favour of the Commission and ruled that SCI had indeed charged excessive prices for these products. However, the CAC overturned this decision, finding in favour of SCI.

As the first excessive pricing case with a ruling since the *Mittal* decision, the CAC judgment in *SCI* presents an opportunity to revisit old debates and engage in new concepts that arose, particularly around the interpretation of economic value and the determination of a long-run competitive equilibrium (LRCE) as the benchmark for economic value. In this chapter, we explore whether, and how, the judgment takes the debates on determining economic value forward. We also discuss the pertinent issue of the treatment of special cost advantages that a dominant firm has in an excessive pricing determination and the implications of the CAC's decision in this regard in the South African context.

The next section evaluates the debates on the need for intervention and sets out the South African legislative framework in this light. Thereafter we provide a brief background on the SCI case, followed by consideration of whether the LRCE as referred in CAC *Mittal* is a conceptual framework or a new test, and to what extent this concept takes the debate on measuring economic value forward by providing a coherent understanding and measurement of economic value. The treatment of special cost advantages in determining economic value is then debated before providing some conclusions.

South Africa's legislative framework: When is intervention warranted?

The divergence in approaches to excessive pricing can partially be explained by the nature of the markets in the different jurisdictions. Different countries' choices regarding excessive pricing reflect decisions about the relative balance between risks of over- and underenforcement in the context of their unique economic challenges and conditions. The US and the European Union have large markets where it is unlikely for a single firm to be able to act truly independently and unconstrained by the threat of new entry. On the other hand, in South Africa and other smaller economies in southern Africa which are faced with overwhelmingly dominant firms and where there are barriers to entry, it is possible for firms to extract high rents from their positions. These smaller markets mean that when there is a need to achieve economies of scale, the industries will typically be more concentrated. For example, the scale of sugar production by Zambia Sugar, producing approximately double the domestic demand, means that there is only one very large firm in Zambia and others of similar size are unlikely (Chisanga, Meyer, Winter-Nelson and Sitko, 2014). Similarly, the scale of production required for integrated flat steel production is far above the size not just of demand in South Africa, but of demand in neighbouring economies also. In the case of wheat milling in South Africa, scale economies mean that there can only be a few firms, implying that in smaller markets there may well be unilateral dominance (Grimbeek and Lekezwa, 2013). In such instances the cost of underenforcement is high, particularly where the relevant product is an intermediary input into other markets. Recognising that the different jurisdictions have different market characteristics, it is then appropriate that there is a divergence of approaches to excessive prices (Evans, 2009).

In recognition of the risks of overenforcement, economists have identified circumstances that may require intervention by competition authorities (Evans, 2009; Lewis, 2009; Motta and de Streel, 2007; O'Donoghue and Padilla, 2013; Roberts, 2008). There has been some debate about the nature of barriers to entry that should be adopted in the limiting principles. The requirement for legal barriers to entry (Evans and Padilla, 2005a) would, in a literal reading, exclude a number of firms that have entrenched (near) monopoly positions and are not subject to regulation. Lewis (2009) argues that in instances where barriers to entry were established by historical circumstances, or by technological and commercial considerations, the effect is at least as insurmountable as legal barriers. In a similar vein, O'Donoghue and Padilla (2013, p. 775) move away from the position on legal barriers to argue that intervention should be limited to those industries '(1) that are protected by high barriers to entry; (2) where one firm enjoys considerable market power; and (3) where investment and innovation play a relatively minor role'. In such markets, the high prices that a firm with significant market power can charge will not result in new entry, while the danger of chilling innovation and risk taking does not arise as a legitimate concern. The excessive pricing provision should therefore be aimed at pricing that is not 'the legitimate rewards of monopoly power as the fruits of successful investment, innovation or efficiency' (Rose and Bailey, 2013: 10.107). Such pricing might be the result of exploitation of market power bequeathed to a firm through state support, or current or past exclusive rights.

As noted, although generally cautious about intervention in such matters, particularly in innovative industries, the EC intervenes in certain situations. A 2016 speech by the EC's commissioner of competition, Margrethe Vestager, highlighted that intervention was necessary in the Gazprom gas case, where restrictions on resale between geographic markets resulted in Gazprom charging excessive prices for gas in certain countries (European Commission, 2016). There is less fear of stifling innovation in a 'commodity'-type product market like gas than there is in more dynamic, hi-tech markets like electronics, computers or smartphones.

The formulation of excessive pricing in the South African Competition Act broadly follows that of European case law, with the definition of an excessive price having been taken directly from the *United Brands* decision.[3] Although the European legislation does not directly refer to excessive pricing, the term has been a product of case law (Lewis, 2009). Article 82(a) of the EC Treaty prohibits a dominant firm from engaging in 'unfair' pricing practices, which has been interpreted as including excessive and predatory prices.

The South African legislation not only explicitly prohibits excessive pricing but has also included a definition of the term. Section 8(a) of the Act provides that it is prohibited for a dominant firm to charge an excessive price to the detriment of consumers, where an excessive price is defined in section 1(1)(ix) as 'a price for a good or service which bears no reasonable relation to the economic value of that good or service' (aa) and 'is higher than the value'(bb). The assessment set out in the Act comprises the factual determinations of the price of the good or service that is alleged to be excessive, and the economic value of that good or service and value judgements on the reasonableness of the difference between price and economic value, as well as whether the price is to the detriment of consumers.

As noted, the Act does not define economic value and this is a key area of debate in the South African case law. The interpretation of economic value is developed through jurisprudence. We argue that economic value must be interpreted in line with market conditions prevalent in South Africa and that this is what the legislature must have intended by the inclusion of this provision in the Act (see also Lewis, 2009; Roberts, 2008).

The preamble of the Act explicitly recognises the excessive concentrations of ownership and control as a result of the apartheid regime and the Act's objective to address the consequences thereof, further reflected in the purpose of the Act. This includes prohibiting practices that undermine a competitive economy, and promoting outcomes that support employment and equitable participation of small and medium enterprises in the economy. Addressing exploitative conduct by dominant firms in the form of excessive pricing is an important objective of the Act under these circumstances. Other countries that have not had the same history and outcomes in their economies as South Africa may have less motivation to include the excessive pricing provision in their respective competition laws.

As a result of the sanctions imposed on South Africa during the apartheid regime, the government heavily protected and supported the growth and development of state-owned enterprises, often supporting one firm per industry with no clear conditionalities on the behaviour of firms. This support extended to a range of strategic industries, including steel and petrochemicals, creating entrenched dominant firms with significant market power. After privatisation, these firms continued to operate as private monopolies and oligopolies facing little or no effective rivalry. As the CAC in *Mittal* noted, 'a history of such state largesse cannot be permitted to subvert competition nor should the market power inherited from the erstwhile status as a state enterprise be exerted with continued impunity'.[4] Thus, at least in the South African context, the competition authorities ought to be most concerned with pricing in markets with high and non-transitory barriers to entry, that is, where the dominant firm's position is entrenched, and where the dominant firm's position in that market is not the result of any innovation or risk taking by the firm but rather due to current or past exclusive rights or state support (Motta and de Streel, 2006; Vickers, 2006).

Background to the SCI case

The Commission investigated the case against SCI on request from the Department of Trade and Industry (the dti). The dti was concerned about the poor growth of labour-absorbing downstream industries, such as plastic products manufacturing. High input prices were identified as a major challenge to downstream beneficiation in the plastics value chain for household products like buckets, chairs, tables and cooler boxes, and for industrial products such as car parts and water tanks.

SCI is a wholly owned subsidiary of Sasol Limited, a previously state-owned company that is a vertically integrated fuel and petrochemicals business. The complaint against SCI was on its pricing practices for key inputs into downstream plastics manufacturing. These included purified propylene, where SCI has overwhelming dominance in South Africa, and polypropylene, where SCI is dominant in terms of the Act but competes with Safripol. Safripol's ability to effectively compete with SCI in the polypropylene market is limited, given that it is principally reliant on SCI for its propylene input and is capacity constrained. Purified propylene is made from feedstock propylene, which is produced as a by-product from Sasol's synthetic fuels business, Synfuels, through its coal-to-fuel and gas-to-fuel processes.

South Africa (and Sasol) has been a net exporter of polypropylene for over 20 years. South African demand for polypropylene is less than 300 000 tonnes/annum. In November 2016, Sasol announced an expansion of its polypropylene production by 103 000 tonnes/annum to just over 625 000 tonnes/annum, reinforcing its strong net exporter position going forward (Van Wyngaardt, 2016).

It was common cause between the Commission and SCI that SCI is one of the lowest-cost producers in the world, with its feedstock propylene costs around 25–30% lower than typical producers in Europe. Synfuels' processes mean that it produces more propylene relative to a typical oil refinery. Sasol can, and does, convert some of the propylene into fuel. However, there are limitations on the extent to which it can do this cost-effectively if it is to meet the country's clean fuels regulations. Sasol acknowledges its very low-cost advantage in propylene feedstock, which has underpinned expansions in capacity to serve export poly-propylene markets, no doubt including its latest 2016 expansion.

Feedstock propylene prices depend on its alternative uses, including keeping the feedstock (or refinery grade) propylene in the fuel pool, or extracting and purifying the propylene to chemical grade or polymer grade propylene for conversion into various chemical products and polypropylene. Sasol's pricing of polymer-grade propylene did not reflect its actual alternatives, which are limited, given the large amounts of feedstock propylene that are produced as a by-product. Instead, its polymer-grade propylene prices were linked to local polypropylene prices through a pricing formula based on an import parity price of polypropylene sold in the local market.

This derived price is in no way reflective of SCI's very low cost of producing feed-stock propylene. SCI argued that its low-cost feedstock is a 'special cost advantage'. The *SCI* case turns, in particular, on how the low costs should be treated, especially in the context where those costs are derived from historical decisions which advantage the firm, in this case including policy decisions and extensive support by the apartheid state (see below on the treatment of special cost advantages).

While in the mid-1990s polypropylene to local customers was priced at export parity prices, Sasol moved to import parity levels in 2002/2003, which it has maintained ever since. The costs of importing polypropylene into South Africa are not trivial, and include shipping, transport, insurance, wharfage and a 10% import duty (although the duty has since been reduced to zero). These notional costs of importing were then added to a free-on-board pricing point to arrive at an import parity price for local customers. This meant a substantial increase in prices of polypropylene, and, in turn, of purified propylene. The impact of this was seen in the declining output of the local plastics industry. The price of both purified propylene and polypropylene, as intermediate products into plastics production, has significant implications for the price and competitiveness of a range of domestically produced plastic products.

The price charged by SCI to local buyers of polypropylene has thus been substantially above the prices earned on its actual exports, reflecting the inclusion of all the notional costs to import. The price to local buyers competing in the domestic market has also been substantially above the prices SCI has provided to other categories of customers, such as export customers of polypropylene products (who were not allowed to redirect product back into South Africa).

Determining economic value

The determination of economic value has been a point of contestation in excessive pricing literature and case law. As the legislation has not defined the term or established tests for its calculation, the case law has, over time, developed both.

Reviews of literature in this area show that there is no generally accepted definition of economic value (Calcagno and Walker, 2010; Evans and Padilla, 2005a). However, case precedent has been instructive in interpreting economic value. In *United Brands*, the courts defined economic value as the price that would arise under conditions of 'normal and sufficiently effective competition', while in *NAPP*[5] economic value was understood to be determined under conditions of 'effective competitive pressure'. In light of these cases, in the literature excessive prices have been understood as those which could not be charged under conditions of effective competitive rivalry (Ezrachi and Gilo, 2009; Motta and de Streel, 2007). All the definitions given by the case law refer to the counterfactual to be used in the assessment as the outcomes of effective competition. However, the concept of effective competition itself has taken different meanings over time, which has added to the difficulties in assessing economic value.

One understanding is that it is the absence of market power where market power is understood as the ability to raise prices above marginal cost in the short run and above average total cost in the long run (Mehta and Peeperkorn, 2007). The reference to the short run is not particularly useful as it suggests a requirement of perfect competition. It is unlikely that the intention of the legislature was to characterise any price above marginal cost as excessive. A more useful understanding of effective competition is where there is sufficient rivalry to ensure that prices are not raised significantly above a measure of average total cost. The levels of competition for it to be deemed effective are thus dependent on the outcomes it produces rather than the form of competition (Bishop and Walker, 2010). The use of comparators in assessing economic value is in line with this approach by comparing an allegedly excessive price to the price that is an outcome of more competitive, comparable geographic or product markets.

The European case law has established a range of comparators that are commonly used as the benchmark for economic value (Motta and de Streel, 2007). These comparators can be grouped into two broad sets and have also been accepted by the South African courts.[6] First, prices of the same firm for substantially the same product in different markets (after correcting for transport and related costs in the case of different geographic markets), and/or prices to different customers in the same market can be used as comparators. This includes prices of products sold into export markets. Second, prices can be compared of same/similar products sold by different firms in competitive or international markets. These are typically known as international price comparators.

Other measures of economic value used in the European case law include direct price-cost tests and profitability tests. These are subject to empirical challenges in measuring costs for an efficient firm, as inefficiency cannot be a justification for charging high prices, as well as identifying what are reasonable levels of profit and how to measure the relevant asset base. These are challenges that economic regulators grapple with.

The *Mittal* case was the first case in which the CAC sought to clarify the standards to be applied in South Africa. In *Mittal*, the CAC defined the 'economic value' of a good or service as 'the notional price of the good or service under conditions of long-run competitive equilibrium'. The CAC cautioned that this is not to be understood as a price set under conditions of perfect competition in the short run, 'but rather competition that would be effective enough in the long run to eliminate what economists refer to as "pure profit" – that is a reward of any factor of production in excess of the long-run competitive norm which is relevant to that industry or branch of production'.[7]

The *SCI* case was the first time that the precedent set by the CAC in *Mittal* could be tested. Key new questions were added to the economic value debate, especially around what LRCE is and what it means in relation to economic value.

In the *SCI* case, the parties involved interpreted the CAC *Mittal* definition to establish two tests. A distinction was drawn between i) a test based on a price that would allow for entry (SCI's primary test – 'the LRCE test'), which determines the notional price of the good or service under assumed conditions of LRCE, and ii) the prices which would be charged if there were existing competitors under a notional competitive norm (the Commission's approach – the 'effective competitive rivalry' test). Whether there is indeed a distinction between the LRCE test and effective competitive rivalry is dependent on the interpretation of the conditions of LRCE. This brings into question whether the CAC intended the prices under LRCE as a framework or as a test in itself.

In the rest of this section, we explore whether the LRCE approach takes us forward in determining economic value by considering whether the CAC's reference to the competitive benchmark was intended as an end or as a means to an end. This is assessed by testing whether the LRCE test, as interpreted by SCI, corresponds to the intention of the legislature and whether it is capable of practical application.

LRCE: A framework or a new test?

The LRCE benchmark obviously turns on how 'long run' and 'competitive equilibrium' are understood. On the one hand, SCI argued that it should be interpreted as the prices at which firms would enter the market without necessarily having access to inputs at the same costs as the incumbent firm in question. On the other hand, as the Commission argued, it should be understood as the pricing which would have prevailed had there been established effective competitors in the market with similar costs to the incumbent.

The 'long run' can be defined in a textbook sense as where factors of production are variable, where there is free entry and exit in an industry, and where normal profits, and not 'pure profit', are made (Blaug, 1997). In this case, pure profit is understood as any profit above the 'normal' rate of profit, which includes depreciation and return to shareholders. The normal rate of return rewards the investor at the opportunity cost of the investment. The conditions of no 'pure profit' and free entry and exit were at the heart of the debate on what the CAC intended by LRCE.

At a return based on the opportunity cost of the investment, investors would be indifferent as to which industry they are in and would have an incentive to invest in the relevant industry only if the profits were above the normal rate. The CAC's guidance in *Mittal* was very clear that the meaning of LRCE is that there are zero 'pure profits'. SCI's interpretation of the LRCE then appears to be at odds with the zero pure profits condition. SCI's interpretation of LRCE as the costs of an entrant necessarily requires that there is some profit above the normal rate to be able to attract the entrant in the first place.

This interpretation is inconsistent with the literature on understanding LRCE in the context of economic value. Though there is no agreement on the exact interpretation of LRCE, what is consistent across the different contributions is that LRCE should be calculated with reference to existing firms rather than to new entrants (Calcagno and Walker, 2010; Davis, 2011; Lewis, 2009). Calcagno and Walker (2010) understood LRCE to mean the costs of an efficient (not necessarily the most efficient) firm in the long run and proposed that economic value can then be calculated by means of a profitability test (as was used by the defendant in *Mittal*). The efficient firm test here refers to the costs of either the dominant firm or an (existing) competitor. Davis (2011: 328) held that when determining economic value in line with the conditions of LRCE, the assessment should consider, among other things, the dominant firm's production costs.

In addition to whether to consider the costs of an entrant or those of notional established competitors, SCI's interpretation of the LRCE test also requires parameters to be specified in determining this equilibrium, and there could be multiple equilibria. As such, a monopoly is a possible equilibrium if the hypothesised market is small relative to scale economies (such as if the existing market size is used in the case of a developing country with a relatively small national demand). This approach is inconsistent with accepted principles in determining economic value. Even in circumstances where economic value is to be determined for differentiated products, it has been argued that economic value of the product must first be determined by a method which assumes competition between producers of the identical product (Petersen, Maenetje and Le Roux, 2008). That is, economic value should be determined 'as if' there had been competitors producing the same product rather than the actual situation where differentiation can mean firms produce variations of the product that differ materially (and a rival firm would have to invest in making its product a closer competitor to the dominant firm in question). However, this may not necessarily arise where there is monopolistic competition as, in the long run, monopolistic competition can produce outcomes similar to perfect competition where all pure profit is competed away, albeit under specified assumptions (Chamberlin, 1933).

SCI's interpretation of long run in the LRCE test also means that excessive prices would be temporary as entrants would compete the price down to the level of zero pure profits after entry. This is not consistent with durable entry barriers which are not necessarily specific to the firm – there could well be several firms with the same durable advantages over entrants. The idea of free entry and exit is rooted in a model which assumes away such barriers and this is often inconsistent with reality.

In economic textbook models of the 'long run' all factors of production are variable and firms can enter and exit. This needs to take into account barriers to entry beyond simply making the necessary capital investment, including, for example, access to key inputs at competitive prices. In the SCI case, the incumbent firm has access to low-cost feedstock that is not available on equal terms to potential entrants. This represents an absolute cost advantage in the sense that the entrant cannot secure as low a cost of production as the incumbent firm, thus creating a barrier to entry (see Bain, 1956, as cited in Gilbert, 1989). These low feedstock costs are a result of a legacy of extensive former state support which bestowed SCI its market position and not a result of risks or innovation undertaken by the firm (discussed later).

SCI's modelled LRCE price outcomes were also set in the very market in which the dominant firm is alleged to be charging excessive prices (including, pertinently, the size of the market). This fundamentally undermines the entire analysis because it disregards the fact that the very basis of the complaint was that in that given market there is never going to be more than one firm operating at scale and therefore there will never be effective competition. Markets in which excessive pricing is likely to happen are precisely those where there will never be entry and exit by new entrants, as acknowledged by SCI's economic expert.[8] This is fundamentally the reason why the Act requires regulating exploitative abuses such as excessive prices – because these high prices will not automatically result in new entry.

SCI's approach is consistent with neither the realities of the South African economy nor the purpose of the Act, which has a strong focus on correcting previous excessive concentrations that resulted from state support. Thus, the CAC could not have intended 'long run' in the textbook sense but rather under particular circumstances. The equilibrium price resulting from competition is dependent on the relevant market characteristics and, even in the 'long run', the size of the market and scale economies are relevant. SCI's LRCE test was calculated with the actual conditions where excessive prices can potentially arise, that is, where there is already a quasi-monopoly (or, in theory, given that the dominance threshold is 35 or 45%, a duopoly). However, for the CAC in *Mittal*, LRCE appeared to mean that the level of competition was sufficient to compete away all supernormal/pure profits. This is in line with Alfred Marshall's (1920, pp. 617–619) discussion of the fair or normal rate of profit for each branch of trade under the 'long period or true normal results of economic forces'. By definition, this cannot include a monopoly price as a possible outcome of the LRCE modelling, or, in the absence of restrictive assumptions, a duopoly. In fact, this interpretation of economic value may restrict the application of the test in precisely the industries where market structure ensures the incumbent has a strong position as the facts of the market will mean an LRCE with positive economic profits.

It appears therefore that SCI's conceptualisation of the LRCE as a test does not provide for a coherent analysis of economic value for an excessive pricing determination as suggested in the literature. It is necessary for the tests for economic value to have practical application. For a new test to take the debate forward, it should have fewer difficulties in application than the currently accepted tests for economic value. The LRCE test does not meet either of these criteria. It yields prices, and hence economic values, which are a function of the number of firms, the size of the market and assumptions as to how the firms compete. In short, these are not prices that reflect pure profits having been competed away nor are they prices which are cost-reflective.

SCI's interpretation of the LRCE divorces the test from the particular firm and circumstances. A reading of CAC *Mittal* in its entirety strongly suggests that the reference to LRCE was to provide a broad conceptual framework for the analysis of economic value and that it endorsed comparators and price-cost analyses, which are widely accepted measures of economic value. This is confirmed by the CAC in *SCI* where it states that in the *Mittal* decision the Court's inclusion of paragraphs 40 and 43 (defining economic value as prices under LRCE) sought to provide a framework to evaluate this evidence and thereby determine whether the price so charged was excessive.[9]

In our view, the appropriate approach to the reference to LRCE by the CAC is to consider what pricing would be under conditions of effective competitive rivalry between firms with similar costs to the incumbent. Thus, the competitive equilibrium concept is a means to an end (effective competitive rivalry) and not an end in itself. The Tribunal in *SCI* also interpreted the reference to LRCE as the conceptual framework that should be applied when thinking through the assessment of economic value.[10] CAC in *SCI* rejected the modelling of a notional equilibrium and, like the Tribunal, used the dominant firm's economic costs as a measure of economic value.[11]

We propose that the appropriate analysis is based on effective competitive rivalry, where effective competition yields cost-reflective prices and the cost of a good or service is indicative of its economic value.[12] When thinking about the counterfactual to determine economic value, one has to imagine a market that adds the dimension of effective rivalry to the industry under review using the dominant firm's actual costs as a starting point. However, it is necessary to evaluate to what extent the dominant firm's accounting costs as reflected in their financial statements are representative of economic costs and whether there is a need to make any adjustments. In other words, the price under LRCE is an outcome that can be expected when existing firms are competing effectively with one another and the costs of the dominant firm are indicative of the costs of the existing firms. This interpretation was accepted by the Tribunal in *SCI*, noting that in economic terms effective competition means rivalry between established firms in a given relevant market.[13] The CAC was unfortunately silent on this.

The implication of adopting effective competitive rivalry as the understanding of LRCE is that the thought exercise should be conducted on the costs of the existing firm, given that the existing firm could have plausibly been 'replicated' under situations of competition (and not where the position was due to firm-specific innovation). As a result, the LRCE and effective competition tests would collapse into one test. There is no substantial difference between the two, other than the differentiation being a gloss put on by economists. The discussion on whose costs are relevant for the analysis then becomes central to this debate. The notional entrant approach is also inconsistent with other areas of competition assessment that employ a counterfactual analysis, such as in cartel damages and merger assessment. These also do not involve notional entrants, but rather counterfactuals that are based on the facts of the specific firms in the market in question. For example, in mergers the consideration of potential entrants is within a specific context. Before a potential entrant/expansion can be included in the counterfactual, it must be shown that the entry or expansion is likely to occur; that the anticipated entry or expansion is of a nature, scale and scope to prevent or reverse the anticompetitive effects that the merger otherwise would have; and that the entry or expansion is likely to occur within a reasonable time period (ICN, 2006). Similarly, in margin squeeze cases there are two tests, the 'as-efficient competitor' test (relying on the costs of the dominant firm) and the 'reasonably efficient' test (relying on the costs of an existing competitor).

The difficulties in the practical application of the LRCE approach are immediately evident in the SCI case in the treatment of firm-specific cost advantages (which it terms 'special cost advantages'). SCI's reading of the LRCE approach led it to discard the very favourable low input costs of feedstock propylene in favour of hypothetical feedstock costs a notional entrant would face (which, in SCI's view, would be considerably higher than its own) (see later for our evaluation of this).

Same approach to economic value, different answers: The devil is in the detail

Both the Tribunal and the CAC found that economic value could be determined through different methods, an approach consistent with the literature and the approach in other jurisdictions. The Tribunal evaluated the following methods put forth by the parties to determine the economic value of purified propylene: price-cost tests (using the dominant firm's economic costs); comparison of domestic prices with prices in other geographic markets; and a comparison of SCI's export prices with domestic prices. Though the CAC emphasised that economic value can be determined using a range of comparators, quoting the European case law at length, it did not engage with the comparators put forward by the parties as a measure of economic value.[14] Instead, the polypropylene international comparators were considered only in the reasonableness discussion, which was effectively moot as the Court had already found that the prices charged by SCI were not substantially above economic value. In other words, the CAC in *SCI* considered only those disputes relating to the price-cost assessments. In determining the dominant firm's economic costs, the two judgments agreed on the valuation of feedstock propylene for the calculation but differed on the valuation of SCI's capital assets, the level of capital reward/return on capital to be applied, the allocation of group costs, and the allocation of fixed costs between domestic and export sales.

The choices on each of these four factors led the Tribunal and the CAC to make different findings. The Tribunal found in favour of the Commission, with purified propylene mark-ups over economic costs during the complaint period in the range of 25.1–41.5% for sales to Safripol. Regarding polypropylene, the Tribunal found the price mark-up over economic costs in the range of 17.6–36.5% (which includes both a conservative and a more realistic measure range). SCI's local prices for polypropylene were also found to be 23% higher than average deep-sea export prices, and between 41 and 47% above discounted prices charged in Western Europe.

The CAC found that the average purified propylene mark-ups were between 12.1 and 14.3% and the polypropylene mark-ups between −28.9 and −24.4%. The Court concluded that SCI had not engaged in excessive pricing and over-turned the Tribunal judgment.

The implication of the precedent set by the CAC in *SCI* on these specific factors is not the subject of this chapter. However, the quantum of the differences between the Tribunal's and the CAC's mark-ups suggests that South Africa is still a long way from having a clear framework for assessing excessive prices.

The treatment of special cost advantages

Central to the debate on what a competitive price would be in our view is what the costs of production are. Although there are fundamental disagreements on the determination of economic value, there is common recognition that the concept of economic value encapsulates cost considerations. The point of departure is, as highlighted, on *whose* costs and *what* costs.

With regard to whose costs should be considered, the question is whether it is the costs of the dominant firm in question, those of a notional entrant or costs which would prevail if there were effectively competing firms in the market (discussed above).

This section reviews the contrasting viewpoints on *what* costs should be considered and whether the CAC's decision in *SCI* provided any further clarity on how to treat special cost advantages. The key debate is whether all costs should be taken into account or certain costs excluded on the basis that they are not representative of the 'notional competitive norm' or costs that the notional entrant would incur, because they confer a 'special cost advantage' to the particular firm in question. This debate emerges directly as a result of the different interpretations of LRCE discussed above.

As noted, we do not enter here into other debates raised in the case about the inclusion and exclusion of certain cost categories and the measurement of cost of capital. Although the latter dispute resulted in significant cost differences, as seen in the large differences in price-cost margin calculations, the most fundamental dispute was on the treatment of special cost advantages and whether these should be excluded when determining economic value. The issue of the treatment of special cost advantages is core because it determines how SCI's low feedstock propylene costs are accounted for in price-cost tests or profitability analyses. Given SCI's very low feedstock costs of propylene, price-cost tests taking into account these low costs result in high margins.

Economic value in relation to costs
It is unclear what the CAC's final position on special cost advantages is. Its treatment of special cost advantages in the *SCI* judgment is at odds with its own statements in the *Mittal* judgment. In *SCI*, the CAC in effect held that special

cost advantages should *not* be considered and that the actual price at which Synfuels sold its feedstock to SCI should be used in calculations.[15] This actual price is not the true valuation of the feedstock and the Commission argued that it was well above the true fuel alternative value, and therefore had to be adjusted downwards.

SCI's interpretation of the CAC in *Mittal* was that these costs should instead be adjusted upwards as they serve to reduce the dominant firm's costs below the notional competitive norm. In particular, SCI sought to partially use the CAC's approach in *Mittal*[16] in that the relevant costs can be calculated by determining the costs that would prevail in LRCE.[17] The CAC further held that while the dominant firm's costs were an important evidential ingredient in such an inquiry, they were not conclusive.[18] This is because some of the dominant firm's cost advantages may be 'unique' to it, and not available to a notional entrant or existing competitor.

> It seems to follow that, in determining the economic value of a good or service, the cost savings to the firm resulting from the subsidised loan or the lower than market rental – or indeed any other special advantage, current or historical that serves to reduce the particular firm's costs below the notional competitive norm ought to be disregarded. Thus economic value is a notional objective competitive-market standard, and not one derived from circumstances peculiar to the particular firm. If the firm's price is no higher than economic value, no contravention of s 8(a) can arise.[19]

However, the CAC in *Mittal* did not suggest that such special cost advantages ought to be completely disregarded in an excessive pricing assessment. In fact, paragraph 43 goes on to state:

> If, however, the firm's price is in fact higher than economic value so determined, the test of reasonableness in respect of the difference remains to be applied. The expression 'reasonable profit', when dealing with economic value, should be avoided. The test of reasonableness applies to the excess of price over economic value, and thus only to the element of 'pure profit' (over and above 'normal profit') implicit in that price. It is at this stage of the enquiry that circumstances peculiar to the particular dominant firm would rationally come into the reckoning.

This brings into the spotlight the consideration of state support. The CAC itself emphasised in the *SCI* judgment that it had, in *Mittal*, stated that the advantages of state support should be examined at the reasonableness stage of the inquiry because 'it was here that it was appropriate to take into account how the firm's cost affected the reasonableness of its price in relation to the value of the good and whether the high price of the good represented a reward for risk and innovation'.[20]

Yet, the CAC did not take the significance of state support into account even at this stage of the assessment in the SCI case, seemingly because (although it is not clear in the judgment) the calculated price-cost margins were too low to warrant further consideration of special cost advantages.[21] The CAC's approach suggests that the reasonableness assessment takes place in sequential steps where one first determines whether the mark-ups over economic value based on a notional firm are reasonable, and, if they are found to be unreasonable, only then does the next step of the inquiry kick in – that is, whether special cost advantages, such as those bequeathed by state support, are considered. We argue that this is the wrong approach and the SCI case clearly reveals why this is so.

What constitutes special cost advantages?

We begin with what can be considered a special cost advantage. The CAC in *Mittal* provided certain broad examples of what might be special cost advantages. It mentioned benefits flowing to the firm from subsidised loans, long-term low rentals or other special advantages which may serve to reduce its own long-run average costs below the notional norm.[22] But as the Tribunal highlights in the *SCI* decision, the CAC did not explain how the examples provided in the ruling arose from the particular facts of the *Mittal* case.[23] A number of things remain unclear, and the CAC's *SCI* judgment has unfortunately not gone any further in clarifying these issues for future cases in which they may be relevant. The issues include: what exactly does a benefit from a subsidised loan and long-term low rental refer to and how would these be quantified in practice? If these advantages were available to more than one firm in the industry, assuming there was competition, would it still be a 'special' cost advantage? (See below.) What other types of costs could be categorised as special cost advantages under this category and can the circumstances of the industry affect the consideration of a particular type of special cost advantage (i.e., can a type of cost advantage that is 'special' in one industry not be 'special' in another)?

Furthermore, there is no indication of how such cost advantages could be 'corrected for' in an excessive pricing assessment. Sylvester (2014) demonstrates that the method of correcting for special cost advantages by simply adding costs onto those of the dominant firm's costs (to bring costs up to the notional competitive norm as suggested by Langbridge and MacKenzie, 2010) results in several distortions. He shows that this overestimates costs and prices that would result under a competitive market structure and possibly even overestimates the cost of the monopolist if it did not enjoy the special cost advantage at all, if certain assumptions of the shape of the cost curve are taken into consideration. Irrespective of whether the nature of the cost curve in such industries is upward or downward sloping, simply adding the 'special cost advantage' back onto the dominant firm's costs does not produce the appropriate counterfactual cost level (Sylvester, 2014). Considering special cost advantages when assessing reasonableness instead, according to the latter part of paragraph 43 in CAC *Mittal*, avoids such challenges of adding back costs. The determination then reduces to a value judgement of whether the price-cost margins are justified given the source of the special cost advantages.

Sylvester (2014) also attempts to understand the possible meaning of special cost advantages and suggests that the *amici curiae* in the *Mittal* case appear to have conflated the notions of opportunity costs and costs that occur under the notional competitive norm. Sylvester highlights that the *amici curiae* explained at length why accounting and economic costs can differ if opportunity costs are present and that any special cost advantage should be valued at the opportunity cost rather than the actual amount paid. The *amici curiae* then reach the conclusion that the CAC adopted in its decision at paragraph 43, where, instead of using the wording 'opportunity cost' (following from their descriptions and reasoning), they use the wording 'notional competitive norm' as the standard to evaluate costs (Petersen, Maenetje and Le Roux, 2008, para. 23.1, cited in Sylvester, 2014). Sylvester's argument is that these are two different notions, and not just a matter of semantics. He argues that the opportunity cost is in fact a firm-specific cost, while the notional competitive norm suggests a market-related price which is not firm-specific.

The Tribunal held in *SCI* that given its specific circumstances, special cost advantages could not be assessed according to the general examples provided by the CAC in *Mittal*. Doing so would not take into account a situation where pure profit was not as a result of innovation and own risk taking.[24] The latter was indeed the Commission's stance on special cost advantages. The CAC's response to this in the *SCI* judgment unfortunately does not add any further clarity.[25]

We argue that it is crucial to understand the history of how SCI attained its dominant position and whether this was due to innovation and risk taking or whether it was bequeathed through extensive former state support. Only once this is understood can the treatment of special cost advantages be determined. The Commission led extensive evidence in this regard, including the various forms of state support received throughout the history of Sasol.[26] The Commission's expert witness highlighted that given the strategic nature of the sector, the state ensured that Sasol would not fail, including through extensive protection of the fuel industry, which extended to marketing arrangements with other oil companies that ensured offtake and marketing of Sasol's fuel; funding of Sasol through revenue from fuel levies;[27] support in terms of access to infrastructure; the strategic inland location of Natref and exemptions from paying crude oil transport costs. The state also bore much of the risk during the privatisation process. The Commission concluded that Sasol was created and supported by the state and that any advantage that it presently enjoys is a result of this and not of innovation and own risk taking. Similarly, SCI's dominant position in purified propylene and polypropylene was a direct result of such support. The Tribunal found in favour of the Commission in this regard,[28] highlighting that SCI's own witness confirmed that Sasol had leveraged its protected position in fuel to enter the chemicals business.[29] The CAC in the *SCI* judgment simply did not engage in this critical debate.

Special or not? What makes sense in the South African context?

Cost advantages bestowed through extensive state support cannot be separated from the technology that SCI employed in its operations and whether this conferred any special cost advantage to it. On this aspect, SCI's fundamental dispute arose again from its interpretation of CAC *Mittal*, categorising its low propylene feedstock cost as a special cost advantage which, according to its interpretation of LRCE in CAC *Mittal*, ought *not* to be considered in any calculations. SCI's position was that its Synfuels operations (using the Fischer-Tropsch process) were unique and could not easily be duplicated. The resultant low feedstock cost advantage conferred on SCI was therefore 'special' and not the industry 'norm'. To equate this to the industry norm, its costs would have to be adjusted upwards, the effect of which would result in lower price-cost margins.

The Commission's industry expert witness argued that there was nothing 'special' about the Fischer-Tropsch process and that it was in fact a standard technology and production process. The Tribunal also held that SCI's witness conceded the purification process of SCI was not special in that it was not very different from US producers in terms of costs, and was in fact a 'standard distilla-tion technology'. The witness further conceded that SCI had undertaken limited innovation in purified propylene and polypropylene.[30]

Importantly, the Commission argued that the low feedstock cost that resulted from the process was not a 'unique' or 'firm-specific' advantage to SCI. If there was greater competition at the downstream level (in competition to SCI), then it would be expected that Synfuels would supply all these firms with feedstock propylene at prices that it supplies SCI and it would not then be a 'unique' cost advantage to SCI only. In this sense, the lack of competition in the domestic market should not confer a special cost advantage to SCI (see also Sylvester, 2014, regarding the facts of the *Mittal* case).

Furthermore, while SCI commended the CAC's approach in equating eco-nomic value to the *notional* price of the good or service under conditions of LRCE, it held that the CAC was mistaken in then suggesting[31] that any special advantage should be taken into account in considering the reasonableness of the relationship between the dominant firm's prices and economic value.[32] SCI's expert witness claimed that taking the special cost advantage back into the reck-oning at this stage was nonsensical when it had been removed in the first place as it did not represent the costs of a notional entrant.[33]

Ultimately, the CAC in *SCI* did not take into account special cost advantages at *any* stage of the inquiry. This appears entirely at odds with the purpose of section 8(a) of the Act in the context of South Africa's history of economic development. The Act aims to ensure efficient outcomes in the economy and in this sense aims to achieve cost-reflective prices. But equally important in the South African context, the preamble of the Act clearly sets out the concerns arising from the previous economic and social imbalances of the economy (dis-cussed above).

The Tribunal concluded, correctly in our view, that SCI's cost advantage ought to be taken into account at some stage of the inquiry.[34] The Tribunal noted that SCI's approach instead leads to an artificial result, and that it was not practical that if in SCI's notional exercise prices were found not to be above economic value, special cost advantages could never be considered ever again in the analysis. The Tribunal's interpretation of the CAC's decision in *Mittal* was that a broader and more holistic view, including the realities of the market, must be taken when considering special cost advantages.[35] Unfortunately, this appears not to be what the CAC itself ultimately employed in its approach in *SCI*.

The importance of history and how a firm attained its dominant position has nonetheless been recognised by Judge Davis in other platforms (Davis, 2011), who noted that South Africa's past industrial policy did not cater for competitive rivalry. Motta and de Streel (2007), Roberts (2008) and Evans (2009) also suggest that those markets in which monopolies established dominance due to current or past exclusive or special rights are the very markets in which competition authorities should be concerned about excessive pricing in the first place, as high prices are usually merely a rent unrelated to market conditions.

Given this manifest purpose of the Act, the widespread recognition that there are circumstances in which competition authorities should intervene in excessive pricing cases, and the circumstances of this case closely fitting these criteria, an approach in which special cost advantage should never be considered at any stage in an excessive pricing case is entirely at odds with the spirit of the Act. Never considering special cost advantages would vindicate exactly the types of firms whose conduct could potentially fall foul of this provision and where intervention should occur. These include present and former state-owned enterprises that attained their 'special cost advantage' not through innovation and own risk taking but through state support.

In our view, two general insights on the treatment of special cost advantages can be drawn from the above discussion. First, the history of how the firm attained its advantageous position is fundamentally important in an excessive price assessment. If it was through extensive innovation and own risk taking, then one could argue that the cost advantage that arises from this is indeed 'special' to the firm. In this regard, one could consider, as the Tribunal did, evidence or lack thereof on investments in technology in the affected business. The nature of the technology can also be evaluated as part of the broader argument. If the advantage is instead because of past and current state support, then this should not be considered special, because if a different industrial policy model had been employed by the state at the time, more than one firm could have potentially benefited from such support.

Second, what may appear to be a 'unique' input cost to a downstream firm may not be unique to it at all if there was competition in the downstream market and every firm could potentially benefit from the low input in question.

Conclusions

Excessive pricing provisions are important for smaller markets (such as markets in many developing countries) as economies of scale and barriers to entry imply a greater likelihood of dominant firms that are not always subject to regulation and that can charge supra-competitive prices. This is the case in the South African economy, which is characterised by concentrated industries and an economy skewed to resource-based and capital-intensive production due to previous exclusionary policies. In instances where excessive pricing is of an intermediary product, it can be particularly harmful and the risk of overenforcement needs to be balanced against the needs of the economy and the harm from underenforcement. In the *SCI* case, the Tribunal held that the dominant firm's conduct resulted in missed opportunities for innovation and development for the domestic manufacture of plastic goods downstream. Considering the employment potential of a medium-technology industry such as plastics conversion in a developing economy, South Africa cannot afford these missed opportunities. Though the Tribunal decision was overturned, the decline of the downstream sector has been linked to the increase in prices following the change in SCI's pricing strategy in 2002/2003 (Beare, Mondliwa, Robb and Roberts, 2014; Mondliwa and Roberts, 2014).

Though there has been extensive debate on whether or not it is necessary for competition authorities to pursue excessive pricing, there is a growing body of literature which recognises the substantial potential impact of an excessive price in an economy, and, as such, this literature proposes that different jurisdictions should choose paths that are most appropriate for their particular circumstances. Otherwise, in countries like South Africa where there is a history of concentrated industries, particularly in upstream intermediate input product markets like steel and polymers, excessive prices will seriously inhibit the transformation and growth path of these economies. We note, however, that it is important for authorities to consider the implications of making type one or type two errors. False convictions can have the effect of chilling investments while false acquittals can inhibit growth of downstream industries. The growing consensus in the literature is that excessive prices should be limited to industries where there are high barriers to entry, where the dominant firm has and can exercise its market power and where there is little or no innovation.

Others have taken the argument further by identifying markets that are likely to allow a dominant firm to charge excessive prices. These are markets in which firms attained dominance due to current or past exclusive or special rights, and in which high prices usually reflect a supra-competitive rent (Evans, 2009; Motta and de Streel, 2007; Roberts, 2008).

The controversies in excessive pricing are not limited to whether or not it should be pursued as an abuse of dominance but also encompass debates on the appropriate assessment thereof. As this chapter highlights, excessive pricing is one of the most difficult contraventions to prove given that a central concept in its assessment, the determination of economic value, is not defined in most jurisdictions. The accepted measures of assessing economic value include price-cost tests, comparators and profitability analyses. The determination of economic value in the CAC's decision in *Mittal* would have been further elucidated after the matter was remitted to the Tribunal. Unfortunately, the parties settled the matter before this happened and these issues were not clarified. The SCI case then presented the first opportunity to revisit the definition of economic value as the notional price under LRCE.

While SCI interpreted economic value based on LRCE by modelling the price that would allow for notional entrants, we have understood it to be a counterfactual where there is effective competition. We considered whether LRCE as first referred in CAC *Mittal* was a conceptual framework or a new test and are of the view that the distinction made between effective competition and LRCE is an artificial one. As we argued, modelling notional entrants may result in a number of challenges, some of which may lead to false acquittals. Setting economic value at prices which cover high costs of entry (including higher input prices or poorer access to inputs) simply defines away the basis for the concern. In such models, the equilibrium could be a monopoly if there are scale economies and a relatively small market. Monopoly pricing against this benchmark would most likely not be found to be excessive. This implies that excessive pricing could only be a very short-term exploitation or only due to legal barriers to entry, as the market would otherwise be effectively competitive. This approach is at odds with the circumstances of smaller economies like South Africa's.

Given that the purpose of the Competition Act in South Africa includes economic efficiency, increased participation and redistributive objectives, the CAC's reference to economic value as the notional prices under conditions of LRCE cannot be understood as modelling prices that would allow for notional entrants in circumstances where the market conditions do not allow for entry and the dominant firm is entrenched. The continued exertion of pricing power implies ongoing welfare losses and distortion of relative prices in the economy. We have argued that the appropriate interpretation of economic value in CAC *Mittal*, which is also consistent with other passages in the decision, is prices that would arise under conditions of effective competitive rivalry.

Notes

1   Both authors were part of the team of economic experts for the Competition Commission. The views expressed in this chapter are the authors' own and do not necessarily reflect the views of the Commission.

2   Several states, however, have anti-'price gouging' laws that prohibit short-term steep price increases during periods of unexpected high demand, such as following natural disasters or emergencies.

3   *United Brands v EC Commission* [1978] 1 CMLR 429.

4   Mittal Steel South Africa Limited, Macsteel International BV, Macsteel Holdings (Pty) Limited vs Harmony Gold Mining Company Limited, Durban Roodepoort Deep Limited at [29]; Case number: 70/CAC/Apr07. See also Davis (2011).

5   *Napp Pharmaceutical Holdings v DG of Fair Trading* [2002] CAT 1; [2002].

6   CAC *Mittal*, fn 82.

7   Para. 40.

8   Padilla cross-examination at 2127, 3–2128, 12.

9   Para. 111.

10   Para. 50.

11   Para. 115.

12   See CAC *Mittal*, para. 51.

13   Para. 70.

14   CAC *SCI*, paras. 102–104.

15   Para. 115.

16   Para. 43.

17 *Mittal*, fn 70.

18 *Mittal*, fn 70.

19 *Mittal*, para. 43.

20 Para. 171.

21 CAC *SCI*, paras. 172–174.

22 Para. 43.

23 Para. 90. The Tribunal highlights that the CAC didn't have to explain this as it remitted the matter to it.

24 Para. 90.

25 See para. 172.

26 See Expert Witness statement of Dr Rustomjee, 2012, chief pp. 3394–5, p. 3399, p. 3400, pp. 3403–4m, p. 3406.

27 Tribunal decision, para. 106, drawing from evidence presented by Rustomjee.

28 Paras. 104–108.

29 Para. 116, citing MacDougall of SCI: 'Sasol is establishing that it is using the Synfuels operation as a platform for growth. It is holding Synfuels neutral so that it is not making additional profit, but it is not losing anything and then that creates the opportunity to build a significant downstream petrochemical industry.'

30 Tribunal decision, paras. 111–113, citing evidence from MacDougall of SCI.

31 Later in para. 43.

32 CAC *Mittal*, para. 43.

33 Padilla cross-examination at 2059, 14–2060, 9.

34 Paras. 120, 121.

35 Para. 95.

References

Bain J. 1956. *Barriers to New Competition.* Cambridge, MA: Harvard University Press.

Beare M, P Mondliwa, G Robb and S Roberts. 2014. Report for the Plastics Conversion Industry Strategy, prepared for the Department of Trade and Industry. Mimeo.

Bishop S and M Walker. 2010. *The Economics of EC Competition Law: Concepts, Application and Measurement* (3rd edition). London: Sweet & Maxwell.

Blaug M. 1997. *Economic Theory in Retrospect* (5th edition). Cambridge: Cambridge University Press.

Calcagno C and M Walker. 2010. Excessive pricing: Towards clarity and economic coherence. *Journal of Competition Law and Economics* 6: 891–910.

Chamberlin EH. 1933. *The Theory of Monopolistic Competition* (Vol. 6). Cambridge, MA: Harvard University Press.

Chisanga BF, H Meyer, A Winter-Nelson and NJ Sitko. 2014. *Does the Current Sugar Market Structure Benefit Consumers and Sugarcane Growers?* IAPRI Working Paper No. 89. http://ageconsearch.umn.edu/bitstream/188569/2/wp89.pdf.

das Nair R. 2008. Measuring excessive pricing as an abuse of dominance: An assessment of the criteria used in the Harmony Gold/Mittal Steel complaint. *South African Journal of Economic and Management Sciences* 11: 279–291.

Davis D. 2011. Abuse of dominance, competition law and economic development: A view from the southern tip of Africa. In B Hawk (ed.), *2010 Annual Proceedings of the*

Fordham Competition Law Institute, International Antitrust Law and Policy, pp. 325–338. Huntington, NY: Juris Publishing.

European Commission. 2016. 'Protecting Consumers from Exploitation'. Speech of the EC's Commissioner on Competition, M. Vestager, at the Chillin' Competition Conference, Brussels, 21 November (online document).

Evans D. 2009. Why different jurisdictions do not (and should not) adopt the same antitrust rules. *Chicago Journal of International Law* 10: 161–188.

Evans D and J Padilla. 2005a. Excessive prices: Using economics to define administrable legal rules. *Journal of Competition Law and Economics* 1: 97–122.

Evans D and J Padilla. 2005b. Designing antitrust rules for assessing unilateral practices: A neo-Chicago approach. *University of Chicago Law Review* 73: 76–80.

Ezrachi A and D Gilo. 2009. Are excessive prices really self-correcting? *Journal of Competition Law and Economics* 5: 249–268.

Ezrachi A and D Gilo. 2010. Excessive pricing, entry, assessment and investment: Lessons from the Mittal litigation. *Antitrust Law Journal* 76: 873–897.

Gilbert RJ. 1989. Mobility barriers and the value of incumbency. In R Schmalensee and RD Willig (eds), *Handbook of Industrial Organization* (Vol. 1), pp. 475–535. Amsterdam: Elsevier Science Publishers.

Grimbeek S and B Lekezwa. 2013. *The Emergence of More Vigorous Competition and the Importance of Entry: Comparative Insights from Flour and Poultry*. Centre for Competition Regulation and Economic Development Working Paper Series No. 1.

ICN (International Competition Network). 2006. 'ICN Merger Guidelines Workbook'. Prepared for the Fifth Annual ICN Conference in Cape Town (online document).

Langbridge S and N MacKenzie. 2010. Excessive pricing: Guidance from South Africa. *European Competition Law Review* 31: 354–361.

Lewis D. 2009. 'Exploitative Abuses – A Note on the *Harmony Gold v Mittal Steel* Excessive Pricing Case' (online document).

Marshall A. 1920. *Principles of Economics* (8th edition). London: Macmillan.

Mehta K and L Peeperkorn. 2007. The economics of competition. In J Faull and A Nikpay (eds), *The EC Law of Competition* (2nd edition), pp. 1.01–1.304. Oxford: Oxford University Press.

Mondliwa P and S Roberts. 2014. Excessive pricing and industrial development: The recent Competition Tribunal finding against Sasol Chemical Industries. *New Agenda: South African Journal of Social and Economic Policy* 55: 48–51.

Motta M and A de Streel. 2006. Excessive pricing and price squeeze under EU law. In C-D Ehlermann and I Atanasiu (eds), *European Competition Law Annual, 2003: What Is an Abuse of a Dominant Position?* pp. 91–126. Oxford: Hart Publishing.

Motta M and A de Streel. 2007. Excessive pricing in competition law: Never say never? In *The Pros and Cons of High Prices*, pp. 14–46. Stockholm: Konkurrensverket – Swedish Competition Authority.

O'Donoghue, R and AJ Padilla. 2006. *The Law and Economics of Article 82 EC*. Oxford: Hart Publishing.

O'Donoghue R and AJ Padilla. 2013. *The Law and Economics of Article 82 EC*. Oxford: Hart Publishing.

Petersen R, H Maenetje and M le Roux. 2008. Submissions by Amici Curiae on the interpretation of section 8(a) of the Competition Act, Competition Appeal Court ruling on the

Harmony Mittal appeal. Available from the registrar of the Competition Appeal Court upon request.

Roberts S. 2008. Assessing excessive pricing: The case of flat steel in South Africa. *Journal of Competition Law and Economics* 4: 871–891.

Roberts S. 2012. 'National dominant firms, competition law, and the implications for economic development in Southern Africa: Case studies of energy, beer and food'. Paper presented at the 3rd International Conference of the Instituto de Estudos Sociais e Económicos, Maputo, Mozambique, 4–5 September.

Rose V and D Bailey (eds). 2013. *Bellamy and Child: European Union Law of Competition* (7th edition). Oxford: Oxford University Press.

Sylvester A. 2014. Excessive prices legislation in developing markets: Some problems that arise when importing the law from developed jurisdictions. *Journal of Economics and Financial Sciences* 7: 607–619.

Van Wyngaardt M. 2016. 'Sasol unveils R1.1bn polypropylene expansion project', *Engineering News*, 21 November, http://www.engineeringnews.co.za/article/sasol-unveils-r11bn-polypropylene-expansion-project-2016-11-21.

Vickers J. 2006. How does the prohibition of abuse of dominance fit with the rest of competition policy? In C-D Ehlermann and I Atanasiu (eds), *European Competition Law Annual, 2003: What Is an Abuse of a Dominant Position?* pp. 147–156. Oxford: Hart Publishing.

5 Competition and regulation interface in energy, telecommunications and transport in South Africa

Reena das Nair and Simon Roberts

Introduction

Economic regulation is largely about regulating the natural monopoly parts of value chains and generally involves the regulation of enterprises that are, or were, state-owned. Regulating access to, and pricing of, essential infrastructure, key inputs and bottleneck goods and services that cannot be easily replicated is considered necessary to ensure that fair access is provided and that monopoly prices are not charged (Viscusi, Vernon and Harrington, 1998). Economic regulation is also seen as a mechanism by which significant market failures can be corrected, or entrenched dominant positions kept in check. In certain industries, such as network infrastructure, the private sector will underinvest as the social returns are generally greater than the private returns, given the large externalities generated. In such industries, economic regulation is necessary to ensure sufficient investment. Therefore, the scope of economic regulation is broader than just controlling access and pricing. Dynamic considerations such as the impact on investment decisions, the impact of infrastructure on the development path of the economy, and the creative role of competitive rivalry all need to be part of an effective economic regulatory regime.

While economic regulation is often viewed as the control of market power in instances where competition is either not possible or not desirable, competition policy is about regulating the potentially anticompetitive behaviour of dominant players and addressing structural changes through the merger regime or through conditions. In this sense, economic regulation is predominantly *ex ante*, where the rules of the game are set out upfront, while competition law enforcement is largely *ex post*, where past anticompetitive conduct is prosecuted after the fact, except for the merger regime where accretions of concentration which could potentially lead to anticompetitive outcomes are curbed *ex ante*. However, this dichotomy is imprecise, as even economic regulation mainly uses past conduct and data to determine the future course of action and competition policy aims to influence future conduct through changing past undesirable behaviour. The two are even further interrelated – regulation is required for competition to flourish, for instance, to ensure access to essential facilities or inputs. A regulatory regime that favours incumbents over new entry hinders competitive objectives and it is important that regulators take into account dynamic gains from greater competitive rivalry in setting the rules of regulation and when making decisions. Similarly, it is important that competition authorities appreciate the rationale for, and forms of, economic regulation and, at the same time, understand that some matters regarding competitive outcomes are more effectively resolved through regulatory intervention.

This chapter draws lessons from experiences in three regulated industries in South Africa: energy, telecommunications and transport (ports and rail). These sectors were selected as part of a national government-funded project aimed at building regulatory entities' capacity (CCRED, n.d.).[1] The project reviewed the performance of regulators in the wider context of their mandates and powers; the challenges they face in terms of regulatory capacity, accountability, credibility and other constraints, including fiscal constraints; and industry performance in terms of pricing outcomes, investment in the sector and allocative and productive efficiency. The reviews further assessed whether economic regulation in these industries has contributed to, or been in conflict with, other economic development mandates aimed at sustainable development and inclusive growth. We draw on these reviews to identify important lessons for the interface between competition and regulation in these sectors. This is useful for economic regulators in terms of learning from one another, for engagement between economic regulators and competition authorities, as well as for policy makers.

The different industries reflect a diversity of approaches from which insights can be drawn. In electricity we have an integrated state-owned enterprise (SOE) with an independent regulator, and the introduction of new participants in the form of renewable energy generators. In rail freight and ports there is an integrated SOE without a regulator until the recently established Ports Regulator. In telecommunications, the main operator has long been effectively privatised, and there are private operators in mobile telephony, with a long-established regulator and enforcement actions by the competition authorities.

In the remainder of this chapter, we evaluate the outcomes and performance of the electricity, transport (ports and rail in particular) and telecommunications sectors of South Africa, highlighting how certain decisions of the relevant regulator encouraged competitive outcomes while others discouraged it. We conclude by comparing and contrasting the similarities and differences of each regulatory regime and drawing together key lessons learnt.

Energy

The electricity supply industry (ESI) of South Africa is dominated by state-owned utility Eskom, which operates across the entire electricity value chain in generation, transmission and distribution.[2] Eskom generates 95% of the electricity consumed in the country, with independent power producers (IPPs) representing a much smaller portion of electricity generation.

After the corporatisation of Eskom, there were concerns around its dominance in the ESI, and around the poor performance on a technical level throughout the value chain.[3] Even though Eskom was funded by government, alternative sources of funding were needed to invest in and develop the ESI. These factors culminated in developing a hybrid model in which, on the one hand, Eskom was given the responsibility for immediate new investment, and, on the other, private IPPs were given an opportunity to participate in electricity generation. However, the industry is still dominated by Eskom in terms of the size of its contribution to electricity generation, its ownership and operation of transmission network services and its role in distributing electricity. Eskom distributes around 60% of the country's power, with municipalities distributing the balance. Although Eskom distributes more power than municipalities do, it serves fewer end users, focusing on long-term contracts with mining companies and other large industry players at more favourable rates.

The ESI has been regulated by an independent regulator since 1995, first by the National Electricity Regulator, followed by the National Energy Regulator of South Africa (Nersa) since 2005. Nersa is tasked with price determination, licensing, dispute resolution and the compliance of electricity suppliers.

Outcomes in the ESI and the regulator's role

The outcomes observed in the ESI, particularly in terms of the supply and pricing of coal-generated electricity, are linked to investment patterns in generation infrastructure which, in turn, are a product of regulatory decisions. But these outcomes have also been influenced by political pressure, Eskom's market power and large electricity-intensive user groups. Policy uncertainty and institutional complexity (several players with divergent views involved in decision making and no clear energy policy[4]) have further resulted in certain detrimental impacts on the sector and the economy as a whole, particularly during the 2008 load-shedding crises. However, the success story of the ESI on the generation level has been the Renewable Energy Independent Power Producers Procurement Programme (REIPPPP) (discussed later). The evolution of the renewable energy industry emphasises how challenges can be effectively addressed through proactive regulation that takes into account competition principles.

The key question relating to average and relative prices charged to different electricity customers is how the legacy of overinvestment in generation capacity in the 1980s has influenced the structure of the economy and, in particular, its capital-intensive bias. As discussed below, overinvestment in generation capacity led to power stations being built and then mothballed in the 1980s. This meant that it was worth selling electricity as long as the price earned was above the variable costs of generation and made some contribution to the fixed costs. In a sense, the overinvestment in capacity – which could clearly not be reversed – created the basis for some buyers to receive a subsidised price. The question is which buyers received this advantage. The easiest way to increase demand was by incentivising large energy-intensive industries such as smelters, which is largely what happened. However, the unintended consequence was a skewing of the economy towards a very capital-intensive structure. In effect, the cheap electricity amounted to an export subsidy for these types of businesses, with the knock-on effect of supporting the exchange rate, which in turn made other producers of traded goods less competitive. The second key implication is that when electricity demand outstrips capacity then new capacity needs to be built, and the rationale for the very cheap pricing no longer exists – pricing needs to cover the costs of building the generation plant and not just the cost of operating the power station. The lack of conditions linking the low pricing to availability meant that the economy was rationed in its electricity usage, and Eskom had to compensate large energy-intensive users for reducing their consumption.

The result of the historic decisions regarding investment and pricing is that there has been a path dependency on relatively cheap and non-renewable electricity. The adjustment towards new priorities and appropriately priced electricity has been slow and riddled with difficulty. In addition, the costs of the new-build programme and the electricity prices required for the financial sustainability of Eskom demonstrate just how big the effective subsidies have been.

Average real prices declined over the 1980s and 1990s (figure 5.1), although the average price conceals the differences in prices to different users. The steep increases in average prices coinciding with large infrastructure build are also evident.

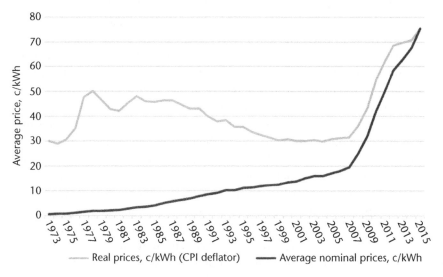

Figure 5.1 Average electricity prices and increases, 1972–2015

Sources: Eskom (Average nominal prices from http://www.eskom.co.za/CustomerCare/ TariffsAndCharges/Pages/Tariff_History.aspx); StatsSA (CPI from http://www.statssa.gov.za/ publications/P0141/CPIHistory.pdf); average real prices: authors' calculations (2015=100)

Note: The average price is a simple average across all tariffs Eskom charges, calculated by taking the total value of sales divided by the number of kilowatt-hours (kWh) sold per year. It is assumed that this includes sales through special pricing deals.

Suboptimal investment decisions in terms of planning, timing, size and technology choices of power plant investments have affected the pricing trajectory. Between 1974 and 1978, electricity prices rose steeply in real terms due to capacity shortage, along with increasingly frequent load shedding up to 1981.

In response, Eskom started a large new-build programme. By 1983, the SOE had 22.26 gigawatts (GW) of generation capacity under construction or on order (Steyn, 2006). Failure to properly plan and oversee investment decisions resulted in an excessive capacity expansion programme and inefficiency in investment by Eskom (Kessides, Bogetic and Maurer, 2007). To service Eskom's soaring debt, costs were passed on to consumers, leading to steep average nominal price increases in the 1980s while the SOE benefited from a monopoly position, government guarantees, open-ended Reserve Bank forward cover and an exemption from taxes and dividends.

By the late 1980s/early 1990s, Eskom faced severe political pressure to reduce prices as soon as declining debt levels would allow it (Steyn, 2003). Increased internal efficiency and huge excess generation capacity (due to the economic downturn and the commissioning of new power stations in the 1980s) allowed Eskom to reduce real electricity price increases for the following 15 years. Moreover, in the 1990s, Eskom entered into a compact with its customers to keep its prices low and to reduce the real cost of electricity by 20% over the period 1991–1996. A reduction of 16.6% was achieved. This kept prices at a level that was relatively low compared to global standards and, as noted, these low prices did not adequately cover costs or allow for reinvestment.

One solution was to increase demand by incentivising large energy-intensive industries such as smelters and other heavy users. In the 1990s, Eskom entered into favourably priced long-term supply agreements[5] with aluminium smelters (Alusaf, BHP Billiton's predecessor) and with ferrochrome smelters[6] to ensure offtake of excess electricity capacity and to promote downstream industry. These pricing structures, increasingly favourable to large industrial users, were not amended by Nersa over the years according to changing supply and demand balances and economic conditions. When the balance changed and the country faced an electricity shortage in 2008, these contracts caused considerable controversy. They were seen to favour big foreign-owned business that contributed little to local downstream beneficiation (as they largely exported unbeneficiated products) and to employment, at the expense of the local economy which suffered serious electricity shortages and escalating prices. Prices to heavy users of electricity arguably should increase relative to light users in tight supply situations so as to discourage the use of electricity and encourage investment in energy efficiency and renewable energy. While these selected dominant customers received significantly cheaper prices[7] compared to households and smaller industry, partly due to lower costs to supply/serve,[8] there appeared to be few other cost-related reasons for these prices. This practice in effect created a path dependency on cheap, dirty energy by heavy industry. These decisions further had implications for economic participation as they favoured heavy users of electricity and limited participation for those who could not secure these favourable rates.

When demand once again outstripped supply the South African government, through Eskom, started a massive generation expansion programme in 2005.[9] This reaction to the increased demand on the grid was delayed and not in time to prevent the 2008 crisis. Although the programme considered the objectives of the latest Integrated Resource Plan, especially the need to diversify the technology and fuel mix of generation, technology choices were predominately influenced by the objective of 'keeping the lights on' at the cheapest cost (at the time of decision making). Hence, the programme still favoured large coal-fired generation plants.

As in the 1980s, the financing requirements of this colossal investment programme contributed to pushing prices up, ultimately resulting in a trebling of the average price from 2009/2010 to 2017/2018 (Nersa, 2010, 2013). The repetition of a suboptimal investment pattern (over- and underinvestment) could have been avoided through effective (and implemented) policy learnings and prudent investment decisions. A proactive strategy for new generation capacity based on timely progressive building (rather than lumpy, large-scale build) and matching demand trends and forecasts would have delivered a much smoother price trajectory.

However, these outcomes were not because of Nersa's actions (or inactions) alone. Government made a number of public statements bypassing Nersa, compromising its independence. For instance, government sent out mixed messages on whether Eskom should invest in generation capacity or not. Initially, the blueprint for a competitive ESI, which included a power exchange, the unbundling of distribution and transmission and a partial unbundling of generation, was produced for Cabinet in May 2001. The document recommended that 30% of the generation capacity be sold to the private sector, with Eskom retaining 70% of the market. It was stated that Eskom would not build any additional generation capacity from 2001, thus transferring this to the private sector (Pickering, 2010). But this message was reversed when government then announced that Eskom should build power stations. This created uncertainty for private sector IPP investors about whether or not to invest. Further, with Cabinet approval, Eskom bypassed Nersa's review process of the construction of Kusile power station, again compromising the regulator's credibility.

Regarding unbundling, in 2011 the Independent Systems and Market Operator (ISMO) Bill approved by Cabinet envisaged that an ISMO would invest, operate and maintain the country's high-voltage transmission grid separately from Eskom to ensure that independent generators would receive fair access to the transmission network. The ISMO had the potential to accelerate the development of renewable energy and increase participation of IPPs in the country, empowering them to sell electricity directly to customers without having to be routed through Eskom and allowing for any surplus generation to be sold back to the utility or to third parties. The ISMO Bill was stalled in parliament.[10] This lack of progress in introducing competition can be attributed to vested interests in the industry and an attempt to protect Eskom's dominant position (das Nair, Montmasson-Clair and Ryan, 2014).

At several points, there has been political pressure in the pricing of electricity. In the 1980s and 1990s, there was pressure on Eskom to suppress prices. In 2004, the minister of public enterprises announced that Eskom was prohibited from increasing prices above inflation. This announcement questioned the independence of the regulator and tarnished the credibility of the administrated pricing system. As the actions of the minister contradicted the principles of the legislation, it created a sense of unease regarding 'the government's respect for the role of independent regulatory processes' (Steyn, 2003, p. 3).

During the implementation of the Multi-Year Price Determination (MYPD) mechanism,[11] Eskom did not always receive the price increase it sought through the required revenue pricing mechanism. In some instances, this was because an objective of lowest possible electricity prices was prioritised. In other instances, it was because Nersa more strictly questioned Eskom's costs submissions (prices were determined based on covering full costs and allowing a rate of return). It is argued that not allowing full cost recovery through the tariff mechanism jeopardised Eskom's ability to finance new generating capacity (Steyn, 2012). Nersa has nonetheless made significant progress in reducing uncertainty for customers by making different Eskom tariff structures more transparent, user friendly and cost-reflective over the years.

The pricing of electricity sold through municipalities has been a further area of contention, one in which some headway has been made by Nersa but more could be done in terms of ensuring investment in maintenance and repair of the distribution system. Municipalities are primarily responsible for distribution and retail activities in urban areas, and they purchase power from Eskom for resale to consumers within their boundaries. Households and industry have raised serious concerns that electricity prices are excessively marked up by municipalities, over and above Eskom's tariffs, with no consistency across municipalities. This is said to impact negatively on the competitiveness of small industrial end users, such as foundries and light manufacturing, supplied by municipalities. Some estimates are that municipality mark-ups can be between 50 and 100% above the direct Eskom price (Clark and Van Vuuren, 2013), placing those that source from a municipality immediately at a competitive disadvantage to rivals sourcing directly from Eskom.

The reasons for this appear to partly stem from municipality funding models, where funds generated from electricity sales are used to cross-subsidise other municipal activities, creating perverse incentives to inflate electricity tariffs through high mark-ups to earn more revenue to fund other activities. In addition, there is regulatory uncertainty or misalignment when it comes to who is ultimately responsible for regulating municipal activities. The constitution grants municipalities the executive authority and the right to administer electricity reticulation. While Nersa has the mandate to set the tariff at which municipalities can price electricity sales, the constitution allows municipalities the right to apply surcharges or mark-ups over and above this Nersa-determined price for municipal services.[12]

One of the biggest issues, however, remains the lack of maintenance and investment in distribution infrastructure. Ageing infrastructure operating at maximum capacity is overloading the system, resulting in supply interruptions.[13] A major refurbishment backlog estimated at R27 billion exists in the ESI and continues to grow at an estimated R2.5 billion per annum (Louw, 2012; Noah, 2012; Rustomjee, 2013). Nersa could potentially play a much stronger role in ensuring that municipalities invest in maintenance and refurbishment of distribution infrastructure.

The renewable energy experience

The REIPPPP is an interesting case study which highlights ways in which challenges in the ESI can at least partially be addressed through effective regulation which proactively introduces competitive rivalry.[14] Gaylor Montmasson-Clair and Reena das Nair provide an in-depth assessment of the renewable energy experience in South Africa in chapter 8 in this volume.

The evolution of the renewable energy programme has been a learning curve for stakeholders. The early programmes to facilitate entry by IPPs were conceptualised, designed and administered by Eskom in 2007/2008. In each of these programmes[15] there were no power purchase agreements (PPAs) between Eskom and IPPs. This made the commercial banks reluctant to finance them as it placed considerable risk solely on the IPPs. Further, there was also reluctance on the part of project developers to participate in the programmes given Eskom's dual role as the dominant industry player and administrator of the process.

Changing strategy given the poor results of the initial programmes, Nersa developed a Renewable Energy Feed-In Tariff (REFIT) mechanism which sought to procure power output from qualifying renewable energy generators at predetermined prices. Under this programme, IPPs were to sell renewable energy-based electricity to Eskom (as the exclusive buyer) under a PPA, and were entitled to receive regulated tariffs based on the particular generation technology. However, this was also unsuccessful and the feed-in tariff was never implemented as industry considered it to be too low. In 2009, Nersa revised the tariffs to allow greater returns on investment, but subsequently lowered them again in line with international benchmarks. There were significant other teething problems with the REFIT programme, where again it was felt that too much risk was allocated to IPPs. IPPs, developers and financiers insisted on a PPA underwritten by the government to reduce this risk. Because of this and for a range of other reasons, including concerns around Nersa's ability to coordinate and administer such a system[16] and conflicts with public finance and procurement laws, the REIPPPP, which was a competitive bidding procurement programme, came into being. This programme is run by the Department of Energy (DoE) and the National Treasury.

The auction system designed in the REIPPPP encourages both competitive pricing and local manufacturing, given local content requirements. The programme has been hailed a success in many parts of the world and implementation of the system has been recognised to encourage maximisation of dynamic returns of competition.

Bids are evaluated on their price competitiveness (70%) and a set of economic development/inclusivity criteria (30%). Economic development criteria are designed to advance government policies on socioeconomic development, such as job creation, procurement of locally manufactured inputs and community ownership of renewable energy project companies. Notably, to secure local participation, the project company must comprise 40% participation by a South African entity. The localisation requirements and the funding support from the Department of Trade and Industry (the dti) to local manufacturers have encouraged an important emerging industry in South Africa.

Further, projects that meet a set of minimum requirements (in terms of environmental, land, commercial, legal, economic development, financial and technical criteria) are selected as preferred bidders in the REIPPPP. Following this, various stakeholders, including the DoE, Nersa, Eskom, commercial banks, development finance institutions and IPPs work together to finalise the financial aspects of the project. Then PPAs between preferred bidders and Eskom are signed and underwritten by the National Treasury, which includes details about the terms on which the project company sells electricity to Eskom.

PPAs backed by Treasury greatly improved risk allocation, gave much-needed certainty to financiers and enabled lenders to provide financing on competitive terms to IPPs. Further, the REIPPPP is conducted in a transparent manner, providing detailed feedback to unsuccessful candidates to improve the quality of successive bids. Additionally, the private sector has played an important role in supporting the DoE to develop the PPAs and economic development criteria of the programme.

The positive impact of encouraging competition is seen in the falling tariffs for various sources of renewable energy in successive bidding rounds (table 5.1). In addition to increased competition, this was due to a combination of tariff caps imposed by the DoE, reduced price ceilings for wind and solar, increased experience of bidders in successive rounds, increased maturity of technologies and allocation of a capacity limit for each technology from round 2. The first four rounds of the programme were oversubscribed, revealing the interest in the programme. In total, over 100 projects have been selected, accounting for more than 6 300 megawatts (MW) of nominal generation capacity amounting to close to R200 billion.

Table 5.1 REIPPPP tariffs over bidding rounds, in rands per kWh

Technology	Round 1	Round 2	Round 3	Round 4
Onshore wind	1.14	0.89	0.66	0.52
Concentrated solar power	2.68	2.51	1.46	n/a
Solar photovoltaic	2.75	1.65	0.88	0.66
Biomass	n/a	n/a	1.24	1.22
Landfill gas	n/a	n/a	0.84	n/a
Small hydro (≤10 MW)	n/a	1.03	n/a	0.94

Source: Adapted from Montmasson-Clair, Moilwa and Ryan (2014)

The outcomes of the REIPPPP highlight the importance of proactively encouraging competitive rivalry between producers, as well as the state's and the regulator's roles in creating a framework conducive to this. This was a deliberate and coordinated strategy by relevant stakeholders to design the auction such that it introduced 'synthetic competition' through the scorecard method (see Ginsburg, 2009, on synthetic competition). Further, the REIPPPP is an excellent example of how multiple economic and social objectives can be incorporated into energy policy through appropriate structuring of bidding processes.

Freight rail and ports

The regulation of ports and freight rail (see Baloyi, 2014; TIPS, 2014a) shares much in common with electricity in that the provision is under an SOE which has been corporatised, and operates within a policy framework determined by a line department. There are also similarities in terms of the historic investment patterns which were oriented to heavy, mining and energy-intensive industry (Fine and Rustomjee, 1996). Rail infrastructure was also developed for grain farmers, with rail sidings linked to silos built for the agricultural cooperatives.

Transport infrastructure exhibits very substantial externality effects, however, given its network and partial public-good nature. This is why the state has constructed the transport infrastructure in almost all countries. The returns from the infrastructure investment are realised across the economy in the activity that is enabled and thus it is appropriate to finance the investments out of tax revenues.

In competition terms, elements of the transport infrastructure can be considered essential facilities as they cannot be easily replicated and access is required to provide a good or service. The provision of the infrastructure and the terms of access are therefore critical to participation in the economy by different groups and by location. In South Africa, excellent infrastructure was constructed for the prioritised groups under apartheid. To evaluate the regulatory framework and its implications for competition, it needs to be considered in light of the historical context. How has the regulatory framework taken the inherited structure into account and incorporated social returns and incentives for investment? Has it opened up opportunities for increased participation and, if so, how?

We specifically consider rail freight and ports, both of which form part of state-owned corporation Transnet. The evaluation is thus how the governance framework has impacted on the decisions of Transnet, including the resources at its disposal.

The 1996 Transport White Paper envisaged an intermodal transport system with a greater role for general rail freight and greater private participation in the system as a whole. It was based on the potential gains from a more diversified and open national economy. As such, it had to be understood in terms of the wider economic and industrial policy goals of the first democratic government.

At the same time, in 1996 the shift in fiscal policy signalled by the Growth, Employment and Redistribution strategy meant that funding was not made available for investment in transport infrastructure and, indeed, government investment in infrastructure overall was cut back sharply (Roberts, 2004). This was compounded by the pension fund deficit which Transnet had to cover on its own balance sheet for former employees of the South African Transport Services.

Over the last two decades, the outcome has been that general freight movements have shifted significantly away from rail to road. General freight prices have been increased to levels which are above road freight charges (figure 5.2). Port charges (discussed below) have been far above international norms for general cargo. By comparison, the transport costs for primary commodities such as coal and iron ore remained relatively low. The outcomes have thus not been consistent with the objectives set out in 1996.

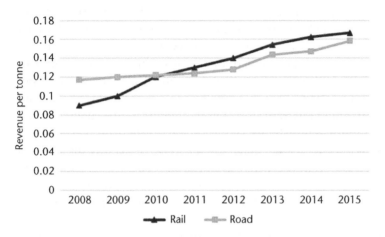

Figure 5.2 Average revenue per tonne for freight rail and road, 2008–2015
Sources: Statistics South Africa, Land Transport Surveys (available online for each month)

Transnet is responsible for setting rules on access, tariffs and investments. The state, as owner, monitors performance and sets objectives for Transnet, with this responsibility lying with the Department of Public Enterprises (DPE). The governance of Transnet as a state corporation is the responsibility of the Transnet board. The policy framework lies with the Department of Transport, and the widespread linkages of transport with economic activity mean there are substantial coordination challenges with, for example, industrial policy. The DPE sets objectives through the shareholder compact. These objectives can in principle be set with a view to the longer-term economic objectives, which would require careful specification and monitoring of non-financial measures of performance, alongside consideration of investment plans.

From the late 1990s the main objectives were focused on the financial performance of Transnet. Not surprisingly, this meant that the Transnet focus was not on investments which would yield returns in the future, through enabling new economic activity, and where the economic returns could not be captured by Transnet. Instead, the focus was on where revenues could be earned from the existing infrastructure. This implied that the focus on the mining sector was effectively increased, rather than being reoriented to more diversified economic activities. Upgrades and expansions to the coal and iron ore lines were made.

The historic investments in the existing coal and iron ore lines naturally made incremental expansions more financially profitable, in a simple path dependency effect. Cost-reflective tariffs further meant that historically privileged interests locked in their advantages as the costs of these lines were lower given the existing base and the volumes already being transported. Considering pricing and investment in a mature rail infrastructure, which simply needs to be maintained and upgraded, is different from the investment decisions for an industrialising economy where much of the infrastructure needs to be constructed with a view to the changing structure of the economy.

The apparent lack of coordination between the DPE and the Department of Transport, greater emphasis on short-term financial measures and lack of public finance for investment meant that governance and decision making were not consistent with the wider needs of economic development. For example, the proportion of citrus moved by rail fell from 80% in 2005 to 5% in 2013 (Baloyi, 2014, p. 31). Even grain has seen a substantial fall, from 90 to 30%. The one sector of manufacturing aside from heavy industries such as basic metals and basic chemicals that has seen growth is automotive. It also relies on local and international transport for inputs and finished vehicles. While there have been some improvements in transport of built-up models, automotive components (not contained in completely knocked-down packages) are not well catered for by rail freight.

With regard to the pricing of different cargoes at ports, a somewhat different picture emerges since 2009. This may be at least partly attributed to the establishment of a Ports Regulator.

Outcomes in the ports sector and the role of the regulator

South Africa's geographic location and size means that access to efficient port infrastructure is of critical importance for growth.[17] Approximately 96% of South Africa's exports (by volume) are by sea, so the competitiveness of the country's ports has a direct bearing on the competitiveness of its industrial and export activities. There have been concerns around the skewed pricing and high tariffs of South African ports, highlighted in recent government economic policy documents.[18]

The ports infrastructure in South Africa is 100% state-owned through Transnet National Ports Authority (TNPA). The majority of port operations are run by Transnet Port Terminal (TPT). Until 2002, almost all infrastructure and services were provided by public sector entity Portnet, owned by Transnet. In 2002, the port infrastructure was separated from the services to form the National Ports Authority (NPA) and the South African Ports Operator, later renamed TPT, both continuing to be owned by Transnet.

As was the case with rail freight, port tariffs were used to improve the income of Transnet as a whole, cross-subsidising other activities. However, this had serious negative consequences on investments in port infrastructure and competitiveness of tariffs, and has been to the detriment of promoting industrial policy objectives. Tariffs in South Africa were higher than those internationally, efficiency levels lower and ports provided fewer and lower quality services. Further, the prices charged at the different ports within South Africa, for equity reasons, are fairly uniform despite their different locations, demand drivers and features. This limits competition between ports, as well as for services within ports, and reduces the incentive to invest in infrastructure and increase productivity. Competition between ports remains weak, largely because TNPA is the only entity permitted to develop, manage and set tariffs for ports in South Africa. Intra-port competition is also low given the dominance of TPT in service provision, such as in cargo handling and for highly specialised terminals, and, in most instances, traffic volumes are insufficient to support more than one terminal of any type. Competition in container freight/handling is also weak.

Many of these problems stem from the conflict of interest in Transnet owning both the landlord company (NPA) and the company that is the main user of the ports (TPT). That conflict, linked to the approach of Transnet to use the profit generated by the ports operation to subsidise other operations in the group, led to underinvestment in port infrastructure, again highlighting the short-sighted outlook on developing facilities through investments.

In 2002, the gazetted National Commercial Ports Policy laid out the framework for the role of the different players in the sector, the challenges that needed to be addressed and the approach to regulation.[19] The policy highlighted the strategic importance of ports in contributing to the growth and development of the South African economy and put forward key principles for effective ports regulation. The core of these was the need for the NPA, which was within Transnet, to be separated from Transnet and to be established as a new, independent state-owned corporate entity. This was to ensure that the ports operate in the best interests of the country, in line with the mandate spelt out in the legislative framework, rather than in the narrower, profit-maximising interests of Transnet. The NPA would then report to the DPE.

Recognising the complexity and financial implications for Transnet in setting up separate institutions, a National Ports Regulator was established in 2009 as an interim measure until the full separation could take place.

The Ports Regulator has made significant progress in reducing tariffs through changing tariff structures to different user groups. This it started implementing without a full staff complement or sophisticated pricing mechanisms. While the approach taken by the Ports Regulator in the initial years was to limit the tariff increases to below or at inflation levels, the 2013 tariff decision saw a significant reduction in key tariff lines. This is in contrast with the approach of the regulator in the electricity supply industry, where, although Nersa has tried to keep tariffs at cost-reflective levels, it has done little to change the pre-existing relative tariff structures to different user groups. The result is that historically prioritised industries are still favoured with regards to lower electricity pricing.

The Ports Regulator decreased the tariff on cargo dues in certain areas. For instance, container full export cargo dues were reduced by 43.2% and container full import cargo dues by 14.3% (TIPS, 2014a). It also undertook a tariff comparator study or benchmarking exercise in April 2012, called the Global Port Pricing Comparator Study, which revealed that the total general cargo tariffs at the ports of Durban and Cape Town were very high by world standards. For instance, TNPA charges US$275 000 for an average vessel, while the global average is US$150 000. The average cost per vessel call in Durban and Cape Town was around US$450 000 compared to around US$200 000 for Singapore. The study, which also looked at specific sectors, found that the tariffs for export of primary commodities, mainly coal and iron ore, were well *below* the global average, while the tariffs on containers and automotive were significantly *higher* than the average (table 5.2). A specific study on the automotive sector in South Africa was undertaken by the regulator, comparing South African ports to 16 other ports. It found that Durban was considerably higher-cost than most of the others, even after rebates and discounts. This again highlights the historic bias towards certain industries, which is at odds with the present-day developmental agenda of the country.

Table 5.2 South Africa's ports tariffs deviation from the global average, 2012

Sector	Deviation from global average (%)
Containers (total ports authority pricing including cargo dues with rebates)	294
Containers (cargo dues with rebates)	721
Automotive sector (ports authority tariffs with rebates)	212
Automotive sector (cargo dues with rebates)	710
Coal (TNPA costs faced by cargo owners)	−50
Iron ore (TNPA costs faced by cargo owners)	−10

Source: TIPS (2014a) citing Ports Regulator of South Africa (2012, p. 6)

The Ports Regulator and the National Association of Automobile Manufacturers of South Africa engaged with each other regularly to find a solution to high port tariffs. The Association highlighted the significance of the automotive sector, which contributes 12–15% to South Africa's manufacturing industry output and 6% to the country's GDP (TIPS, 2014a). A reduction in the automotive manufacturing sector's port charges would directly improve the export competitiveness of the automotive industry, in turn resulting in increased exports as well as the opportunity to secure contracts from within the global operations of their members. Improved port tariffs would therefore contribute to the economic development objectives of the country to create jobs and increase investment. The Ports Regulator continues to consider these submissions seriously. In the tariff year 2013/2014, it reduced the automotive tariff charges in the tariff book adjustments, with motor vehicles exported 'on own wheel' cargo dues reduced by 21.1%. Although tariffs need to reduce further to bring them closer to international levels, this is a positive movement towards aligning tariffs while taking into account government economic (and social) policy objectives. According to the Ports Regulator,

> It is clear from the data that South African cargo owners and logistics operators face significantly higher infrastructure costs than the rest of the sample when using containers to move cargo. With the bulk of

> South Africa's manufactured goods arguably exported through containers this is clearly contradictory to current industrial policy aiming to incentivise value addition, broadening of the manufacturing base and increasing manufactured exports. (TIPS, 2014a, citing Ports Regulator of South Africa, 2012, p. 9)

The revised pricing strategy has been in effect since 2015 and has enabled ongoing investments in the maintenance and extension of the South African ports system, ensuring cost recovery across all national ports. There is one basic rate for cargo dues for each different cargo handling type (i.e., containers, dry bulk, break bulk, liquid bulk, automotive), replacing the previous differentiation of cargo dues by commodity. Cargoes moving in large shiploads, such as dry bulks, continue to pay lower cargo dues per tonne than cargoes using smaller vessels such as general cargo ships. Further, deviations from the base rates for cargo dues were introduced in line with government priorities for promoting exports and beneficiation industries, but these reductions have been determined fairly arbitrarily. Beneficiation rebates have also been introduced, where lower tariffs are charged for exports produced through the beneficiation of South Africa's natural resources. This is in line with the dti policy objective of increasing local value addition. TNPA's beneficiation contributions for the metals sector are that iron ore, a raw material, would receive no rebate, while pig iron would receive a 10% discount, rolled steel and pipes a 60% discount, and structural steel, machinery and white goods an 80% discount. The broad principles of this pricing mechanism are set to continue in 2017, although situation-specific variations have been introduced, such as discounts on the cargo dues for maize for the first five million tonnes in 2016/2017, given the drought.[20] These developments are due to dynamic and bold steps by the Ports Regulator to increase the competitiveness of South African ports and align pricing to support other industrial policy objectives. The regulator has achieved this in a short space of time and faced with substantial limitations in resources and regulatory capacity. Through relatively simple benchmarking exercises and proactive decisions, it has reduced tariffs and reversed past asymmetry in a short time period.

The issues in rail and ports are essentially the same and yet changes have been made in ports through the introduction of a regulator. However, lest this be interpreted simplistically as an argument for regulation, the ports case contrasts with electricity where the regulator has not adjusted the relative prices of heavy mineral processing and diversified industry to rectify the historical bias.

Another contrast, in the opposite direction, is that the REIPPPP example in electricity demonstrated the potential learning from opening up access, even while pursuing non-financial objectives. In ports, access to facilities could be widened. This is not only about private ownership – some of the terminals are private (such as for bulk chemicals) and have been bottlenecks undermining competitors. Separating different levels even while maintaining state ownership can change the incentives of managers (as was intended with the NPA and contemplated in the ISMO for electricity).

Telecoms

Telecommunications is often used as an example of where technology change means that what was once a natural monopoly (and in almost all countries state-owned, due to the need to invest in a fixed-line network) is no longer so.[21] Mobile telephony is not subject to the same utility-type cost structure and provides an alternative to relying on the fixed-line network. It was even proposed that the need for regulation would wither as competition took root (Cave, 2006). South Africa has followed the orthodoxy in this regard with relatively light regulation of mobile telephony and an expectation that as this segment expanded, coupled with entry into fixed-line, competition would generate efficient economic outcomes.[22]

Reflecting these prior beliefs, regulation has been focused on interconnection to ensure that newer participants can link with the existing networks so that their subscribers can make and receive calls with subscribers on other networks. However, the call termination rates were simply to be set between the parties subject to broad principles. There are also provisions for facilities leasing so that entrants can gain access to the facilities in existence but, similarly, the terms and mechanisms for this were not specified.

On the face of it, the issues appear to be quite different from those in transport and energy. After reviewing the outcomes and assessing the role of economic regulation and the links to competition, we point to areas of common concern. In particular, we argue that the South African experience of telecommunications regulation points to the need to regulate for increased competitive rivalry and participation in the economy, recognising the implications of the past state investment.

Outcomes in telecommunication

In terms of South Africa's rankings in the information and communications technology (ICT) sector, the World Economic Forum's Network Readiness Index ranked South Africa 65th out of 139 countries in 2016, while the International Telecommunications Union ICT Development Index ranked South Africa 88th out of 175 countries. These indices combine a number of measures but to a large extent these outcomes reflect relatively poor broadband coverage, speeds and pricing. The number of broadband internet subscribers is substantially below South Africa's peers (figure 5.3). This could be attributed to the very unequal income distribution in South Africa. However, in terms of broadband speeds, South Africa has also been falling behind other BRICS[23] countries, aside from India (figure 5.4). Prices for fixed broadband are also substantially higher in South Africa, and four times those in India (figure 5.5).

Mobile phone prices have also been relatively high, and above the Southern African Development Community (SADC) average until the reductions in prices from 2008 (Hawthorne, 2014a). There were larger reductions from 2010 onwards following the reductions in call termination (voluntary at first), with the largest reductions in 2013 following the imposition of lower call termination charges.

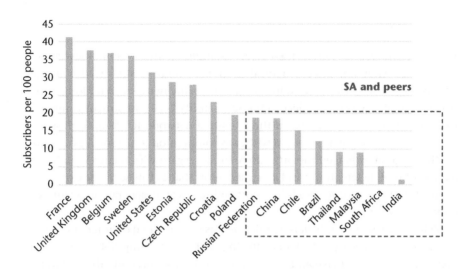

Figure 5.3 Fixed broadband internet subscribers per 100 people, 2015

Source: World Bank (n.d.)

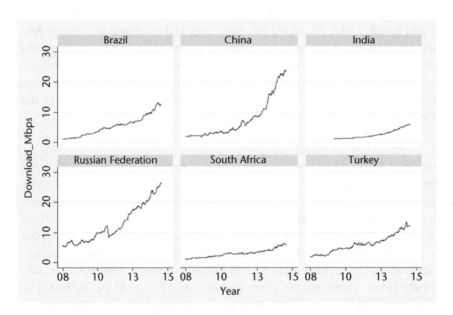

Figure 5.4 South Africa's broadband speeds compared to those in Brazil, China, India, Russia and Turkey

Source: Analysis of Ookla (2015). Accessed from 'Netindex',
http://www.netindex.com (this data source has since been discontinued)

Note: Mbps = megabits per second

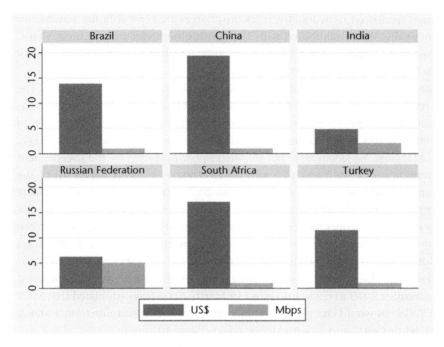

Figure 5.5 Prices for fixed broadband, US$, 2014

Source: Analysis of ITU (2014)

Note: Mbps = megabits per second

Regulation and competition in mobile telephony: Interconnection and call termination

South Africa appears to have relatively strong rivalry in mobile telephony, with four operators in 2014. And, there have been three operators for more than a decade following the entry of Cell C. Why then have South Africa's mobile rates remained higher than in many other countries which have a similar number of competitors? Developments in recent years reveal the importance of strong regulatory action for smaller rivals to be effective competitors. It is well established in economic theory that a duopoly may well not mean vigorous competition, even without there being an explicit collusive agreement. In the case of mobile telephony, the historic South African model of two-year contracts and the obstacles to number portability meant subscribers were unlikely to switch, dampening price competition (ICN, 2006). Cell C's entry was thus meant to be competitively significant.

The mobile-to-mobile call termination rates were originally set at R0.20/minute between Vodacom and MTN by their mutual agreement, when the mobile operators were licensed in 1993 (Hawthorne, 2014b; Knott-Craig, 2009). Prior to Cell C's entry in 2001, however, the call termination rate had been increased to R1.19/minute for peak hours and R0.65/minute for off-peak.[24] This effectively placed a floor under the price that Cell C could offer to attract subscribers, as with a small subscriber base a majority of the calls made by Cell C subscribers would be terminating on the networks of other operators. The call termination charges reinforced network effects, as the charges are obviously not payable for on-net calls. When combined with the existing obstacles to switching, Cell C remained a marginal player with an insignificant impact. Competition did not work in terms of prices to consumers.

Regulation has an important role to play in understanding these outcomes. The interconnection guidelines of 1999, 2000 and 2002 under the Telecommunications Act required major operators to set their call termination rates at the long-run incremental cost of call termination (Aproskie, Hodge, Lipschitz and Sheik, 2008). But, MTN and Vodacom were not declared major operators by the Independent Communications Authority of South Africa (Icasa).[25] Under Chapter 10 of the Electronic Communications Act (No. 36 of 2005) Icasa can, in general, regulate prices where markets are characterised by ineffective competition. It is also specifically empowered under section 41 to prescribe regulations for wholesale interconnection rates. After a public inquiry into interconnection in 2006 and 2007, Icasa decided it had to develop regulations for Chapter 10 before it could regulate interconnection. This effectively stalled the process until regulations were published in November 2010 to come into effect in March 2011. Icasa stipulated that MTN and Vodacom would charge call termination rates of R0.40/minute from 1 March 2013, while Cell C and Telkom Mobile could charge 10% more.

Actual call termination rates were reduced earlier than stipulated in the regulations. The Parliamentary Portfolio Committee on Communications held hearings in 2009 which led to reductions being agreed by the operators with the minister of communications, to reduce peak rates to R0.89/minute (McLeod, 2009). This political pressure then provided the base for Icasa's subsequent regulations. While the agreed reductions in 2009 supported Cell C, in particular, in being a somewhat more effective competitor, reflected in increased subscribers and some competitive pressure on prices, the really big change in prices towards those at the lower end of SADC countries was only in 2013 (figure 5.6), after the Icasa regulation came into force.

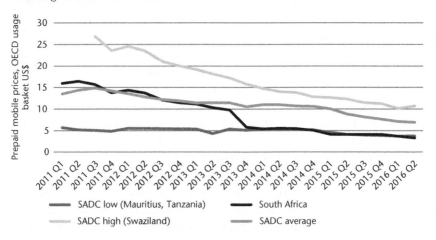

Figure 5.6 Prepaid mobile prices, US$, 2011–2016

Source: Analysis based on data prepared by Research ICT Africa (n.d.)

Note: OECD = Organisation for Economic Cooperation and Development

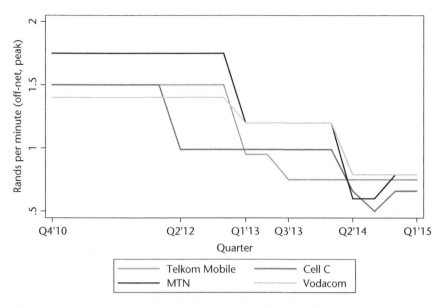

Figure 5.7 Reductions in call termination rates, 2010–2015

Source: Research ICT Africa. Lowest available retail prepaid voice prices (off-net, peak), 2010–2015 (data not available publicly)

Subsequent final regulations in 2014 lowered termination rates further and increased the asymmetry (figure 5.7). The new regulations also, however, lowered the rates that Cell C and Telkom Mobile are able to charge Vodacom and MTN, down from R0.44 to R0.31. Cell C subsequently objected to this (Paelo, 2015).

A number of lessons can be drawn from the South African experience over the past two decades. First, competition requires appropriate regulation. This includes incorporating principles related to addressing market power and the ability to enforce. Second, competition does not equate to the number of competitors and we cannot be complacent about technology changes meaning competition will blossom of its own accord, even while technical natural monopoly factors become less significant. Third, entrenched first movers can protect their advantages. This motivates for asymmetry in call termination between incumbents and entrants, although only for a relatively short time (Hawthorne, 2014b). In other words, regulation is required to change the rules of the game to foster effective competitive rivalry. Fourth, the de jure independence of institutions is less important than their mandate, powers and political support. In this case, the change appears closely linked to a shift in the balance of interests evident in the portfolio committee hearings. This is possibly linked to the interest of Telkom as a new mobile entrant. The change in call termination certainly contrasts with the developments in facilities leasing where Telkom is the incumbent.

Regulation and competition: Facilities leasing

If anything, the competition and regulation issues related to the position and market power of the fixed-line incumbent Telkom have been longer running than those of the mobile operators. They are also arguably more important as they underpin the poor ICT performance of the South African economy. There have been many reviews of these issues (e.g., Aproskie et al., 2008, Gillwald, Moyo and Stork, 2012; Makhaya and Roberts, 2003). The South African fixed-line telecommunications utility, Telkom, was incorporated in 1991 as an SOE governed by the Department of Posts and Telegraphs.[26] The privatisation of Telkom was presented as a solution to attract investment and to assist a financially ailing SOE, through a 30% stake sold to a consortium (Thintana) comprising Malaysia Telecommunication and SBC Communications as 'strategic equity partners'.[27]

The privatisation of these entities coincided with the extension of Telkom's monopoly in voice telephony for five years, from 1997 to 2002, justified by the imposition of universal service obligations.[28] The monopoly period was also seen as necessary for Telkom to prepare itself for the onslaught of competition. Competition was effectively delayed by a further five years to 2007, due to various factors including a protracted licensing process (Horwitz and Currie, 2007). The Second National Operator, Neotel, was licensed in 2005, launched in August 2006 and commenced services in 2007.

As with the entrant into mobile telecommunications, the presence of a competitor to the incumbent did not realise apparently competitive outcomes. While the competition authorities have taken on a number of matters, these are *ex post* evaluations of past conduct and the rulings are many years after the conduct being complained of. They relate to conduct by Telkom which undermined downstream competition (see Hawthorne, 2014a; Makhaya and Roberts, 2014).[29] One rationale for this conduct is to inhibit the growth of the upstream rival as downstream firms may support and provide custom to the upstream entrant.

Facilities leasing, on which we focus here, is a more direct challenge for an entrant. To address the incumbent's position, regulators have developed means of separating the upstream and downstream divisions of vertically integrated upstream incumbents and have developed open access frameworks – local loop unbundling (LLU) – for third parties to make use of monopoly inputs. In South Africa, the facilities-leasing regulations under the telecommunications legislation are designed to ensure that new entrants are able to gain access to the existing facilities in order to build their own infrastructure linked into the existing infrastructure and thus to climb the 'ladder of investment' (Hawthorne, 2014a).

The Electronic Communications Act of 2005 makes provision for the leasing of Telkom's facilities by other parties. However, Telkom declined to conclude an infrastructure-sharing agreement with Neotel, favouring a case-by-case approach to managing access. In 2007, a policy decision was taken to commence with LLU. According to the Ministerial Policy Directive of 2007, Icasa was given until November 2011 to publish LLU regulations.[30] In 2010, Icasa issued regulations for general facilities leasing, but not for LLU. By 2011, Icasa had not instituted any significant steps to effect the orderly implementation of LLU, save for issuing a discussion paper and holding public hearings into the matter. The discussion paper outlined various methodologies to effect the policy directive on LLU. Telkom raised various objections to this process. In its Findings Note,[31] issued after its hearings on LLU, Icasa found that the obligation to lease facilities applies to all licensees providing electronic communications network services. The Findings Note also sets out a timetable for fixed-line LLU, with numerous steps including further industry consultation and engagement, a regulatory impact assessment on the costs and benefits of the various forms of LLU, followed by market reviews and the introduction of supplementary LLU regulations. The Department of Communications (DoC) set a deadline for Icasa to implement LLU by the end of 2011 but Icasa did not achieve this target and has not to date implemented LLU.

In the midst of this vacuum, in December 2011, Neotel made a request to Telkom to lease local loop infrastructure at two specific sites. Neotel framed this request under the provisions of the Electronic Communications Act. Telkom rejected this approach by Neotel on the basis that the regulatory framework envisages a separate process for LLU and, in any event, Neotel had not framed its request according to the provisions of the Act. Neotel's subsequent complaint against Telkom[32] was referred by Icasa to the Complaints and Compliance Committee (CCC).[33] The CCC[34] is a mechanism for resolving disputes. Alternatively, Icasa could impose a remedy unilaterally or negotiate with the parties to resolve a matter. The CCC issued an interim order that acknowledges that Neotel's request is legally valid and holds that Telkom's response to Neotel is inadequate. Thus Telkom has contravened Regulation 3(2) of the Act's Facilities Leasing Regulations of 2010. However, as a matter of practicality, the CCC decided that it would be necessary for the LLU regulations to be in place to enable the leasing of copper infrastructure.[35] The CCC instructed Icasa to develop terms and conditions consistent with Chapter 8 of the Act within a period of three months from its decision, which was taken on 18 May 2012.

The LLU process, and the dispute between Telkom and Neotel regarding the leasing of infrastructure, demonstrates the privileges of incumbency enjoyed by Telkom and the difficulties faced by an entrant in competing with such an incumbent. It also illustrates that the rules have not properly addressed the conduct they were meant to, while more attention needs to be paid to the way institutions work in practice.

The actions of the state as owner have been contradictory to its aims as a reformer and economic policy maker. Unlike with entities such as the transport and electricity parastatals, the government shareholding in Telkom is held by the DoC, which is also responsible for the policy framework. This compounds the conflict of objectives and adds to the inclination to retard the development of Icasa into a strong regulator. For example, Telkom's long battle to keep competitors from offering voice services was assisted by DoC delays in providing clarity regarding the extent to which value-added services providers could also provide voice services.[36]

Common lessons drawn: What is the role of competition in economic regulation?

The reviews of the different regulated industries expose both similarities and differences in the approach to regulation, particularly regarding consideration of competition principles in implementing regulatory rules. Important lessons from the interface between competition and regulation in these sectors can be drawn. These are useful for economic regulators in terms of learning from one another, for engagement between economic regulators and competition authorities, as well as for policy makers.

There are clear differences in regulator structure, capacity and experience, yet some of the most effective decisions which promoted increased participation have been made by relatively new regulators with very limited capacity.

In terms of structure, in electricity the fully integrated and corporatised SOE, Eskom, is regulated by independent regulator Nersa. In rail freight and ports there is also an integrated SOE but without an independent regulator until the recently established Ports Regulator. All operate within a policy framework determined by a line department. In telecommunications, the main operator has been privatised with a long-established regulator and enforcement actions by the competition authorities.

The industry reviews have shown that entrenched interests have frustrated investments in infrastructure that would have otherwise increased participation in line with government's economic and social objectives. Favourable treatment of powerful industries and groupings such as mining and metal smelters (justified by short-term financial performance measures) has resulted in similarities in terms of the historic investment patterns which were oriented to these industries. Regulators in many instances have not taken into account diversified users' needs.

An exception is in the renewable energy sector, where a proactive and coordinated approach by the state and the regulator in the REIPPPP led to introducing greater participation in electricity generation by IPPs, the benefits of which are evident in falling tariffs and encouraging local content. While there are also private operators in mobile telephony, the benefits of increased participation have not resulted in the desired outcomes. Entrenched market power of the incumbent has been protected historically and there is a need to regulate more for increased competitive rivalry and participation in the economy.

With regard to rail and ports, many of the problems of underinvestment need to be understood in terms of the wider fiscal framework and corporatisation of Transnet as owner, user and self-regulator of the infrastructure (until recently for ports), along with the governance exerted by the state as owner through the DPE. These factors are related to the practice of Transnet using the profit generated by the rail and ports operation to subsidise other operations in the group, and have led to underinvestment and inappropriate (and uncompetitive) pricing, especially for diversified container freight. Unlike with other entities, the government shareholding in Telkom is held by the DoC, which is also responsible for the policy framework. This compounds the conflict of objectives and adds to the inclination to retard the development of Icasa into a strong regulator in the telecoms industry.

A lesson from this would be to separate regulators from their line departments. And although the interim Ports Regulator has still not seen a full separation of powers, the benefits of independent regulation in ports are seen in the significant progress made by the Ports Regulator in reducing tariffs through changing tariff structures to different user groups. This contrasts with the approach of the regulator in the electricity supply industry, where Nersa has done little to change the pre-existing relative tariff structures biased to historically favoured user groups.

Also markedly different are the different rates of reform in the sectors reviewed. Positive and pro-competitive outcomes were achieved much faster in renewable energy and in ports compared to rail and telecoms. Further, in the case of ports, this was done with limited capacity. Therefore, it is not necessarily about the capacity and experience of the regulator – effective decisions can be taken quickly with limited capacity.

What is also evident is that there is limited transfer of learning between the regulators from their respective failed or successful experiences. For instance, useful lessons from the auction system design of the renewable energy programme could potentially be adopted in other regulated industries. One way in which this transfer could be achieved is to consider merging the regulators into a single economic regulator, possibly including even the competition authorities.

It is apparent from the sector reviews that effective regulation is necessary to ensure that the competitive space remains open and to govern aspects such as access to critical infrastructure. Even in industries where scale economies would advocate that only one firm operate, regulation that is conducive to creating 'synthetic competition' by ensuring the participation of several competitors has shown positive outcomes in terms of the dynamic gains from rivalry.

Notes

1   All outputs from this project can be accessed at http://www.competition.org.za/regulatory-entities-capacity-building-project/.

2   The energy sector reviews (electricity and renewable energy) were undertaken by Trade and Industrial Policy Strategies (TIPS) on behalf of CCRED – das Nair, Montmasson-Clair and Ryan (2014) for electricity and Montmasson-Clair, Moilwa and Ryan (2014) on renewable energy. There was also a study of liquid fuel, which is not included in this chapter.

3   Transmission and distribution losses averaged 20% compared to the global average of 5%. Eskom was strapped for cash and debt coverage ratios were high. Below-cost tariffs significantly contributed to poor technical and financial performance (Eberhard and Gratwick, 2008).

4   Some of the many key stakeholders in the ESI include the departments of Energy, Public Enterprises, Environmental Affairs and Water Affairs; National Treasury; Nersa; Eskom; IPPs; the Energy Intensive Users Group of Southern Africa; the South African Local Government Association; the Association of Municipal Electricity Undertakings and municipalities.

5   Special/negotiated pricing agreements, where prices to the smelters were fixed in terms of international aluminium prices and exchange rates.

6   The ferrochrome smelter agreements were terminated, but certain of the BHP contracts are still in effect, even after its aluminium operations were sold off to South32.

7   General industrial customers pay Megaflex rates, which are also cheaper than what households pay, although not as favourable as what BHP Billiton pays.

8   There were also interruptability provisions in the contract with BHP that allowed Eskom to cut supply to the smelters when the grid was under stress, which was to the disadvantage of the smelters – pricing has to reflect this.

9   Valued at R340 billion, excluding capitalised borrowing costs. By 2018/2019, the programme will add 17.1 GW of capacity to the 2005 nominal generation capacity of 36.2 GW (Eskom, 2013).

10 While the ISMO Bill has been discussed and agreed on by the Portfolio Committee on Energy on two occasions at least, it was stalled in parliament, being removed from the National Assembly Order Paper twice, in June and November 2013 (Pressly, 2013).

11 The pricing methodology has historically been, and is currently, one of full cost recovery in principle. Nersa currently employs the mechanism of an MYPD method to set electricity prices. The MYPD is essentially a rate of return method of price regulation where price level is set to cover all costs and to allow a fair rate of return on the cost of capital.

12 Through the Municipal Fiscal Powers and Functions Act (No. 12 of 2007). Other legislation governing municipalities includes the Municipal Finance and Management Act and the Municipal Systems Act.

13 The international benchmark for distribution losses (as electricity moves through the network) is 3.5%. Distribution losses in South Africa's best-run metros are significantly above the international benchmark. In 2011/2012 the most efficient municipality, eThekwini, achieved a distribution loss of 5% (National Treasury, 2011), whereas the two largest metros in South Africa, the City of Johannesburg and the City of Cape Town, achieved 11% and 9.3% respectively (National Treasury, 2011).

14 This section draws from TIPS (2014b).

15 Pilot National Cogeneration Programme, the Medium Term Power Purchase Programme and the Multisite Base-load Independent Power Producer Programme.

16 In fact, the DoE and Treasury considered that Nersa was acting beyond its mandate in being the custodian of this programme.

17 This section draws from TIPS (2014a).

18 The New Growth Path emphasises the need to have competitive pricing in ports and the Industrial Policy Action Plan states that high ports charges remain a significant constraint and a threat to the manufacturing industry and employment. The fact that South African ports' charges are among the highest in the world is also highlighted in these documents.

19 Government Gazette, 8 August 2002, Notice 1409, http://www.gov.za/sites/www.gov.za/files/23715_1.pdf.

20 Record of decision, Tariff Application by the National Ports Authority for the Tariff Years 2016/17–2018/19.

21 This section is drawn from Hawthorne (2014a).

22 The Independent Communications Authority of South Africa Act (No. 13 of 2000) provides for the establishment of the industry regulator, Icasa, as well as for the Complaints

and Compliance Committee. The Electronic Communications Act and the Competition Act provide an economic regulation mandate to the competition authorities and Icasa in a number of areas, including interconnection and facilities leasing, spectrum management and universal service and access, and competition and price regulation.

23 Brazil, Russia, India, China, South Africa.

24 The rates were subsequently increased to R1.25 for peak hours by 2005 (Aproskie et al., 2008).

25 Cell C made an application to have Vodacom and MTN declared major operators but later withdrew it.

26 As per the Post Office Amendment Act (No. 85 of 1991). Before this, telecommunication services were provided by the Department.

27 SBC is an American company spun out of the AT&T stable.

28 By the end of the period of exclusivity, there was a net decline in fixed-line and internet penetration (see Makhaya and Roberts, 2003).

29 Tribunal case no. 11/CR/Feb04. See CCSA (2013) for the settlement of the second case.

30 These remained outstanding in February 2014.

31 'Findings Note on the Icasa Framework for Introducing Local Loop Unbundling', http://www.ellipsis.co.za/wp-content/uploads/2011/11/ICASA-Findings-Note-30112011.pdf.

32 Under s43(5)(c) of the Act.

33 The matter was heard on 16, 17 and 18 May 2012. Case no. 59/2011, *Neotel (Pty) Ltd vs Telkom SA Ltd*.

34 Established in terms of s17A of the Icasa Act of 2000 as amended.

35 In accordance with s(44)(3)(m) of the Act.

36 Only when Altech brought a case through the courts was it confirmed that under the Electronic Communications Act value-added network service providers can convert licences into individual electronic communication services and roll out their own networks, as there is no legal monopoly held by Telkom.

References

Aproskie J, J Hodge, R Lipschitz and F Sheik. 2008. 'South African 15-Year Telecommunications Policy Review'. Office of the Presidency (online document).

Baloyi B. 2014. 'The Role of South Africa's Freight Rail Regulatory Framework in General Freight's Sluggish Growth Performance'. Centre for Competition, Regulation and Economic Development, University of Johannesburg (online document).

Cave M. 2006. Encouraging infrastructure competition via the ladder of investment. *Telecommunications Policy* 30: 223–237.

CCRED (Centre for Competition, Regulation and Economic Development). n.d. 'The Regulatory Entities Capacity Building Project' (online document).

CCSA (Competition Commission South Africa). 2013. 'Commission Reaches Settlement Agreement with Telkom'. Media release, 14 June (online document).

Clark A and B van Vuuren. 2013. 'Nelson Mandela Bay Business Chamber NERSA Consultation MYPD3' (online document).

das Nair R, G Montmasson-Clair and G Ryan. 2014. 'Review of Regulation in the Electricity Supply Industry'. Regulatory Entities Capacity Building Project, Centre for Competition, Regulation and Economic Development (online document).

Eberhard A and K Gratwick. 2008. Demise of the standard model for power sector reform and the emergence of hybrid power markers. *Energy Policy* 36: 3948–3960.

Eskom. 2013. *Integrated Report for the Year Ended 31 March 2013*. Johannesburg: Eskom.

Fine B and Z Rustomjee. 1996. *The Political Economy of South Africa: From Minerals-Energy Complex to Industrialisation*. Boulder, CO: Westview Press.

Gillwald A, M Moyo and C Stork. 2012. *Understanding What Is Happening in ICT in South Africa: A Supply- and Demand-Side Analysis of the ICT Sector*. Evidence for ICT Policy Action Policy Paper 7. http://www.researchictafrica.net/docs/Policy%20Paper%207%20-%20Understanding%20what%20is%20happening%20in%20ICT%20in%20South%20Africa.pdf.

Ginsburg, DH. 2009. Synthetic competition. In F Lévêque and H Shelanski (eds), *Antitrust and Regulation in EU and US: Legal and Economic Perspectives*, pp. 1–19. Cheltenham: Edward Elgar.

Hawthorne R. 2014a. 'Review of Economic Regulation of the Telecommunications Sector'. Centre for Competition, Regulation and Economic Development, University of Johannesburg (online document).

Hawthorne R. 2014b. 'Linkages between economic regulation of the mobile sector in South Africa, sector performance and economic development: The call termination rate intervention'. Presented at the Second South African Economic Regulators Conference, Birchwood Conference Centre, Johannesburg, 18–19 March.

Horwitz, RB and W Currie. 2007. Another instance where privatization trumped liberalization: The politics of telecommunications reform in South Africa – A ten-year retrospective. *Telecommunications Policy* 31: 445–462.

ICN (International Competition Network). 2006. 'Report of the ICN Working Group on Telecommunication Services'. Presented at the Fifth Annual Conference, Cape Town, South Africa, 3–5 May.

ITU (International Telecommunications Union). 2014. 'Measuring the Information Society Report 2014' (online document).

Kessides IN, Z Bogetic and L Maurer. 2007. *Current and Forthcoming Issues in the South African Electricity Sector*. World Bank Policy Research Working Paper No. 4197.

Knott-Craig A. 2009. 'Interconnect: The real story', *TechCentral*, 11 August, http://www.techcentral.co.za/interconnect-the-real-story-2/555/.

Louw D. 2012. 'Electricity distribution network collapse three years away', *Engineering News Daily*, 27 July.

Makhaya G and S Roberts. 2003. Telecommunications in developing countries: Reflections from the South African experience. *Telecommunications Policy* 27: 41–59.

Makhaya G and S Roberts. 2014. *The Changing Strategies of Large Corporations in South Africa under Democracy and the Role of Competition Law*. Centre for Competition, Regulation and Economic Development, University of Johannesburg, Working Paper 2/2014. https://static1.squarespace.com/static/52246331e4b0a46e5f1b8ce5/t/54242cdfe4b063a8a548ce80/1411656927180/CCRED+Working+Paper+02-2014_+SA+Large+Corps+ MakhayaRoberts.pdf.

McLeod D. 2009. 'Cellular operators agree to cut interconnection rates', *TechCentral*, 12 November, http://www.techcentral.co.za/cellular-operators-agree-to-cut-interconnection-rates/11233/.

Montmasson-Clair G, K Moilwa and G Ryan. 2014. 'Review of Regulation in Renewable Energy'. Regulatory Entities Capacity Building Project, Centre for Competition, Regulation and Economic Development (online document).

National Treasury. 2011. 'Local Government Budgets and Expenditure Review: 2006/07 – 2012/13. Chapter 9: Electricity' (online document).

Nersa (National Energy Regulator of South Africa). 2010. *NERSA's Decision on Eskom's Required Revenue Application – Multi-Year Price Determination 2010/11 to 2012/13 (MYPD 2)*. Pretoria: Nersa.

Nersa. 2013. *NERSA's Decision on Eskom's Revenue Application for the Third Multi-Year Price Determination Period 2013/14 to 2017/18*. Pretoria: Nersa.

Noah A. 2012. 'Eskom's submission on possible solutions to Electricity Distribution Industry (EDI) challenges'. Presentation to the Portfolio Committee on Energy, 25 July.

Paelo A. 2015. 'Leveling the Playing Field: Asymmetry in Call Termination Rates in SA'. Centre for Competition, Regulation and Economic Development, Quarterly Review (online document).

Pickering M. 2010. 'Towards an Independent System Operator for South Africa'. Energy Research Centre, University of Cape Town.

Ports Regulator of South Africa. 2012. 'Global Port Pricing Comparator Study – 01/04/2012 Research Summary' (online document).

Pressly D. 2013. 'ANC mum on stalled ISMO Bill', *Business Report*, 15 November.

Research ICT Africa. n.d. 'Cheapest Mobile Prepaid Voice Product in Africa by Country' (online document).

Roberts S. 2004. Investment in South Africa: A comment on recent contributions. *Development Southern Africa* 21: 743–756.

Rustomjee Z. 2013. *DTI Electricity Pricing Project, Final Report (Draft)*. 26 November.

Steyn G. 2003. *Administrated Prices: Electricity*. Pretoria: National Treasury.

Steyn G. 2006. 'Eskom: History's unheeded lessons', *Business Day*, 17 March.

Steyn G. 2012. 'The impact of economic regulation on the management and performance of South Africa state owned enterprises.' Presented at the South African Economic Regulators Conference, National Energy Regulator of South Africa, Johannesburg, 21 August.

TIPS (Trade and Industrial Policy Strategies). 2014a. 'Review of Regulation in the Ports Sector'. Regulatory Entities Capacities Building Project, Centre for Competition, Regulation and Economic Development (online document).

TIPS. 2014b. 'Review of Regulation in Renewable Energy'. Regulatory Entities Capacities Building Project, Centre for Competition, Regulation and Economic Development (online document).

Viscusi WK, J Vernon and J Harrington. 1998. *Economics of Regulation and Antitrust*. Cambridge, MA: The MIT Press.

World Bank. n.d. 'Fixed broadband subscriptions (per 100 people)', http://data.worldbank.org/indicator/IT.NET.BBND.P2.

Part Three

Competition and regulation in
reshaping African markets

6 How multinational investments in grain trading are reshaping Zambia's market

Nicholas J. Sitko and Brian Chisanga

Introduction

Multinational capital is flowing into African agrifood systems in ways that are dramatically altering how food is produced and consumed in the region. While multinational investments in African food systems are not new, shifts in the political, economic and demographic landscape of the region have expanded the scope and scale of these investments. Over the last decade or so, much of sub-Saharan Africa has witnessed rapid urbanisation, sustained GDP growth, single-digit inflation and the emergence of an African middle class (Chikweche and Fletcher, 2014; Fine et al., 2012; Losch, 2012; Ncube, Lufumpa and Vencatachellum, 2011). These domestic transformations are taking place within a global context of increasing uncertainty over global grain supplies and prices (Dewbre, Giner, Thompson and Von Lampe, 2008). The interactions between these domestic, regional and global factors have created incentives for multinational investment throughout African agrifood systems, from food production to retailing.

To date, research on the transformation of African agrifood systems has focused most intently on the rise of supermarkets (Neven, Odera, Reardon and Wang, 2009; Reardon, Timmer, Barrett and Berdegué, 2003; Weatherspoon and Reardon, 2003) and the growth in demand for African land for commercial agricultural purposes (Cotula, Vermeulen, Leonard and Keeley, 2009; Deininger and Byerlee, 2011; Hall, 2011). This research has highlighted important system-wide benefits of the corporatisation of African agrifood systems, including improved capacity to manage environmental and financial risk, the increased pace of technology adoption, and supply chain modernisation (Collier and Dercon, 2014; Minten, Randrianarison and Swinnen, 2009; Reardon and Berdegué, 2006).

However, there is considerable concern over the potential ramifications of the transformation of African agrifood systems for small-scale producers, who continue to make up the majority of the population in sub-Saharan Africa and among whom poverty levels remain unacceptably high (Haggblade et al., 2012; Weatherspoon and Reardon, 2003). This includes the displacement of traditional food markets by supermarkets, which may weaken the capacity of smallholders to tap into expanding urban-demand opportunities (Reardon et al., 2003; Tschirley, Reardon, Dolislager and Snyder, 2014; Weatherspoon and Reardon,

2003), and the enclosure of smallholder farming areas by commercial agriculture investments (Cotula et al., 2009; Hall, 2011; Jayne et al., 2014).

Missing in the debates over the role of multinational capital in the transformation of African agrifood systems is the growth of multinational investment in African cereal and oilseed trading and associated activities. Investments in grain and oilseed trading in Africa by large multinational firms has been prompted, in large part, by the same sets of incentives driving investments in other aspects of African food systems, including growing urban demand on the continent, increasing uncertainty over global food prices and higher potential profit margins relative to global averages. What are the implications of this wave of investment interest in African grain and oilseed trading? More specifically, can this investment interest be harnessed in ways that are beneficial for smallholders and consumers?

In this chapter, we use Zambia as a case study to examine the effects of multinational investment in cereal and oilseed trading. We argue that these investments are becoming an increasingly important dimension of Africa's agrifood transformation, and, if well managed, have the potential to improve competition within the intermediary markets that most smallholders depend on; to lower margins in food marketing systems; to improve price and supply risk management throughout grain and oilseed supply chains; to stimulate rural non-farm opportunities, particularly in grain assembly and transport; and to add a powerful voice for free cross-border trade and predictable agricultural policies. Yet, our analysis suggests that the potential also exists for a less positive outcome. In particular, this investment wave may squeeze out domestic competition in the sector, as well as provide a conduit for multinational firms to gain vertical control of domestic food markets through ancillary investments in input supply, domestic processing and production (Anseeuw and Ducastel, 2013). By highlighting the potentially divergent pathways this investment wave can stimulate, we hope to provide concrete recommendations to policy makers on how to effectively manage this investment interest in order to maximise its beneficial effects.

Data sources and methodology

The data for this chapter are predominantly qualitative and were derived from multiple sources. To understand the ways in which smallholder grain markets function and the effects of multinational investment in grain trading on these markets, we carried out interviews with smallholder farmers, small-scale assembly traders and local grain wholesalers in five districts in Zambia (table 6.1). These districts were selected because they are high-production areas and have witnessed recent investments from multinational firms in domestic grain trading.

Farmers selected to participate in focus group discussions were identified with the help of local Ministry of Agriculture and Livestock extension officers. Only farmers who sold grain in the previous year were selected to participate in the discussions. During these discussions, farmers were asked to identify local traders in their area. This snowball sampling strategy enabled the identification of local assembly traders and the primary local wholesaler(s) in each market.

Table 6.1 Interview respondents

Districts	Chipata Katete Choma Mpongwe Mkushi
Farmer focus group discussions with smallholders	25
Total number of farmers	382
Assembly traders	44
Local small- and medium-scale wholesalers	7
Large-scale multinational wholesalers	5

To understand how and why multinational firms have begun investing in Zambia's grain-trading markets, we conducted interviews with representatives of five of the major firms in Zambia, which we complemented with online research of company websites. Both local and multinational wholesalers also provided data on trading costs and prevailing prices that enabled us to calculate trends in wholesale margins over time. We also interviewed a representative of the Grain Traders' Association of Zambia (GTAZ), who provided key informant data on broader industry trends and changes in association membership composition.

We supplement this qualitative data with nationally representative survey data on production and marketing collected by the Zambian Central Statistical Office. We utilise the Crop Forecast Survey in 2012 and 2014, which collects anticipated sales volumes from over 14 000 small- and large-scale producers, and the 2012 and 2015 Rural Agricultural Livelihoods Survey (RALS), which collects actual sales behaviour by small-scale farmers. The RALS captures specific marketing behaviour. However, it does not effectively disaggregate multinational large-scale traders from domestic ones. The survey response for sales channel is simply 'large-scale trader'. Still, there are several reasons why we are confident that this market channel is almost exclusively multinational large-scale traders. First, when we examine sales volumes through different market channels by province, we find that the large-scale trader purchases occur almost exclusively where multinational firms operate – primarily in Eastern and Central Provinces, and, to a far lesser extent, in Southern.[1] Second, large-scale domestic traders in Zambia focus mostly on the commercial farming sector. To the extent that they buy from the smallholder sector, this occurs through small- and medium-scale traders that aggregate for them. A farmer would not recognise these as proxies for larger buyers. Finally, only one large-scale domestic wholesaler operates a buying depot in a rural part of Zambia, and this is located within Lusaka Province. Direct purchases by large-scale traders in Lusaka Province accounted for a small fraction of total large-scale trader purchases in our data. For these reasons, we believe that our data do provide insights into smallholder marketing to the multinational sector.

Substantiating the investment wave in grain and oilseed trading

In Zambia, ten multinational firms of various national origins have made substantial investments in cereal and oilseed trading and associated services, including input and asset financing, collateral management and post-harvest management. While private investments in food crop origination began soon after market liberalisation in the 1990s, uncertainty over government trade policies, coupled with limited tradeable supplies and domestic market opportunities, pushed most of these initial investors out of the market (Dorosh, Dradri and Haggblade, 2009; Nijhoff, Jayne, Mwiinga and Shaffer, 2002). According to GTAZ, by 2002 multinational firms played an inconsequential role in Zambian grain wholesale markets. Yet this all changed in 2008, in the wake of the global food price spike. Beginning in 2008, multinational firms began establishing trading operations in Zambia or initiated an expansion of existing agricultural operations into grain trading. The scale of these investments has been impressive.

Using a combination of smallholder household survey data and interviews with industry experts, table 6.2 indicates that in the 2011/2012 crop marketing season large-scale grain trading firms directly handled approximately 500 000 metric tonnes (mt) of maize, soybeans and wheat. This amounted to 25% of the total marketed surplus for these three crops. Using estimated nominal 2012 farm-gate prices for these commodities (ReNAPRI, 2015), the purchase value amounts to US$260 million spent in direct payments to farmers, of which over US$18 million went directly to small-scale farmers. By 2015 these firms were handling 621 000 mt of grain, with a significantly expanded presence in the smallholder market. Household survey data show that these firms increased their smallholder market presence by nearly 178 000 mt. This amounts to US$233 million in payments to farmers, with US$53 million going to small-scale farmers.

This national-level picture obscures the significant regional (provincial) dimensions of the investment. Multinational investments in grain wholesaling from the small-scale sector were almost completely confined to two Zambian provinces (Eastern and Central) in 2014/2015. In these two provinces, firms such as Cargill, Afgri and NWK Agri-Services all operate smallholder origination operations. The geographic clustering of these investments is evident from household survey data. As shown in table 6.3, these two provinces account for 93% of all soybean sales to large-scale trading firms and 79% of all maize sales.

The figures on the share of small-scale sales procured by large-scale traders underestimate the scale of these traders' operations in this sector. This is because only direct sales to large-scale traders are accounted for in this estimate. As discussed in more detail below, small-scale intermediaries that bulk crops from small-scale farmers for onward sale frequently sell to large-scale multinationals, either directly under contract or independently. These small-scale traders accounted for 58 and 7% of the total volume of small-scale soybean and maize sales, respectively, in 2012. By 2015 this figure had changed to 48% for soybeans

Table 6.2 Maize, soybean and wheat sales volume and quantities purchased by large-scale traders, 2011/2012 and 2014/2015

Farmer category	Sales 2011/2012 (mt)			Share of total purchases by large-scale grain traders (%)		
	Maize	Soybean	Wheat	Maize	Soybean	Wheat
Large scale	120 993	188 586	250 629	80	80	80
Small scale	1 446 262	14 452	0	4	22	0
Total (mt)	1 567 255	203 038	250 629	154 645	154 048	200 503
	Sales 2014/2015 (mt)			**Share of total purchases by multinational grain traders (%)**		
	Maize	Soybean	Wheat	Maize	Soybean	Wheat
Large scale	122 691	162 675	192 514	80	80	80
Small scale	2 047 642	35 993	0	11	38	0
Total (mt)	2 170 333	198 668	192 514	323 393	143 817	154 011
Total change 2011/2012 to 2014/2015 (mt)	603 078	-4 370	-58 115	168 749	-10 231	-46 492
Change in smallholder purchases (mt)	601 380	21 541	0	167 390	10 498	0

Sources: Large scale from Crop Forecast Survey 2012 and 2015 (not currently publicly available). Share small-scale purchases calculated from RALS 2012 and 2015 (IAPRI, 2016). Share of large-scale purchases estimated by GTAZ.

Table 6.3 Sales to large-scale trading firms by province, 2014/2015 (%)

Province	Soybeans %	Maize %
Central	48.3	34.9
Copperbelt	0.4	2.8
Eastern	44.5	43.9
Luapula	0.8	0.7
Lusaka	2.4	3.3
Muchinga	0.3	3.3
Northern	1.9	1.5
North-Western	0.0	0.1
Southern	1.4	9.4
Western	0.0	0.0

Source: IAPRI (2016)

and 17% for maize. The declining role of small-scale traders and the increasing role of multinational traders in the context of rapidly expanding smallholder soybean production are likely due to increased input financing and forward contracting for soybeans by some multinational firms. We return to this point below.

The timing of the current multinational investment wave in Zambia is not a coincidence, nor is it occurring only in Zambia. Interviews with representatives from multinational firms in Zambia suggest that similar investments in grain trading are occurring in all major grain-producing countries in eastern and southern Africa, including Malawi, Tanzania, Kenya and Mozambique. This has been partly driven by increased uncertainty over global grain supplies and prices, which has made the region's historical reliance on cheap grain imports from abroad more costly and tenuous. This uncertainty, combined with growing and more affluent urban populations, has prompted firms to explore opportunities to tap into domestic production to meet a greater share of domestic and regional demand.

Firms also indicate that margins in Zambia's grain markets, like those in neighbouring countries, tend to be higher than in more advanced markets, due to the large number of intermediaries involved in the markets, high transactions costs associated with limited economies of scale and poor infrastructure, and limited market information leading to opportunities for rents to be earned through asymmetrical market information. Through various marketing network arrangements, including diffuse smallholder procurement networks and forward contracting arrangements, multinational firms see opportunities to overcome some of these transaction costs in ways that enable them to capture higher margins relative to more established global grain markets.

This wave of multinational investment into trading has occurred along three primary paths. The first is through an expansion of existing cash crop operations – particularly cotton in Zambia – into the grain sector. Changes in Cargill Corporation's investment strategies in Zambia, and Africa more broadly, reflect this investment pathway into grain trading. Cargill's initial African investments focused on traditional cash crop procurement and processing, including tea handling and storage in Kenya, cotton procurement and ginning in Zimbabwe, Zambia and Uganda, and cocoa in Ghana and Ivory Coast. As global grain prices began to rise in 2007/2008, Cargill began a 'process of strategic growth into grains and oilseeds'.[2] This included expansion into maize and soybean origination and trading in Zambia (2010), Zimbabwe (2011), Mozambique (2013) and Kenya (2013).

The second pathway is through an extension of established African operations into new African markets. This pathway includes the migration of established South African firms, such as Afgri and Senwes, into other African grain markets, including Zambia. Yet it is not just South African firms moving north. Two large East Africa firms – Export Trading Group and the Metl Group – have entered Zambia's grain wholesale markets. These firms are also well established in other major production areas in sub-Saharan Africa.

The final pathway for multinational firms to establish a presence in new African markets is through the acquisition of an existing domestic firm or the establishment of a new domestic subsidiary. For example, in Zambia, the South African firm NWK Agri-Services, in partnership with Louis Dreyfus, acquired Dunavant Cotton Company and then subsequently expanded operations into grain trading and financing. Other companies, such as Holbud Limited based in the UK, have established grain-trading subsidiaries in Zambia, mostly trading in wheat produced on commercial farms. In this case, Holbud Limited operates in Zambia under the name DomZam.

It is important to note that many of the firms making investments in Zambian and other African cereal and oilseed markets have diverse investment interests and expertise, which may have important implications for their broader impact on domestic food markets. These include interests in production financing, input supply, direct food and fibre production and food processing. Their diverse areas of interest and expertise enable these firms to generate margins all along the supply chain. In some cases this enables the firm to take risks in the market that it wouldn't otherwise be able to take, because losses in one part of the chain, for example input financing, can be made up elsewhere, for example in cooking-oil processing.

However, this integration raises concerns that by establishing a foothold in African grain markets through investments in trading, these firms will seek to gain greater control of the production and marketing systems through the vertical integration of input supply, marketing, storage and processing, thereby limiting competitiveness in the system (Anseeuw and Ducastel, 2013). There are indications that this process is under way in Zambia. Of the ten multinational firms currently operating in Zambia, two have acquired shares or outright ownership of grain- and oil-processing firms, two are involved in commercial agricultural production in Zambia and other African countries, three offer financing services and three are involved in input supply. While this provides opportunities to develop institutional arrangements to overcome persistent smallholder market failures, it also raises concerns about smallholders' loss of control over production and marketing decisions (Key and Runsten, 1999; Kirsten and Sartorius, 2002).

Ultimately, the specific outcome of this investment wave for smallholders is contingent on the policy decisions being made today. To guide these policies, it is critical to examine how these firms are integrating into domestic wholesale markets and what this means for the structure and performance of the markets.

Multinational integration into domestic markets

Grain markets in sub-Saharan Africa are often characterised as embedded within social networks, where repeated transactions and local reputations enable the markets to function in the absence of statutory contract enforcement mechanisms or structured trading platforms (Fafchamps, 2004). Understanding how multinational firms, which often lack the local social capital that domestic firms enjoy, integrate into these markets is important for assessing their implications for domestic and regional food markets.

The primary comparative advantage that multinational firms enjoy relative to domestic firms is their ability to access significantly cheaper financing than is available in domestic credit markets. In Zambia, lending from domestic banks to the agricultural sector is limited, and interest rates on short-term loans can exceed 20% on dollar loans and are even higher for loans in the local currency. This high cost, combined with large collateral requirements, makes access to commercial credit for domestic actors difficult. Multinational firms do not face the same sorts of credit constraints. Due to their considerable scale and global reach, these firms can access credit from numerous sources, including from within their own corporate structures or from commercial banks outside of Zambia that offer significantly cheaper credit terms. Indeed, many of these firms maintain headquarters or subsidiary branches in the US, Singapore or Dubai, which facilitates access to low-cost lending.

Access to low-cost financing enables multinational firms to engage in grain procurement and storage strategies that are generally not available to their domestic counterparts. Multinational firms routinely use their access to cheap financing to provide credit to smaller-scale grain buyers in surplus regions to buy grain on their behalf. In most surplus regions of Zambia, several medium-scale local traders have traditionally competed for smallholder maize. These medium-scale traders have well-established networks of small-scale grain assemblers that operate in smallholder production areas. By providing credit to these medium-scale local buyers, multinational firms are able to tap into existing procurement networks without necessarily establishing a physical presence in these regions.

These grain assembly networks are complex and require substantial amounts of local knowledge to navigate. In particular, these networks enable the aggregation of marketable lots of grain from extremely dispersed smallholders with limited surpluses to sell and who lack the economies of scale to ferry their grain to district markets (Poulton, Kydd, Wiggins and Dorward, 2006; Sitko and

Jayne, 2014). The complexity of this aggregation market is a function of the prevailing smallholder market participation structure in Zambia. In 2010/2011, which was a very good production year, only 40% of Zambian smallholders sold maize, though nearly 90% grew maize. Of these, 5.4% accounted for 50% of the total marketed surplus, with the other 50% provided by the remaining 35% of surplus producers (Chapoto and Jayne, 2011). Thus, the bulk of the maize being sold is sold in very small quantities. Without effective grain aggregation and intermediation services, most surplus producers in Zambia would find it difficult to engage in the market since they lack the economies of scale to justify transportation to external markets.

Data suggest that Zambian intermediary assembly markets are widespread and competitive. As shown by Chapoto and Jayne (2011), 75% of maize sellers travelled less than three kilometres to sell their grain. When farmers sell through these markets, they are paid roughly 82% of the prevailing price in nearby wholesale markets (Sitko and Jayne, 2014). Interviews with assembly traders and local wholesalers suggest that the influx of multinational capital into these markets has enabled both an expansion of the number of assembly traders and greater price competition. Sustaining these competitive assembly markets that poorer rural households depend on will require continued competition at the wholesale level. As Barrett (1997) has shown, competition at the assembly stage of grain markets is conditioned by the degree of competition at the wholesale stage (see also Sitko and Jayne, 2014). To the extent that multinational capital injections into local wholesale markets can continue to drive competition in assembly markets, this investment will prove beneficial for both smallholders and other types of rural non-farm economic activities, including assembly trading and transport. However, there is concern that by utilising local traders to buy on their behalf, multinational firms may in the medium to long term decrease competition in these assembly markets by limiting available downstream markets. Prior to the infusion of multinational investment, local traders sold grain to a wide range of downstream buyers, including commercial processors and local, informal consumer markets. If the provision of capital to these local traders limits their available markets, then the effect will be to decrease price competition throughout the local market networks.

While the majority of multinational firms operate their smallholder grain-purchasing operations through the sorts of local contractual arrangements discussed above, a growing number of these firms have established buying points in key production areas. Most of these are firms with established cash crop buying operations, such as Cargill and NWK, which have been adapted to handle grain trading. For these firms, there is a significant incentive to spread the cost of risk of operating cash crop outgrower programmes over a wider range of crops, including maize and soybeans. Afgri has also opted to bypass local trader contracts and instead source grain from established buying points in the major smallholder production regions of Eastern and Central provinces.

Established local buying points enable these firms to more fully integrate into smallholder markets and production systems. In particular, these firms often link their buying activities to other sorts of investments, including input credit and extension services. These sorts of linked production and marketing activities are primarily being explored by firms with long-standing relationships to smallholders through cash crop outgrower operations (Chamberlin et al., 2014). Through these cash crop operations, firms have already assumed many of the costs associated with screening potential input-credit recipients. With cheap credit to acquire inputs and an established group of farmers with a record of input-credit repayment under cash crop outgrower schemes, these firms have begun exploring opportunities for input credit for grains and oilseeds. For example, since 2013, Cargill in Zambia has provided nearly US$12 million in input financing for maize and soybean to approximately 45 000 smallholder farmers. Cargill is able to use various financial instruments to hedge some of the price risk associated with this investment and the repayment risk associated with contract non-compliance. These risk management tools are not available to local, less sophisticated firms.

Cheap financing also supports multinationals' integration into domestic grain market structures by enabling investment in grain storage and seasonal arbitrage. In Zambia, storage infrastructure has traditionally been concentrated in the hands of the state, as part of its Food Reserve Agency (FRA), and the commercial milling sector. Few domestic wholesalers or small-scale traders are willing or able to store grain. In rain-fed, unimodal agricultural systems like Zambia's, grain storage is critical for smoothing seasonal price fluctuations and limiting crop losses. The lack of domestic investment in grain storage is, therefore, detrimental to grain price stability. Due to the high cost of domestic credit, most domestic wholesalers utilise their own capital to purchase grain. Obstacles to grain storage are further exacerbated by the price uncertainty created by the government's involvement in maize markets resulting from ad hoc releases of subsidised grain into domestic consumer markets and from trade restrictions (Jayne, Zulu and Nijhoff, 2006). As a result of the costs and risk to storage, domestic traders rely primarily on earning smaller margins from back to back trades spread over as much volume as possible. Yet, as one domestic wholesaler stated during an interview, 'storage is where the money is'.

Seasonal grain price movements in Zambia are substantial. Figure 6.1 shows the average monthly price index for real wholesale maize prices in Zambia between 2000 and 2013, with a score of 100 representing the average annual price. It shows that wholesale maize prices tend to be their lowest in May, as the smallholder maize harvest begins, and reach their peak in January, the middle of what is called the hunger period in Zambia. On average, wholesale maize prices in Zambia increase by 48% between May and January, representing a substantial profit opportunity for firms willing and able to store grain.

Access to cheap financing enables multinational trading firms to more easily assume the costs and risks of storing smallholder grain than their domestic competitors. Moreover, they are capable of utilising their access to finance to enter into collateral management arrangements with commercial farmers in Zambia, thereby providing production financing to commercial farms and ensuring themselves access to grain during the smallholder production season. Through these two mechanisms, multinational wholesalers are able to play a beneficial

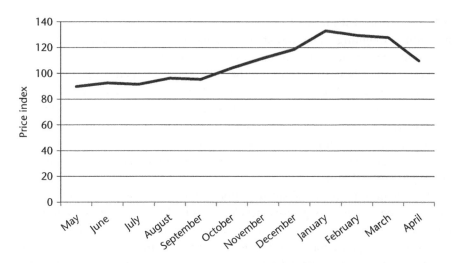

Figure 6.1 Zambian wholesale maize price index, 2000–2013

*Source: Central Statistical Office, Price Bulletin Data, Zambia
(monthly bulletins available at http://www.zamstats.gov.zm/)*

role in Zambia's grain markets, both in terms of supporting commercial producers to access inputs and in smoothing supplies in Zambia's seasonal markets.

Effects of multinational investment on grain markets

In this section we examine the effects of the multinational investment wave on the performance of grain markets in four different ways. First, we explore smallholders' perceptions of how grain markets have evolved as a result of the establishment of multinational firms in their areas. Second, we use household survey data to examine the extent to which these market channels are available to poorer segments of the rural population. Third, we examine how domestic wholesalers, both medium and large scale, perceive these investments. Finally, we investigate trends in trading margins for maize over the period of multinational firms' expansion in Zambia. Taken as a whole, these assessments highlight both the benefits of multinational investments in grain trading, as well as areas of concern.

Smallholders' perceptions

Focus group discussions with smallholders operating in regions that have seen an expansion of multinational investment in grain trading evidence a broadly positive view of this market transformation. Farmers were asked to compare the experience of selling to these firms relative to selling to local wholesalers and to the parastatal FRA. Smallholders' responses to these questions were surprisingly consistent. Respondents stated that relative to local market actors, multinational firms provide a higher level of professionalism and trustworthiness in their interactions with farmers. Several key points were repeated: multinational firms utilise weighing scales and are more reliable than local traders; they provide additional services, including SMS-based market updates, input credit in some cases and extension advice; and they offer more competitive prices.

Relative to the FRA, these firms are generally thought to offer low prices, but they provide a valuable alternative because farmers are paid cash on delivery, while the FRA is notorious for delayed payments due to lack of available funding. Moreover, some respondents indicated that accessing FRA markets frequently required making payments to FRA depot managers, a problem not encountered with multinational firms.

The enhanced professionalism and efforts to build trust among smallholders can be viewed as a broadly positive development for local grain markets. If these attributes become sources of comparative advantage, they may force local actors and government parastatals to improve the ways they engage with smallholders in order to retain market share. However, the accounts described here relate only to farmers selling directly to depots operated by these firms. As discussed previously, many of the firms use local buyers and their assembly agents to purchase on their behalf. Moreover, the majority of maize sellers do not enjoy the economies of scale needed to transport their maize to an established buying point. This raises some concern, as the contractual arrangements that exist between the firms and local buyers are such that they may actually increase incentives for the sorts of unscrupulous market behaviours that farmers frequently complain about. In particular, cash advances to local traders are typically for a predetermined quantity of grain, with the local traders' margins coming from the cash remaining after the specified quantity is acquired. In this context, incentives exist for local traders to maximise their margins through manipulating weighing scales and by offering lower prices than were anticipated in the contract. Thus, while focus group discussions were clear that the presence of multinational firms in local markets is beneficial to those farmers able to sell directly to their depots, the broader impact on smallholder marketing is less clear.

Market participation: Do the poor participate?

The influx of multinational capital into small-scale grain and oilseed markets raises concerns about its potential effects on income inequality. Given the significant asset and production heterogeneity and concentration within most African smallholder systems, including in Zambia, there is reason to be concerned that the potential market benefits described above will only accrue to a minority of already better-off smallholders. To determine whether or not poorer households are able to engage with these markets directly, we disaggregate the smallholder sector into net household income quartiles. In tables 6.4 and 6.5, we use these income groups to quantify the share of total soybean and maize sales by market channel.

Several important findings emerge. First, of the total volume of soybeans purchased directly by large-scale trading firms (row %), 25% is supplied by households in the bottom half of the net income distribution. This is considerably larger than the 15% supplied to large-scale traders by the lower-income groups

Table 6.4 Soybean sales quantity by market channel and income quartile, 2014/2015

Market channel	Net income quartiles											
	1st			2nd			3rd			4th		
	kg sold	Row N%	Column N%	kg sold	Row N%	Column N%	kg sold	Row N%	Column N%	kg sold	Row N%	Column N%
Small-scale trader	3 826 441	20.5	68.0	4 52 971	23.3	59.9	4 211 704	22.6	40.0	6 277 555	33.6	54.7
Large-scale trader	1 400 375	9.9	24.9	2 259 237	16.0	31.1	5 813 616	41.2	55.2	4 646 150	32.9	40.5
Miller/processor	314 869	24.0	5.6	434 216	33.0	6.0	230 953	17.6	2.2	334 144	25.4	2.9
Other HH	86 261	14.0	1.5	202 081	32.8	2.8	202 693	32.9	1.9	125 587	20.4	1.1
Govt (FRA)	0	0.0	0.0	0	0.0	0.0	0	0.0	0.0	0	0.0	0.0
Other (schools, NGOs, etc.)	2 205	1.9	0.0	15 541	13.3	0.2	6 137	5.2	0.1	93 219	79.6	0.8

Source: IAPRI (2016)

Table 6.5 Maize sales quantity by market channel and income quartile, 2014/2015

Market channel	Net income quartiles											
	1st			2nd			3rd			4th		
	kg sold	Row N%	Column N%	kg sold	Row N%	Column N%	kg sold	Row N%	Column N%	kg sold	Row N%	Column N%
Small-scale trader	49 960 868	14.5	26.9	77 807 308	22.6	24.0	85 541 599	24.9	17.2	130 655 955	38.0	13.5
Large-scale trader	9 270 485	3.8	5.0	26 640 550	11.1	8.2	58 891 483	24.4	11.9	146 268 771	60.7	15.1
Miller	1 722 344	2.1	0.9	4 016 964	4.9	1.2	7 357 384	8.9	1.5	69 261 551	84.1	7.2
Other HH	14 394 216	23.6	7.8	16 438 935	27.0	5.1	12 849 159	21.1	2.6	17 226 394	28.3	1.8
Govt (FRA)	108 563 990	8.8	58.5	194 870 347	15.8	60.1	328 200 849	26.6	66.1	603 280 721	48.9	62.3
Other (schools, NGOs, etc.)	1 803 141	16.7	1.0	4 455 102	41.3	1.4	3 534 801	32.7	0.7	1 006 836	9.3	0.1

Source: IAPRI (2016)

in the maize market. As shown in table 6.4, within the lower-income groups, large-scale traders are the second most important market channel behind small-scale traders (column %). Conversely, as shown in table 6.5, large-scale traders are the third or fourth most important market channel for maize sellers in the lower-income groups.

Taken together, these data suggest that there is solid evidence that poor households do sell directly through this emergent market channel. However, the crop context matters. Several important differences exist between maize and soybeans, which likely influence market behaviours. First, maize is both a staple food and a cash crop. As such, poor households will retain the bulk of the maize they produce for consumption. This is not the case for soybeans, which are grown almost entirely as a cash crop in Zambia (Lubungu, Burke and Sitko, 2013). Maize market participation is also closely associated with the size of the area cultivated, while this relationship is much weaker for soybeans (Lubungu, Burke and Sitko, 2013). Thus, poorer, more land-constrained households that grow soybeans are still likely to sell. The fact that such a large volume of surplus soybeans purchased by large-scale traders comes from poorer households with smaller surpluses to sell also suggests that the sorts of origination networks described above are reasonably good at linking to these farmers. This is less so for maize. While this is certainly a reflection of the difference between crops in terms of volumes sold across income group, the role of the state marketing board is important. As shown in table 6.5, the FRA purchases substantial volumes of maize, limiting the amount available for private sector actors.

Local wholesalers' perspectives

Whether or not multinational investment in grain trading triggers improvements in smallholder marketing conditions depends in large measure on the extent to which this investment improves competitive conditions in local assembly markets. There are two primary ways in which multinational investment can affect market competition. The first is through the expansion or contraction of wholesale market opportunities within local markets. This comes down to whether or not the entry of a multinational wholesaler into a local market serves to expand the number of existing wholesalers or whether it leads to consolidation. Although other mitigating factors are also likely at play, including the large and unpredictable role of the FRA in smallholder markets, three attributes of multinational firms' integration into local markets suggest that they may contribute to local wholesale market consolidation: access to cheap finance and larger economies of scale, which enable these firms to operate on smaller margins than local traders; the use of local traders to procure on their behalf, which from a competition standpoint is functionally equivalent to these traders exiting the market; and a seeming preference among smallholders for multinational firms over local domestic traders, leading to less trade volume passing through local traders' hands.

Although we are unable to directly measure changes in the number of small- and medium-scale domestic traders in Zambia, we are able to infer how the sector has changed by examining their contribution to GTAZ. Membership in

GTAZ is required for traders to acquire import and export permits and is the primary conduit for licensing a grain-trading firm in Zambia. Thus, changes in membership fees likely reflect changes in actual trader numbers. According to GTAZ, from 2008 to 2014, the contribution of small- and medium-scale domestic traders to GTAZ dropped from over US$3 000 to less than US$1 000. This is indicative of a substantial decline in active domestic trading. This decline is, of course, not solely the result of an inability to compete with multinational firms. During this same period the FRA substantially expanded its role in smallholder grain markets. However, local traders confirm that their business has been placed under pressure by multinational entry into their markets, thus limiting tradeable volumes and leading to some traders exiting the market. Because this wave of investment is in an early stage in Zambia, it is unclear if the apparent consolidation of local trading will prove beneficial to the grain-trading sector by forcing out high-margin, inefficient traders, or whether it will limit competitive market opportunities for smallholders.

The second mechanism by which multinational firms influence competition in local domestic trading is through their policy advocacy efforts. Trade and price policies for agricultural commodities in Zambia are characterised by high unpredictability, which increases risks for grain traders and limits incentives to develop transparent, structured trading platforms such as commodity exchanges (Sitko and Jayne, 2012). While this policy-induced uncertainty can generate rents for those with asymmetric knowledge about government's intentions, the overall effect on the sector is to limit investment and willingness to take riskier positions in the market. As such, multinational firms have invested considerable time and effort into advocating for policy mechanisms that can improve the predictability of government trade policies, the scope and scale of the FRA in domestic markets, and put in place legislation to enable the creation of a functional commodity exchange. To the extent that these advocacy efforts are successful, they can enable a more level playing field for all actors in the market to participate.

In 2014, advocacy efforts of large-scale trading firms, both domestic and multinational, succeeded in convincing the minister of agriculture to sign a statutory instrument that enables the trading of warehouse receipts in Zambia. The warehouse receipts, which will be linked to a commodity exchange, can theoretically help both small and large domestic wholesalers to access lower cost financing and improve their capacity to store grain. Thus, through their advocacy efforts, multinational firms may support the development of more competitive market conditions for local traders.

Trends in grain-trading margins

Thus far we have highlighted the potentially divergent ways in which the multinational investment wave can affect the performance of domestic grain markets. Whether or not the effects of this investment are positive or negative for the performance of the market can be gauged by examining trends in trading-market margins. A decline in trading margins over time would indicate increasingly competitive conditions, which would be beneficial to both producers and consumers. Conversely, an increase in margins would indicate a decline in competitive forces and would reflect market concentration.

To measure trends in trading margins, we conducted a survey of twelve grain wholesalers, five multinational and seven local, drawn from seven provinces of Zambia. This survey sought to determine trends in costs and margins in grain trading from the 2008/2009 marketing season to the 2013/2014 season. The major cost items identified during the survey were labour/handling, fumigation, transport and the farm-gate cost of maize grain. Table 6.6 summarises trends in the maize costs and marketing margins from the 2008/2009 to the 2013/2014 marketing seasons.

Table 6.6 Cost and margin estimates for maize trading in Zambia in real US$ per tonne

Cost item in US$ per tonne	Marketing season					
	2008/09	2009/10	2010/11	2011/12	2012/13	2013/14
Labour and handling	14	12	12	12	12	12
Fumigation	1.3	1.0	1.0	1.0	1.0	1.3
Transportation	36	30	31	31	31	31
Maize purchase price	192	164	195	203	212	224
Total	243	206	238	247	256	268
Selling prices (into-mill price)	312	252	259	284	286	282
Margin	69	46	21	36	31	14

Source: Authors' calculation

Between 2008/2009 and 2013/2014, wholesale margins for maize in Zambia declined from US$69/tonne to US$14/tonne. Though the decline has not been spectacular in dollar terms, it has been in local kwacha terms. The volatility of dollar costs and margins is associated with sharp movements in exchange rates during this period. The substantial declines in margins are driven by both an increase in the price paid to acquire grain, which rose 16% in this period, and a decline of 9.6% in average selling prices. Costs associated with storage and transport all remained stable over this period.

This trend in marketing margins is therefore beneficial to consumers and producers, and is indicative of an increasingly competitive wholesale grain market. The decline in margins coincides with the expansion of multinational investment in grain trading. Yet, there is concern that this decline in margins could be short-lived. With prevailing margins as low as US$14 per tonne, smaller-scale domestic wholesalers suggest it is increasingly difficult to remain in business. The concern is that as these margins begin to force smaller volume but otherwise relatively efficient traders from the market, competition within Zambia's whole-sale and assembly markets will decline. If that is the case, then the positive trends in marketing margins may reverse.

Yet it is important to note that the entry of multinational capital into Zambian grain trading is not the only factor driving declining trading margins. Another important contributing factor is government price controls. Over the period of interest, the government expanded its role in smallholder grain mar-kets through its FRA operations, purchasing up to 80% of the smallholder maize crop in 2010 (Sitko and Kuteya, 2013). The FRA offers pan-territorial prices and therefore tends to pull up average farm-gate prices. Thus, grain wholesalers are forced to raise their buying price from farmers in order to compete with the government price. At the same time, the government sells maize to millers at prices lower than the purchase price in order to maintain the low consumer prices of mealie meal (a staple food in Zambia). In order for grain wholesalers to sell their grains locally, they have to match the lower government price. The net effect is that wholesale margins are squeezed, thus substantially undermin-ing the capacity of wholesalers, particularly lower-volume local traders, to be profitable.

Conclusion and recommendations

Our analysis suggests that the wave of multinational investment into Zambia's grain-trading sector has thus far proved broadly beneficial to the performance of the market. Smallholder farmers who sell grain suggest that the influx of these multinationals has provided them with more cost-competitive, trustworthy and professional market outlets than before. These are markets that are avail-able to both rich and poor households. Moreover, some of these firms provide ancillary services to farmers, including market price information, input credit and extension advice. In addition, these firms are in some cases pumping credit into local wholesale markets through contractual arrangements with small-scale local traders, which enables an expansion of assembly trading activities. Finally, this investment wave has coincided with a sharp decline in marketing margins, which is beneficial for both consumers and producers.

Yet this positive story must be read with some caution. While the sharp decline in trading margins has likely helped to improve efficiency in the market and forced higher-margin traders out, there is concern that relatively efficient, lower-volume traders cannot profitably remain in the market under current con-ditions. If this is the case, we would anticipate a steady rise in trading margins as these traders exit the sector and competition for grain begins to dwindle.

What can policy makers in Zambia, and other African countries facing the same sort of investment interest, do to capitalise on the beneficial aspects of this investment while managing its risks? Our analysis suggests that address-ing differences in the cost of credit for domestic and multinational firms is a potentially important point of leverage, which can enable domestic firms to be cost-competitive with multinationals. Addressing these differences requires developing strategies to lower both the cost of domestic borrowing and collateral requirements for domestic wholesalers to borrow.

However, in Zambia the opposite is occurring. Interest rates in Zambia are high and rising, due in large part to a rapid increase in government borrowing from domestic credit markets. Treasury bill yields on 182-day bills increased from a low of 2.6 in April 2010 to 17.5 in August 2014. This had the effect of mopping up much of the available capital in domestic credit markets and pushing up the cost of what remains. Greater fiscal discipline is therefore needed to improve the competiveness of domestic lending and to support domestic industry growth.

More specifically to the grain-trading sector, policy makers must provide the necessary enabling environment to support the development of a warehouse receipt system linked to a functional commodity exchange. While the Zambian commodity exchange has languished in recent years, the government recently designated a warehousing authority, which is seen as the last legal hurdle to implementing a warehouse receipt system (Sitko and Jayne, 2012). Warehouse receipts can enable local wholesalers to utilise grain stocks held in certified warehouses as collateral to access commercial credit (Coulter and Onumah, 2002). This has the dual advantage of improving credit conditions for these traders and enabling them to store grain in anticipation of higher prices later in the season.

However, while these strategies offer potential instruments to improve lending to the sector, the effectiveness of these interventions ultimately requires a more predictable policy environment. Current state interventions in grain markets are not only driving down margins in the trading sector, and thus putting substantial pressure on smaller-scale local wholesalers, but the unpredictability of these interventions also stymies lending to the sector. Banks may be unwilling to lend against warehouse receipts, or will only lend a small percentage of the current value of stocks held in warehouses if future price uncertainty is high due to policy unpredictability.

Thus, in many ways Zambia's grain markets, and indeed the grain markets of the region, are at a critical juncture. If the policy status quo is maintained, Zambia is likely to see industry consolidation and a substantial decline in competition in the grain-trading sector, which will have long-run detrimental effects on producer and consumer prices. Yet, if proactive steps are taken to improve policy predictably and increase credit availability to local wholesalers, the opportunity exists for a truly radical and pro-poor transformation in the functioning of these markets. It is hoped that by elevating the visibility of this ongoing transformation, this chapter can play a role in informing current policy discussions on grain market development.

Notes

1 During the reporting period only Afgri operated buying centres in Southern Province.
2 See http://www.cargill.com/worldwide/index.jsp#africa.

References

Anseeuw W and A Ducastel. 2013. 'Production grabbing': New investors and investment models in agriculture. *QA Rivista dell'Associazione Rossi-Doria* 2: 37–55.

Barrett CB. 1997. Food marketing liberalization and trader entry: Evidence from Madagascar. *World Development* 25: 763–777.

Chamberlin J, N Sitko, A Kuteya, M Lubungu and S Tembo. 2014. *Maize Market Coordination in Zambia: An Analysis of the Incentives and Obstacles to Improved Vertical and Horizontal Coordination.* IAPRI Technical Report 2. http://www.iapri.org.zm/index.php/research-reports/technical-reports.

Chapoto A and TS Jayne. 2011. *Zambian Farmers' Access to Maize Markets.* Food Security Research Project Working Paper No. 57, Lusaka, Zambia.

Chikweche T and R Fletcher. 2014. Marketing to the 'middle of the pyramid' in emerging markets using a social network perspective: Evidence from Africa. *International Journal of Emerging Markets* 9: 400–423.

Collier P and S Dercon. 2014. African agriculture in 50 years: Smallholders in a rapidly changing world? *World Development* 63: 92–101.

Cotula L, S Vermeulen, R Leonard and J Keeley. 2009. 'Land Grab or Development Opportunity? Agricultural Investment and International Land Deals in Africa'. IIED/FAO/IFAD, London/Rome (online document).

Coulter J and G Onumah. 2002. The role of warehouse receipt systems in enhanced commodity marketing and rural livelihoods in Africa. *Food Policy* 27: 319–337.

Deininger KW and D Byerlee (with J Lindsay, A Norton, H Selod and M Stickler). 2011. *Rising Global Interest in Farmland: Can It Yield Sustainable and Equitable Benefits?* Washington, DC: World Bank.

Dewbre J, C Giner, W Thompson and M von Lampe. 2008. High food commodity prices: Will they stay? Who will pay? *Agricultural Economics* 39: 393–403.

Dorosh P, S Dradri and S Haggblade. 2009. Regional trade, government policy and food security: Recent evidence from Zambia. *Food Policy* 34: 350–366.

Fafchamps M. 2004. *Market Institutions in Sub-Saharan Africa: Theory and Evidence.* Cambridge, MA: The MIT Press.

Fine D, A van Wamelen, S Lund, A Cabral, M Taoufiki, N Dörr, A Leke, C Roxburgh, J Schubert and P Cook. 2012. 'Africa at Work: Job Creation and Inclusive Growth'. McKinsey Global Institute (online document).

Haggblade S, V Theriault, J Staatz, N Dembele and B Diallo. 2012. 'A Conceptual Framework for Promoting Inclusive Agricultural Value Chains'. International Fund for Agricultural Development (IFAD), mimeo (online document).

Hall R. 2011. Land grabbing in southern Africa: The many faces of the investor rush. *Review of African Political Economy* 38: 193–214.

IAPRI (Indaba Agricultural Policy Research Institute). 2016. 'Rural Agricultural Livelihoods Survey: 2015 Survey Report' (online document).

Jayne TS, A Chapoto, N Sitko, C Nkonde, M Muyanga and J Chamberlin. 2014. Is the scramble for land in Africa foreclosing a smallholder agricultural expansion strategy? *Journal of International Affairs* 67: 35–53.

Jayne TS, B Zulu and JJ Nijhoff. 2006. Stabilizing food markets in eastern and southern Africa. *Food Policy* 31: 328–341.

Key N and D Runsten. 1999. Contract farming, smallholders, and rural development in Latin America: The organization of agroprocessing firms and the scale of outgrower production. *World Development* 27: 381–401.

Kirsten J and K Sartorius. 2002. Linking agribusiness and small-scale farmers in developing countries: Is there a new role for contract farming? *Development Southern Africa* 19: 503–529.

Losch B. 2012. 'Agriculture: The Key to the Employment Challenge'. Perspective Development Strategies, CIRAD (online document).

Lubungu M, WJ Burke and N Sitko. 2013. 'Challenges of Smallholder Soybean Production and Commercialization in Eastern Province of Zambia'. Presented at the Provincial Agricultural Policy Dialogue, Protea Hotel, Chipata, Zambia, 22 November (online document).

Minten B, L Randrianarison and JF Swinnen. 2009. Global retail chains and poor farmers: Evidence from Madagascar. *World Development* 37: 1728–1741.

Ncube M, CL Lufumpa and D Vencatachellum. 2011. *The Middle of the Pyramid: Dynamics of the Middle Class in Africa*. African Development Bank Market Brief, 20 April. http://www.afdb.org/fileadmin/uploads/afdb/Documents/Publications/The%20Middle%20of%20the%20Pyramid_The%20Middle%20of%20the%20Pyramid.pdf.

Neven D, MM Odera, T Reardon and H Wang. 2009. Kenyan supermarkets, emerging middle-class horticultural farmers, and employment impacts on the rural poor. *World Development* 37: 1802–1811.

Nijhoff JJ, TS Jayne, B Mwiinga and J Shaffer. 2002. *Markets Need Predictable Government Actions to Function Effectively: The Case of Importing Maize in Times of Deficit*. Policy Synthesis 6. Lusaka: Food Security Research Project.

Poulton C, J Kydd, S Wiggins and A Dorward. 2006. State intervention for food price stabilisation in Africa: Can it work? *Food Policy* 31: 342–356.

Reardon T and JA Berdegué. 2006. 'The Retail-Led Transformation of Agrifood Systems and Its Implications for Development Policies' (online document).

Reardon T, CP Timmer, CB Barrett and J Berdegué. 2003. The rise of supermarkets in Africa, Asia, and Latin America. *American Journal of Agricultural Economics* 85: 1140–1146.

ReNAPRI (2015) 'Anticipating the Future of Agriculture in the Region: Outlook for Maize, Wheat, Sugar and Rice' (online document).

Sitko NJ and TS Jayne. 2012. Why are African commodity exchanges languishing? A case study of the Zambian Agricultural Commodity Exchange. *Food Policy* 37: 275–282.

Sitko NJ and TS Jayne. 2014. Exploitative briefcase businessmen, parasites, and other myths and legends: Assembly traders and the performance of maize markets in Eastern and Southern Africa. *World Development* 54: 56–67.

Sitko NJ and AN Kuteya. 2013. *The Maize Price Spike of 2012/13: Understanding the Paradox of High Prices Despite Abundant Supplies*. Indaba Agricultural Policy Research Institute Working Paper No. 81. http://fsg.afre.msu.edu/zambia/wp81.pdf.

Tschirley D, T Reardon, M Dolislager and J Snyder. 2014. *The Rise of a Middle Class in East and Southern Africa: Implications for Food System Transformation*. UN WIDER Working Paper No. 119. http://www.saipar.org:8080/eprc/handle/123456789/417.

Weatherspoon DD and T Reardon. 2003. The rise of supermarkets in Africa: Implications for agrifood systems and the rural poor. *Development Policy Review* 21: 333–355.

7 Competition and incumbency in South Africa's liquid fuel value chain

Anthea Paelo, Genna Robb and Thando Vilakazi

Introduction

There is an ongoing debate in South Africa regarding the transformation of the liquid fuel sector value chain, which has historically been controlled by a handful of large multinational oil companies.[1] The petroleum sector is strategic in terms of its wider impact on consumers, as a provider of inputs into other productive sectors of the economy and as an important influence on the trajectory of economic development. In South Africa, the sector benefited from substantial investments and support from the apartheid government for security of supply and national security reasons, particularly in light of widespread sanctions in the years prior to the democratic transition in 1994. A favourable policy environment over the years has created a sector characterised by a handful of large fuel-importing oil companies with refining capacity in strategic port locations, as well as a national champion, Sasol, producing fuel inland. Importantly, all of the incumbent firms exhibit high levels of vertical integration into activities spanning the entire value chain, including importing, refining, production, distribution and retail.

Following the democratic transition, greater emphasis began to be placed on transforming the sector to be more inclusive at different levels of this value chain, culminating in the attachment of the Liquid Fuels Charter as an addendum to the Petroleum Products Act (No. 120 of 1977). The entry and growth of new, independent wholesalers as part of this process of transformation is of particular importance, as distribution and retail are the activities in the value chain with the lowest level of capital requirements for entry. With time, the goal should be to allow entrants at the wholesale level to develop capabilities that allow for their gradual migration up the value chain, creating competition with the incumbent oil companies.

These goals around transformation are not only important for their own sake. They fit within the context of a growing global body of literature on the significance of inclusive economic growth and broadening economic participation. A central component of achieving this increased participation is removing structural and strategic barriers to new entry at different levels of the economy (see Ianchovichina and Lundstrom, 2009; Spence, 2008). In South Africa and elsewhere, research highlights the importance of addressing the market power of large and entrenched firms to stimulate economic growth and the key role of competition authorities in this process (see Acemoglu and Robinson, 2012; Makhaya and Roberts, 2013; North, Wallis, Webb and Weingast, 2007; Roberts, 2012). South Africa's National Development Plan and industrial policy framework also emphasise the importance of creating a dynamic and entrepreneurial economy and addressing high levels of concentration in the economy (NPC, 2013).

Barriers to entry, by creating and reinforcing the market power of large firms, tend to lead to higher prices, lower levels of innovation and a less competitive economy. Incumbent firms have an incentive to lobby and employ strategies to retain high barriers to entry and protect their position in the market. Ultimately, the focus of policy makers should be on creating a market in which firms compete to introduce better prices or products, reduce costs and achieve returns which reward dynamism, innovation and effort, rather than trying to maintain their position by handicapping potential rivals. In a country like South Africa where there are significant unemployment, poverty and inequality challenges, it is particularly important to understand the nature and extent of barriers to entry in the economy in order to ensure that regulatory and policy interventions have a meaningful impact on creating inclusive and shared growth.

Progress in lowering barriers to entry and encouraging transformation has been limited in the liquid fuel sector. While over 1 000 licences have been issued to potential entrants in fuel wholesaling, less than 10% of them are being used effectively by firms that have been able to enter and survive in the industry. Independent wholesale firms are able to enter the market. However, they are typically restricted to supplying less profitable regions and are limited in terms of their expansion as they are highly dependent on the major fuel companies for supply and access to customers.

In this context, this chapter aims to unpack the barriers to entry in the wholesale of liquid fuels in more detail, in order to understand what prevents new entrants from growing into effective competitors to the major fuel companies. The chapter draws directly from a recent study by the Centre for Competition, Regulation and Economic Development on the same subject. As such, all references to industry knowledge and interviews are based on data and information from the broader study.[2] In the remainder of this chapter, we consider literature on barriers to entry before providing an overview of the fuel sector in South Africa and the various barriers to entry that were identified by the study. After concluding, we discuss policy recommendations arising from the findings.

Theoretical discussion of barriers to entry

In economic theory, free entry and exit are important conditions for competition to prevail. When the likelihood of new entry or expansion by existing firms in the market is high, incumbent firms will be constrained by the fear that increased prices would lead to actual or potential rivals expanding their output (O'Donoghue and Padilla, 2006). However, if it is difficult, time consuming or costly for new entrants to come into a market, incumbents may be able to profitably raise prices without a new firm entering the market and driving prices and profits back down.

There has been a debate over the years about the importance of barriers to entry in determining the level of competition in an industry (see Banda, Robb, Roberts and Vilakazi, 2015). Recent theories highlight the importance of economies of scale, imperfect information and strategic behaviour by incumbent firms in deterring entry, leading to a lessening of efficiency and overall welfare. These theories place particular emphasis on the idea of strategic barriers. Strategic barriers are created when incumbent firms use their dominant position to foreclose or exclude entrants in order to undermine competitive rivalry. Other types of barriers that exist because of factors inherent in the nature of the market are termed structural barriers.

Structural features of the market which influence the ease of entry are sunk costs, absolute cost advantages, economies of scale and switching costs. Sunk costs are investments that must be made on entry (e.g., in technology, marketing, research and development), which the investor will not be able to recoup if the firm exits the market. Such costs obviously increase the risk of entry. Whether or not a cost is fully sunk may not be clear-cut, but will depend on what portion of the value of the investment the firm has a reasonable expectation of recouping, should exit occur.

An absolute cost advantage is present where an incumbent firm has an inherently lower cost of production than an entrant, for example, because it has preferential access to raw materials or technology (Church and Ware, 2000). This may be due to a historical advantage in terms of geographic location, rights to certain inputs or preferential contracts with input suppliers.

Scale economies also represent a type of structural barrier to entry. A firm enjoys economies of scale in the production (and/or distribution) of a product when its average costs fall as output increases (O'Donoghue and Padilla, 2006). In an industry where the economies of scale are very high relative to market demand, a large incumbent firm will have an advantage over smaller entrants, since a new entrant selling smaller volumes than the incumbent will have higher costs and make lower margins than the incumbent. If customer switching is low due to brand loyalty or long-term contracts, for example, then it may be very difficult for a new entrant to win customers initially, and, if combined with economies of scale, this may make it difficult for a new entrant to compete sustainably.

Legal or regulatory barriers may also exist, such as tariffs, licensing requirements or weak or badly designed economic regulations. Licensing, for example, can raise barriers to entry if it is associated with onerous requirements on prospective licensees. Regulatory barriers are an interesting category of entry barriers as they can be influenced by policy interventions. Economic regulation is particularly important as it is explicitly aimed at dealing with a lack of competition. Access regulations seek to ensure that vertically integrated monopolies provide access to essential inputs or facilities to rivals on fair terms. This is usually necessitated when there is a natural monopoly at one level of the value chain but competition is feasible at other levels of the chain. Access regulations which are inadequate or poorly enforced can allow vertically integrated dominant firms to leverage their market power to restrict new entry, helping them to maintain their dominant position. The other major type of economic regulation which can impact entry is price regulation in that it may limit the margins that can be earned by a new entrant, which then reduces the incentive for new firms to enter the market and makes it difficult for smaller competitors to survive. By contrast, effective economic regulation will encourage entry and competition wherever feasible.

As noted, when an incumbent firm's conduct creates barriers to entry, these are termed strategic barriers. If the entry of a new competitor is likely to reduce the profits made by the incumbent, either because prices fall or its share in total output is reduced, the incumbent may have an incentive to try to deter entry or ensure that it is unsuccessful. Incumbent firms may employ a wide range of strategies to these ends.

Entry deterrence refers to a situation where the incumbent firm employs a strategy in order to make entry seem unattractive to a prospective entrant. This type of strategy may take a number of forms – for example, pricing below cost or overinvesting in capacity – but always with the aim of persuading the entrant firm that it is unlikely to be successful and that the incumbent firm is strong and committed to fighting any entrant (see Bishop and Walker, 2010; Cabral, 2000; Dixit, 1979, 1981; Motta, 2004). These theories typically rely on the entrant firms' lack of perfect information about the incumbent's costs.

Strategic barriers can also arise from the behaviour of firms through practices that raise rivals' costs and/or induce customers or suppliers not to deal with rivals (reduce rivals' revenue). Again, there are a number of ways in which incumbent firms can try to create these barriers. They may do so by restricting competitors' access to inputs or to customers. If the incumbent is vertically integrated, it may be able prevent the competitor from gaining access to a vital input or charge a very high price for it so that the competitor cannot be profitable. Economists have shown that the incumbent firm could have an incentive to do this for a number of reasons, but particularly if it perceives a threat that an entrant may vertically integrate into its monopoly market (Carlton and Waldman, 1998; Rey and Tirole, 2007). Another strategy which an incumbent may employ is to tie up key customers into exclusive contracts so that an entrant cannot acquire sufficient customers to reach an efficient scale of production. An incumbent may employ a combination of these strategies to deter or defeat entry.

Effective rivalry between firms to win over customers that have scarce resources encourages firms to produce better-quality goods and offer lower prices. This rivalry requires firms to be more prudent in their use of the resources available to them by eliminating inefficient use of resources, cutting down wastage and thus reducing their costs (Evans and Joekes, 2008). It is therefore not surprising that firms will compete aggressively, and at times unfairly, to prevent rivals from gaining a foothold in the market. Firms can choose to compete on the basis of improved product offerings and investments in improving their capabilities, in which case efficiency, effort and ingenuity are rewarded. On the other hand, firms can compete (unfairly) by leveraging their incumbency and engaging in practices that seek to raise rivals' costs and ultimately diminish the significance of rivals as effective competitors. This can also be described as the difference between 'performance competition' and 'handicap competition' (seeking to handicap rivals) (Gerber, 2010).

Strategic barriers to entry are often relevant where there is a vertically integrated monopolist who has an incentive to protect the rents being earned in the monopoly market through attempting to frustrate entry at another level of the market. This is particularly acute where the incumbent firm or firms have control over key inputs required by entrants. In these circumstances, the incumbent firms may find it profitable to engage in strategies to raise rivals' costs or reduce rivals' revenues. They may also choose to accommodate entrants but to attempt to force them into a particular market niche where they can operate at a smaller scale, without threatening the incumbents' main market.

Strategic entry barriers are also important in concentrated markets, which are prone to coordination among firms. Vertical restraints such as exclusive contracts, exclusive territories, retail price maintenance and restricting supply can be used to support a coordinated agreement by preventing downstream firms from undermining a collusive agreement (Levenstein and Suslow, 2014). Cartels have used vertical restraints to foreclose entrants from access to inputs and to markets (Levenstein and Suslow, 2014). Close relationships between firms, including through historical ties and information exchange, tend to make such outcomes more likely. Thus, strategic barriers to entry may be employed by a group of firms with joint market power as well as by individual dominant incumbents.

Strategic barriers to entry are considerably more difficult to evaluate, partly because there is often more than one possible interpretation of the observed behaviour. For example, exclusive contracts can be an efficient way of incentivising investment by suppliers or their distributors, but they may also be intended to deny a new entrant access to customers. The nature and effects of the conduct therefore need to be carefully assessed and weighed against any efficiencies it generates.

Although the consideration of barriers to entry in competition law is largely technical, the discussion has tried to illustrate the mechanisms by which barriers to entry impact on competition and participation in an industry. The following case study on the liquid fuel sector in South Africa highlights the ways in which these barriers can work in practice.

Case study: Liquid fuel sector in South Africa

In this section we provide background to the liquid fuel sector in South Africa, and then discuss the structure of the market and the main strategic barriers to entry which illustrate the concepts raised in the literature review.

Overview of the sector

The liquid fuel sector in South Africa presents an interesting case study in that it has historically enjoyed protection from the state due to the strategic objective of ensuring security of supply in the country. This has created a market where there is an established set of incumbent firms and significant barriers to entry for newer entrants.

The sector is governed by two main bodies: the Department of Energy (DoE) and the industry regulator, the National Energy Regulator of South Africa (Nersa). The DoE mostly deals with issues pertaining to licensing and the pricing structure. Nersa sets tariffs for petroleum pipeline operations and approves tariffs for petroleum storage and loading facilities. The Petroleum Pipelines Act (No. 60 of 2003) also gives Nersa the authority to compel operators of pipeline, loading and storage facilities to allow independents access to unused or 'uncommitted' capacity, although Nersa is unable to compel the owners or operators to expand their facilities.

The country's overriding concern in the liquid fuel sector has been to ensure security of supply. The DoE's legislated mandate is 'to ensure secure and sustainable provision of energy for socio-economic development' (Department of Energy, 2015). This concern was emphasised even more prior to 1994, as the apartheid government needed to ensure supply of fuel, particularly during the period of sanctions. As such, the government created a protected environment where a small number of oil companies were allowed to grow, acquire key infrastructure such as refineries and depots in strategic locations and thus develop considerable market power. This led to vertical integration across all levels in the fuel sector, from importing, refining and production to distribution and retail, further entrenching the market power held by these few oil companies. The industry is thus characterised by seven oil majors – Total, Sasol, Engen, Chevron, Shell, PetroSA and BP – that still account for about 70% of the retail volumes of fuel sold (Lewies, 2013). The other 30% of the retail volumes sold are by independent players in the retail market. However, even the independent players source their fuel almost exclusively from the seven major oil companies, which, by virtue of their refineries and control of the port and storage facilities, also control the supply of fuel at the upstream level.

Figure 7.1 shows the different levels of the value chain in liquid fuel distribution. The wholesaling of fuel takes place once crude oil imports have been refined and distributed (mostly via pipeline) to the different depots and storage facilities in the country. The fuel is then sold on a wholesale basis to commercial customers through three main channels: the oil company's own distribution, branded marketers and independent wholesalers. Through the first channel, the oil companies sell directly to large-volume customers. In the second channel, the oil companies first sell the fuel to their branded distributors or marketers, who act as contracted agents of the oil companies and sell only in allocated regions. The independent wholesalers have supply contracts with the branded distributors and/or oil companies. However, they do not operate under the brand or policies of the major oil companies and are free to distribute fuel to customers in different geographic areas.

Market structure and competitive dynamics in the petroleum sector

Of particular interest in this sector is how the major oil companies have come to jointly control critical stages of the value chain, and how the vertically integrated

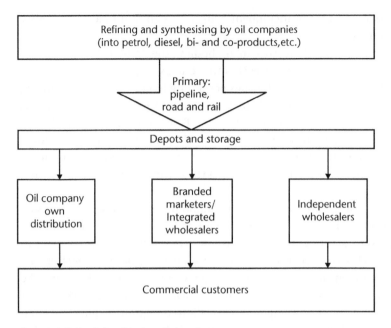

Figure 7.1 Fuel distribution (inland)

Source: Authors' interpretation

nature of their operations has allowed the incumbents to control competitive outcomes not only at the refinery level, but in distribution and retail as well. The findings of various competition cases in the past decade illustrate the overarching concern regarding the joint market power and intricate bargaining relationships which exist between the major oil companies in South Africa.

In 2005, a proposed merger between Sasol and Engen was prohibited by the Competition Tribunal on the basis of concerns regarding the market power which the merger would likely grant to the merged entity in the context of the structure and history of the sector. At the time, Sasol had 82% of the inland wholesale supply and was a part owner in Natref,[3] whereas Engen had refining capacity at the coast. The inland region represented over 60% of national demand and, through the Main Supply Agreement (MSA), the other oil companies had been required to purchase Sasol's product in the inland region but Sasol was prevented from entering the retail market. At the downstream level, therefore, Engen had a large network of retail outlets which, together with Sasol's extensive inland refining and wholesale capacity, would have led to significant control of the inland market in particular. At the time, government was talking about deregulating the retail market and the pipeline capacity from the coast to the inland region was potentially going to be expanded. In this context, Sasol gave five years' notice of the termination of the MSA in 1998 and subsequently entered negotiations with Engen.

The Tribunal found that there was a credible threat of foreclosure as a result of the merger and that Sasol would have the incentive and ability to foreclose competing retailers inland. The Tribunal considered that it would be some time still before increased pipeline capacity came on stream and, in the meantime, Sasol could self-supply and exclude downstream competitors in the inland region. The other oil companies would not be able to retaliate at the coast as Sasol had access to Engen's Durban refinery. According to the Tribunal, this was likely to result in other oil companies 'suing for peace' and agreeing not to compete with the merged entity. In other words, a coordinated outcome was likely. The Tribunal considered that the characteristics of the petroleum industry lend themselves to a collusive outcome:

> all the conditions for cartel formation and maintenance pertain: the structure of the markets is oligopolistic; the products are homogenous and technologically mature; entry barriers are very high; cost structures of the various oil companies are similar...the rate of growth in demand is moderate and demand is highly inelastic; there is no countervailing buyer power to speak of; the markets are highly transparent; there is an extensive history of co-operation both at the level of the MSA and also in a range of joint ventures and ubiquitous swap and hospitality arrangements.[4]

The close contacts between the major oil companies have also been facilitated through various exemption applications, which have enhanced coordination between the companies. In 2005, following a period of fuel shortages, a task team appointed by the minister of minerals and energy recommended that there be increased coordination over issues such as supply lines and shutdowns. The petroleum industry was encouraged to apply for an exemption from the Competition Act through the South African Petroleum Industry Association (SAPIA). An exemption was granted for a period up to 31 December 2015. A short-term exemption was also granted in 2010 to coordinate supply for the World Cup.

In addition to the fact that these arrangements facilitated coordinated outcomes in the sector, an information exchange case involving Chevron, Engen, Shell, Total, Sasol, BP and SAPIA was referred to the Tribunal by the Competition Commission in 2012. The Commission's expressed reasons for the referral were summed up as follows:

> The disaggregated sales information exchanged between oil companies in the case being referred here removed any element of surprise in strategic decision making and functioned as a reliable substitute to direct cartel interactions insofar as it made monitoring of rivals possible. This, together with the history of coordinated behaviour and other characteristics that exist in the petroleum industry, made achieving cartel outcomes post the exemption period possible. (CCSA, 2012)

Together, these cases show the effect of state-sanctioned protection on the competitive dynamics in the sector. Furthermore, they describe a market wherein incumbent operators, through close contacts with one another, have effectively established a position of joint market power in which rivalry between companies is restricted. This is significant when considering the likelihood of entry of new companies and their ability to eventually expand up the value chain in direct competition with the incumbents. It is also relevant to the question of whether entry at the wholesale level will encourage rivalry between the main suppliers by playing them off against one another. We return to this issue in the discussion below.

The Sasol/Engen merger decision also illustrates the significance of the ownership of key infrastructure by the major oil companies and how that has contributed significantly to the creation of structural barriers to entry and expansion in the sector. The sunk investments made into building the refineries and depots, investing in technology, marketing, and research and development reduce the returns the incumbents need to stay in the market compared to those an entrant needs to invest in entering and successfully competing in the market. The oil majors enjoy economies of scale and absolute cost advantages such as preferential access to fuel and infrastructure, which puts them in a much better position than entrants.

Furthermore, entrants at various levels of the value chain face structural barriers in the form of access to finance as well as environmental and pricing regulation, although some of these factors affect all players in the industry in a similar manner. It is worth noting that although the pricing regulation is in itself not an impediment to entry, it does act as a barrier to growth according to wholesalers in the sector. The current system is known as the Regulatory Accounting System (RAS). It separates all activities in the value chain with a view to compensating investment in all activities by allocating the margins to be earned at each level of the chain. While this assures that independent wholesalers in particular earn a margin for their activities and investment, they are still required to compete with the oil majors, which are vertically integrated at every level of the value chain, as well as the branded distributors of these companies. As such, these major rivals earn margins throughout the value chain (discussed below).

Strategic barriers to entry in the liquid fuel sector

Strategic barriers to entry arise from the incumbent firms' reaction to entry, which in some circumstances may constitute anticompetitive conduct. As noted above, this conduct could take the form of aggressive post-entry behaviour or entry deterrence, raising rivals' costs and reducing their revenues. Our study of the liquid fuel wholesale sector found that there are a range of strategic barriers which make it difficult for entrants to compete in the sector. These include a variety of arrangements relating to access to customers, access to infrastructure and facilities, as well as the vertically integrated nature of the sector. This section considers the main barriers identified.

Scale, pricing and access to customers

One of the primary challenges facing wholesalers is that major oil companies provide better discounts and payment terms to customers than smaller rivals are able to. As incumbents with direct control of the input as well as a bigger balance sheet, the fuel majors are able to give much more favourable terms to their customers, such as longer periods of credit to pay for the fuel. Related to this is the fact that the oil companies also deal with large volumes of fuel, thus enjoying significant economies of scale in their operations.

While this aspect is characteristic of most industries where entrants need to compete with established incumbents, the challenge here is that the major companies are vertically integrated and also control the supply of fuel, and so it is even more difficult for downstream rivals to compete because in most cases they would be competing directly with their suppliers. This is exacerbated by the fact that the major oil companies have established relationships and hold long-term supply agreements with several of their large customers, so that competing wholesalers, who rely on the same companies for supply, are not able to match the terms or discounts in order to compete for these customers. Another difficulty is the majors' supply agreements with branded marketers, which often give them exclusive rights to distribute within a given region. Independent distributors may have to purchase fuel from these branded marketers, introducing another layer of cost and making it more difficult to compete for customers.

Wholesalers have argued that they are left to compete through deriving efficiencies in their own operations, offering better service to customers than their larger rivals, and offering additional services and support to customers as value-added products. While customers can benefit substantially from this approach, in the medium to long term the ability of these wholesalers to expand their businesses is restricted, at least partly because they may incur additional costs in providing value-added services, and customers in the industry generally remain focused on price as the primary determinant of whom they will source their fuel from.

Control of key inputs (security of supply)

As noted, rivals' costs can be raised by incumbent firms through various mechanisms. One aspect is through leveraging control of key inputs to increase the input costs or reduce supply to downstream rivals, thus potentially foreclosing them. In the fuel sector, the main oil companies exercise significant control of several key inputs.

The major suppliers generally do not supply product to small new entrants as the volumes they require when starting out are considered to be too low. New entrants are usually directed to acquire supply from branded wholesalers or to first acquire sizeable contracts before they can deal directly with the major suppliers. Once the new entrants establish supply contracts with either the majors or the branded marketers, they are still at a disadvantage because during shortages they are often the last to get access to fuel after the major operators and their branded marketers. The wholesalers generally have limited leverage for negotiating with their suppliers and no real possibility of playing one supplier off against another because of the very transparent nature of costs and pricing in the industry. Information obtained in the study suggests that if a wholesaler competes too strongly or presents a competitive threat to an incumbent oil company, there is a risk that the wholesaler could be foreclosed from supply. Thus, independent wholesalers are kept in a particular market niche.

Control of key infrastructure

The discussion above suggests that wholesalers, and particularly large ones, should seek alternative sources of supply. However, one of the main challenges, particularly with importing fuel directly, is oil companies' ownership of key infrastructure such as port facilities, depots and storage. The main port facilities for landing fuel in Durban are owned by the major oil companies, including through part-ownerships of refineries and other facilities. Thus, in order to land fuel currently, an independent player would have to negotiate with the major oil companies for access to this infrastructure. Similarly, the existing storage facilities in Durban are mainly owned by the major oil companies and there is no commercial imperative for them to construct more storage capacity than they expect to use. In addition, even when there is apparently spare capacity in their facilities, it may not be practical to rent it out to independents since the major oil companies need to ensure that there is always sufficient available capacity for the arrival of their next fuel shipment.

Independent storage facilities are available through companies like Vopak. However, in general, even the independent facilities are contractually bound to the major oil companies. Based on data from Nersa, only 6% of storage capacity for petrol and diesel at the port in Durban is currently independent (Nersa, 2014). The remaining 94% is owned by the major oil companies. Storage facilities are extremely expensive to build and, in order to get financing, storage companies are usually required to acquire long-term use-or-pay contracts with customers for at least 80% of the capacity to be built. This generally means engaging the major oil companies, which would have substantial volume requirements and the ability to guarantee volumes for five or six years. Smaller companies, by contrast, take on a substantial risk by signing up for a long use-or-pay contract. In addition, storage companies sometimes require guarantees to be paid upfront while the capacity will only come online in 18 months to two years. This is onerous for a small firm and as a result only 1.7% of storage capacity is currently used for independent wholesalers and other rivals to major oil companies, despite efforts by Nersa to force facility owners to have explicit allocation mechanisms for sharing uncommitted capacity.[5]

There has been a recent effort to increase access to independent storage. In December 2014, Nersa gave approval for an independent company to put up independent storage in Cape Town despite opposition from Chevron. Chevron alleged that putting up another facility would result in loss of jobs as there would be too much storage. Nersa, perhaps realising the benefit to security of supply, approved the construction of the facility (Monteiro, 2014).

Alternatively, independent wholesalers could decide to import fuel from the world market on their own but this is very expensive and often fraught with complications. First of all, importing fuel is a risky endeavour requiring a large balance sheet and well-managed cash flow. A small tanker-load of fuel could take at least three weeks to reach the port, in which time currency and oil price fluctuations may have changed the economics of the deal. Once the fuel has landed, there are often problems with its quality, which is difficult for an independent wholesaler to manage without refining capacity. The major oil companies have refineries in the country and therefore can fairly easily rectify any deficiencies or changes in the quality of landed fuel. The view of wholesalers is that even if several independents took on the venture collectively, there is still a substantial risk in importing fuel directly from the world market.

If an independent wholesaler were to successfully import fuel through the port and gain access to storage facilities, it would still need access to the fuel pipeline to transport the fuel inland. The pipeline infrastructure is owned and operated by Transnet Pipelines which, as part of its mandate, has to ensure access to this infrastructure. The pipeline infrastructure is particularly important when considering that 60% of fuel demand in South Africa is in the inland regions such as Gauteng, while the remainder is coastal (Naidoo, 2011). The challenge in this regard is that the current pipeline infrastructure is connected to the storage facilities of the major oil companies at the port, which again requires negotiations with the major suppliers that carry far larger volumes. Furthermore, once the fuel is transported by pipeline to the inland region, storage facilities are required once the fuel is offloaded from the various inland pipeline depots. Currently, fuel is transported by road and rail from the depots to the storage facilities of the main oil companies.

There have been efforts to import fuel through Mozambique and then transport it via rail or road. The quality of this fuel, however, is questionable and the channel unreliable. A number of firms have had bad experiences with this channel of supply, including in terms of the reliability and quality of the product. Furthermore, given the costs involved, it is not sustainable to transport this fuel to inland regions other than Mpumalanga and Limpopo.

Pricing and transport

The issue of transportation is especially important in this sector. For wholesalers, the ability to achieve scale in transporting loads of fuel to various customers can determine whether the operator is able to make a profit. Given that margins in the industry are controlled and that wholesalers do not have the control of supply or the scale of operations to afford to obtain fuel at heavily discounted prices, it is increasingly important to be able to reduce costs and derive efficiencies in their operations. Due to changes in the pricing regulation over time, most of the major oil companies have given away less profitable wholesale businesses in peri-urban and rural areas to branded and independent wholesalers. This in fact led to the entry of several firms to the wholesale level of this sector. These areas are less profitable primarily because of the distances travelled to service customers in these markets. However, wholesalers have argued that RAS, the current pricing mechanism, is not calculated based on all the costs experienced in servicing customers in distant rural areas and delivery to small customers requiring small volumes. Instead, the mechanism is said to be based on the costs of an average operator largely based in urban areas where transport distances from depots are less, and demand is higher.

RAS assumes a benchmark service station through averaging the costs of 50 depots. Wholesalers have argued that service stations located farther from the benchmark station bear higher transport costs, which reduces the margin they can receive. Distributors that are closer to the benchmark station receive higher profit margins than those farther away. It is for this reason that the major oil companies chose to sell off the less profitable sites that were in the rural areas and far from the benchmark station. The major oil companies therefore retain the sites with the highest profit margins. This arrangement affects both branded and independent wholesalers in so far as branded wholesalers have also been allocated less profitable peri-urban and rural areas in accordance with the policies of the oil company that they are contracted with.

Conclusions

The combined effect of the barriers to entry noted above is that while a large number of entrant wholesalers have been licensed, very few are actually operating in the industry and still fewer are operating successfully. Even if a new entrant does manage to secure both fuel supply and customers for the product, the environment remains challenging and most struggle to grow beyond a small scale of activity.

Competition appears to be relatively muted in the industry due to a combination of factors, including the vertical agreements between the major oil companies and their branded marketers and retailers, ongoing coordination between the major oil companies, cost and price transparency and the nature of economic regulation in the sector. The major oil companies have been able to coordinate the supply of fuel to different parts of South Africa through various mechanisms, including an exemption from the Competition Act. Although in theory it is possible for an independent player to import fuel, in practice there are a series of constraints which make this very difficult, if not impossible. These constraints mainly relate to the availability of storage infrastructure.

This results in a situation where new entrants at the distribution level are usually accommodated into the industry by existing players, rather than entering independently and challenging the status quo. For example, a well-established wholesaler may agree to supply fuel to a new entrant if the entrant can deliver a new customer that the established player would not otherwise have served, but would be unlikely to do so if the new entrant plans to compete for existing customers. Similarly, the more established wholesalers do not typically compete with the major oil companies for customers as they are usually tied in to a branded-marketer agreement which dictates the area in which they may trade. Even where this is not the case, it is difficult for wholesalers to compete with the major oil companies for customers when they are dependent on them for the supply of fuel. These dynamics would not matter if there were strong competition between the major oil companies themselves and therefore between the different vertical chains present in the market. However, this does not seem to be the case. Such competition as does take place is typically based on service levels and there is no vigorous price competition in the market.

This may be attributable in part to the economic regulation of the industry. The fact that prices are regulated serves as a further disincentive for competition in the industry. Even though prices are directly regulated at only one level of the value chain, the price formula includes wholesale and retail margin components, which means that the compensation level for the average wholesaler is common knowledge throughout the industry. Similarly, the return that the average retailer should make is published as part of the formula. The fact that the retail price (of petrol) is regulated means that the total rents available are determined by the regulator. The major oil companies in turn have control over supply so that they generally do not allow wholesalers and retailers any more than these average amounts, no matter whether the wholesaler or retailer in question is located in a high- or low-cost area to service.

The price regulation system may also explain why wholesalers report that they are generally unable to play the major oil companies off against one another, as it provides a focal point around which the major oil companies can easily tacitly coordinate. Coordinated outcomes in oligopolistic markets are the result of repeated games where the market conditions mean that competitors find it more profitable to adhere to the collusive agreement (whether tacit or explicit) than to compete strongly with one another. For this to be the case, firms must have a means of reaching agreement and a mechanism for detecting and punishing deviations from that agreement. This suggests a set of conditions in which coordination is more likely, including high levels of concentration, symmetry between firms, transparency in the market and product homogeneity.

As discussed by the Tribunal and highlighted above, all of these conditions are met in the petroleum industry. Transparency, in particular, is very high in this market as a result of the swap agreements between the major oil companies, the pricing formula used by the regulator and the need to coordinate supply in the interests of security of supply. Market transparency enhances the ability of firms to monitor the behaviour of competitors and detect any deviation from the coordinated outcome. The information-sharing arrangement which the major oil companies were party to until recently would have further enhanced their understanding of one another's businesses and avoided head-on competition. As noted, the transparent pricing formula published by the regulator provides an easy means for firms to reach a tacit understanding on price.

In this context, the long-term exclusive contracts which the major oil companies sign with their branded distributors could also be interpreted as a means of committing to maintain the agreement, as the agreements effectively prevent the firms from undercutting one another to customers and allow them to maintain high margins upstream. This may also partially explain the major oil companies' decision to disinvest from the wholesale level. Independent wholesalers, on the other hand, are prevented from competing effectively by the control which the major oil companies hold over supply. They have neither the ability nor the incentive to compete strongly on price, as the major oil companies control the price at which they receive the product, and the independent wholesalers are effectively reliant on them for their existence. Unless the independent wholesalers are able to access an alternative source of supply, the major oil companies' control of the market and ability to extract the majority of the available rents is likely to continue. This ties in with the earlier discussion of strategic barriers raising the costs of rivals and reducing their ability to compete.

The liquid fuels industry is one where there are a number of competing imperatives. In addition to stimulating transformation in the industry, DoE is also concerned with ensuring security of supply and preventing costly shortages of fuel in the country. Furthermore, the goal of ensuring that fuel is affordable to consumers across the country could be thwarted if consumers in outlying areas had to face the full costs of distributing fuel to these areas, which would therefore necessitate some cross-subsidisation. In this environment, competition concerns may be relatively low down on the list of priorities. However, the study has shown that to a large degree the problems with competition and increased participation and transformation in the industry are interlinked, and the constraints in wholesaling are in fact directly linked to the broader market structure, regulatory environment and resulting constraints to greater competition in the industry as a whole.

Recommendations

We consider a set of recommendations, drawn from the study, that not only focus on the wholesale level of the market and the barriers discussed, but also consider aspects of the sector as a whole that affect the wholesale level.

It is clear that developing alternative sources of supply would undermine returns to the incumbent oil companies, which would be expected to adjust their competitive strategies in response to this. Significant benefits would accrue to downstream operators and consumers if distributors could play oil companies off against one another to get better prices and terms. Furthermore, oil companies would most likely have to compete with one another more aggressively, which it appears is not currently happening in the market. In order for this to be possible, however, interventions are required at the transport and storage levels.

In this regard, facilitating access for independent wholesalers to storage infrastructure is critical to enabling alternative sources of supply into the market, and hence to allowing for greater levels of competition in the value chain. In the short term, Nersa should continue to make efforts to enable independents to gain access to existing uncommitted capacity. In the longer term, it is necessary to ensure that there is sufficient uncommitted capacity in the market for independents to use. DoE and Nersa could do this by leveraging storage facility licence conditions to mandate that players set aside a certain proportion of capacity for independents to use. Alternatively, investment in new independent storage capacity can be facilitated, either through providing guarantees or through funding support from the Department of Trade and Industry's initiatives, such as the Black Industrialists Programme. Nersa should also continue to promote competition through its regulatory decisions, as was done in the recent *Burgan vs. Chevron* case.[6]

Some interventions could be made in the short term to assist independent wholesalers to be effective competitors. For instance, it does seem that a review of the implementation of RAS would be beneficial and could include consideration of situations where wholesalers are not receiving the full margins recommended in the RAS pricing mechanism, and the adequacy of the allocated margins over-all. In addition, increased efforts in terms of capacity building and assistance for new entrants could help to address any skills deficiency in the industry, including in the management of finances and on strategies to derive efficiencies in entrant businesses given the current pricing and cost environment.

A long-term intervention could be to address the exclusive and long-term nature of the agreements between the major oil companies and their branded distributors. The agreements between wholesale distributors and the major oil companies serve to restrain competition by specifying geographic territories (in the case of branded marketers) and, in some cases, the customers which a whole-sale firm is required to service. In the case of independent wholesalers, the supply relationships with the oil companies would probably not exist if the oil company thought that those wholesalers threatened to compete with them directly. If supply contracts were known to be for a shorter period of time, then it is more likely that oil companies would have to compete to retain those wholesalers as distributors for them in specific areas and especially those that they would rather not service themselves. However, this would potentially be constrained by the fact that oil companies would most likely remove their infrastructure from a wholesaler's site if they could no longer supply that wholesaler, for competitive and environmental reasons.

It is of course important to keep in mind the issue of security of supply in considering interventions that impact on the sector. However, with well-designed policies, it should be possible to meet the objectives of competition, transformation and security of supply simultaneously.

Notes

1   See, e.g., http://www.parliament.gov.za/live/content-mobi.php?C_Item_ID=4777&Item_ID=3536.
2   See http://www.competition.org.za/barriers-to-entry/.
3   An inland crude oil refinery.
4   Competition Tribunal, case no. 101/LM/Dec04, para. 526.
5   National Energy Regulator Application Reference No. PPL.sf.lf.F1/173/2014 and PPL.sf.lf.F3/174/2014, para. 72.
6   National Energy Regulator Application.

References

Acemoglu D and J Robinson. 2012. *Why Nations Fail: The Origins of Power, Prosperity and Poverty*. New York: Crown Business.

Banda F, G Robb, S Roberts and T Vilakazi. 2015. 'Review Paper 1: Key Debates in Competition, Capabilities Development and Related Policies: Drawing the Link between Barriers to Entry and Inclusive Growth'. Centre for Competition, Regulation and Economic Development, University of Johannesburg (online document).

Bishop S and M Walker. 2010. *The Economics of EC Competition Law: Concepts, Application and Measurement* (3rd edition). London: Sweet & Maxwell.

Cabral LMB. 2000. *Introduction to Industrial Organization*. Cambridge, MA: The MIT Press.

Carlton DW and M Waldman. 1998. *The Strategic Use of Trying to Preserve and Create Market Power in Evolving Industries*. National Bureau of Economic Research (NBER) Working Paper No. 6831.

CCSA (Competition Commission South Africa). 2012. 'Competition Commission Refers a Case of Collusion against Oil Companies', 24 October (online document).

Church J and R Ware. 2000. *Industrial Organization: A Strategic Approach*. New York: McGraw-Hill.

Department of Energy. 2015. 'Strategic Plan: 2015–2020' (online document).

Dixit A. 1979. A model of oligopoly suggesting a theory of entry barriers. *Bell Journal of Economics* 10: 20–32.

Dixit A. 1981. The role of investment in entry deterrence. *Economic Journal* 95: 95–106.

Evans P and S Joekes. 2008. *Competition and Development: The Power of Competitive Markets*. Ottawa: International Development Research Centre.

Gerber D. 2010. *Global Competition: Law, Markets and Globalisation*. Oxford: Oxford University Press.

Ianchovichina E and S Lundstrom (with L Garrido). 2009. 'What Is Inclusive Growth?' World Bank, Economic Policy and Debt Department (online document).

Levenstein M and V Suslow. 2014. How do cartels use vertical restraints? Reflections on Bork's *The Antitrust Paradox*. *Journal of Law and Economics* 57: 33–50.

Lewies G. 2013. 'Downstream liquid fuel sector'. Presentation to the Portfolio Committee on Energy on behalf of the South African Petroleum Retailers' Association (SAPRA), 24 July.

Makhaya G and S Roberts. 2013. Expectations and outcomes: Considering competition and corporate power in South Africa under democracy. *Review of African Political Economy* 40: 556–571.

Monteiro A. 2014. 'Burgan gets approval to build Cape Town fuel-storage plant', *Bloomberg*, 9 December, http://www.bloomberg.com/news/articles/2014-12-09/burgan-gets-approval-to-build-cape-town-fuel-storage-facility.

Motta M. 2004. *Competition Policy: Theory and Practice*. New York: Cambridge University Press.

Naidoo L. 2011. 'Future fuel distribution strategies for Southern Africa: How road, rail together with pipelines can work together to guarantee security of supply to Gauteng'. Presented for Transnet Pipelines, Southern Sun OR Tambo, Kempton Park, 2–3 November.

Nersa (National Energy Regulator of South Africa). 2014. 'Petroleum storage facility database' (unpublished document).

North D, J Wallis, S Webb and B Weingast. 2007. *Limited Access Orders in the Developing World: A New Approach to the Problems of Development*. World Bank Policy Research Working Paper WPS4359.

NPC (National Planning Commission). 2013. 'National Development Plan 2030: Our Future – Make It Work' (online document).

O'Donoghue R and J Padilla. 2006. *The Law and Economics of Article 82 EC*. London: Hart Publishing.

Rey P and J Tirole. 2007. A primer on foreclosure. In M Armstrong and R Porter (eds), *Handbook of Industrial Organization* (Vol. 3), pp. 2145–2220. Amsterdam: North Holland.

Roberts S. 2012. 'National dominant firms, competition law and implications for economic development in southern Africa: Case study of energy, beer and food'. Presented at IESE Conference, Maputo, 4–5 September.

Spence M. 2008. 'Commission on Growth and Economic Development'. *The Growth Report: Strategies for Sustained Growth and Inclusive Development* (online document).

8

South Africa's renewable energy experience: Inclusive growth lessons

Gaylor Montmasson-Clair and Reena das Nair[1]

Introduction

As a middle-income country with high levels of poverty, inequality and unemployment, and a legacy of historically skewed economic participation, South Africa has been grappling with socioeconomic issues since the democratic dispensation in 1994 (NPC, 2011). As in many other developing countries, economic growth, even when sustained for a period of time, has not translated into equal opportunity and equal access to markets and resources for poor and marginalised groups, perpetuating high inequality levels (see De Mello and Dutz, 2012).

This entrenched situation has precluded inclusive growth. The term 'inclusive growth' is often used interchangeably with 'broad-based', 'shared' or 'pro-poor growth', referring to growth which encapsulates both improved participation and benefit sharing (Ranieri and Ramos, 2013). Broader, more dynamic perspectives of inclusive growth further include opening up new sectors and harnessing existing sectors to produce more value-added offerings. These rely on significant investments in productive capabilities and skills (Khan, 2012).

It is fairly uncontroversial that growth must be broad-based to be sustainable in the long run, both across sectors in the economy and across a large proportion of a country's labour force (Acemoglu and Robinson, 2012; Ianchovichina and Lundstrom, 2009; Khan, 2012). While economic growth is a prerequisite for poverty reduction, it is well recognised that it does not guarantee that everyone benefits equally. South Africa seeks to achieve more inclusive growth as envisioned in the country's New Growth Path (EDD, 2010). The country's strategy to achieve inclusive growth, particularly increased employment growth and lower income inequality, is set out in the *National Development Plan: Vision for 2030* (NPC, 2011). These policy drivers recognise the importance of a competitive, diversified and more inclusive economy in improving trade performance, job creation and revenue generation (National Treasury, 2013).

Achieving such inclusive goals requires government intervention through appropriately designed, coordinated and implemented policies, with the aim of creating new economic opportunities and ensuring greater participation.

Intervention, including through regulation, can take the form of removing barriers to participation and creating a more level playing field or actively formulating policies that, by their very design, mandate participation by previously marginalised groups (Ianchovichina and Lundstrom, 2009). As argued in chapter 5 in this volume and in Roberts and Mondliwa (2014), a view of regulation which focuses only on existing infrastructure and static considerations of efficiency is a narrow one and there is a strong rationale for regulation to actively introduce competition, dynamism and transformation into an industry.

Infrastructure development – the procurement of large-scale infrastructure – is one area in which the state and economic regulators can, by setting the example, leverage economic regulation to foster inclusive growth. Infrastructure development in South Africa, however, has so far not been done in an inclusive manner and the potential of economic regulation has not been harnessed. It can be argued that, in order to foster inclusive growth through infrastructure development, a change in practice is required, one in which economic regulation can play an active role. Makhaya and Roberts (2013) highlight that past policy intervention has largely failed to stimulate effective competitive rivalry and tip 'the balance of power' in favour of new entry and increased participation (see also chapter 5, this volume). However, the role that regulation can play in fostering inclusive growth through creating opportunities and removing barriers to entry by stimulating competitive rivalry remains largely underresearched.

This chapter investigates the interplay between economic regulation, competition policy and inclusive growth in South Africa, using as a case study the utility-scale renewable energy sector. Through South Africa's Renewable Energy Independent Power Producer Procurement Programme (REIPPPP), the government is procuring utility-scale renewable energy-based electricity generation capacity from independent power producers (IPPs). The REIPPPP provides a perfect frame to investigate the impact of economic regulation on inclusive growth. The scheme was specifically crafted (through economic regulation) to promote competitive outcomes and foster inclusive growth. While South Africa's renewable energy experience has been substantially researched (Eberhard, Kolker and Leigland, 2014; Montmasson-Clair, Moilwa and Ryan, 2014; Montmasson-Clair and Ryan, 2014; Papapetrou, 2014), this chapter presents a new prism of analysis, assessing outcomes in the sector through both an economic regulation and an inclusive growth lens.

In the remainder of the chapter, we first discuss how economic regulation can be harnessed to foster inclusive growth through competitive outcomes. We then analyse the potential to use economic regulation to spur broader inclusive growth outcomes, such as socioeconomic objectives, before concluding.

Harnessing economic regulation for inclusive growth through competitive outcomes

The first step in evaluating the capacity of economic regulation to foster inclusive growth objectives is to ascertain its impact on competition-related outcomes.

This section reflects on the interplay between economic regulation and competition policy, highlighting competitive outcomes as one of the core functions of economic regulation. It then applies these findings to South Africa's experience in renewable energy, showing strong consistency with historical trends.

Economic regulation, competitive outcomes and inclusive growth

The presence and persistence of a range of market failures is the most prominent justification for economic regulation. Market failures arise when resources are not allocated or priced efficiently, and when a more optimal outcome would result from reallocating resources and altering prices. Market failures, along with other constraints, impede the poor and marginalised from accessing markets and benefiting from growth, thereby perpetuating inequality and non-inclusive growth (Ali and Son, 2007; Ianchovichina and Lundstrom, 2009; see also chapter 5, this volume).

One type of market failure, and a persuasive justification for regulation, is the presence of natural monopolies. Typical industries that have natural monopoly characteristics and that are commonly subject to regulation include electricity transmission, liquid fuel pipelines, telecommunication infrastructure and water supply systems. In South Africa, economic regulation has focused on regulating the natural monopoly parts of these value chains, which were formerly state-owned and subsequently privatised (Roberts and Mondliwa, 2014).

Another type of market failure arises from non-competitive markets. This can occur when a single firm or groups of firms possess persistent market power which results in less than optimal output being produced with higher resultant prices. The lack of effective competition could result in dominant firms abusing their market power or engaging in collusive behaviour, obtaining rents at the expense of consumers and potential competitors. This has negative implications for productivity and job creation. Uncompetitive markets also result in lower levels of innovation, reduced choice for consumers and poorer quality of goods or services. Not only are direct consumers harmed, but the viability of downstream industries is affected if the product in question is an intermediate input. Furthermore, firms with market power that control essential facilities that cannot easily be replicated or that control key inputs could abuse their dominance by limiting access to their facilities, thereby creating barriers to entry. Regulation can be a way to curb excesses in market power by regulating access to infrastructure as well as other market outcomes, including prices (Viscusi et al., 2000, in Roberts and Mondliwa, 2014).

South Africa's history and economic policies under apartheid created markets that are highly concentrated, with a few firms in strategic industries possessing considerable market power. Economic opportunity only catered to the interests of minority groups. The state owned and controlled several strategic sectors, such as energy, telecommunications, mining, agriculture and several intermediate industrial product markets. Even following the liberalisation and privatisation trends of the 1990s, most of these industries continue to be highly concentrated while some remain state-owned (Makhaya and Roberts, 2013). Participation by new entrants has typically been constrained through structural or strategic barriers to entry (or both).

Barriers to new entry also present themselves if there are political and/or vested interests at play that serve to protect the incumbents. While in theory increased competition should allow greater and more inclusive economic participation, in reality the power and vested interests of large firms and linkages to the political economy pave the path in which countries develop and often undermine efforts of economic regulators and well-intended policies (Roberts, Vilakazi and Simbanegavi, 2014, citing Acemoglu and Robinson, 2012, and North, Wallis and Weingast, 2009).

In South Africa, powerful conglomerates have shaped the development trajectory of industry. Even in regulated industries where competition could be actively introduced, such as in energy and telecommunications, broad-based participation has remained muted given the presence of structural and strategic barriers. Makhaya and Roberts (2013) suggest that it is both the political connections of the incumbents and the strategic behaviour in these sectors that serve to restrict entry, allowing entrenched dominant positions to be maintained. This influence extends to the ability to shape the new regulatory frameworks in favour of dominant incumbents.

More broadly, Rodriguez and Menon (2010) have argued that, in developing countries, blindly promoting competition laws and policies ignores the actualities of prevailing political settlements and institutional realities (in Roberts, Vilakazi and Simbanegavi, 2014). Regulators are exposed to lobbying by powerful interest groups and outcomes of this may be that the development trajectory of the industry is short-sighted.

The clout of such vested interests has critical implications for the pursuit of inclusive growth. Khan (2012) and De Mello and Dutz (2012) reiterate the importance of understanding political settlements when evaluating inclusive growth. This is further highlighted by Levine (2012) who, when assessing the financial sector, stresses the political economy challenges to the creation of policies that would stimulate inclusive growth. Levine explains that powerful individuals or circles in society may not want the financial sector to perform well as this would empower the previously economically disenfranchised, creating competition and potentially diluting the importance of their wealth and political influence (De Mello and Dutz, 2012).

Economic regulation, competitive outcomes and inclusive growth in South Africa's electricity sector

The renewable energy experience in South Africa demonstrates a deliberate attempt to harness economic regulation to actively generate competitive outcomes. The REIPPPP, initiated in 2011, is the first meaningful endeavour on the part of the government to open up the electricity generation market and introduce IPPs alongside the state-owned utility, Eskom, which generates about 95% of the country's electricity.

Structured around successive bidding rounds, REIPPPP started with an initial allocation of 3 625 megawatts (MWs) to be procured from IPPs over a maximum of five bid windows by 2016. In December 2012 and August 2015, the

Department of Energy (DoE) published additional determinations, bringing the total determination to 14 725 MW. As of September 2016, 6 376 MW of generation capacity (102 projects) had been approved for total investments of over R194 billion, with a collective capacity of 2 738 MW already operational.

While opening the generation market to the private sector constitutes a positive development, it has had no real impact on competition *in* the electricity market, only introducing competition *for* the market. This is owing to Eskom's sustained control over the industry through holding most of the generation capacity (Pickering, 2010) and the limitation of the role of IPPs to supply through government-run procurement programmes only. Nevertheless, the REIPPPP did create a precedent and the electricity market is now being opened to IPPs for other technologies. Similar IPP procurement programmes for baseload electricity from coal, natural gas and hydroelectricity, as well as for co-generation, are being rolled out (as of January 2017) by government.

Through increased competition, the REIPPPP aims to procure renewable energy-based electricity at the lowest cost possible while fostering maximised economic development outcomes. The evaluation framework of the REIPPPP, composed of two clear-cut phases (a prequalification stage and an evaluation stage), ensures a fair and levelled playing field for all participants. In a first prequalification stage, bidders have to satisfy minimum threshold requirements in six areas: financial, technical, commercial and legal, land, economic development and environmental. They must, inter alia, demonstrate the readiness of the project (land acquisition, funding, technologies, suppliers, ability to meet deadlines, environmental consent, etc.), its financial viability and the arrangements to meet minimum requirements in terms of economic development.

As a rule, and in order to secure local participation, the project company must also comprise 40% participation by a South African entity (Campbell, 2012). The DoE (via teams of independent experts) requires detailed and comprehensive bids. Failure to include all required information, and not having this information available on request during the evaluation period, is grounds for elimination.

Bids meeting all these initial requirements are admitted to the second stage – the actual auction – where they are assessed on a competitive basis. Bids are reviewed based on weighted criteria: 70% for their price offer and 30% for their additional contribution to economic development (detailed later).

Stringent criteria also aim to ensure the sustainability of the newly generated competition by limiting the participation to serious players. To avoid low-quality or unreasonable bids and the phenomenon of 'winner's curse', which has plagued a number of auction mechanisms, such as the British Non-Fossil Fuel Obligation scheme in the 1990s (Mitchell and Connor, 2004), project developers have to pay at bid submission a deposit (reimbursed to unsuccessful projects) of R100 000 per MW (Campbell, 2012). Furthermore, successful bidders are required to pay a grid guarantee of R200 000 per MW as well as factor into their budget a development fee (to be used to run the programme) of 1% of total project costs (Campbell, 2012).

The REIPPPP and competition outcomes

The REIPPPP has generated substantial positive competition-related outcomes, primarily in terms of market entry and pricing. Vested interests have nevertheless delayed and limited the scope of the impacts.

Vested interest in South Africa's renewable energy journey

South Africa's road to large-scale, renewable-energy-based electricity generation has been a haphazard and convoluted path, illustrating the difficulty in overcoming vested interests. From the publication of the 2003 White Paper on the Renewable Energy Policy of the Republic of South Africa, which set the objective of generating 10 000 gigawatt-hours of renewable energy by 2013 (approximately 4% of the energy mix), to the procurement of the first MW of generation capacity in 2011, a long and complex policy development process took place in the country. It is intrinsically intertwined with the opening of the electricity supply industry to the private sector.

Several initial attempts that were conceptualised, designed and administrated by the state-owned, vertically integrated monopoly Eskom, such as the Pilot National Cogeneration Programme, the Medium Term Power Purchase Programme and the Multisite Base-load Independent Power Producer Programme (see DoE, 2009; Yelland, 2009), failed to effectively procure power from IPPs. The National Energy Regulator of South Africa (Nersa) then developed a Renewable Energy Feed-In Tariff (REFIT) mechanism to procure power output from qualifying renewable energy generators at predetermined prices. Faced with political and legal challenges, the REFIT policy was abandoned in favour of an auction system (Baker, 2012; Creamer, 2011). Following a lengthy transition process, the DoE, with assistance from National Treasury's Public-Private Partnership Unit, launched the REIPPPP in August 2011.[2]

Unlike previous attempts, the REIPPPP has benefited from a number of key overarching success factors on political (e.g., the policy space), organisational (e.g., the institutional arrangements) and operational (e.g., the power purchase agreement [PPA]) levels.[3]

Indeed, only when policy certainty on the role of renewable energy and the associated investment strategy (i.e., the role of the private sector) were achieved could the procurement framework be successfully implemented. IPP participation in electricity generation was secured in 2007 with Cabinet designating Eskom as the single buyer of power from public and private producers and mandating the state-owned enterprise to ensure that 'adequate generation capacity is made available and that thirty per cent of the new power generation capacity is derived from IPPs' (GCIS, 2007).[4] Large-scale commitment to renewable energy was achieved in 2010 with the Integrated Resource Plan for Electricity 2010–2030 (IRP 2010). The IRP 2010 intended for renewable energy technologies (solar and wind essentially) to supply 42% of the new additional capacity over the 2010–2030 period or 9% of the total electrical energy in 2030 (DoE, 2011).

Institutional arrangements, which were central to the failure of previous programmes, have also been at the crux of the success of the REIPPPP. The programme has benefited from effective institutional leadership and political will from the DoE and the National Treasury, and the active participation of all relevant stakeholders, from other government departments (such as the departments of Trade and Industry and of Environmental Affairs) to Nersa, Eskom, financial institutions and project developers. Had just one of these vital players been missing from the programme design and consultation, the scheme would have been less successful.

In addition, under the REIPPPP, the risk allocation has been adequately balanced between all stakeholders. While previous programmes aimed at promoting the development of renewable energy in South Africa largely failed due to a risk allocation severely in favour of government and the national utility (i.e., pushing most risks onto the private sector), the REIPPPP relies on a more distributed risk profile. The PPA, which constitutes the only source of revenue for developers and for commercial banks financing IPPs (to ensure debt repayment and adequate return on investment), meets international standards, although the financial close phase could be improved.

The PPA is held for 20 years and in local currency, and allocates risk between the parties based on investment-friendly terms.[5] It guarantees payment of an agreed tariff for power generated on a take-or-pay basis (Stemple, 2013).[6] The tariff is agreed upon the award of the preferred bidder status and is indexed to the rate of inflation over the duration of the contract with Eskom. The agreement is underwritten by the National Treasury should Eskom default on the terms. The DoE separately contracts with the project companies to offer recourse for project investors in the event that Eskom fails to meet its obligations under the PPA.

The project developer and its financiers are, however, responsible for building and operating the plant. In the case of IPPs defaulting on supplying the agreed amount of electricity due to weather instability or plant degradation or destruction, the liability falls on the IPP and the project financiers. Should the project company fail to generate the contracted energy, the lenders are asked to step in and find a replacement project company, if feasible. If not, the allocation for that project could be put up for bid in subsequent rounds (Stemple, 2013).

Although the above account suggests successful outcomes, vested interests in the electricity sector can be argued to have contributed to the slow pace of introducing competition. In addition, Eskom remains a vertically integrated utility with little incentive to treat IPPs fairly. In 2015, uncertainty arose around Eskom's issuance of budget quotes, which are a prerequisite for IPPs' bids to reach financial close, for the connection of new renewable energy IPPs to the grid. Since 2015, the utility has displayed a strong reluctance to provide such budget quotes. This can arguably be considered a negotiation strategy to slow the development of IPPs and obtain additional funds from the regulator (Slabbert, 2015; Tshabalala, 2015). Additional resistance occurred in 2016 with Eskom's CEO publicly indicating its unwillingness to sign further PPAs with REIPPs (Creamer, 2016).

Further opening of the electricity supply industry is still required to introduce meaningful market competition, notably at the generation stage. The opportunity to invest in large-scale renewable energy generation capacity is currently limited, outside of the REIPPPP. The passing of the Independent Systems and

Market Operator (ISMO) Bill, aimed at introducing an unbundled ISMO (i.e., outside of Eskom) to invest, operate and maintain the country's high-voltage transmission grid, was meant to address this blockage (see also chapter 5, this volume). It would empower IPPs greatly to sell electricity directly to third-party consumers, such as mining and industrial complexes, and provide the platform for South African companies to generate their own electricity and sell potential surplus to the utility and a third party. As of January 2017, the Bill has been stalled in parliament since 2011 and is likely to remain so in the short to medium term, seemingly owing to vested interests and an attempt to protect Eskom's dominant position.

Reduced barriers to entry and stimulated increased participation

The programme has largely been oversubscribed, a testament to the interest in it, and has resulted in committed investment of over R194 billion (DoE, NT and DBSA, 2016). As illustrated in table 8.1 and figure 8.1, the number of bid responses has increased dramatically with each round, along with a decrease in the number of successful bidders, illustrating the growing interest in the programme as well as its increasingly competitive nature.

On the one hand, the programme's design has been conducive to market entry, considerably widening the number of electricity producers in the country. The number of bids increased from 53 to 93 across the first three rounds. The fourth round saw a stabilisation effect with a total of 77 bids received (Creamer, 2015).

On the other hand, a high degree of competitive rivalry has made success particularly hard for developers (figure 8.1). In the first round, 53% of received bid responses were selected as preferred bidders. This proportion decreased to 24% in the second window and further to 20% in the third bid window. While it originally stood at 17% in the fourth bid window, the additional allocation as part of round 4.5 increased the success rate to 34%.

Practically, the programme has also been efficient in mitigating the risk of winner's curse. All projects selected as preferred bidders have so far reached financial close and the first REIPPPP project, Scatec Solar's 75 MW solar photovoltaic plant, was connected to the grid three months ahead of schedule in September 2013 (Clover, 2013).

As illustrated in table 8.1, over the first seven bid windows (1, 2, 3, 3.5, 4, 4.5 and 1S2), a total of 6 376 MW of generation capacity was procured.

The success of the programme has been evidenced by the positive response received from developers, investors and financiers, as well as local and international manufacturers, who have actively participated in the programme. As such, the programme has attracted a large number of international and domestic project developers, sponsors and equity shareholders. Across the first 64 projects, more than 100 different shareholding entities participated in the programme. Some have been particularly active, with 46 and 25 institutions, respectively, participating in more than one project and in three or more projects. South African insurance company Old Mutual has been the most active entity, supporting 16 projects (Eberhard, Kolker and Leigland, 2014).

Table 8.1 Total MW awarded per technology in the REIPPPP, September 2016

Awards (MW)	Total determination	Round 1 allocation	Round 2 allocation	Rounds 3 & 3.5 allocation	Rounds 4 & 4.5 allocation	Round 1S2	Total allocation
Wind	6 360	649	559	787	1 363		3 357
Solar PV	6 225	627	417	435	813		2 292
Concentrated solar power (CSP)	1 200	150	50	400	0		600
Small hydro	195	0	14	0	5		19
Landfill gas	25	0	0	18	0		18
Biomass	210	0	0	17	25		41
Biogas	110						0
Small-scale	400					49	49
Total	14 725	1 425	1 040	1 657	2 205	49	6 376

Source: Authors, based on DoE (2012a, 2013a); DoE, NT and DBSA (2016)

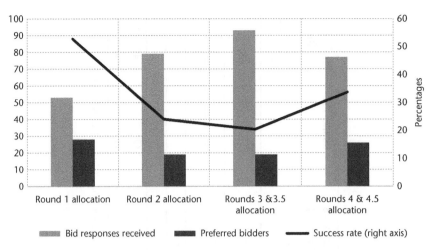

Figure 8.1 Bid responses, preferred bidders and success rate in the REIPPPP as of September 2016

Source: Authors, based on DoE (2012a, 2013a); DoE, NT and DBSA (2016)

In addition, the existing mechanisms have resulted in some degree of competition regarding engineering, procurement and construction (EPC) contractors and equipment suppliers, with 49 companies servicing the first 64 projects. Most companies are involved in more than one project, as the primary or secondary contractor. According to Eberhard, Kolker and Leigland (2014), main EPC contractors with three or more projects include South African (Consolidated Power Projects, Group Five Construction, Murray & Roberts), Danish (Vestas), Spanish (Acciona, Abengoa, ACS Cobra, Iberdrola Engineering and Construction), German (Juwi Renewable Energies, Nordex Energy), Norwegian (Scatec), Italian (Temi Energia) and Indian (Suzlon) companies. The number of technology suppliers is also fairly diverse. Wind turbine suppliers have included European, Chinese and Indian companies such as Vestas, Siemens, Nordex, ABB, Guodian and Suzlon. European, Chinese and Korean manufacturers constituted the main solar photovoltaic suppliers: Siemens, SMA Solar Tech, BYD Shanghai, Hanwha Solar, 3 Sun, AEG and ABB (Eberhard, Kolker and Leigland, 2014).

These positive achievements were no accident and result from continual policy and regulatory learnings from previous initiatives, international experience as well as the iterations of the current programme (Montmasson-Clair, Moilwa and Ryan, 2014; Montmasson-Clair and Ryan, 2014). Stakeholders have commended the extensive due diligence required of developers in their bids and the programme's clarity and reliability. The publication of transparent, consistent and independently reviewed evaluation criteria has emerged as a critical condition for the private sector. The evaluation mechanism has contributed to creating certainty and ensuring the participation of project developers in the programme. Clear and consistent criteria have further enabled fair competition in the renewable energy market and the selection of the most competitive bids.

Stringent criteria have, however, impacted on participation in the programme. The rigour required to meet evaluation criteria and each step in the bidding process, while welcomed by the private sector, has proven to be extremely time consuming and expensive. Key advisors such as legal experts are costly for project developers and can represent up to 15% of project development costs (Montmasson-Clair, Moilwa and Ryan, 2014). The need to reduce the cost of meeting all requirements has arisen for IPPs. Particularly, mechanisms to prevent the winner's curse phenomenon have constituted a hindering factor for the participation of new and/or smaller, previously disadvantaged players. As such, the design of the evaluation criteria, particularly their stringency, is reviewed between every bidding window, factoring market dynamics and local capabilities.

The design of the REIPPPP has therefore been efficient in lowering the barriers to entry and introducing a number of new participants into the electricity generation market. While further analysis is required to fully grasp the implications for inclusive growth, preliminary conclusions nevertheless suggest that market entry has primarily favoured established domestic and international companies, with limited room for the participation of small and medium-sized enterprises. Notably, there has been subdued participation of South African firms, even by means of partnerships or joint ventures with more experienced international players. In sum, the programme constitutes a noteworthy improvement but further efforts are required to widen the spectrum of entities participating in the market.

Substantial reduction in prices

The REIPPPP has resulted in considerable progress over time in terms of prices. Tariffs have significantly dropped over the rounds, well below the required price ceilings (see figure 8.2). For example, prices fell on average from R2.75/ kilowatt-hour (kWh) to 66c/kWh for solar photovoltaic projects, and from R1.14/kWh to 52c/kWh for wind projects.

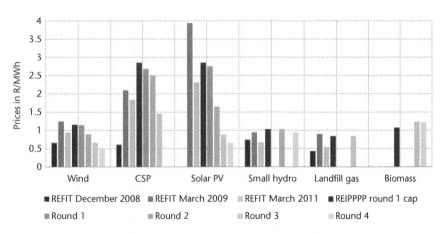

Figure 8.2 Evolution of REFIT tariffs, 2008–2011, and REIPPPP prices, in R/MWh

Source: Authors, based on DoE (2013a); Greyling (2012); Nersa (2011); DoE, NT and DBSA (2016)

Notes: REIPPPP prices are fully indexed on an April 2011 basis.
Due to a change in tariff structure, prices for CSP in round 3 are not directly comparable with rounds 1 and 2. In round 3, projects received a base price for 12 hours every day and 270% of base price for five 'peak' hours every day. Round 4 data exclude round 4.5 projects.
MWh = megawatt-hour

In the first bid window, which was utilised in many ways as a round of observation, prices were relatively high compared to the previous REFIT mechanism. No capacity cap (other than the total allocation of the programme) was set, price caps were publicly released and new developers were not yet ready to put forward competitive bids. These combined factors resulted in a lack of competition and the absence of pressure on the bidders to reduce their price offering. As a result, prices in the first round were high and ended up very close to the prescribed ceilings, raising caution with regard to publishing price caps.

Prices received for the second and third auction rounds were significantly more competitive and even lower than expected (Lucas, Ferroukhi and Hawila, 2013). This trend was confirmed in the fourth round too. The trend essentially resulted from aggressive price competition, project developers being more experienced and familiar with the programme, an increased maturity of technologies, reduced price ceiling for some technologies, such as wind and solar, and the allocation of a capacity limit for each technology from the second round onwards.

The use of an auction system, with the appropriate risk mitigation mechanisms, has reduced the complexity of price setting for the South African government and allowed for prices to decrease rapidly as a response to increased competition, technology maturity and improved developer experience. This success story, resulting from a well-crafted combination of price caps, maximum project size and determined allocation, has been one of the REIPPPP's major achievements. Price caps must, however, be set appropriately so as not to prevent participation. Price caps set too low played a part in the absence of successful projects in the first two rounds for some technologies, such as landfill gas and biomass.

Economic regulation for inclusive growth through socioeconomic development outcomes

The second step to evaluate the potential of harnessing economic regulation to stimulate inclusive growth outcomes is assessing the role of economic regulation in promoting socioeconomic development.

Economic regulation, socioeconomic development and inclusive growth

Proactive economic regulation, including effective competition policy, has an important role to play in promoting inclusive growth outcomes through socioeconomic development. Effective competitive rivalry is a means by which participation in different sectors in the economy can be widened to be more inclusive. Broad-based growth is unlikely to materialise if left solely to the market; the state and economic regulators have active roles to play in this regard.

If competition policy as a form of regulation is effectively designed and implemented, it can foster inclusive growth (UNCTAD, 2015). Several countries, including South Africa, have competition policies. They aim to curb excessive concentrations in the economy (*ex ante* through the merger regime) and prohibit anticompetitive conduct resulting in the exploitation of customers or the exclusion of competitors, ultimately to the detriment of consumers and the competitive process (*ex post* through abuse of dominance and cartel provisions).

While greater economic efficiency (resulting in lower prices, better quality, increased choice and innovation) is a key desired outcome of competition policy, the South African Competition Act (No. 89 of 1998, as amended) has a broader purpose which specifically addresses public interest criteria/goals of greater participation and economic and social inclusivity. This is clearly set out in the Act, where the purpose includes 'to promote employment and advance the social and economic welfare of South Africans' and 'to ensure that small and medium-sized enterprises have an equitable opportunity to participate in the economy; and to promote a greater spread of ownership, in particular to increase the ownership stakes of historically disadvantaged persons'.

The merger regime in South Africa requires consideration of similar public interest criteria. It considers the effect of the merger on a particular industrial sector or region; the impact on employment; the ability of small businesses, or firms controlled or owned by historically disadvantaged persons, to become competitive; and the ability of national industries to compete in international markets. Mergers that are not found to substantially lessen competition may still be prohibited on public interest grounds.

Economic regulation can also be harnessed to foster inclusive growth through socioeconomic development. Economic regulation is largely viewed as *ex ante*, where the aim is to control market power in instances where competition is either not possible or not desirable (such as where industries are characterised by natural monopolies and certain market failures are present). It aims to do this by setting out the rules of the game upfront (see also chapter 5, this volume). Economic regulation can also often encompass multiple objectives, of which competition may be just one. Others could include economic, environmental and social objectives, in addition to core infrastructure functions (Steyn, 2012).

But economic regulation and competition policy are not mutually exclusive. For competition to flourish, effective economic regulation is necessary and can be designed to create what has been termed 'synthetic competition' even in natural monopoly situations (Ginsburg, 2009). Indeed, Newbery (2002, p. 28) cautions against the mantra 'competition where feasible, regulation where not', highlighting that even the potentially competitive elements of a network industry, such as electricity generation, often still need regulatory oversight so that market power is not abused and inclusive outcomes can be achieved. Changing the rules of the game, or 'regulating for competition' to ensure that the dynamic benefits of competition are part of the long-term vision, is necessary to ensure wider economic participation and inclusive growth. Actively encouraging investment in the energy sector is an area in which previously disadvantaged individuals could participate and this requires regulators to design the rules of the game upfront so that participation is encouraged.

It is, however, important to emphasise that competition policy and other forms of economic regulation ought to complement, and not be expected to substitute, other government policies in trying to attain inclusive growth objectives. In general, the record of regulatory intervention in telecommunications, liquid fuels, rail and electricity supply in South Africa has not yielded the desired degree of competitive and inclusive growth.[7]

Economic regulation, socioeconomic development and inclusive growth in South Africa's renewable energy sector

The development of renewable energy appears as a key area where economic regulation has been (tentatively) mobilised in South Africa to generate socioeconomic outcomes. Competitive rivalry triggered by economic regulation has been harnessed to promote inclusive growth. The economic development objectives of the REIPPPP have focused on ensuring that South Africans (notably previously disadvantaged citizens) participate in, own and benefit from renewable energy activities in the country.

The structure of the REIPPPP has been explicit in facilitating this (although economic development criteria remain secondary to price). Traditionally, government's procurement has been based on 80–90% price consideration and 10–20% for developmental objectives such as black economic empowerment. The REIPPPP, in advancing a greater proportion to economic development considerations (30%), has attempted to stimulate socioeconomic goals.

Within the 30 points (out of 100) awarded for economic development, different components are weighted as follows: job creation (25%), local content (25%), ownership (15%), management control (5%), preferential procurement (10%), enterprise development (5%) and socioeconomic development (15%) (DoE, NT and DBSA, 2016). For each category, points are allocated based on minimum desired targets, over and above minimum thresholds. In a given category, meeting only the minimum threshold translates into zero points while reaching the target grants the maximum number of points. From the threshold to the target, a linear relationship determines the total points awarded to the bid. This system is meant to ensure minimum economic development contributions from project developers while encouraging them to aim for higher targets (Montmasson-Clair, Moilwa and Ryan, 2014). Table 8.2 summarises the qualification thresholds for the third bid window, highlighting the diversity of socioeconomic objectives attached to the programme.

The REIPPPP and socioeconomic outcomes

In line with international experience (see Azuela and Barroso, 2011; Cozzi, 2012; Del Río and Linares, 2014; IRENA, 2013), South Africa's renewable energy journey illustrates both the difficulty and the possibility of fully harnessing the potential of economic regulation to foster socioeconomic objectives. Despite a design geared towards promoting local economic and social development, direct outcomes have been uneven but generally improving and encouraging.

Valuable but limited job creation

Job creation accounts for 25% of the economic development criteria embedded in the programme (DoE, NT and DBSA, 2016). Three main areas which create

Table 8.2 Economic development criteria and targets set for the REIPPPP

Economic development element	Description	Bid window 1		Bid window 2		Bid windows 3, 3.5 and 4	
		Minimum (%)	Target (%)	Minimum (%)	Target (%)	Minimum (%)	Target (%)
Job creation	Jobs for citizens	50	80	50	80	50	80
	Jobs for black citizens	30	50	30	50	30	50
	Jobs for skilled black citizens	18	30	18	30	18	30
	Jobs for local communities	12	20	12	20	12	20
Local content	Value of local content as a percentage of total project value	24 or 35 depending on technology	45 or 50 depending on technology	24 or 35 depending on technology	60	45 or 50 depending on technology	65
Ownership	Shareholding by black people in the project company	12	30	12	30	12	30
	Shareholding by local communities in the project company	2.5	5	2.5	5	2.5	5
	Shareholding by black people in the EPC contractor	8	20	8	20	8	20
	Shareholding by black people in the operations contractor	8	20	8	20	8	20
Management control	Black top management	n/a	40	n/a	40	n/a	40

continued →

Economic development element	Description	Bid window 1		Bid window 2			Bid windows 3, 3.5 and 4		
		Minimum (%)	Target (%)	Minimum (%)	Target (%)		Minimum (%)	Target (%)	
	Broad-based black economic empowerment procurement	n/a	60	n/a	60		n/a	60	
Preferential procurement	QSE and EME procurement (up to R35 million in turnover)	n/a	10	n/a	10		n/a	10	
	Women-owned vendor procurement (businesses + 50% owned by women)	n/a	5	n/a	5		n/a	5	
Enterprise development	Enterprise development contributions	n/a	0.6	n/a	0.6		n/a	0.6	
	Adjusted enterprise development contributions (local communities)	n/a	0.6	n/a	0.6		n/a	0.6	
Socioeconomic development	Socioeconomic development contributions	1	1.5	1	1.5		1	1.5	
	Adjusted socioeconomic development contributions (local communities)	1	1.5	1	1.5		1	1.5	

Source: DoE, NT and DBSA (2016)

Note: EME = exempted micro enterprise; QSE = qualifying small enterprise direct jobs are equipment manufacturing, project construction and installation, operation and maintenance, covering the standard divisions of project life.

Project developers have committed to noteworthy job creation as part of their bids. As detailed in figure 8.3, solar photovoltaic is set to be the technology generating the largest number of jobs judging by the successful projects from the first four rounds. Solar photovoltaic projects should create a total of 37 307 employment opportunities, followed by onshore wind and CSP projects.

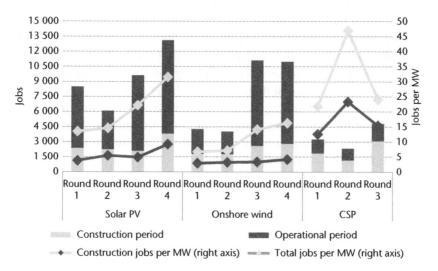

Figure 8.3 Committed job creation for selected technologies over REIPPPP bidding rounds 1–4

Source: Authors, based on Montmasson-Clair, Moilwa and Ryan (2014);
DoE (2013a); DoE, NT and DBSA (2016)

Note: Job creation is expressed in 12 person-months and 12 person-months per MW capacity of generation procured. Round 3 data exclude the two CSP projects of round 3.5. Round 4 data exclude round 4.5 projects.

While project developers have committed to job creation, employment opportunities in the construction and operation of renewable energy-based power plants remain limited. In addition, trade unions have raised concerns about the quality and precarious nature of the jobs generated by the projects, with most employment opportunities created in the communities surrounding projects being for low-skilled security guards (Montmasson-Clair, Moilwa and Ryan, 2014).

The allocation of jobs at the community level also appears lacking in transparency. Skilled employment is generally sourced from the economic centres of the country (such as Gauteng), notably owing to the lack of available skills at the community level (McDaid, 2014). While deemed local by the programme, these employment opportunities do not benefit the community in which the projects are located. Although some skills transfer takes place, it appears to be project-specific and not common practice.

In sum, the contribution of the programme to job creation, while noteworthy, remains limited. Employment is primarily short term and low skill and does not benefit local communities. While job creation is (rightfully) not the main objective associated with developing renewable energy, further efforts are required to maximise the potential for local job creation and to foster inclusive growth.

Noteworthy (constrained) local industrial development

The design of the REIPPPP aims to stimulate the development of local industries through local content requirements. While such requirements internationally have generally not had a positive record, local content targets, and accordingly the local content share of projects in South Africa, have increased over each bid window to encourage further industrialisation, manufacturing and job creation (figure 8.4). Local content calculations cover all stages of the value chains, except land costs and finance costs. All domestic expenditure qualifies as 'local'. This includes civil works, engineering, project management, assembling imported parts, manufacturing some or all components, local technology development through innovation and research and development, and technology transfer from overseas firms via licensing agreement.

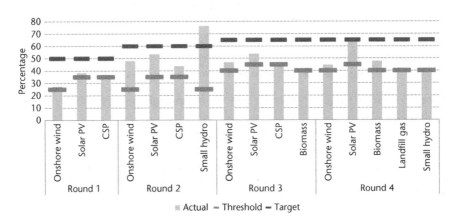

Figure 8.4 Local content requirements and achievements across REIPPPP bidding rounds

Source: Authors, based on Montmasson-Clair, Moilwa and Ryan (2014); Campbell (2012); Eberhard, Kolker and Leigland (2014); DoE (2013a); DoE, NT and DBSA (2016)

Note: Round 3 data exclude the two CSP projects of round 3.5. Round 4 data exclude round 4.5 projects. Technologies where no bid was successful in a particular round have been omitted.

For example, the rand value for local content inputs and processes for onshore wind increased by 33% from the first to the second round and by 37% from the second to the third round. Accordingly, these costs as a share of total project costs have risen from around one-fifth to nearly half. The first bidding round had set a 25% local content target for onshore wind (DoE, 2012b).

Most developers found the 25% target easy to meet as the majority of civil and electrical activities are undertaken by local companies and a large percentage of local transport is used to achieve this target. However, local content requirements increased to 40% in round 3. Turbines, which are generally imported, make up 60–70% of project costs, rendering the local content requirements more difficult to achieve for developers due to the limited local manufacturing base (Vermeulen, 2012).

Looking at solar PV, the local content costs have increased to over half of total project costs, while the rand value of these inputs and processes is falling, in line with smaller allocation and decreasing local content costs due to heightened competition across the entire value chain, from module manufacturers to developers (DoE, NT and DBSA, 2016).

Altogether, solar PV, onshore wind and CSP technologies brought up local content of R32.2 billion over the first four rounds of the programme, with solar PV (R19.5 million) and onshore wind (R19.0 million) leading the way. With local content thresholds increasing progressively for all three technologies, the local content costs as a share of total project costs increased accordingly over the four bid windows.

However, the industrialisation envisioned as part of the programme remains constrained owing to the limited MW capacity allocated per technology (to create sufficient aggregate demand for international companies to set up manufacturing sites in the country) and the small existing manufacturing base. While the existing allocations represent a substantial volume, the overall capacity is spread across several technologies as well as numerous competing developers and suppliers, thus failing to create enough aggregate demand to encourage large investments in local manufacturing. For example, in the absence of critical mass, manufacturing wind turbines in South Africa remains challenging as every wind turbine model requires a different blade, which means a different mould will be needed for each blade (DLA Piper and CD Hofmeyr, 2012). The lack of long-term certainty about the programme has also hindered the development of local manufacturing, leading to some facilities established at the onset of the REIPPPP already closing down (such as the SMA plant in the Western Cape).

Additionally, local content requirements involve short-term trade-offs. As the localisation of new technologies raises the costs of goods, local content requirements can hinder the growth of new sectors if they are not in line with the country's capacity and capability, and impede the decrease in prices. The ability of developers to meet local content requirements largely depends on whether the local industry can manufacture the components of equipment required for their facilities. As such, due to a specific domestic context, all raw (unprocessed) steel, regardless of origin, is considered to be 100% local. It is further recommended that all raw (unprocessed) aluminium, regardless of origin, be considered 100% local (dti, 2013).

Going forward, long-term certainty on the future of the procurement scheme, in terms of MW capacity and technology, must be maintained to maximise industrialisation benefits. The publication in November 2013 of an updated IRP, while advocating that the current renewable energy programme should be continued with additional annual rounds, reintroduced a degree of uncertainty by modifying the allocation per technology included in the IRP 2010 (DoE, 2013b). A new iteration of the IRP was released in November 2016 and is currently going through the consultation process.[8] While reviewing and updating the country's electricity plan is a necessary ongoing exercise, further certainty on the allocations per technology must be ensured to provide clarity to the sector (Montmasson-Clair and Ryan, 2014). The new allocation of 6 300 MW announced in April 2015 is a step in the right direction to establish increased long-term certainty and local investment.

South African companies are also well placed to supply blades, gearboxes, generators and controllers for main wind turbines, although they still source some parts internationally (Baker, 2012). The programme has triggered some noteworthy manufacturing investments which would have been extremely unlikely without it. For example, multi-sector company Corporación Gestamp's wind industrial division, GRI Renewable Industries, invested €22 million in a wind tower manufacturing facility in Cape Town (Kolver, 2014), while engineering group DCD Wind Towers built a R300 million wind tower manufacturing facility in the Coega industrial development zone in the Eastern Cape (Moodley, 2014). At least five photovoltaic panel assembly plants have also been established in South Africa over the last few years, and some international suppliers have used these to achieve localisation targets (Eberhard, Kolker and Leigland, 2014). These investments have triggered some skills transfer towards South Africa at the manufacturing level.

Failed attempts at spurring community development

Finally, the REIPPPP includes community development as one of its key objectives. To encourage social development in neighbourhoods that surround renewable energy projects, community trusts need to be made up of members that live within a 50 km radius of the project site (Van den Berg, 2013). This is to prevent nepotism over how community beneficiaries are selected, as well as to ensure that the surrounding communities, which often bear the unaccounted ecological, social and economic costs of the project, benefit from the developments. Most communities hold a stake of up to 5% on average, per project, through community trusts. These community trusts are fully funded by the Development Bank of Southern Africa (DBSA), the Industrial Development Corporation and/or the Public Investment Corporation, while some are classified as free carry. For example, the DBSA provides low-interest financing to community trusts to buy shares in the project company. The shares are managed by the DBSA and the community trust leadership, and these two parties decide on how the revenue is to be spent.

Community trusts are set up with the financial assistance of development finance institutions for communities living near the projects to buy shares in the project companies. Associated revenues, estimated at R9.5 billion collectively over the first three bid windows, are set aside for community-led projects (Montmasson-Clair, Moilwa and Ryan, 2014).

The management of community trusts established to meet social development outcomes has created some unintended consequences. Concerns have been raised about the concentration of these funds in a limited number of communities, their monitoring and evaluation, and the capacity of the DoE and development finance institutions to manage the funds and ensure IPPs meet their commitments.

In addition, the concern is that many community trusts have been established merely to serve the requirements of the request for proposals. Project developers and the local development finance institutions have little experience in working with communities and municipalities in these areas to ensure that development programmes are aligned with community interests and municipal plans. Community participation and ownership aspects of the project can indeed promote perverse development by concentrating large funds in community trusts, without having well-thought-through developmental objectives. The risk is that such community trusts will receive excessive financial flows with little knowledge of the communities in which they are working.

An implementation agreement signed with the DoE is meant to ensure that preferred bidders adhere to their commitments. Each bidder is required to report to the DoE on a quarterly basis regarding these commitments (DoE, 2012c). The REIPPPP awards more points to communities located closer to the renewable energy project and does not place a limit on multiple community trusts for one community. This results in a small number of communities having multiple community trusts assigned to them. The developmental aspects of the community trust projects come second to concentrating community trusts in lucrative areas.

Due to the competitively sensitive nature of the programme, developers are not able to share their socioeconomic development plans, resulting in several developers engaging with similar communities and confusion for all parties. In addition, no structured partnership with the local municipality exists and local government is only engaged in a fragmented, peripheral and uncoordinated manner. Dissatisfaction is further compounded as a result of the mistrust between councillors and community representatives and the lack of transparency surrounding the selection of socioeconomic projects (McDaid, 2014; Tait, Wlokas and Garside, 2013).

Furthermore, some developers have attempted to retain control of the trusts, while claiming that they are 'owned' by the community. The appointment of the trustees and the management of the funds remain problematic and appear far from the standards of good governance, with evidence of nepotism, political arrangement, elite capture and lack of communication, transparency and accountability (McDaid, 2014). The quality and relevance of social investment projects have also been questioned at the local level (McDaid, 2014; Tait, Wlokas and Garside, 2013).

Social issues such as the rising cost of living, indebtedness and diseases have reportedly increased around project sites, notably during construction, because of increased employment and the influx of workers. Gender issues are also not being considered by the programme as no gender specialist is included in the programme team. Preliminary evidence shows that women may not enjoy many of the benefits (such as employment), but may bear a disproportionate amount of the burden (e.g., an increase in gender-based violence). Overall, little feedback is provided to project developers on their social development plans as no social scientists or labour specialists are present in the team of independent experts (McDaid, 2014).

Renewable energy projects have the capacity to generate substantial amounts of money for local communities. Clearly, the expectation that these projects, unlike projects based on other energy sources, should take on a complex and onerous responsibility for community development, has introduced numerous unintended consequences. The lack of adequate structures at the local level and of monitoring and evaluation at the national level, along with the inexperience of project developers in this space, has led to the further marginalisation of, and division within, already marginalised and vulnerable communities.

Conclusions

This chapter highlighted the important role that economic regulation could have in attaining inclusive growth outcomes through greater participation and the promotion of socioeconomic development. This is particularly relevant for South Africa, given the country's history of non-inclusive participation in the economy and skewed access to economic opportunities. The importance of 'regulating for competition' is emphasised, dispelling the notion that regulation and competition can effectively function independently of each other. The coordination of the state, independent economic regulators, competition authorities and the private sector is essential to reduce barriers to entry and to stimulate inclusive growth. However, this should be done with cognisance of the political and vested interests at play.

The renewable energy experience in South Africa highlights the deliberate and successful attempt to introduce competition and inclusive growth objectives in the formulation of regulatory policy for the electricity supply industry. The REIPPPP has been a success in competitively procuring large-scale renewable energy-based electricity generation capacity. Economic regulation has been particularly efficient in driving prices down in a limited amount of time. It has also opened up the market to a large array of new participants in the electricity generation market, lowering considerably the barriers to entry. Beyond prices and market entry, the direct translation of the increase in competition into inclusive growth does not appear automatic, although first results are encouraging. Although limited in scope, the REIPPPP provides a first successful attempt at managing vested interests in South Africa's electricity supply industry. Furthermore, while the REIPPPP has had noteworthy positive impacts in terms of job creation and industrial and community development, these positive outcomes remain limited (and in some cases hampered by unintended consequences), illustrating the difficulty of maximising several objectives at the same time.

In line with international experience, the preliminary findings from the case study illustrate the potential, as well as the difficulty, in channelling economic regulation to stimulate competition for economic development and inclusive growth. In this respect, this case study carries substantial lessons for the procurement of large-scale infrastructure in South Africa and other developing and emerging economies. Going forward, the REIPPPP and similar programmes could notably strengthen their impact on inclusive growth, particularly in terms of local manufacturing and community development, by establishing strong monitoring and evaluation frameworks and further capacitating project developers in meeting economic development requirements. Setting the appropriate instruments to create aggregate demand (required for the development of local manufacturing) could further contribute to enabling the type of economic development and skilled employment envisioned for such programmes. In the short term, however, this is likely to come at the expense of other policy objectives, such as cost affordability, and trade-offs between various objectives must be carefully considered to maximise national benefits.

Notes

1   The authors wish to thank the Research Project on Employment, Income Distribution and Inclusive Growth (REDI3x3) for supporting the work published in this chapter.
2   See Montmasson-Clair, Moilwa and Ryan (2014) for a detailed analysis of South Africa's renewable energy journey.
3   Many more factors contributed to the success of the programme. See Montmasson-Clair, Moilwa and Ryan (2014), Montmasson-Clair and Ryan (2014) and Eberhard, Kolker and Leigland (2014) for more details.
4   Cabinet further specified that over the 2007–2027 period, 'Eskom will build all nuclear power plants in South Africa and the IPPs will build more than 50% of all non-nuclear power plants' (GCIS, 2007).
5   A multitude of risks can be associated with the construction and profitable operation of a power plant, from fuel price and supply (this risk is by definition not applicable to renewable energy-based plants), foreign exchange, environmental assessments and authorisations, the connection to the transmission and distribution networks, revenue collection, to timely and on-budget plant construction and plant operation.
6   Essentially, this means that irrespective of power demand by the grid, if the power is generated by the renewable project, the tariff will be paid by Eskom for each kilowatt of energy produced.
7   Nevertheless, the Ports Regulator in South Africa has in recent years made significant regulatory decisions with positive impacts on competitiveness. See Reena das Nair and Simon Roberts' chapter in this volume for a review of ports regulation in South Africa.
8   See http://www.energy.gov.za/IRP/irp-2016.html.

References

Acemoglu D and JA Robinson. 2012. *Why Nations Fail: The Origins of Power, Prosperity, and Poverty*. London: Profile Books.

Ali I and HH Son. 2007. *Defining and Measuring Inclusive Growth: Application to the Philippines*. Asian Development Bank, ERD Working Paper No. 98, July.

Azuela GE and LA Barroso. 2011. *Design and Performance of Policy Instruments to Promote the Development of Renewable Energy: Emerging Experience in Selected Developing Countries*. Washington, DC: World Bank.

Baker L. 2012. *Power Shifts? The Political Economy of Socio-Technical Transitions in South Africa's Electricity Sector*. Norwich: School of International Development, University of East Anglia.

Campbell A. 2012. 'Funding Projects in REIPP – Lessons Learnt from BD1' (online document).

Clover I. 2013. 'Scatec Solar connects South Africa's first renewable independent power project to the grid', *pv magazine*, 10 September, http://www.pv-magazine.com/news/details/beitrag/scatec-solar-connects-south-africas-first-renewable-independent-power-project-to-the-grid_100012682/#axzz2vfQwZchi.

Cozzi P. 2012. *Assessing Reverse Auctions as a Policy Tool for Renewable Energy Deployment*. Medford, MA: Center for International Environment and Resource Policy.

Creamer T. 2011. 'Fresh concern that SA will abandon Refit in favour of competitive bids', *Engineering News*, 23 June.

Creamer T. 2015. 'More than 70 bids received for fourth renewables bid window', *Engineering News*, 24 February.

Creamer T. 2016. 'Eskom letter sends shock waves through private power sector', *Engineering News*, 21 July.

De Mello L and MA Dutz (eds). 2012. 'Promoting Inclusive Growth: Challenges and Policies'. OECD Publishing (online document).

Del Río P and P Linares. 2014. Back to the future? Rethinking auctions for renewable electricity support. *Renewable and Sustainable Energy Reviews* 35: 42–56.

DLA Piper and CD Hofmeyr. 2012. EPC Contracts in the Renewable Energy Sector – South African RE IPP Programme – Lessons learned from Phases 1 and 2. See https://www.dlapiper.com/~/media/Files/Insights/Publications/2012/10/EPC%20contracts%20for%20South%20African%20wind%20farms/Files/epccontractswindenergyprojectssouthafrica/FileAttachment/epccontractswindenergyprojectssouthafrica.pdf.

DoE (Department of Energy). 2009. *Creating an Enabling Environment for Distributed Power Generation in the South African Electricity Supply Industry*. Pretoria: DoE.

DoE. 2011. *Integrated Resource Plan for Electricity 2010–2030*. Pretoria: DoE.

DoE. 2012a. 'IPP Procurement Programme 2012: Determination under Section 34(1) of the Electricity Regulation Act 4 of 2006' (online document).

DoE. 2012b. 'PPC-Energy: Update on Window 1 RE-IPP Procurement Programme'. PowerPoint presentation (online document).

DoE. 2012c. 'Postponement of 3rd bid submission date for the REIPPP', *EE Publishers*, 27 September, http://www.ee.co.za/article/deptenergy-359-10-postponement-of-3rd-bid-submission-date-for-the-reipppp.html.

DoE. 2013a. 'Renewable Energy IPP Procurement Programme: Bid Window 3. Preferred Bidders' Announcement' (online document).

DoE. 2013b. *Integrated Resource Plan for Electricity (IRP) 2010–2030: Update Report*. Pretoria: DoE.

DoE, NT (National Treasury) and DBSA (Development Bank of Southern Africa). 2016. 'Independent Power Producers Procurement Programme (IPPPP): An Overview as at 30 September 2016'. Pretoria: DoE, NT and DBSA.

dti. 2013. 'REIPPP Bidders Conference 16 August 2012 Green Industries, Department of Trade and Industry' (online document).

Eberhard A, J Kolker and J Leigland. 2014. *South Africa's Renewable Energy IPP Procurement Program: Success Factors and Lessons*. Washington, DC: Public–Private Infrastructure Advisory Facility.

EDD (Economic Development Department, South Africa). 2010. *The New Growth Path: Framework*. Pretoria: EDD.

GCIS (Government Communication and Information System). 2007. 'Statement on Cabinet Meeting of 5 September 2007' (online document).

Ginsburg DH. 2009. Synthetic competition. In F Lévêque and H Shelanski (eds), *Antitrust and Regulation in the EU and US: Legal and Economic Perspectives*, pp. 1–19. Cheltenham: Edward Elgar.

Greyling A. 2012. 'Renewable Energy'. Independent Power Producer (REIPP) Procurement Programme – An Eskom perspective. Presentation at the Sustainability Week conference, Sandton Convention Centre, Johannesburg, 27 July.

Ianchovichina E and S Lundstrom (with L Garrido). 2009. 'What Is Inclusive Growth?' World Bank, Economic Policy and Debt Department (online document).

IRENA (International Renewable Energy Agency). 2013. 'Renewable Power Generation Costs in 2012: An Overview' (online document).

Khan M. 2012. The political economy of inclusive growth. In L de Mello and MA Dutz (eds), 'Promoting Inclusive Growth: Challenges and Policies' (Chap. 1). OECD Publishing (online document).

Kolver L. 2014. 'GRI to start manufacturing wind towers in Cape Town in H2 2014', *Engineering News*, 20 January.

Levine R. 2012. Finance, regulation and inclusive growth. In L de Mello and MA Dutz (eds), 'Promoting Inclusive Growth: Challenges and Policies' (Chap. 2). OECD Publishing (online document).

Lucas H, R Ferroukhi and D Hawila. 2013. *Renewable Energy Auctions in Developing Countries*. Abu Dhabi: International Renewable Energy Agency.

Makhaya G and S Roberts. 2013. Expectations and outcomes: Considering competition and corporate power in South Africa under democracy. *Review of African Political Economy* 40: 556–571.

McDaid L. 2014. 'Renewable Energy: Independent Power Producer Procurement Programme Review 2014'. Electricity Governance Initiative of South Africa, Cape Town (online document).

Mitchell C and P Connor. 2004. Renewable energy policy in the UK 1990–2003. *Energy Policy* 32: 1935–1947.

Montmasson-Clair G, K Moilwa and G Ryan. 2014. 'Review of Regulation in Renewable Energy'. Regulatory Entities Capacity Building Project, Centre for Competition, Regulation and Economic Development (online document).

Montmasson-Clair G and G Ryan. 2014. Lessons from South Africa's renewable energy regulatory and procurement experience. *Journal of Economic and Financial Sciences* 7: 507–526.

Moodley S. 2014. 'Wind-tower manufacturing facility on track for 2014 opening', *Engineering News*, 17 January.

National Treasury. 2013. 'Medium Term Budget Policy Statement. Chapter 1: Securing Inclusive Growth' (online document).

Nersa (National Energy Regulator of South Africa). 2011. 'Review of Renewable Energy Feed-In Tariffs'. Nersa Consultation Paper, March (online document).

Newbery D. 2002. Regulating unbundled network utilities. *The Economic and Social Review* 33: 23–41.

North DC, JJ Wallis and B Weingast. 2009. *Violence and Social Orders: A Conceptual Framework for Interpreting Recorded Human History*. Cambridge: Cambridge University Press.

NPC (National Planning Commission). 2011. 'National Development Plan: Vision for 2030' (online document).

Papapetrou P. 2014. *Enabling Renewable Energy in South Africa: Assessing the Renewable Energy Independent Power Producer Procurement Programme*. Cape Town: World Wide Fund for Nature South Africa.

Pickering M. 2010. *Towards an Independent System Operation for South Africa*. Cape Town: Energy Research Centre, University of Cape Town.

Ranieri R and RA Ramos. 2013. 'After All, What Is Inclusive Growth?' International Policy Centre for Inclusive Growth (online document).

Roberts S and P Mondliwa. 2014. Fuelling the economy: A critical review of liquid fuels regulation in South Africa. *Journal of Economic and Financial Sciences* 7: 547–568.

Roberts S, T Vilakazi and W Simbanegavi. 2014. 'Understanding competition and regional integration as part of an inclusive growth agenda for Africa: Key issues, insights and a research agenda'. Paper submitted for the Eighth Annual Competition Commission and Tribunal Conference, 4–5 September.

Rodriguez A and A Menon. 2010. *The Limits of Competition Policy: Shortcomings of Antitrust in Developing and Reforming Economies*. The Hague: Kluwer Law International.

Slabbert A. 2015. 'Budget quotes: Eskom board to consider solution', *Moneyweb*, 3 November.

Stemple R. 2013. *Sustainable Growth from a Renewable Source*. Cape Town: Futuregrowth Asset Management.

Steyn G. 2012. 'The impact of economic regulation on the management and performance of South Africa state owned enterprises'. Presented at the South African Economic Regulators Conference, National Energy Regulator of South Africa, Johannesburg, 21 August.

Tait L, HL Wlokas and B Garside. 2013. *Making Communities Count: Maximising Local Benefit Potential in South Africa's Renewable Energy Independent Power Producer Procurement Programme (REIPPPP)*. London: International Institute for Environment and Development.

Tshabalala R. 2015. 'Eskom budget can't support new independent power producers: Molefe', *Timeslive*, 20 October.

UNCTAD (United Nations Conference on Trade and Development). 2015. 'The Role of Competition Policy in Promoting Sustainable and Inclusive Growth', UN Doc. TD/RBP/CONF.8/6, Geneva, 27 April (online document).

Van den Berg J. 2013. 'Submission to NERSA: Eskom MYPD 3 Application'. South African Renewable Energy Council (online document).

Vermeulen A. 2012. Localisation might be a challenge in future REIPPP bidding rounds. *Engineering News*, 14 December.

Yelland C. 2009. 'Independent power producers (IPPs) organise collectively to take on Eskom', *EE Publishers*, 29 August, http://www.ee.co.za/article/independent-power-producers-ipps-organise-collectively-to-take-on-eskom.html.

9 Competition and regulation in Zimbabwe's emerging mobile payments markets

Genna Robb, Isaac Tausha and Thando Vilakazi

Introduction

Mobile money has attracted global attention because of its ability to bring people from the cash-based, 'unbanked' economy into modern systems of 'book-entry money'. This process is commonly referred to in the industry as 'banking the unbanked' (Klein and Mayer, 2011). It involves the use of mobile phone technology to make financial transactions. Generally, this allows users to engage in transactions ranging from buying and transferring airtime, to transferring funds and making payments from their mobile devices (ITU, 2011). A 'traditional' form of this is where banks have mobile phone applications which allow their customers to interact with their bank accounts on their phones.

As a subset of mobile banking, and of particular interest to this chapter, is the ability to transfer money in person-to-person (P2P) transactions, that is, from the bank account or mobile operator 'wallet' of one person, to the mobile number or mobile operator wallet of another.[1] These services allow customers to use their mobile device to send and receive monetary value – to transfer money using their phone, which in some cases includes international, cross-border and/or domestic remittance transfers.[2] Importantly, these services can be provided even when the sender and/or recipient does not have a bank account. In Zimbabwe, this led to rapid adoption by users since NetOne and Telecel both launched their mobile money transfer (MMT) services in January 2011, followed by Econet in September 2011. Users include customers in rural areas where access to banking services has been limited and remittance transfers from large cities and abroad are an important source of income (Dermish, Hundermark and Sanford, 2012). This is especially relevant given the withdrawal of the majority of Zimbabweans from formal banking services during the prolonged period of economic distress over the past decade, leading to a largely cash-based economy and the use of direct, informal cash transfer mechanisms, such as through minibus taxi services and travelling relatives or friends (Dermish, Hundermark and Sanford, 2012).

These aspects of mobile money have important implications in terms of competition and economic development. The ability to draw in subscribers that are unbanked and marginalised by formal financial services through simple, affordable, convenient and safe platforms contributes to greater financial inclusion (Klein and Mayer, 2011), and facilitates transactions between individuals (e.g., remittances) as well as between enterprises.[3] However, the gains in welfare can easily be undermined where markets are concentrated and dominant incumbents are able to unfairly abuse their strength in adjacent markets, such as mobile money services, to bolster their market power in primary markets (mobile telecommunication services). This is especially the case where rival operators face high barriers to entry related to network effects in particular, which makes it difficult for as-efficient rivals to effectively compete for customers. In the case of the Zimbabwean market, where Econet is the dominant player in traditional services and MMTs, customers have a strong incentive to use the mobile money services of the largest network (primarily due to lower costs and convenience), which requires them to also subscribe to Econet's traditional mobile services offering through purchasing a sim card. This relationship between the two markets makes it especially difficult for rivals to encourage customers to switch, which has important implications for competition between operators in the Zimbabwean market (discussed later).

This chapter takes a broad look at the competition and regulatory environment related to mobile money in Zimbabwe. It explores the nature of the mobile payments market in Zimbabwe and theory and literature around network effects and possible competition problems which can arise in this type of market, including through international comparisons with the Zimbabwean market. It also deals with the issue of interoperability and the conditions where it is likely to develop versus situations where regulatory intervention is likely to be required. This is then all related to the Zimbabwean context in order to present possible ways forward for regulators.

In the remainder of the chapter we provide a background to the market for MMT services in Zimbabwe and its development in recent years before reviewing the literature on competition and regulatory issues in network industries and mobile money markets in particular. Thereafter we assess competition and regulatory issues specific to the Zimbabwean market and draw comparisons with developments in other countries in South and East Africa. After concluding, we provide recommendations for policy making and enforcement through agencies such as competition authorities and sector regulators.

The Zimbabwean mobile money market

The provision of mobile banking – relying on mobile network operator (MNO) infrastructure – by banks, and the provision of MMTs by MNOs, relies on the use of the Unstructured Supplementary Service Data (USSD) codes held by MNOs, which are issued and licensed by the Postal and Telecommunications Regulatory Authority of Zimbabwe (Potraz). This refers to a short code such as '*200#', which, when dialled, presents the customer with a menu of functions, including the option to conduct a P2P transaction. We include the process outlined for Econet customers as an example (box 9.1).

Box 9.1 Method for sending money over the EcoCash platform

6 Send Money: How do I send money (transfer cash) using my EcoCash account?

1. Dial *151*200# and enter your **pin** to access their EcoCash menu
2. Go to **Option 4-Send Money**
3. Select either **Option 1-Registered Customer** or **Option 2-Unregistered Customer**
4. Enter receiving mobile number using the following form at (071xxxxxxx, 077xxxxxxx, 073xxxxxxx)
5. Enter the amount that they wish to transfer (*e.g.* 2 for $2 or 2.10 for $2.10)
6. You will receive a notification on your screen advising you of how much you have said they wish to send and the mobile number you wish to send to. From there you can either Select **Option 1-Approve** or **Option 2-Cancel** the transaction.
7. On approval of the transaction, a confirmation messages will be sent to both lines with the following details:
    *   **Sender:** Amount transferred, recipient's name (if the recipients number is registered for EcoCash) or mobile number (unregistered), approval code and their new wallet balance.
    *   **Recipient:** Amount transferred sender's name and the transaction approval code.
8. Keep these confirmation messages as reference and only dispose of them when you are certain that you no longer need them and the recipient has managed to collect the money

Source: EcoCash (n.d.)

Customers are generally required to register at an outlet of the chosen network provider in order to have access to a mobile wallet and the MMT service, by simply producing proof of identity, filling in an application form and being in possession of an active sim card for that network. Across all MNOs in Zimbabwe, recipients of funds are then required to go to an agent of the sender's network operator to collect any transferred funds, unless the recipient is a registered wallet customer on the same network, in which case they have the option of retaining the funds received in their mobile wallet. For example, an EcoCash customer who is a recipient of funds transferred from another EcoCash customer can go to an EcoCash agent to collect the funds in cash ('cash-out') or can retain the funds in their EcoCash wallet. Recipients on a different network to the sender need to present confirmation of the funds transferred to them (the message received contains a unique reference number) to an agent of the sender's network, who will then cash-out to the recipient. As of 2016, Potraz expects MNOs to implement interoperability between mobile wallets across networks as well, so that subscribers to other mobile money services can send money directly to an EcoCash wallet and vice versa.

Agents have therefore been a critical part of the value chain for providing MMT services. These agents effectively act as the equivalent of bank branches for sending and receiving money transfers. Most MNOs operate agent networks that include the owners, operators or employees of small retailers or postal outlets (USAID, 2010). Some agents are contracted as exclusive or non-exclusive agents of an MNO, whereas others, such as postal service branches and large grocery retailers, in most cases can be contracted by several MNOs. The Reserve Bank of Zimbabwe (RBZ) issued a directive in 2014 prohibiting agent exclusivity unless the operator could demonstrate the need to have exclusivity over a particular agent.[4] Currently, Econet has by far the largest network of agents in Zimbabwe, based on data from Potraz (table 9.1).

Table 9.1 Agents by mobile network operator

MNO	2012	2013	2014	2015
Telecel	–	–	4 586	6 984
NetOne	32	61	1 612	2 262
Econet	2 301	9 108	17 181	24 013
Total	2 333	9 169	23 379	33 259

Source: Potraz quarterly reports (http://www.potraz.gov. zw/index.php/categorylinks/120-quarterly-reports)

Note: For 2014 and 2015, totals for the fourth quarter are used.

The growth of Econet's EcoCash facility into the leading mobile banking platform in Zimbabwe, well ahead of its rivals, was fuelled by the ability to attract previously unbanked customers. Although a significant proportion of Zimbabwe's population of 13.7 million people do not have bank accounts (around 30% are banked), many have access to a mobile phone and are subscribers of one of the three MNOs. The total number of mobile network subscribers in Zimbabwe at the beginning of 2014 was just under 14 million, according to Potraz, which includes multi-simming by customers.[5] This had grown to more than 19 million by the end of 2015. In addition, Econet's growth in this area is at least partly due to its established position and brand presence in traditional mobile services.

Based on data from Potraz, the largest share of the market among the three players in mobile services (by number of subscribers) (table 9.2) and in MMT service provision is held by Econet (table 9.3).[6] Rivals to Econet gained market share in 2014 and 2015, which may be attributable to their growth in MMT services, among other factors.

As these services grow in popularity in Zimbabwe, banks are looking to broaden their offering to enable their clients to not only use traditional banking services, including mobile banking, but also to execute MMTs to unbanked people directly from their bank accounts. This presents a dynamic growth area in the sector. Banks may also perceive a competitive threat from MNOs providing MMT services, particularly because a proportion of their traditional customers also use MMT services due to their convenience and lower price, for instance. We discuss the interactions between banks and MNOs below.

Table 9.2 Market shares by number of mobile money subscribers, 2012–2015

	2012 (%)	2013 (%)	2014 (%)	2015 (%)
Telecel*			13.3	14.3
NetOne	0.1	0.5	9.9	11.4
Econet	99.9	99.5	76.8	74.3

Source: Potraz quarterly reports

Note: * Telecel discontinued its MMT platform and relaunched it as Telecash in 2014.

Table 9.3 MNO market shares by number of registered subscribers, 2010–2015

	2010 (%)	2011 (%)	2012 (%)	2013 (%)	2014 (%)	2015 (%)
Telecel	18	17	20	19	22	24
NetOne	17	18	16	17	23	28
Econet	65	65	64	64	55	48

Source: Potraz quarterly reports

The provision of MMT services in Zimbabwe

In terms of the supply of MMT services, MNOs have back-office links to the payments system through host banks. In Zimbabwe, it is a requirement of the RBZ that MMT service providers have to partner with a bank which 'hosts' them, at least partly because RBZ is not empowered by the National Payments System Act (No. 21 of 2001) to supervise MNOs.

Following the introduction of NetOne's OneWallet (with FBC Bank) and Telecel's Skwama product (with Kingdom Bank) in January 2011, Econet introduced EcoCash in September of that year. The early growth of OneWallet and Skwama was much slower relative to that of EcoCash. Telecel subsequently withdrew its product, which required users to also be clients of the host bank, on the grounds that partnering with a single bank limited the potential market size for the product as many of its subscribers were also clients of other banks (Kabweza, 2012). Telecel apparently made a strategic decision to connect its mobile platform to more banks by partnering with the ZimSwitch Mobile platform. NetOne has also partnered with ZimSwitch, although Econet has not.

ZimSwitch is a financial switching company which was formed in 1994 through a partnership between six financial institutions to connect nineteen of Zimbabwe's banks.[7] The company processes domestic card-based automated teller machine and point of sale transactions among member financial institutions in real time online. The ZimSwitch Mobile platform enables all financial institutions connected to ZimSwitch to offer mobile banking services through USSD technology (mobile) via the internet, and also integrates with service providers such as utility companies (Kabweza, 2011). The platform enables users to transfer money through ZimSwitch Instant Payment Interchange Technology, which acts as an aggregator that facilitates transactions when customers look to move money to and from their bank accounts for mobile payments.

By connecting via the ZimSwitch platform, MNOs obviate the need to contract with individual banks or service providers in terms of providing mobile financial services (and gaining access to the national payments system) as they did before. The fact that both Telecel and NetOne partnered with the ZimSwitch platform allowed customers of different banks two options in terms of which network to use to access the mobile financial services. In this way, interoperability created benefits for customers, although, as noted, the largest MNO, Econet, has not partnered with ZimSwitch for P2P transactions. In fact, the subject of complaints by various banks in Zimbabwe relates primarily to Econet's initial refusal to partner with ZimSwitch and its insistence that banks should instead integrate with its own EcoCash platform (for which a fee of $0.30 would be levied per transaction) should they want their customers to be able to link their accounts to EcoCash and send money using this method (Kabweza, 2014; Makichi, 2014).

Econet followed a different strategy in implementing its mobile money services. It acquired shareholding in TN Bank in November 2012 in a transaction which was conditionally approved by the competition authority. The condition required Econet to ensure that it continues to avail mobile connectivity to other competing financial institutions. TN Bank later rebranded to Steward Bank in 2013. TN Bank served as Econet's implementing partner or host bank for the growth of its EcoCash platform.

The provision of MMTs has evolved significantly over a short period in Zimbabwe. This dynamic in the sector seems to have a great deal to do with the model followed by the MNOs in delivering this service. For instance, Econet applies what is termed an 'MNO-led' model, which means that the MNO is in control of the full process of facilitating an MMT, including running the mobile network, performing cash-ins or cash-outs, transferring funds and settling (USAID, 2010). This is in contrast to bank-led models wherein MNOs are only involved at the level of providing the primary network infrastructure for facilitating transactions. Importantly, although MNOs still require banks to 'host' them with regard to accessing the payments system, there has been an evolution in the sector in so far as customers are not required to hold an account with a specific bank in order to access these services. Furthermore, the ability of Econet to introduce its own rival platform and not partner with banks initially is likely to have influenced the patterns of growth in the sector by allowing Econet to directly leverage its strength in the mobile services market into the MMT environment.

Econet's ability to control interoperability with and access to its own platform, which is by far the largest, also places it in a position to drive the growth of 'on-network' transactions in the context of significant network externalities (discussed below). Until recently, there were difficulties in the market relating to the ability to send money to recipients on other networks, although Potraz sought to address this. In the first phase, the regulator required operators to ensure the ability to send money to the sim or number of a recipient on another network, and in the second phase transfers will be enabled between mobile wallets. Technical and contractual issues need to be resolved between the operators, including linking of trust accounts, before full implementation can take place.

Competition and regulatory issues in mobile money markets: Literature and theory

Network effects, also referred to as network externalities or demand-side economies of scale, are the effects that one user of a good or service has on the value of that product to other users. In products or industries characterised by network effects, the value of a product or service is dependent on the number of others using it (Shapiro and Varian, 1999). A number of industries exhibit network effects, including telecommunications, where users benefit directly from the size of a network as it dictates the number of others with whom they can communicate (Economides, 2010; Srinivasan, Lilien and Rangaswamy, 2004).

Network effects can be classified into two types: direct (or same side) network effects and indirect (or cross-side) network effects. Direct network effects are present when adoption by different users is complementary, so that each user's adoption payoff and incentive to adopt increases as more people adopt based on horizontal compatibility (Farrell and Klemperer, 2007). In the case of mobile money solutions in Zimbabwe such as Econet's EcoCash, Telecel's Telecash and NetOne's OneWallet, the more that consumers use the mobile money solution on one side of the network the greater the utility the consumers on the same side of the network attain. This is typically through being able to more conveniently and cheaply connect with or send money to users that are on the same network and mobile money platform versus those that are subscribers to different platforms.

Indirect network effects arise if adoption of the product improves opportunities to trade with another side of the market. Markets that exhibit indirect network effects are commonly known as two-sided markets. A two-sided platform refers to products and services that bring together different groups of users in two-sided networks. Indirect network effects imply that customer utility from the primary product increases as more customers or suppliers exist on the other side of the market. For example, in transaction markets the adoption of MasterCard by consumers depends on the number of merchants who accept it for transacting. On the other hand, the merchants can adopt the card on condition that it has many subscribers using it. Similar indirect network effects manifest in the mobile money sector in that the adoption of a particular mobile money system may be dependent on the number of merchants or billers who accept it. Mobile money agents and merchants are more willing to adopt a mobile money system with a higher subscriber base (Anderson, 2009).

Network effects can significantly affect competition among firms by creating a barrier to entry for new firms that may find it difficult to compete with the incumbent's much larger network. When network effects are present, the firm's installed customer base can be considered a key asset to gain supra-competitive returns (Economides, 2010). Network industries are prone to dominance and therefore often associated with the existence of monopolies (Motta, 2004). Due to network effects, a firm with a larger number of users will become increasingly attractive to existing users and this will attract new users. Network effects may thus create winner-takes-all outcomes (Arthur, 1996). Market tipping off may occur, where a dominant firm manages to gain advantage in consumer preference, thus becoming more and more popular and eventually becoming the dominant solution in the market. Network effects can also be deliberately leveraged by a dominant firm wishing to maintain its position in the market and make life difficult for smaller rivals.

What makes mobile money markets particularly prone to high barriers to entry is their close connection to the market for traditional mobile services (voice, sms and data), where network effects are also present. Indeed, one motivation for MNOs' provision of mobile money services is to retain and grow market share in the market for traditional mobile services. In this way, a high market share in the market for traditional MNO services tends to give an MNO an advantage in the roll-out of mobile money services, which can lead to a dominant position in the mobile money market, further strengthening the firm's market position in the original market. This is borne out in practice in a number of markets where large MNOs have achieved dominant positions in developing mobile money markets.

Economists from the Chicago School have argued that a dominant firm has no incentive to leverage its market power into adjacent vertical or horizontal markets. This is explained using the One Monopoly Profit theory, which states that a firm which has a monopoly in one market can extract all the possible rents from its original monopoly position, and will not gain anything from extending that monopoly power into related markets (O'Donoghue and Padilla, 2006). This theory rests on strong assumptions, however, including that the adjacent market is perfectly competitive and the monopolist can credibly commit to charging the monopoly price to all customers.

Post-Chicago economists have since pointed out a number of situations where these assumptions are not met and where, consequently, it is possible for anticompetitive foreclosure to occur. One such case is where a dominant firm is concerned that through allowing entry into a complementary market, it may in future face greater competition in its primary market, through entry or expansion of the competitor into this market (Carlton and Waldman, 2002). Carlton and Waldman's theory relies on entry into the complementary market being costly. However, O'Donoghue and Padilla (2006) note that the incumbent may have an incentive to monopolise the complementary good market even when entry is costless, provided there are network externalities. In fact, both factors are present in the Zimbabwean markets for mobile payments and mobile services, as a substantial upfront investment in infrastructure is required to enter the market and, as discussed above, network effects are substantial.

The defensive leveraging theory is particularly strong in industries with network externalities, as the possibility of market tipping in the complementary product market (e.g., mobile payments) provides a threat to the incumbent monopolist's position in the primary market (e.g., mobile services), because a successful entrant in the complementary product market would then be in a much stronger position to grow in the primary market.[8] To remove the threat to its monopoly position in the primary market, the incumbent then attempts to exclude competitors in the market for the complementary product so as to ensure that its product becomes the dominant standard.

One way that a dominant firm in one side of a network market can do this is to make its products partially or fully incompatible with components produced by other firms. This can be done through actual product incompatibility or explicit exclusion or refusal to interconnect with other firms, particularly competitors. If a firm is dominant in one of the markets it has no incentive to allow full compatibility of its products with those of its competitors. Compatibility is dependent on the intensity of the network effect, that is, the more intense the network effect, the stronger the incentive for a firm to make its products incompatible with substitutes (Economides, 2010). The decision to choose to remain incompatible with the rival ensures that the dominant firm can keep all the network effects it creates to itself. As in the example above, the dominant MNO has higher chances of attracting more subscribers to its mobile network services if it chooses incompatibility on its mobile payment system.

If, on the other hand, there are a range of smaller firms in the market, interoperability is more likely to develop naturally as each player has more to gain and less to lose from 'pooling' the network effects. In this scenario, interoperability should result in a larger overall market as a linked network is more attractive and hence attracts larger demand. Therefore, there are gains to all from interoperability, but if there is one very large player, its losses due to weakening the network effects may outweigh these gains, and hence interoperability is not in its interest.

Mobile money markets are prone to all these features, and in Zimbabwe the market structure is particularly skewed, with one firm, Econet, having very high market shares in both the mobile services and the mobile money markets until recently. This creates concern that barriers to entry and expansion for smaller rivals may be difficult to surmount. In most countries, including Zimbabwe, interconnection in the mobile network services and compatibility at the level of voice and low-capacity data transmission are mandated by law (Nyaga, 2014). However, in most developing countries, mobile money is a relatively new development which is very dynamic and interoperability has not advanced in most markets. Until recently, simple aspects of interoperability, such as the ability of mobile wallets to connect across networks, had not been implemented although regulators have now instituted measures to address this.

Emerging competition and regulatory issues in the Zimbabwean market

How does the theory apply to Zimbabwe?

As the largest MNO in Zimbabwe and by far the largest provider of mobile payments services, Econet is in a very strong position. As noted, markets for traditional mobile telecommunications services and those for mobile payments are strongly interlinked and the provision of mobile payments services can provide a way for MNOs to induce customer loyalty and prevent customer switching. In this case, part of Econet's strategy with regard to EcoCash may be to provide such a ubiquitous service that most consumers want to use EcoCash, thereby locking them in as Econet subscribers. The network effects inherent in both markets will tend to reinforce this, as the more subscribers EcoCash and Econet have, the more attractive they become to customers (and the less attractive competitors become). Econet's annual report describes EcoCash as 'a key value driver, subscriber retention and loyalty product' (Econet, 2014, p. 23). This indicates that part of the value of EcoCash is derived from its ability to help Econet retain subscribers in the mobile services market and to reduce subscriber switching.

If Econet perceives a threat from Telecel and NetOne to its market power in the mobile services market, it may have a further incentive to strengthen EcoCash in order to ensure that subscribers stick with Econet in the market for mobile services.

Furthermore, to the extent that Econet expects a dominant standard to emerge in the mobile payments market, it may have a further incentive to ensure that this is EcoCash, to protect its position in the mobile services market. The banks, on the other hand, present a potential threat to the position of EcoCash, which is important in itself but also because this could reduce the value of EcoCash as a means of retaining and attracting subscribers in the traditional mobile services market. With a 65% share in the MNO market and a share of over 90% in the mobile payments market, Econet has been in a strong position for many years to exploit these network externalities. Subscribers may be reluctant to switch away from Econet to a smaller network, although it does appear that rival operators have increasingly been able to compete with Econet in traditional services as well as in mobile money services through aggressive marketing and pricing in recent years. Telecel's Telecash platform, for example, has grown significantly since its relaunch in 2014, which suggests that the operator has been able to draw in Econet and EcoCash customers, and, importantly, to draw in new demand as the total number of subscribers grows. Multi-simming in the market may also mean that customers are increasingly registering as subscribers of mobile money and mobile telephony services across different networks.

A competition complaint

In 2014, a competition complaint was laid against Econet by the Bankers' Association of Zimbabwe, which submitted a complaint to the Zimbabwe Competition and Tariff Commission (ZCTC) relating to Econet's conduct with regard to its EcoCash platform.[9] The complaint raised a number of concerns. Of particular interest are the concerns relating to the provision of USSD services whereby Econet allowed banks to use the USSD service for the provision of other mobile banking services (balance checks, bill payment, bank account to bank account transactions, etc.) to banked clients, but not for P2P transactions requiring a link between mobile wallets and bank accounts.

Econet initially refused to allow the banks access to its EcoCash platform for P2P transactions, meaning that it was not possible for bank customers using

Econet to draw money from their bank account to send money via EcoCash in a P2P transaction. In February 2014, Econet finally agreed to grant the banks access to the platform. However, this was subject to a number of terms which the banks argued to be unfair. The most important of these was the cost for P2P transactions, which would be charged at a rate of 30c per session compared to 5c or zero for all other mobile banking transactions. This was a key aspect of the complaint. In contrast, Telecel and NetOne charged the banks a much lower amount or zero for using the same USSD facility on their mobile payments platforms. There were also requirements that EcoCash imposed on the banks and their clients in terms of the way that the USSD service was to be used, such as on session times and supplementary codes, which made the service increasingly inconvenient for bank clients.

The ZCTC did not publish a decision on the matter although certain regulatory solutions were sought to resolve the concerns based on cooperation between the ZCTC, RBZ and Potraz.

Interoperability in the Zimbabwean market

Until around 2015 there was no interoperability between EcoCash and the other mobile money platforms in Zimbabwe. EcoCash customers could not send money to the mobile wallet of a NetOne or a Telecel customer, although money could be sent to the mobile number (sim) of a recipient on another network. Similarly, Telecel customers could not send money to an Econet sim or EcoCash wallet. It is therefore significant in terms of the development of the market that value can be sent to recipients across networks, albeit not to their wallets.

A lack of interoperability implied that if customers wanted to be able to be sent money by EcoCash customers, which was highly likely given that EcoCash held 90% of mobile payment subscribers, they had no option but to also be with EcoCash. If they wanted to be able to send money to EcoCash customers, also very likely, they could not be with Telecash. Given the network effects in the industry, this put EcoCash in a very strong position in the market.

Even if EcoCash customers could send money to the other MNO sim cards at the time, customers would still have to cash-out the money at an EcoCash agent. If they then wanted to transfer the money to their Telecash wallet or OneWallet, they would have to go to a Telecash or NetOne agent and pay the money back in. Thus, while this would provide interoperability of a kind, there are transaction costs as it would be inconvenient and costly to customers.

As noted, interoperability is usually beneficial for smaller firms that struggle to combat the market power and network effects enjoyed by larger incumbents. Incumbents may, however, have the incentive to resist interoperability to the extent that it will enable them to preserve their dominance. In a situation where there are a number of firms of similar size, interoperability is more likely to evolve naturally than where there is one dominant firm and other smaller players (Andes, 2012). The Zimbabwean market structure obviously reflects the latter example quite closely, which suggests that there was a need for regulatory intervention to ensure a level playing field for smaller mobile money providers. In this regard, the question for policy makers is how best to balance the need to promote competition against the need to preserve the incentives to invest.

While Telecel's fast growth in terms of subscriber numbers suggests that entry into the mobile payments market is possible without interoperability, its relative size is much smaller than Econet's and its growth may be constrained in future as the market growth slows. To avoid this, the operator would need to develop strategies to entice customers away from Econet – unless there was full interoperability in the market. This suggests that it is indeed difficult to grow in the market without interoperability.

On the other hand, there is an argument that multi-homing or multi-simming is common in Zimbabwe and that this effectively means that interoperability is not important as customers can simply switch between sims to send money to customers of different mobile money platforms. We do not have data on the prevalence of multi-homing in this market so it is hard to test this. We note, however, that even to the extent that customers have more than one sim, there is still inconvenience and cost attached to having to register for more than one platform and transfer balances into and out of each wallet.

The lack of interoperability may be restricting the growth of this new market. As discussed above, there is substantial latent demand for mobile financial services in Zimbabwe. To the extent that the lack of interoperability limits competition, it will lead to higher prices and less innovative products for consumers, which will in turn limit uptake.

Contrast with other countries in the region

In order to understand why the Zimbabwean mobile money market has evolved as it has, we present a comparison with other countries in the region. What is striking is that the markets in all countries are highly concentrated and, in all countries except Rwanda and Tanzania, the leading firm has more than 50% market share (figure 9.1).

The Kenyan market is particularly concentrated, with the leading firm, Safaricom, having a market share of 80%. Zimbabwe also has a highly concentrated market, with Econet enjoying a 75% market share. In Zambia there is a duopoly: MTN with a 59% market share and Airtel with 41%. In Uganda, MTN is also the largest player with 58% of the market, but there are three additional competitors, one of whom (Airtel) has a 27% market share. The most competitive markets appear to be Rwanda and Tanzania, where there are three and four significant players, respectively: Vodacom (38%), Tigo (33%), Airtel (27%) and Zantel (2%) in Tanzania, and MTN (49%), Tigo (35%) and Airtel (16%) in Rwanda. These market shares translate into high HHI[10] figures in all six countries, again with the HHI figures for Kenya being the highest at 6 486 (table 9.5).

In a market with network effects, one would expect that where there is one very large player, interoperability is unlikely to develop naturally. In the case of the six countries considered here, only one has implemented interoperability. In Tanzania, interoperability developed as an industry-led process. In 2014, Airtel, Tigo and Zantel agreed to allow their platforms to interoperate. Subsequently, the industry worked on a set of standards governing P2P payments across the

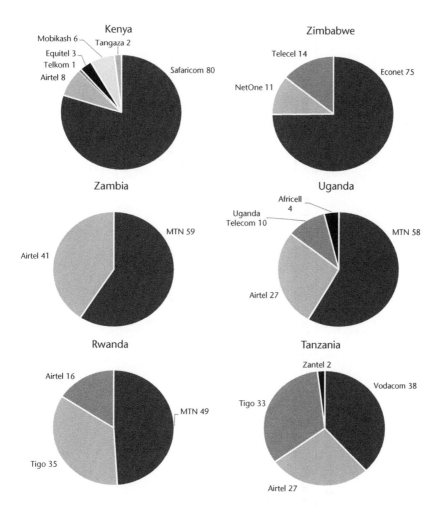

Figure 9.1 Mobile money market shares in Uganda, Zimbabwe, Kenya, Zambia, Tanzania and Rwanda (%)

Source: Various online sources including telecommunications and financial regulators of the various countries, company websites and publicly available data

Notes: All market shares are measured by mobile money subscriber numbers. It is assumed that the figures reflect the total number of registered subscribers and not those that are active. The number of active subscribers is not typically reported on by various authorities and operators. The data used are from 2015, except for Zambia, which is 2014.

various networks, and finally, in 2016, it appeared that all four operators, including Vodacom, would implement interoperability between their systems. It is unsurprising that this development arose in Tanzania, since it has one of the least concentrated markets of the countries in the sample and has three significant players in the mobile money market.

As shown in table 9.4, Tanzania also has the least concentrated market for traditional mobile services (measured in terms of subscriber numbers). By contrast,

Table 9.4 MNO market shares by mobile network subscribers, 2015

Kenya (%)		Zimbabwe (%)		Uganda (%)		Zambia (%)		Rwanda (%)		Tanzania (%)	
Safaricom	67	Econet	54	MTN	51	MTN	51	MTN	47	Vodacom	35
Airtel	19	Telecel	15	Airtel	37	Airtel	34	Tigo	35	Airtel	30
Telkom	11	NetOne	31	Uganda Telecom	10	Zantel	15	Airtel	18	Tigo	30
Equitel	2			Africell	3					Zantel	4
										TTCL	1

Sources: Various online sources including telecommunications regulators of the various countries, company websites and publicly available data

Note: Shares do not always add up to 100% due to rounding.

Kenya and Zimbabwe both have one firm with a much higher market share than the others in the MNO market as well as the mobile money market. In both cases, the dominant player in the MNO market has been able to establish a similarly strong position in the mobile payments market. As discussed, the large incumbent firm may have the ability and incentive to protect its position in the MNO market through maintaining its dominance in mobile payments, particularly if it feels threatened by growing competitors in the MNO market. This presents it with an incentive to resist interoperability.

Another way that firms can enhance rather than reduce the network effects in mobile payments is to charge a higher price for transfers to unregistered recipients than to registered recipients. This means that to send money to another customer of the same mobile money platform is cheaper than to send money to someone who is not a customer and may be a customer of a competing platform. Thus customers can send money more cheaply to customers of the same network, creating incentives for subscribers to stick with the platform with the most users. This is similar to the effect of high interconnection charges between MNOs in the market for traditional mobile services.

In order to see how different market structures influence the rates charged to send money to unregistered recipients, we calculated the average price to send $20 to registered and unregistered recipients in the six countries, for the largest player in each country. We then calculated the percentage difference between what is charged for transfers to registered and unregistered recipients. As shown in table 9.5, there is a substantial difference in cost in all countries, with the exception of Tanzania. Transfers to unregistered recipients in Zimbabwe and Kenya are 29% and 83% more expensive, respectively, than transfers to registered recipients. Tanzanian transfers to unregistered recipients are the same price as to registered recipients. This reflects the difference in market dynamics in the two countries, where there is an incentive for Econet, the largest player in Zimbabwe, to try to make other networks seem unattractive.

Table 9.5 Features of mobile money markets in six countries

	Kenya	Zimbabwe	Zambia	Uganda	Rwanda	Tanzania
Number of players	6	3	2	4	3	4
Market share of largest firm (%)	80	75	59	58	49	38
Industry HHI	6 486	5 918	5 170	4 275	3 882	3 266
Interoperability	No	No	No	No	No	Yes
% difference between registered and unregistered (largest player)	83	29	88	32	25	0

Sources: Market shares and HHI (see figure 9.1); price differential, websites of MMT providers listed in figure 9.1

The brief country comparison set out above has illustrated that other countries face similar challenges to those faced by Zimbabwe in regulating the fast-growing mobile payments market. Where there is asymmetry already in the MNO market in terms of one player that is much larger than the rest, this seems to lend itself to an even more unbalanced market for mobile payments, where the network effects in both markets are mutually reinforcing. Zimbabwe, however, appears to be an extreme case. At the other extreme, Tanzania, where the MNOs have more even shares of the market, seems to be developing a more competitive mobile payments market and even moving naturally towards interoperability between the different mobile payments platforms. This suggests that in the more asymmetric markets such as Zimbabwe and Kenya, attention needs to be given to possible regulatory solutions that will prevent the dominance of the main player becoming entrenched and difficult to undermine. In these cases, the pressure for interoperability may need to come from the regulator rather than the market.

Conclusion and possible policy implications for Zimbabwe

The growth of MMTs in Zimbabwe is directly linked to developmental objectives in terms of increasing the access of all individuals in the society to a safe, secure and affordable means of transacting. This is consistent with the increased emphasis globally on inclusive economic growth which speaks largely to participation and the ability of people to play a part in the process of growth as well as sharing in its benefits. However, the benefits derived from MMTs to poor customers in particular can be eroded over time where MNOs in dominant positions can leverage that dominance to make it difficult for rival operators to compete. This can take place through various mechanisms, including defensive leveraging, which is enhanced where there are market tipping and network effects, where the product of the incumbent firm becomes the dominant standard, and when it can use its pricing and strategies in both sides of a market to protect its position.

In this regard, the Zimbabwean market is particularly interesting when considering the strong position of Econet in the primary market for traditional mobile telecommunications services, as well as its strong position in the adjacent market for MMTs. The comparisons above of EcoCash with the platforms of other providers in the region suggest that as in Kenya, the incumbent firm is able to leverage its strong position in the market to charge prices (to unregistered users, for instance) that enhance the network benefits of customers switching to its platform. Furthermore, through limited interoperability with rival MNO platforms, customers face an incentive to join the MMT platform, which they perceive to have the largest subscriber base, thus requiring the customer to purchase the sim of that network as well. In contrast, the market in Tanzania has tended towards interoperability to the benefit of consumers, as reflected in the pricing comparisons.

This scenario presents some interesting challenges for regulation. In most cases, competition law enforcement cannot, on its own, mandate interoperability between providers of mobile services generally. Additionally, competition law cases tend to be drawn out and litigious, which is a resource-intensive process. Instead, there may be a direct role for other regulatory agencies in changing the set of rules in the market to encourage greater rivalry, including through interoperability. This is through the ability of sector regulators to facilitate and stipulate arrangements between players that support smaller operators while also encouraging and rewarding investment by large incumbents. One example of this is the use of asymmetric call termination rates in the South African telecommunications sector (see Paelo, 2015).

In a 2014 effort to increase competition and facilitate the growth of smaller operators in the market, given the strong position of South Africa's major operators Vodacom and MTN, the Independent Communications Authority of South Africa (Icasa) introduced lower, asymmetric call termination rates. These asymmetric rates allowed the smaller operators to charge their larger competitors a higher price for termination while the small operators pay a lesser fee. Despite the mobile operators' concerns about Icasa's intervention in setting asymmetric call termination rates, the regulation does not appear to have had a damaging effect on the market. Instead, consumers have benefited from the lower rates, while subscriber numbers and operator profitability have also increased.

In Zimbabwe, recent developments suggest that a regulatory solution is being pursued, correctly in our view, to address some of the concerns raised in the complaint discussed above. The ZCTC has recently been able to facilitate interactions between the RBZ and the sector regulator for telecommunications, Potraz, in addressing competition concerns regarding pricing and access in MMT services (see *The Herald*, 2015). The ZCTC identified potential competition concerns as well as issues that could best be resolved by sector regulators. RBZ and Potraz have been responsive to this approach and regulatory solutions have been arrived at in an expedient manner, suggesting that regulatory coordination is important for dealing with restrictions on participation and competition where there are likely to also be significant efficiency gains to consumers through the strategies and investment of large incumbents. This approach is important in the discussion about interoperability, where the authorities need to balance sanctions for abuses of a dominant position in a market against the pro-competitive benefits of firm strategies. For instance, regulators need to consider the right of firms to benefit from their investments in infrastructure and technology, which tend to be substantial in telecommunications markets. If the authority wishes to encourage greater interoperability, for instance, then terms need to be reached that still reward the innovation and investment of the incumbent firms, such as Econet. This may involve some form of compensation being paid by rival operators to the dominant player.

Further to this, where there are network effects, consumers do benefit from lower fees, for instance, for transacting over the same network as the person they are sending money to. This is an important efficiency which accrues to customers that would need to be weighed against the likely medium- and long-term effects of reduced rivalry in the sector. Other things being equal, regulating for a fairer and more competitive environment in the short term is more likely to result in sustainable efficiencies, innovation, variety and favourable prices in the future.

Notes

1   Mobile wallets are broadly defined as digital or virtual applications that allow mobile device users to store money and credit on their phones (see Andes, 2012).

2   Throughout this chapter, we refer to mobile payments, P2P or mobile money transfer (MMT) services interchangeably.

3   The latter takes place through person-to-business payments, business-to-business payments or government-to-person payments made via mobile phone, although these are not the focus of the chapter.

4   See National Payment Systems Directive: NPS 01/2014.

5   Where customers use sim cards from more than one MNO.

6   Potraz cautioned that the estimates are based on the submissions of the operators themselves and Potraz currently does not have a mechanism for validating these estimates. See information from Econet's website stating that the firm holds over 65.3% of the mobile telecommunications market (http://ewzinvestor.co.zw/).

7   See http://www.zimswitch.co.zw/.

8   Econet's loss of market share in recent years may be related to these effects.

9   This section is based on information from Kabweza (2014) and Makichi (2014).

10   The Herfindahl-Hirschman Index (HHI) is a commonly accepted measure of market concentration (http://www.investopedia.com/terms/h/hhi.asp).

References

Anderson J. 2009. *M-Banking in Developing Markets: Regulatory Implications of Two-Sided Networks*. Tias Nimbas Business School Working Paper, University of Tilburg.

Andes S. 2012. Making the market: How interoperability and tipping points can influence network size. *The Heinz Journal* 9, http://journal.heinz.cmu.edu/wp-content/uploads/2012/05/Final-Making-the-Market.pdf.

Arthur WB. 1996. Increasing returns and the new world of business. *Harvard Business Review* 74: 100–108.

Carlton W and M Waldman. 2002. The strategic use of tying to preserve and create market power in evolving industries. *RAND Journal of Economics* 33: 194–220.

Dermish A, B Hundermark and C Sanford. 2012. 'Mapping the Retail Payment Services Landscape: Zimbabwe'. FinMark Trust (online document).

EcoCash. n.d. 'How to Transact' (online document).

Econet. 2014. 'Econet Wireless FY2014 Financial Results Presentation', 5 May (online document).

Economides N. 2010. Antitrust issues in network industries. In I Kokkoris and I Lianos (eds), *The Reform of EC Competition Law: New Challenges*, pp. 343–376. Alphen aan den Rijn: Kluwer.

Farrell J and P Klemperer. 2007. Coordination and lock-in: Competition with switching costs and network effects. In M Armstrong and R Porter (eds), *Handbook of Industrial Organization* (Vol. 3), pp. 1967–2072. Amsterdam: North Holland.

ITU (International Telecommunication Union). 2011. *The Regulatory Landscape for Mobile Banking*. GSR2011 Discussion Paper. https://www.itu.int/ITU-D/treg/Events/Seminars/GSR/GSR11/documents/04-M-Banking-E.pdf.

Kabweza LSM. 2011. '12 Banks implementing ZimSwitch Mobile. Platform to be mobile network neutral', *TechZim*, 20 October.

Kabweza LSM. 2012. 'Telecel reveals they killed off the Skwama mobile money service', *TechZim*, 24 September.

Kabweza LSM. 2014. 'Econet investigated for anti-competitive behaviour in mobile money business', *TechZim*, 13 June.

Klein M and C Mayer. 2011. *Mobile Banking and Financial Inclusion: The Regulatory Lessons*. World Bank Policy Research Working Paper No. 5664.

Makichi, T. 2014. 'CTC goes after Econet', *The Herald*, 13 June.

Motta M. 2004. *Competition Policy: Theory and Practice*. New York: Cambridge University Press.

Nyaga JK. 2014. Mobile banking services in the East African Community (EAC): Challenges to the existing legislative and regulatory frameworks. *Journal of Information Policy* 4: 270–295.

O'Donoghue R and J Padilla. 2006. *The Law and Economics of Article 82 EC*. Oxford: Hart Publishing.

Paelo A. 2015. 'Leveling the Playing Field: Asymmetry in Call Termination Rates in SA'. Centre for Competition, Regulation and Economic Development, Quarterly Review (online document).

Shapiro C and HR Varian. 1999. *Information Rules: A Strategic Guide to the Network Economy*. Boston, MA: Harvard Business School Press.

Srinivasan R, GL Lilien and A Rangaswamy. 2004. First in, first out? The effects of network externalities on pioneer survival. *Journal of Marketing* 68: 41–58.

The Herald. 2015. 'Zimbabwe: CTC meets RBZ, Potraz over Econet inquiry', 10 February, http://allafrica.com/stories/201502100528.html.

USAID. 2010. 'FS Series #9: Enabling Mobile Money Interventions: Primer, Diagnostic Checklist, and Model Scopes of Work'. Prepared by Chemonics International Inc. for the United States Agency for International Development (USAID) Financial Sector Knowledge Sharing Project (online document).

10 Evaluating the competitiveness of Zimbabwe's poultry industry

Tatenda Zengeni

Introduction

This chapter analyses the competitiveness and performance of the Zimbabwean poultry industry in the context of trade liberalisation, given that both poultry output and the main inputs (animal feed and breeding stock) are tradeable. Poultry is an important product in Zimbabwe as the main source of protein for consumers. It also has strong links to agriculture through the production of animal feed. The Food and Agriculture Organisation (FAO, 2010) notes the rapid growth of the poultry sector globally over the last decade. Despite the rise in chicken demand over the years as a cheap source of protein, the poultry industry in Zimbabwe still faces a number of challenges, which the government claims include stiff competition from cheap imports, rising input costs of maize and soya meal and illegal imports being sold at subeconomic prices (Government of Zimbabwe, 2012). This chapter evaluates these factors and the impact of changing trade protection.

Performance of the poultry industry has been affected by trade liberalisation, which started in 1991 following the adoption of the Economic Structural Adjustment Programme (ESAP), in line with most developing countries, as part of the Washington Consensus policies (Tekere, 2001). However, Zimbabwe maintained a trade surplus in poultry until a deficit started in 2008, due to increasing chicken imports over the previous decade, which reached a peak of US$29 million in 2009. Understanding the reasons for this performance requires evaluating the factors affecting both inputs and outputs, of which protection is one. The concept of effective rate of protection (ERP) is used to assess the impact of changing tariffs. Non-tariff barriers and agricultural policies are also considered, such as the ban on imports of genetically modified (GM) maize, and the ban on poultry imports from South Africa from March 2010 until December 2011 due to an outbreak of Rift Valley fever (RVF). The impact of growth in regional sources of maize (from Zambia) is also taken into account, given the lower transport costs from Zambia. In the 2013 budget statement, the government intervened to protect the poultry industry once again and increased tariffs on chicken to the current rate of 40% or $1.50/kg (Government of Zimbabwe, 2012).

According to the available trade data from 2000–2014, the Zimbabwean poultry industry did not face significant competition from imports prior to 2008. Despite formally adopting trade liberalisation in 1991, Zimbabwe continued to protect its poultry industry. Tariffs were suspended in 2009 due to the macroeconomic crisis and to boost access to food given the collapse in local production. Local production in 2008 fell more than 50% from the previous year. Tariffs were then reinstated in 2012. There are also restrictions to protect the industry, such as import licences and sanitary and phytosanitary measures. The competitiveness of the poultry industry is closely related to the prices and availability of animal feeds, principally maize and soya, and day-old chicks.

Since 2008, the poultry industry has been suffering from stiff competition from chicken imports, which have become a threat to its survival under trade liberalisation. The poor performance under the reduced ERP is obviously due to lack of competitiveness in the face of foreign suppliers. However, it is important to assess the possible underlying causes. Poor competitiveness is partly due to high feed costs, as this is the single largest input, followed by day-old chicks. There are several reasons for high feed costs, including weak agricultural production, resulting in reliance on imports; the costs of sourcing imports; and the ban on GM maize being grown locally. For instance, in 2014 a tonne of maize cost US$364 in Zimbabwe but sold for US$196 in South Africa. Other reasons include low competition at the levels of suppliers of feed and day-old chicks, and in poultry production itself. In light of this background, the present chapter seeks to answer the following question: What is the effect of trade liberalisation on the poultry industry, in the context of a concentrated market structure and factors affecting the price of animal feed, including bans on GM maize?

In the remainder of the chapter, I review theories of trade performance, in particular the Heckscher-Ohlin and value chain theories, before giving a detailed background to the poultry industry in Zimbabwe. I then estimate the ERP, analyse the degree of concentration in the sector, review the industry cost structure and analyse the ban on GM maize.

Theoretical framework

This section first briefly considers the orthodox trade framework based on the Heckscher-Ohlin factor endowments. The implications for the study of the competitiveness of the poultry industry are then considered, given its vertical integration with linked investments required at different levels, and the relatively concentrated nature of the industry. The value chain framework is then reviewed, as it provides a basis for assessing the interrelationship of factors at different levels of processing, along with questions of coordination and governance of the overall value chain and the competitiveness of the end product.

Heckscher-Ohlin theory

The Heckscher-Ohlin theory of comparative advantage, based on factor endowments, is at the core of neoclassical trade theory. This theory is a refinement of

David Ricardo's comparative advantage theory (Todaro and Smith, 2007) and explains patterns of trade between countries in terms of their relative endowments of the two factors of production – labour and capital (Sodersten and Reed, 1994). Following this theory, countries that are rich in capital will produce and export capital-intensive goods, while those richly endowed with labour will concentrate on producing labour-intensive goods. There are substantial gains from global trade as trade allows specialisation in products that are intensive in the country's abundant factor.

However, the theory is based on a number of assumptions, key ones being that there are two factors of production, no transport costs, perfect competition and a homogeneous production function. In this theory, production functions are such that the two commodities produced show different factor intensities, and production functions are different between commodities but the same for both countries (Sodersten and Reed, 1994). While these assumptions enable the theory to work, they are subject to criticism due to the limitations they impose and the lack of realism around assumptions like the existence of perfect competition and of the same production functions in both countries.

According to Todaro and Smith (2007), this theory enables analytical description of the impact of economic growth and trade on trade patterns and on the structure of national economies. Two main conclusions arise from this theory. First, the theory promotes free trade with all countries, as a result of which individual countries gain and world output increases. Second, under free trade, price ratios tend to equalise factor prices across trading countries. Put another way, the theory suggests that prices of factors of production will be the same as countries engage in free trade. Under this theory, any trade protection reduces welfare as it introduces a distortion – meaning that consumers pay more for imports, which affects the exchange rate and reduces trade (and the benefits from exchange and specialisation).

Review of literature on effective rate of protection

The ERP measures the protection provided to domestic value added relative to value added in international (or 'border') prices (Greenaway and Milner, 1993). Its calculation depends not only on the tariff on the final product but also on the input tariff and input coefficient (Corden, 1966). It is widely used as a measure of understanding how nominal tariff rates affect a country's pattern of production (Holden and Holden, 1975). Various studies (Edwards, 2006; Flatters, 2005; Holden, 2001; Holden and Holden, 1975) analysing tariffs show that the ERP is a useful tool for assessing the magnitude of protection. They conclude that effective rates of protection are useful when the structure of tariffs is undergoing change. The measure also shows how the industry's output has been protected against its inputs into the production process.

The ERP is a function of three variables: the nominal rate of protection on the final good, the nominal tariff on imported inputs and the share of imported inputs in the final value of the product (Greenaway and Milner, 1983). It can be concluded that, first, if the nominal tariff on final goods is raised, assuming that all other things remain constant, then that raises the ERP. Secondly, *ceteris paribus*, an increase in the nominal tariff of an imported input will reduce the value added and therefore the ERP. Last, again holding all other things constant, a higher share or an increase in the share of imported inputs will raise the ERP. Greenaway and Milner (1983) also highlight the possibility of a negative ERP. This situation arises when the tariff-distorted value added is less than value added under free trade, a case in which producers will be penalised by tariff intervention by governments. They argue that this situation generally happens in developing countries and arises mainly on exportable goods, which are normally not protected but that rely on imported inputs, which attract duty mainly for revenue purposes. The combined effect of zero duty on final goods and duties on inputs results in a negative ERP.

The concept of ERP is better than nominal rate of protection as it allows analysis of the net protection conferred to a production process rather than to an industry's output (Greenaway and Milner, 1993), and directs attention to the full range of interventions affecting a given production process. These interventions also include the prices of non-tradeable inputs like electricity cost, subsidies that can be offered to the industry by governments and exchange rates in the calculation of ERP to give a more realistic picture of the overall protection accorded to the industry. Of note is that high effective rates of protection tilt resource allocation in favour of that sector against other sectors. The ERP analysis can be a useful input into the process of policy appraisal in both evaluating past policies and assessing the possible impact of policy changes.

The treatment of non-tradeable inputs in calculating the ERP has been analysed in the literature, with two main authors coming up with different proposals. Balassa (1965) argues that the best way to treat non-tradeable inputs is to assume that their price is insensitive to protection. This implies treating non-tradeable inputs as if they are traded inputs, but applying zero tariffs (alternatively, with the imputed effect of other distortions estimated). Corden (1966) proposes that the value added in non-tradeable inputs can be aggregated with all other value added. There has not been a generally agreed way of dealing with non-tradeable inputs in calculating the ERP. As such, different authors use either of these two methods.

In a world where transport costs are significant, where there are vertically related levels of production with investment decisions at each level and where there is imperfect competition, the Heckscher-Ohlin theory is at best too simplified to explore the factors affecting industry performance and the impact of different shocks and distortions.

Value chain theory

The value chain is defined as the full range of activities that firms and workers perform to bring a product from its conception to final use (Gereffi and Fernandez-Stark, 2011). It therefore involves understanding all the different stages of manufacturing, including intermediary phases which a product goes through until it becomes a final product ready for consumption.

The value chain approach to analysis allows one to understand how an industry is organised by examining the structure and dynamics of different actors involved in that industry (Gereffi and Fernandez-Stark, 2011). Its methodology is mainly based on investigating in an industrial context the connections and linkages within the industry. Theoretically, it raises questions of governance and power, which are significant to the operation of an industry or a sector. Three basic components of value chains are important in recognising the concept of a value chain as an analytical tool: value chains are repositories for rent, effectively functioning value chains involve some degree of governance and effective value chains arise from systematic as opposed to point efficiency (Kaplinsky, 1998).

In terms of governance, the value chain framework of analysis argues that there are key actors in the chain. Gereffi, Humphrey, Kaplinsky and Sturgeon (2001) define governance as the non-market coordination of economic activity within the chain through the influence of lead firms along the production chain. For instance, through governance structures, firms can take decisions that may directly or indirectly influence the whole production process. Gereffi et al. (2001) identify four main features of governance in the value chain analytical frame-work. First is the idea that within value chains coordination can take different forms, which can be explained as inter-firm networks. In this case, relationships exist among different firms along the chain. There can also be quasi-hierarchical relationships between powerful lead firms and independent but subordinate firms in the chain; this might be a situation where lead firms control an import-ant raw material or intermediate product. Governance can also take the form of vertical integration within firms. Some firms can decide to invest along the chain and have enterprises that support one another.

The second feature of governance largely shows how the lead firms assume control in the chain. Basically, how lead firms derive their power within the value chain stems from two traits: market power, which is measured in terms of market share, and the degree of concentration. The other crucial aspect is the positioning of such firms in the value chain, which enables them to create and appropriate high returns. Kaplinsky (1998) argues that these two sources of power stem from the barriers to entry that are in force in that particular chain.

The third characteristic of governance arises due to the need for coordination within the chain. First is the coordination that arises as more companies are involved in specifying the products that their suppliers have to make. The more involvement, the more they are likely to create governance structures to coor-dinate supplier activities (Gereffi et al., 2001). The other component concerns how these companies are exposed to risks as a result of supplier failures. The more that firms are exposed to supplier failure, the more they will intervene to coordinate and monitor the supply chain.

Last, governance involves the ability of one firm to influence the activities of other firms in the chain. This position is attained through lead firms defining the products to be produced by suppliers and specifying processes and standards used in the production process. Gereffi et al. (2001) further argue that chains also vary with respect to how strongly governance is exercised, that is, how governance is concentrated in the hands of one firm and the number of lead firms that exercise governance over other chain members. This brings in another aspect of importance in the governance of a value chain – power asymmetry. The form of governance in the chain changes as an industry evolves and matures and governance patterns also vary from one stage to another within the same chain (Dolan and Humphrey, 2004).

In terms of barriers to entry and rent in the value chain, Kaplinsky (2000) argues that economic rent emanates from a situation of differential productivity of factors and barriers to entry, which basically reflects scarcity. Economic rent is mostly dynamic and can be eroded by the forces of competition. In the case of producer rent, it is transferred into consumer surplus through the process of competition. Competition allows for innovation and new ways of organising production. As competition increases within the chain, it may lead to improved efficiency and a reduction in barriers to entry and economic rent.

The final analytical element of the value chain framework is the systemic efficiency that is inherent in analysing a sector as one chooses such an approach. It moves the focus of attention from a point to the whole system, enabling understanding of the different stages that a product has to pass through and the weaknesses associated with each stage. This affords analysts and policy makers an opportunity to reflect on possible policy interventions and to identify the particular stage to target. Such an approach results in appropriate decisions being made, ensuring the long-run success of the whole sector.

Background to Zimbabwe's poultry industry

Zimbabwean poultry industry production relies on both indigenous and imported poultry strains for breeding stock (Faranisi, 1995). As in many developing countries, chicken production in Zimbabwe comprises both large- and small-scale producers (Mapiye et al., 2008). Commercial breeding of poultry is based on imported strains, while the indigenous strains are for small-scale producers, largely in rural areas. Large-scale production is characterised by intensive management, mechanisation and specialisation and dominated by large companies, while small-scale production includes semi-intensive and extensive farming. This section starts by mapping the poultry industry through a value chain analysis before looking at the trade balance of the industry by analysing industry exports and imports. Industry production levels are then analysed, as well as the prices of chicken.

Market structure

The structure of the Zimbabwean poultry industry has evolved substantially over the years, especially after the country's economic recession. The harsh macroeconomic environment between 1999 and 2008 saw traditional chicken-producing firms (Irvine's[1] and Suncrest) nearly collapsing and led to increased vertical integration within the value chain as a means of survival. At the same time, however, new companies entered the sector: Drummonds in 2004, Lunar Chickens in 2007, and Surey Huku, among many other small-scale players.

Broiler production in Zimbabwe is broadly undertaken in four categories: large-scale, fully integrated operations; large-scale, semi-integrated; medium and small-scale (Sukume, 2011). There are two main large-scale producers of chicken – Irvine's and Ostrindo – since the closing down of Suncrest and Lunar Chickens in 2013 and 2015, respectively. Irvine's and Ostrindo are based in

Harare and Bulawayo, respectively. These companies have scale economies associated with their size. The companies are also highly integrated in the poultry value chain. This gives them advantages over medium- and small-scale producers, and ensures the availability of feed and day-old chicks, most likely at lower prices. Irvine's imports breeding stock from Britain and Ostrindo gets its parent stock from Irvine's and Hubbard, since they are the only importers of breeding stock in Zimbabwe. The large-scale, semi-integrated class includes Drummonds Chicken, Soloza Chicken and Hukuru, among others. These companies are semi-integrated in the value chain, do not own breeding operations and sometimes operate small feed mills and slaughter facilities (Sukume, 2011).

The medium-scale producer class produces a cycle[2] of 2 000+ broilers. They are operated by individuals, some of whom are contracted by the large-scale producers. They source their inputs from the open market, including the large-scale producers for day-old chicks. Small-scale producers produce between 50 and 1 500 broilers and also source their raw materials from the open market. Small-scale producers have become increasingly important and are estimated to contribute two-thirds of total production (Ncube, Roberts and Zengeni, 2016).

Poultry value chain

A value chain approach assesses the linkages that exist in an industry. A value chain simply describes the full range of activities required to bring a product or service through the different phases of production, including physical transformation and inputs from various producer services (Kaplinsky and Morris, 2002). Stockfeed manufacturers lie at the heart of poultry production. Poultry feed is a key raw material in production and feed stock is produced in relation to the different stages that chickens pass through, from day old to six weeks. The subsector produces three main types of feed: starter, finisher mash and broiler concentrate. The raw material for stockfeed manufacturing is mainly maize and soya (the composition of these in the feed is discussed later). Nationally, stockfeed manufacturers' interests are represented by the Stock Feed Manufacturers' Association and the poultry industry's interests are represented by the Zimbabwe Poultry Association.

Second in the value chain are the grandparent – the pure lines of day-old chicks – importers (Faranisi, 1995). There are two grandparent importers in Zimbabwe, Irvine's and Hubbard. Hubbard, which is part of the Crest Poultry group, imports the Hubbard breed from France. Irvine's imports the Cobb 500 breed from the UK. Grandparents are used to produce parent stock. The parent stock is used to hatch eggs that produce day-old chicks, which are then sold to poultry breeders. Irvine's and Hubbard are still the main producers at this stage but there are also some small hatcheries, such as Super Chicks and Hukuru, that import fertilised eggs to produce their own day-old chicks. Currently, Zimbabwe has nine[3] registered hatcheries which produce day-old chicks that are distributed evenly around the country. Some of the hatcheries import parent stock from South Africa.

Contract farming arrangements exist in which day-old chick producers provide small producers with chicks, feed and chemicals. The small producers rear the chickens and sell them back to the producers in return for a financial benefit.

After rearing, the chickens are taken to abattoirs where they are slaughtered and dressed (processed) in preparation for selling to wholesalers, supermarkets and fast-food outlets. All the day-old producers mentioned have abattoirs for slaughtering chickens. Figure 10.1 maps the poultry industry value chain.

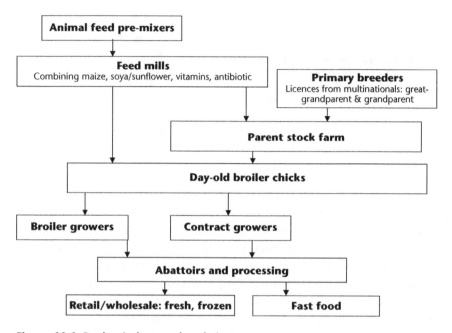

Figure 10.1 Poultry industry value chain

Source: Bagopi et al. (2013)

Of note is that grandparents are imported from Europe. As a major raw material, it is important to analyse the tariffs being levelled for all imports (discussed later). I turn now to the trade balance of the poultry sector.

Trade flows

As noted, Zimbabwe has opened its economy to international trade. It is therefore important to analyse the trade performance of the sector. Zimbabwe is engaged in both bilateral and multilateral trade agreements with its trading partners. Zimbabwe is a member of the Common Market for Eastern and Southern Africa (Comesa) and the Southern African Development Community (SADC) free trade areas. In addition, it is currently negotiating under the tripartite trade agreement between the SADC, Comesa and the East African Community to form a free trade area. The effect of these trade agreements has been to reduce trade barriers, especially tariffs, which impacts on trade flows. Figure 10.2 shows chicken[4] imports for the sector.

As figure 10.2 indicates, between 2000 and 2007 the sector faced hardly any competition from imports. However, there was a sharp increase in imports in 2008. This was due to hyperinflation in Zimbabwe, which affected local

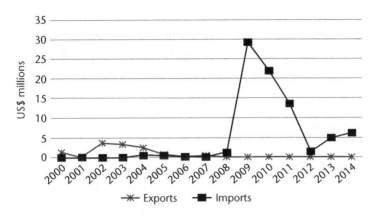

Figure 10.2 Trade balance: Imports and exports, 2000–2014

Sources: Zimstats (2013a) trade data from 2000–2012;
Trade Map data from 2013/2014

production, as well as the launch of the SADC free trade area. Government inter-
vened in 2009 as a result of food shortages and waived duties on all basic goods
as a measure to combat the shortages facing the country. There was thus an economic shock in terms of the macroeconomy and falling agricultural production,
and then a reduction in protection as the government temporarily removed all
duties. In March 2010, the government imposed a ban on chicken imports from
South Africa after an outbreak of RVF. This saw overall imports reduce somewhat.
It also resulted in increased production from local players as they sought to meet
the demand which had been covered by imports. In 2012, the government
reinstated the duties on all South African chicken imports, which continued
to decline. In 2012 they stood at US$1.4 million, and government intervened
further by increasing customs tariffs for all chicken imported from outside the
SADC region from 40% to $1.50/kg or 40%, whichever was higher (Government
of Zimbabwe, 2012). Imports started growing again between 2012 and 2014. A
large component of these imports was frozen cuts and chicken offal, under tariff
line 0207.4000.

Chicken production

This section looks at the industry's performance in relation to production levels.
Figure 10.3 shows dressed broiler production from 2007 to 2015. Chicken production plummeted to a record low of 4 296 metric tonnes in 2008. This was the
period of hyperinflation and the general macroeconomic environment was not
conducive to business due to the political crisis. Imports also increased during
this period.

From 2009 there was a steady increase in production until 2014. During
that time, and especially beginning in 2010, there was strong lobbying by the
Zimbabwe Poultry Association for government to provide protection to the local
industry. In March 2010 a ban was imposed on all chicken from South Africa.
Local production increased during that period (2010–2011) to fill the import gap
and to meet local demand.

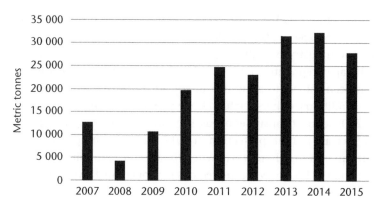

Figure 10.3 Chicken production, 2007–2015

Sources: ZPA (2012, 2015); LMAC (2014)

Note: 2015 data are up to September of that year.

Chicken prices

The chicken market in Zimbabwe, as with all other products, operated under an open market from 2009 to 2011 due to the suspension of duties as a result of shortages. During that period chicken prices were set by imports owing to import penetration. However, since duties were reinstated in 2012 and further increases were implemented in 2013, prices have been largely determined by local supply. Changes in the prices give insight into how price-competitive the sector was in the years in which it experienced high import volumes. This was especially the case in 2008, when local production nearly collapsed. Prices increased in 2012, consistent with higher levels of protection and a sharp decline in imports.

As figure 10.4 shows, prices generally increased marginally after the introduction of the multicurrency in 2009. They fell slightly from US$5.13 in 2009 to US$4.94 in 2010, but monthly price data show that prices in 2010 started increasing from March. This was a result of the ban on imports from South Africa after the RVF outbreak in 2010. South Africa had accounted for a large share of

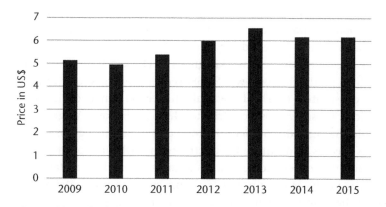

Figure 10.4 Chicken prices per 2 kg, US$, 2009–2015

Sources: Zimstats (2013b); ZPA (2015)

the cheap imports before this ban, reflected in higher average prices in 2011. Prices reduced from US$6.54 in 2013 to US$6.17 in 2014.

In summary, the industry is highly organised, with the Zimbabwe Poultry Association at the apex representing the entire subsector at the national level. The industry has been subject to a number of shocks, some of which relate to macroeconomic conditions. Others relate to trade policy, including the removal of protection in 2009 to meet consumer needs, the ban on South African imports in 2010 and the increase in tariff protection in 2012. Since the inception of the ban on South African imports, there was a switch to new sources of imports from Argentina, Brazil and the US, showing the sector's lack of competitiveness.

Assessing the competitiveness of the poultry industry

Analysing the competitiveness of the sector involves measuring the ERP, the levels of competition in the value chain, specifically in the breeding sector, the impact of low agricultural production and the need to import maize. I look at the cost structure of the sector, giving a detailed analysis of industry cost along the value chain. Thereafter I analyse the ERP accorded the sector. This includes considering the impact of different tariffs on imports from various countries, and assessing the impact of factors affecting the cost of animal feed in addition to tariff protection. I conclude the section by analysing the levels of competition in the sector, specifically in the breeding subsector, and compare prices of day-old chicks with comparable countries in the region.

Industry cost structure

The cost build-up of the poultry industry is an important factor to consider in assessing the competitiveness of the industry. I analyse the cost structure of the whole industry along its value chain in order to evaluate the level that contributes the biggest share of the cost. This enables deeper enquiry into the factors affecting these costs.

Table 10.1 shows the cost structure of producing a dressed two kilograms of chicken. The cost build-up was obtained from the Zimbabwe Poultry Association and compiled as an average for the industry for 2012.

The producer price for a dressed two kilograms of chicken was US$4.80 in 2012, while the total production cost was $3.68. Feed is the largest cost in producing chickens, constituting 64.4% of the total. The second major cost (20.4%) is for day-old chicks. These two costs contribute 84.8% of the total. Wages contribute 2.8% while charcoal adds 6.8% to the total cost of producing the whole bird. (Charcoal is used as a substitute for electricity in fowl runs to warm the birds since the country is experiencing power shortages.) Note that capital costs are included in the producer margin, but transport costs are not measured as these are prices at the factory gate, not delivered to retail outlets.

Given that stockfeed constitutes 64.4% of the total cost of producing a chicken, it is imperative to understand what determines the costs of the main

Table 10.1 Cost structure per 2 kg dressed bird, US$, 2012

Basis of escalation	Cost per bird		
	Cost per bird per variable	Total cost per live bird	% of cost
Day-old chick costs			
Chick price	0.75	0.75	20.4
Stockfeed			
800 g starter crumbs	0.57	0.57	
1 100 g grower pellets	0.76	0.76	
1 500 g finisher pellets	1.04	1.04	64.4
Veterinary costs			
D78 two doses/bird @ $8.60/1 000 doses	0.02		
Clone 30 one dose/bird @ $4.40/1 000 doses	0.00		
Stress pack 100 g per 200 litres for first five days			
In five days 1 000 birds consume 250 ml water	0.00		
Medication allowances 35% of vaccine cost	0.01	0.03	0.8
Litter			
Seven bales per 500 birds	0.01	0.01	0.3
Gas – BOC/BP prices or charcoal			
100 g × price per kg gas BOC/BP	0.00	0.00	0.0
625 g × price per kg charcoal	0.25	0.25	6.8
Subtotal		3.41	
Other costs – statutory			
Wages and salaries/electricity/other		0.10	2.8
Fuel		0.07	1.9
Processing costs per bird			
Packaging – Bag $0.32/Polyprop bag $0.00/12 birds per bag		0.00	0.0
Rentals per bird housed		0.10	2.6
Total costs		3.68	100
Producer price per bird		4.80	
Producer margin (% above cost)		30	30

Source: ZPA (2013)

components of feed. Maize is by far the largest single cost, estimated to account on average for 70% of the cost (Dhliwayo, 2011). The determinants of the maize price are thus very important. In this regard, the effect of low agricultural production, meaning that maize prices are at import levels, needs to be considered. The reasons for the need to import maize go to the debates about the effect of land reform and the continued ban on GM maize and soya in producing stockfeed.

Assessment of maize prices

Since 2002, low maize production in many years has resulted in substantial imports of maize (Zengeni, 2014). The trade deficit has meant that the price of imports has effectively set the local Zimbabwean maize price. Maize is also the staple food of Zimbabwe and as such is one of the most important food crops. There are various reasons for poor maize production, including agricultural policy and land reform. The issues around GM maize are part of the explanation to the extent that utilising GM maize would have meant higher production. Still, it seems doubtful that GM production would have eliminated the trade deficit. In any event, we can treat the trade deficit in maize as resulting from distortions, whether the ban on GM production or the impact of land reform on output levels. Zimbabwe has historically been self-sufficient in maize (as in 2000) and should be again when production fully recovers.

Zimbabwe's reliance on maize imports since 2002 to cover the deficit in supply is potentially hugely significant for the poultry industry, given the importance of maize as an input. The cost of the local maize deficit imposed on local poultry producers depends on the costs of imported maize compared to an international price (or the price being paid in the source country of poultry imports). The cost of imports depends on where the maize is sourced from, and the relevant prices and transport costs. Trade data reveal a switchover from 2009 to 2012 in the main source of maize imports, from South Africa to Zambia, with the big change happening in 2011 (table 10.2). While 74% of maize imports in 2010 came from South Africa, 77% came from Zambia in 2011 and 99% in 2012.

Table 10.2 Maize imports in tonnes by country, 2009–2012

	2009	2010	2011	2012
South Africa (t)	430 990	178 478	24 179	8 732
Zambia (t)	1 621	42 471	373 620	1 217 532
Malawi (t)	643	6 410	82 563	85
Other (t)	1 314	14 520	3 848	586

Source: Zimstats (2013a)

From 2008 to 2010 the Zimbabwe maize price was set by the maize import prices from South Africa. As indicated in figure 10.5, this meant costs at South African prices plus a substantial amount added, presumably reflecting transport and related costs. From 2008 to 2015, Zimbabwe maize prices were between US$90 and US$168 higher than the prices in South Africa, more than 40% higher in relative terms. In 2011 and 2012, however, much smaller price differences (just $12 in 2012) with South Africa were recorded, consistent with the switch in sourcing imports from Zambia. Table 10.3 shows the price differences.

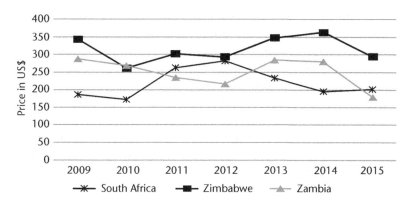

Figure 10.5 Comparison of maize prices, US$ per tonne, 2009–2015

Sources: SAGIS (www.sagis.org.za/); FAOSTAT (www.faostat.org)

Table 10.3 Maize prices in US$ per tonne, Zimbabwe and South Africa, 2008–2015

	2008	2009	2010	2011	2012	2013	2014	2015
South Africa (US$/t)	232	187	172	264	283	234	196	202
Zimbabwe (US$/t)	362	344	262	304	295	349	364	295
Price difference (US$/t)	130	157	90	40	12	115	168	93

Sources: SAGIS (www.sagis.org.za/); FAOSTAT (www.faostat.org)

From 2011 to 2015 there was a relatively consistent mark-up over Zambian prices recorded. This is significant, as the poultry import competition was not coming from Zambia but from South Africa or from deep-sea sources (likely imported through South Africa).

The impact of sourcing from Zambia in 2011 and 2012 was substantial compared to what the prices would have been if the same mark-up on South African prices had been sustained. Prices in Zambia were lower than in South Africa in those years and transport costs appear lower, as the Zimbabwe prices were only around $53 higher than those in Zambia. This meant that in 2012, Zimbabwe maize prices were almost the same as those in South Africa. There was hence no disadvantage from this input for poultry producers in Zimbabwe compared to those in South Africa by 2012. In 2013, however, Zambian prices rose once again compared to South African prices but were lower in 2015.

Despite Zambia sharing the same policy with Zimbabwe on banning the production of GM maize, it is clear from figure 10.5 that its prices have been lower than Zimbabwe's, reflecting Zambia's increasing production and net exports to Zimbabwe (Haggblade, Jayne, Tschirley and Longabaugh, 2008). South Africa, which allows the production of GM maize and which is also the main source of chicken imports into Zimbabwe, has lower maize prices than Zimbabwe for all the years, giving a competitive advantage to the South African chicken producers.

Studies done on GM maize yield per hectare show that net returns are higher than on conventional maize (Mutuc, Rejesus, Pan and Yorobe, 2012; Yorobe and Quicoy, 2006). This is mainly due to lower use of labour and chemicals, which increase the cost of producing maize. This has resulted in the prices of GM maize being generally lower than for conventional maize. In the case of Zimbabwe, a government policy prohibits the importation of GM maize and the inability to produce enough maize has led to reliance on importing maize from neighbouring countries, mainly Zambia.

Effect of higher maize prices

The higher maize price in Zimbabwe than in South Africa has a substantial effect on the competitiveness of Zimbabwean poultry producers. I consider this effect by examining the yearly percentage mark-up of Zimbabwean maize prices compared to South African maize prices as if it was a nominal tariff – the increase over international, or border, prices (table 10.4).

Table 10.4 Maize prices in South Africa and Zimbabwe, 2009–2015

	2009	2010	2011	2012	2013	2014	2015
South Africa (US$/t)	187	172	264	283	234	196	202
Zimbabwe (US$/t)	344	262	304	295	349	364	295
Price difference (US$/t)	157	90	40	12	115	168	93
Mark-up (%)	84	52	15	4	49	86	46

Source: Author calculation based on SAGIS and FAOSTAT price data

Table 10.4 shows that from 2009 to 2015 maize prices in Zimbabwe were higher than in South Africa. The average mark-up of Zimbabwean prices over South African maize prices was 38%. However, the gap declined sharply in 2011 and 2012 due to the imports from Zambia. In 2014 the margin was high due to the bumper harvest in South Africa, which led to prices falling.

Assessment of day-old chick prices

Day-old chicks are the second largest cost in producing poultry. These are produced locally through the breeding operations of vertically integrated poultry producers, as well as other firms that import fertilised eggs. These breeders sell the day-old chicks to independent broiler producers of different sizes, and also use the day-old chicks in their own broiler production.

The breeding subsector of the poultry industry is highly concentrated, with the two main companies, Hubbard and Irvine's, controlling 70% of the market (table 10.5). Hubbard and Irvine's import grandparents from France and the UK, respectively. This gives them a firm position in the value chain as they are the

Table 10.5 Concentration and market shares based on monthly sales, 2012 and 2013

Producer	2012		Concentration		2013		Concentration	
	Chicks/month	Market/share (%)	HHI	CR4	Chicks/month	Market/share (%)	HHI	CR4
Irvine's Zimbabwe	2 493 364	56	3 136	56	2 891 695	58	3 364	58
Crest Poultry Group (Hubbard)	655 133	15	225	71	600 053	12	144	70
Charles Stewart	296 438	7	49	78	424 441	8	64	78
Hukuru Chicks	257 739	6	36	84	388 714	8	64	86
Lunar Chickens	421 350	9	81		265 817	5	25	
Hamara Farm	257 739	6	36		226 724	5	25	
Masvingo Chicks	89 934	2	4		158 530	3	9	
All-Avian					70 033	1	1	
Total	4 471 697	100	3 567	82	5 026 007	100	3 696	86

Source: Author calculation based on Competition and Tariff (2016) data (accessed via private communication)

Note: CR4 = Four-firm concentration ratio; HHI = Herfindahl-Hirschman Index main producers of the primary raw material of the whole industry. However, the subsector has witnessed the entry of new companies such as Hamara and Hukuru, as well as Lunar Chickens in 2007 (which has since closed, in 2015). Hukuru imported fertilised eggs from South Africa for its breeding operations.

The subsector is a highly concentrated market with both the CR4 and the HHI higher than 75% and 1 800 respectively when estimated using actual sales in 2013. Despite the entry of new players, Irvine's remains the biggest player, with a market share of 58% in 2013. The impact of high concentration is assessed below by comparing prices in regional markets.

Regional comparison of day-old chick costs

This section analyses the impact of a highly concentrated breeding subsector on the competitiveness of the whole industry. Using 2012 and 2015 industry data, I compare the prices of producing day-old chicks in Zimbabwe against other countries in the region – Botswana, South Africa and Zambia – to estimate the cost difference (figure 10.6).

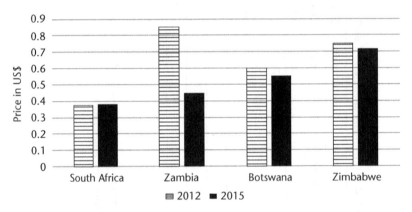

Figure 10.6 Regional day-old chick prices in four African countries, 2012 and 2015

Sources: Bagopi et al. (2013); ZPA (2012, 2015)

Of the countries analysed, in 2015 Zimbabwe had the highest day-old chick prices and Botswana the second highest. However, important to the analysis is the cost of a day-old chick in South Africa, since it is the main source of chicken import competition into Zimbabwe. The price of day-old chicks in Zimbabwe, as a cost to broiler producers, was double that in South Africa in 2012. This improved marginally in 2015. Since day-old chicks constitute 20.4% of the total cost of producing a chicken in Zimbabwe, this finding partly explains why South African chickens are competitive in Zimbabwe.

There are various reasons for this, of which competition is an important one. South Africa has more producers in this stage of the value chain and the low prices might be a result of rivalry among competitors (Grimbeek and Lekezwa, 2013). There may also be cost differences, although South Africa, like Zimbabwe, has to import the genetic breeding stock as grandparents or great-grandparents from multinational companies (Bagopi et al., 2013).

In the next section, I consider the higher day-old chick price as resulting from imperfect competition by including an imputed nominal tariff (103%) on day-old chicks equal to the difference between Zimbabwean and South African prices for 2012.

Trade tariffs and the poultry sector

Zimbabwe regulated foreign trade prior to the 1991 adoption of economic structural adjustment programmes spearheaded by the Bretton Woods institutions (Tekere, 2001). Import substitution was pursued during the Unilateral Declaration of Independence period (1965–1980), during which time domestic industry was protected using high tariffs, quantitative restrictions and embargoes (Rattsø and Torvik, 1998). Zimbabwe's adoption of ESAP led to trade liberalisation in the multilateral context of the World Trade Organisation and in the regional framework under SADC and Comesa, as well as to the signing of bilateral trade agreements with its trading partners (Tekere, 2001). Both SADC and Comesa have attained free trade status. These developments have influenced the poultry sector, as both inputs and outputs are affected by import competition. Below, I present tariff levels on all imported raw materials used by the poultry sector. I then assess the nominal tariffs applying to feed components and to outputs (poultry) to gauge which ones are applicable.

Raw materials
Raw materials used by the poultry industry fall into two categories, those directly linked to the sector and those indirectly linked. Table 10.6 lists raw materials directly used by poultry breeders: breeding stock, feed and vaccines. The rates indicated have remained the same since 2009 and have not been affected by the government's tariff changes.

Stockfeed attracts the highest rate of duty (40%) under the MFN (most favoured nation) rate. The higher duty is due to the need to protect local producers, although impacting negatively on the poultry industry. Under the SADC trade agreements, it still attracts a 15% rate of duty, also to protect local producers. Grandparents, however, attract a 5% rate of duty despite not being available locally. This may be due to the government's need to raise revenue through customs collections. The bilateral trade agreement between Zimbabwe and South Africa and the Comesa trade agreement allow all these raw materials to be imported duty-free.

Maize and soya cake, the two key raw materials, attract duties of 0 and 10% respectively under MFN. The duty on soya is to protect local farmers. Maize is imported duty-free since it is also the staple food, hence the need for it to be cheaply available when farmers fail to meet demand. Zimbabwe has been importing grain in the past years to supplement domestic supply, which has not been able to meet local demand.

Table 10.6 Tariffs on poultry raw materials

Tariff code	Description	MFN (%)	Comesa (%)	South Africa (%)	SADC South Africa (%)	SADC Other (%)
1051100	Fowls of the species *Galluss domesticus/* grandparents	5	0	0	0	0
23099010	Poultry feed	40	0	0	15	15
30023000	Vaccines for veterinary medicines	0	0	0	0	0
1005.9000	Maize	0	0	0	0	0
2304.0000	Soya meal	10	0	0	0	0
2301.1000	Poultry meal	0	0	0	0	0

Source: Zimra (2013)

Note: MFN = most favoured nation

Tariff rates applicable to chicken imports

Tariffs applicable to chicken imports fall under five different trade regimes which Zimbabwe is party to. The duties for all five categories remained unchanged from 2000 to 2008. In 2009, government suspended duties on chicken imports, a measure taken to boost food security after the hyperinflation the country experienced in 2008 (Mudzonga, 2009). The suspension was lifted in 2011 and duties were reinstated at 40% (table 10.7).

Table 10.7 Chicken duties under Zimbabwe's trade agreements

Tariff code	Description	MFN	Comesa (%)	South Africa (%)	SADC South Africa (%)	SADC Other (%)
02071100	Fresh or chilled whole chicken	40% or $1.50/kg	0	0	15	15
02071200	Frozen whole chicken	40% or $1.50/kg	0	0	15	15
02071300	Fresh or chilled cuts of chicken	40% or $1.50/kg	0	0	15	15
02071400	Frozen cuts and offal of chicken	40% or $1.50/kg	0	0	15	15

Source: Zimra (2013)

Under the World Trade Organisation, MFN rates are still very high on all tariff lines, at 40% or $1.50/kg, whichever is higher. However, the bilateral trade agreement between Zimbabwe and South Africa means that the sector is fully liberalised as chickens are imported duty-free. It must be remembered, though, that Zimbabwe banned South African poultry imports from March 2010 until December 2011.

Complicating matters further is that duties were suspended on all poultry imports in 2009 and 2010 due to the economic crisis and the need to make food available to the population. This means that while South African poultry imports were banned in 2010, imports from other sources came in duty-free (i.e., the MFN tariff did not apply due to the duty suspension). In 2011, the ban on South African imports was still in place but the suspension had been lifted, meaning that the 40% MFN duty applied. In 2012, there were once again duty-free imports from South Africa.

Under the SADC free trade agreement, applicable Zimbabwe poultry tariff rates are still at the 15% level, indicating that Zimbabwe classified its poultry industry as a sensitive sector.[5] However, this is not material as the imports within SADC of poultry products come from South Africa and are subject to the bilateral agreement between the countries.

Effective rate of protection of the poultry sector

This section measures the ERP of the whole poultry sector to see how it is protected. The ERP measures the protection provided to domestic value added relative to value added in international (or border) prices (Greenaway and Milner, 1993). As discussed, different factors can be considered in addition to nominal tariffs which increase prices above border prices and hence impact on domestic value added. In particular, I do calculations to take into account the imputed effect of low agricultural production on the maize input price (for animal feed) and estimate the effect of low competition in breeding stock on the price of day-old chicks.

I use the formula below to calculate the ERP of the poultry sector, as well as data from the Zimbabwe tariff handbook for the tariffs on raw materials and output at the HS8 digit level.

$$ERP = \frac{t_i - \Sigma a_{ji} t_j}{1 - \Sigma a_{ji}}$$

Where *ERP* is the effective rate of protection, a_{ji} is the number of units of *j* required per unit of *i* under free trade and t_i and t_j are the tariff levels for output $_i$ and $_j$ respectively.

Data
Tariffs were obtained from the 2012 Zimbabwe tariff handbook and data on the industry cost structure were obtained from the Zimbabwe poultry industry. In

estimating the ERP, the treatment of non-tradeable goods was also considered. In the literature, there are three main ways to deal with this. The first method, proposed by Balassa (1965), assumes that the price of non-tradeable goods will not change if the system of protection is removed, thus meaning their nominal tariff is zero. Thus we treat non-tradeable inputs as tradeable inputs with zero tariffs. The second method, proposed by Scott and Godley (1980), assumes that the non-tradeable goods tariff is equal to the average traded goods tariff. The third approach assumes that non-traded goods are just part of the value added of the manufacturing activity employing them, meaning that their values become domestic value added and traded inputs (Corden, 1966).

This study takes the Corden approach, which is appropriate, given that tradeable inputs are the most significant and the object of focus. Non-traded inputs include a range of small costs like labour, litter and gas. The study does not adjust for exchange rates as Zimbabwe is currently using a multicurrency system after the dollarisation of the economy in 2009.

ERP estimates, without adjusting for maize and day-old chicks

The assessment in this section takes account of the source of import competition, given the duty suspension in 2009/2010 and the ban on imports from South Africa in 2010/2011. This means that the MFN rate applied in 2011. The duties on inputs are, however, not affected in the same way and are zero throughout, as import competition comes from the region and South Africa in particular. In table 10.8, 'weight' is the value of inputs in 2012 prices. The following section introduces measures of imputed nominal tariffs to take account of the effects on maize and day-old chick prices considered above.

Table 10.8 Effective rate of protection without adjusting for inputs

	Weight	2009 (%)	2010 (%)	2011 (%)	2012 (%)
Poultry		0	0	40	0
Day-old chicks	0.75	0	0	0	0
Poultry feed	2.37	0	0	0	0
ERP		0	0	224	0

Source: Author calculation

The ERP for the sector was 0% for all the years except 2011 (table 10.8). The zero rate recorded for these years was due to the zero nominal tariffs on both inputs and outputs. However, in 2011 the 40% duty on poultry resulted in the ERP for the sector increasing to 224%. This was because inputs were still zero-rated. At the same time, the assumption made of maintaining constant prices for chicks and feed while accounting for non-tradeable inputs as part of value added might also explain the high level of protection. Interestingly, for the period under review, the highest production was recorded in 2011, the same year with the highest rate of protection, but production fell by 7% as the ERP fell again to zero in 2012.

ERP estimates, adjusting for maize and day-old chicks, and links with performance

For poultry producers, the effect of higher day-old chick prices from low levels of competition can be considered as if there was a higher import tariff on day-old chicks equivalent to the percentage by which day-old chick prices are above international prices (in this case, South African prices). The following calculations were made before calculating the ERP. I used 2012 cost data to calculate the prices of day-old chicks and feed backwards up to 2009. The impact of the uncompetitive supply of day-old chick tariffs is calculated as the percentage of the cost difference between the Zimbabwean and South African prices. The imputed tariff on maize is calculated as 70% of the cost of feed, factoring in the price changes in the South African prices.

As can be seen from table 10.9, in 2009 there was a negative ERP of –40%. This was due to the high level of nominal tariffs on day-old chicks (103%) and the effect of cheaper maize from South Africa (46.9%). In 2010 the industry again had a negative ERP (–36%) as a result of higher nominal tariffs on day-old chicks (103%) and the impact of cheap maize (31.7%). The output was zero-rated as a result of the ban on chicken imports from South Africa. During this period the industry experienced a surge in imports, further confirming the low levels of protection noted earlier. The ERP increased to 85% in 2011 due to an increase in the nominal rate of protection on the output, from 0 to 40%, combined with the effect of lower maize prices relative to South Africa. Maize prices in 2011 in Zimbabwe were just 15% higher, which translates into a lower imputed nominal tariff on feed of 10%. This substantially higher effective protection is consistent with the increase in production in 2011. In 2012, the ERP was once again negative (–21%), which can be explained by the removal of duties on the output as the ban on South African chickens expired. This is supported by

Table 10.9 Effective rate of protection applying, based on the applicable import, 2009–2012

	Weight	2009 (%)	2010 (%)	2011 (%)	2012 (%)
Poultry		0	0	40	0
Day-old chicks	0.75	0	0	0	0
Poultry feed	2.37	0	0	0	0
Effect of maize imports (as higher Zim price compared to SA price) as imputed feed tariff	2.37	46.9	31.7	10.1	2.9
Day-old chick (SA) impact of uncompetitive local supply	0.37	103	103	103	103
ERP		–40	–36	85	–21

Source: Author calculation

the fact that during the same period, chicken production also declined as local producers were once again subjected to stiff foreign competition.

The low levels of competition among breeding producers also suggest influence over the value chain as they are able to charge what appear to be relatively high prices for day-old chicks. In addition, the importance of this product for consumers was evidenced by the government's decision to suspend all duties in 2009 and 2010 in order to ensure that consumers could access food imports cheaply. A further dimension, which this study has not assessed in detail, is the changing competition landscape in South Africa and its possible effects on the Zimbabwean poultry industry. As assessed in Bagopi et al. (2013) and in Grimbeek and Lekezwa (2013), levels of competition in South Africa increased substantially from 2009. This is reflected in the operating margins of the South African poultry producers, which fell in 2012 and 2013 (with the financial year 2013 overlapping from 2012) (figure 10.7).

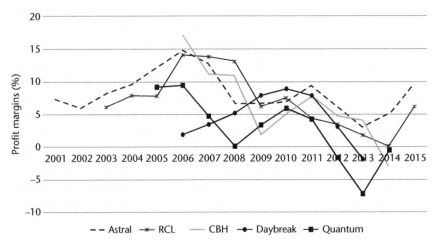

Figure 10.7 Operating margins by company, South Africa, 2001–2015

Sources: Bagopi et al. (2013); annual reports of listed companies

Conclusion

This overview of the poultry industry in Zimbabwe has illustrated the importance of key inputs in the form of stockfeed and breeding stock, as well as the structure of the industry, including the importance of vertically integrated producers.

The study showed that the ERP calculation is complicated by the different trade regimes that exist. If the main international competition is from South Africa, then the existence of the bilateral agreement between Zimbabwe and South Africa means that the poultry sector has not been protected. More recently (2010/2011), the industry felt the effects of the two-year ban on South African imports due to disease, for one year of which the higher MFN tariff was relevant given that deep-sea imports from Latin American countries became the main source of imports. In fact, although in 2009 the government suspended duties on all chicken imports due to the inability of local producers to meet domestic demand, there had already not been any protection against imports from South Africa. The ban on South African imports increased the ERP of the sector from South African producers and the overall rates of protection in 2011 as the suspension of duty was lifted that year.

The nature and impact of protection on inputs and outputs required by the ERP raised a number of questions about what determines the prices of the key inputs relative to prices in South Africa (as the international price used here). The price differences in the main stockfeed component, maize, are substantial, leading to the question of why Zimbabwe imports maize so that the prices are set by imports, which, given transport and related costs, are much higher than in the country of origin.

The study showed that the breeding subsector is characterised by high concentration and that Zimbabwean prices for day-old chicks are above those of comparable countries in the region, such as South Africa. However, it was not possible to evaluate the conduct of the two breeding firms due to data restrictions at the firm level. It is also the case that effects from uncompetitive behaviour at the breeding level are likely to be smaller than the impact of factors relating to stockfeed.

The study highlighted that Zimbabwe has been relying on maize imports since 2002 as it is not able to meet its national requirement. Maize constitutes 70% of stockfeed, thus making it the major cost contributor. Prices for GM maize used in South Africa are substantially lower than Zimbabwean prices. There are different reasons, however, for the higher Zimbabwean maize prices. An important reason for the need to import is the declining local production with the implementation of agricultural policies, in particular land reform. While the ban on GM maize likely meant lower production than would otherwise have been the case, this ban did not represent a change during the period, unlike the agricultural policies. In addition, the study found that reliance on imports depends on the source of those imports, which influences the price. In particular, the examination of maize imports by source country found a shift in 2011 to imports from Zambia. This resulted in a lower mark-up of Zimbabwean maize prices than when sourced from South Africa, as Zambian prices were relatively cheaper in 2011 and 2012 and transport costs lower. Zambia, however, also has a ban on GM maize but has been able to be a net exporter at competitive prices, at least in some years.

The study explored the effects of treating the differences in the key input prices between Zimbabwe and South Africa as being caused by distortions that can be measured as an imputed nominal tariff. In the case of day-old chicks, this reflected the possible impact of low levels of competition at the breeding level. In the case of maize, this was due to falling production for the reasons identified above. The calculation of imputed tariffs on the inputs allowed a calculation of the ERP from 2009 to 2012. This was negative in all years except 2011. The large negative ERPs calculated in 2009 and 2010 were mostly due to the very high price of maize in Zimbabwe and the substantial proportion it accounts for in the inputs to poultry production. In 2011, the difference in the maize price was much smaller (due to imports from Zambia) and the 40% MFN tariff on outputs applied, given the ban on South African poultry imports. In 2012 there was a negative ERP once more as imports from South Africa (with zero duty) were again allowed. The negative ERP was lower than in the earlier years as the maize price difference was very small. The difference in the day-old chick price was available only for 2012 and this disparity was used for the imputed tariff over the four years.

Notes

1   Irvine's Zimbabwe Private Limited is part of Innscor Zimbabwe Limited, a diversified group which has a business interest in milling and manufacturing, distribution, and wholesale and retail.

2   The production cycle is between four and six weeks for a bird to reach 2 kg.

3   All Avian, Irvine's Day Old Chicks, Crest Poultry Group (Hubbard), Lunar Chickens, Nature Best (Strindo), Bulawayo Chicks, Charles Stewart Day Old Chicks, Masvingo Chicks and Chinyika Chicks.

4   Chicken here covers the following tariff lines, representing all forms under which chicken is imported using HS 8: 0207.1100, 0207.1200, 0207.1300 and 0207.1400.

5   This sector is given a longer phase-down period of its tariffs before it is opened to free trade as it is considered to be in need of some protection to enable it to become competitive.

References

Bagopi E, E Chokwe, P Halse, J Hausiku, M Humavindu, W Kalapula and S Roberts. 2013. 'Competition dynamics and regional trade flows in the poultry sector: The case of Botswana, Namibia, South Africa and Zambia'. Paper presented at 7th Annual Conference on Competition, Law and Policy, Johannesburg, 5–6 September.

Balassa B. 1965. Tariff protection in industrial countries: An evaluation. *Journal of Political Economy* 73: 579–594.

Corden WM. 1966. The structure of a tariff system and the effective protective rate. *Journal of Political Economy* 74: 221–237.

Dhliwayo M. 2011. Towards sustainable broiler production: Does use of sorghum (sorghum bicolour) as an adjunct substitute of maize affect broiler performance? *Journal of Sustainable Development in Africa* 13: 225–237.

Dolan C and J Humphrey. 2004. Changing governance patterns in the trade in fresh vegetables between Africa and the United Kingdom. *Environment and Planning A* 36: 491–509.

Edwards L. 2006. Has South Africa liberalised its trade? *South African Journal of Economics* 73: 754–775.

FAO (Food and Agriculture Organization). 2010. 'Agribusiness Handbook: Poultry Meat & Eggs' (online document).

Faranisi AT. 1995. Village chicken breeding in Zimbabwe. In K Dzama, FN Ngwerume and E Bhebhe (eds), *Proceedings of the International Symposium on Livestock Production through Animal Breeding and Genetics*. Harare: University of Zimbabwe.

Flatters F. 2005. Measuring the impacts of trade policies: Effective rates of protection. New York: Mimeo. Com, Inc. http://www.tipmoz.com/library/resources/tipmoz_media/cat3_link_1125323217.pdf.

Gereffi G and K Fernandez-Stark. 2011. *Global Value Chain Analysis: A Primer*. Durham, NC: Center on Globalization, Governance & Competitiveness, Duke University.

Gereffi G, J Humphrey, R Kaplinsky and TJ Sturgeon. 2001. *Introduction: Globalisation, Value Chains and Development*. IDS Bulletin 32.3.

Government of Zimbabwe. 2012. 'The 2013 National Budget Statement: Beyond the Enclave: Unleashing Zimbabwe's Economic Growth Potential' (online document).

Greenaway D and C Milner. 1983. *International Trade Policy: From Tariffs to the New Protectionism*. Basingstoke: Macmillan Press.

Greenaway D and C Milner. 1993. *Trade and Industrial Policy in Developing Countries*. Basingstoke: Macmillan Press.

Grimbeek S and B Lekezwa. 2013. 'The emergence of a more vigorous competition and the importance of entry: Comparative insights from flour and poultry'. Centre for Competition Economics, University of Johannesburg.

Haggblade S, T Jayne, D Tschirley and S Longabaugh. 2008. *Potential for Intra-Regional Maize Trade in Southern Africa: An Analysis for Zambia at the Sub-National Level*. Michigan State University Food Security Research Project Working Paper No. 35, Lusaka.

Holden M. 2001. Effective protection revisited: How useful a policy tool for South Africa? *South African Journal of Economics* 69: 659–673.

Holden M and P Holden. 1975. An intertemporal calculation of effective rates of protection for South Africa. *South African Journal of Economics* 43: 370–379.

Kaplinsky R. 1998. *Globalisation, Industrialisation and Sustainable Growth: The Pursuit of the Nth Rent*. Institute of Development Studies Discussion Paper No. 365, Brighton, University of Sussex.

Kaplinsky R. 2000. Globalisation and unequalisation: What can be learned from value chain analysis? *The Journal of Development Studies* 37: 117–146.

Kaplinsky R and M Morris. 2002. 'A Handbook for Value Chain Research'. Prepared for International Development Research Centre (online document).

LMAC (Livestock and Meat Advisory Council). 2014. '2014 Annual Report' (online document).

Mapiye C, M Mwale, JF Mupangwa, M Chimonyo, R Foti and MJ Mutenje. 2008. A research review of village chicken production constraints and opportunities in Zimbabwe. *Asian-Australian Journal of Animal Science* 21: 1680–1688.

Mudzonga E. 2009. 'The Impact of Imported GMO Chickens on Zimbabwe's Poultry Industry'. Trade and Pro-Poor Growth Thematic Working Group, Trade and Industrial Policy Strategies, Harare (online document).

Mutuc ME, RM Rejesus, S Pan and JM Yorobe, Jr. 2012. Impact assessment of Bt corn adoption in the Philippines. *Journal of Agricultural and Applied Economics* 44: 117–135.

Ncube P, S Roberts and T Zengeni. 2016. *Development of the Animal Feed to Poultry Value Chain across Botswana, South Africa, and Zimbabwe*. WIDER Working Paper 2016/2.

Rattsø J and R Torvik. 1998. Zimbabwean trade liberalisation: Ex post evaluation. *Cambridge Journal of Economics* 22: 325–346.

Scott MF and WA Godley. 1980. 'The arguments for and against protectionism'. Papers presented to the Panel Academic Consultants.

Sodersten B and G Reed. 1994. *International Economics* (3rd edition). Hong Kong: Macmillan.

Sukume C. 2011. Competitiveness Impacts of Business Environment Reform (CIBER): The Poultry Value Chain in Zimbabwe. Zimbabwe Agricultural Competitiveness Programme. DAI/USAID.

Tekere M. 2001. 'Trade Liberalisation under Structural Economic Adjustment: Impact on Social Welfare in Zimbabwe'. Paper Series for the Poverty Reduction Forum, SAPRI (online document).

Todaro MP and SC Smith. 2007. *Economic Development* (8th edition). New York: Pearson.

Yorobe JM and CB Quicoy. 2006. Economic impact of Bt corn in the Philippines. *The Philippine Agricultural Scientist* 89: 258–267.

Zengeni T. 2014. 'The competitiveness and performance of the Zimbabwe poultry industry', unpublished Masters dissertation, University of the Witwatersrand, Johannesburg.

Zimra (Zimbabwe Revenue Authority). 2013. *Integrated Customs Tariff.* http://www.zimra.co.zw/index.php?option=com_phocadownload&view=category&id=6:customs&Itemid=1.

Zimstats. 2013a. Zimbabwe imports and exports trade statistics, CPI data (accessed via private communication).

Zimstats. 2013b. Zimbabwe CPI data (accessed via private communication).

ZPA (Zimbabwe Poultry Association). 2012. December newsletter (accessed via private communication).

ZPA. 2013. May newsletter (accessed via private communication).

ZPA. 2015. Price data (accessed via private communication).

Part Four

Conclusion

11 Competition, regional integration and inclusive growth in Africa: A research agenda

Simon Roberts, Thando Vilakazi and Witness Simbanegavi

Regional integration and inclusive growth: Does competition matter?

In recent years there has been increased attention, once more, on regional integration and its potential contribution to African economic development. However, there are very different emphases and perspectives. On the one hand, regional integration is essentially viewed as removing tariff and non-tariff barriers to trade; in essence, a second-best to unilateral liberalisation. It is also advocated as part of 'defragmenting Africa' – overcoming the legacy of colonial borders – adding the reduction (or even removal) of border controls to the agenda of tariff liberalisation. Other perspectives emphasise the constructive measures required for more meaningful and deeper integration, ranging from investments in improved transport infrastructure to developing effective institutional arrangements. This can include provisions for collaboration on a regional industrial policy, to build capabilities and regional value chains.

A key aspect in the different perspectives is the extent to which natural markets and the behaviour of firms are understood as regional in scope. As firms are internationalised – including through ownership relations, strategic partnerships and distribution arrangements – a regional perspective to firm decision making, such as regarding investment and location of production, is necessary. Given scale economies and relatively small national markets, firms make decisions across countries. However, when trade barriers are raised, firms can protect their market power within countries, which would otherwise be undermined by competition at a regional level.

It is evident that the market power of large firms, whether exerted unilaterally or through coordination with each other, harms economic development and low-income groups. Such power means higher prices for goods and services and distorts the development path of economies where it relates to the pricing of important inputs (such as the effect of fertiliser costs on farmers). The nature of competitive rivalry, and the power and interests of large firms and their owners, is thus at the heart of how countries develop (see Acemoglu and Robinson, 2012; North, Wallis and Weingast, 2009). The decisions of large firms shape the economy as they can make the investments required in productive capacity, provide the upstream inputs and services required by smaller businesses and, in many areas, are also the main routes to market. In crude terms, it is critical whether these firms extract rents through market power, or whether the returns reward effort, creativity and entrepreneurship.

Anticompetitive arrangements can have a regional and international scope. For example, cartels have operated across southern Africa in cement, concrete products and fertiliser (see Makhaya, Mkwananzi and Roberts, 2012; Roberts, 2013). There is thus a close relationship between more competitive outcomes and regional integration. Firms seeking to increase their market power, whether through collusion or abuse of monopoly power, are likely to be better able to do so in smaller national markets.

This points to a critical insight, namely, that the gains from regional integration are much greater when the implications of imperfect competition are taken into account. The gains from trade in models which assume perfect competition are the effects of specialisation and exchange – and there are thus smaller gains from trade between countries that have similar endowments and productive structure. However, with imperfect competition there are potentially very substantial gains from integration of similar economies. Under scale economies a wider market implies lower costs of production as larger-scale production is possible together with more competition (if the market is big enough to support several producers and assuming firms do not collude, or if the market is highly contestable). With differentiated products, integration will mean intra-industry trade and greater variety. There are also dynamic gains from regional trade and competitive rivalry between firms, which stimulate improved products and services and greater management effort.

Harm from low levels of competition (more likely in protected national economies) and the sustained earning of supra-competitive margins also includes the exclusion of rivals – typically smaller firms and entrants who are attracted by the margins to be made but whose increased participation would undermine the anticompetitive arrangements. Anticompetitive arrangements thus typically involve entrenched 'insiders' protecting their position. This has the effect of undermining participation in the economy and stifling the dynamism which comes with it, which goes far beyond simple effects on prices. Active rivalry means improved service, product offerings and ongoing improvements in the capabilities required to deliver these. In other words, effort and ingenuity are rewarded rather than incumbency. This can also be described as the difference between 'performance competition' and 'handicap competition' (seeking to handicap rivals) (Gerber, 2010).

Competition, properly located, therefore means considering the dynamic process of rivalry which has positive dimensions in the form of the ability to develop productive capabilities (such as accessing finance and key infrastructure, investing in skills), as well as the typically considered negative dimensions, such as barriers due to exclusionary conduct by large firms or regulatory barriers. The importance of building and expanding capabilities has been highlighted as being at the centre of a country's economic development (Hausmann, Hwang and Rodrik, 2007; Page, 2012; Rodrik, 2007; Sutton, 2004). Inclusive growth therefore has a competition dimension and, for this to be properly understood, it needs to be viewed from the perspective of regional integration. The links between the fields of competition, trade and regional integration, and inclusive growth have, however, not generally been well developed in the literature.[1] In terms of policy, there are critical insights as it implies choices about competition enforcement across countries relating to the competition regime and the institutional framework.

This final chapter draws on a range of work stretching beyond the chapters in the volume to propose a research agenda which incorporates competition and regional integration as part of an inclusive growth agenda. It builds upon the competition and economic development concerns and themes covered in the Introduction to this volume but homes in on and elaborates the regional economic dimension. As reflected in the contributions to this volume, competition policy and competition enforcement are closely intertwined with the development of industries, regulation and the structure of markets. The focus cannot be on competition policy for its own sake, but on its role as an important microeconomic tool which should form part of broader industrial development strategies.

In the remainder of the chapter, we review the available literature on the linkages between competition, regional integration and inclusive growth. Thereafter, we consider recent empirical evidence on the regional dynamics of competition in the context of southern and East Africa before concluding and making recommendations on the key elements of a new research agenda which incorporates competition and regional integration as part of an inclusive growth agenda.

Competition, regional integration and inclusive growth

We focus here on three main areas where there is an interface between competition, inclusive growth and regional integration. We start by briefly sketching recent developments in competition economics and reflecting on the implications for economic development in African economies, as a foundation for our discussion of questions of inclusive growth and regional integration. The second area considers the relationships between competition and inclusive growth, particularly focusing on the ways in which different interests influence the economic policy agenda and shape the nature of economic outcomes. This points to the important role that research can play in identifying the costs of anticompetitive arrangements protected by political influence, and those groups within society that bear the costs.

The third area is the consideration of regional integration, regional trade and the nature of rivalry, especially dynamic rivalry where firms' strategies seek to shape markets and the impact that this has on investments in productive capabilities. Much of the theoretical literature focuses on the static effects of competition, yet competition evidently relates to the ability of actual and potential market participants to bring improved products and services to the market, and whether effort and creativity are rewarded or whether rewards largely reflect incumbency. Exporting more sophisticated and diversified higher-value products has been highlighted in the trade literature as being a central driver of economic growth. Through drawing on the existing literature, we examine the ways in which the development of capabilities depends on the stimulus of competitive rivalry in the domestic or regional market.

Developments in competition economics and implications for African economies

Empirical studies have shown that a fall in concentration leads to a fall in prices and in price cost margins (see Schmalensee, 1989). The results with regard to profits, taking into account returns on initial investments made, are much weaker, however. Cross-industry regressions find scale economies to be a strong explanatory factor for concentration (Sutton, 2006). Other things being equal, smaller markets relative to the minimum efficient scale (MES) of production in an industry mean that concentration will be higher. Most empirical studies have focused on manufacturing.

Other characteristics put forward to explain concentration include the intensity of advertising and research and development (R&D), although R&D has typically been found to be uncorrelated with concentration (Sutton, 2006). Additionally, these are not exogenous but are part of firms' strategies. Imperfect information and consumer brand loyalty can underpin marketing strategies linked with (exogenous) distribution scale economies to raise the costs of entrants, even where the MES of the actual manufacture of the product is not very large.

Regarding services, network effects have been found to be very important, depending on the industry in question. Where the value to a consumer of a network service depends on how many others are part of the same network, there are substantial first-mover advantages. The impact of these effects also depends on whether there are regulatory interventions to mandate interoperability and interconnection.

The features of an industry, together with market imperfections associated with imperfect information, are now recognised to provide scope for strategic behaviour (Vickers, 2005).[2] Dominant firms can lock in advantages through a range of strategies (Rey and Tirole, 2006; Whinston, 2006). Models can explain possible anticompetitive exclusion with either scale economies or imperfect information (in real-world markets both may well be present). In addition, a dominant firm does not necessarily engage in a single strategy but can adopt multiple and mutually reinforcing strategies. Of course, there are also possible efficiency rationales for conduct, such as exclusive dealing, which means a case-by-case analysis is necessary. Whether there should be presumptions depending on considerations such as market conditions, the extent and durability of dominance and whether the position was the result of innovation is an important question to which we return.

It is now also increasingly recognised that strategies which appear different on the surface may be equivalent.[3] For example, targeted, individualised loyalty rebates can amount to de facto exclusive dealing. A vertically integrated firm with a monopoly in an indispensable input which engages in a margin squeeze over its non-integrated rival through a higher input price is effectively refusing to supply. In the latter case, the downstream firm may well lodge an accusation of predation if it perceives the downstream price to be below its costs. This has implications for attempting to 'pigeon-hole' conduct, as the South African Competition Act does.

The Chicago critique asked why a dominant firm would have the incentive to foreclose, even where they may have the ability to do so. An upstream monopolist, vertically integrated into the downstream market, can earn the one monopoly profit through its upstream pricing and does not need to foreclose downstream rivals. However, this ignores the fact that an entrant upstream – to undermine its monopoly position – may be much more likely if allied with a downstream firm which understands the product and consumer characteristics. Similarly, there may be an anticompetitive rationale for tying and bundling where entrants are likely from adjacent markets.

These theories of exclusionary conduct can explain why dominant firms may be able to protect their position. This is different from concentration, as such. Persisting dominance of the incumbent suggests that effort and creativity are not being rewarded but rather the legacy position. As Geroski and Jacquemin (1984: 22) caution: 'when, however, small asymmetries can be solidified into dominant positions that persist, the inequities they create become institutionalized, creating long-term problems in the performance of the economic system which cry out for policy attention'.

The likelihood of entrenched dominant firms depends on the country conditions and history. This implies a different balance in enforcement from country to country, as has been reflected in comparisons between the appropriate priorities and standards in North America and Europe, as well as comparisons with Asian countries such as Japan and South Korea (Evans, 2009; Fox, 2002, 2003; Hur, 2004; Vickers, 2007).

What are the implications for developing economies and African countries, in particular? There are reasons why the durability of dominance is greater. Scale economies are more significant given the smaller size of markets; information is likely to be poorer; and the costs of building brand awareness, advertising, distribution and marketing may be higher relative to sales. The first movers in many countries are likely to have gained their position either through state support and ownership (even if now privatised) or by being a subsidiary of a multinational corporation that established its footprint under colonial rule. However, while the effect of scale economies is well established, we should be cautious about generalisations in other areas, instead seeing these issues as important ones for future research. There is a growing field of work on the appropriate competition policy for developing countries (see Brusick and Evenett, 2008; Dabbah, 2010; Gal, 2003, 2009) but relatively little regarding African economies.

While greenfield entry by a new investor appears less likely, the learning from models and cases suggests that entry may also be more likely from adjacent geographic markets if the market conditions are similar, and the firm can leverage its existing capabilities. This has implications for regional integration. In addition, there are links with development policies. As highlighted below, Hausmann, Hwang and Rodrik (2007) find that productive capabilities migrate – a firm which has developed capabilities in one product such as cutting machinery for forestry (in the case of Finland) can more readily develop capabilities in cutting machinery for other materials. This suggests that at the regional and country levels we need to consider how the 'optimal level of competition' can be fostered, which links to capabilities development (Amsden and Singh, 1994; Singh, 2004).

Competition, political economy and inclusive growth

Competition is a key component of inclusive growth (in Acemoglu and Robinson, 2012) or 'open access orders' (in North, Wallis and Weingast, 2009).[4] Competitive markets as an existing state mean markets with many participants, low barriers to entry and returns which just reward the investment made and cover the costs of production. But, a country does not arrive at this state by magic. Indeed, it seems obvious that market power, imperfect competition and market failures, which can reinforce positions of market power, are intrinsic features of economic life. We therefore need to understand how the *process* of evolving competitive rivalry is related to the nature of economic opportunity and outcomes.

At the heart of North, Wallis and Weingast's assessment is the combined importance of competition in both the economic and political spheres. Indeed, they argue that '[b]y studying democracy in isolation of markets, political scientists have missed these forces [competitive markets] of political stability' (2009: 129). By this they mean that competitive markets generate long-term prosperity and allow for dynamism in terms of different social groups and interests, which feeds into politics. Conversely, they contend that distortions, such as from rent seeking, impact on relative prices which, in an economy with competitive markets, generate a response from forces in society that recognise the economic costs that are imposed. But, why and how will such competitive markets arise?

North, Wallis and Weingast (2009) believe that progress towards an open access order involves competition-eroding rents, and that this involves liberalisation and independent institutions. However, this fails to recognise the important role that industrial policies and tariffs have played in industrialising countries and does not take us forward in understanding how interests are aligned with the policy frameworks that are adopted (see Khan, 2006). The construction of markets and the main participants reflect a country's economic history. How does competition law and policy then relate to moving towards meaningful increased access?

It has been argued that the vigorous promotion of competition law for developing countries disregards political and institutional realities – in simple terms, because institutions are weak and concentrated business interests are too strong (Rodriguez and Menon, 2010). The strength of those behind anticompetitive arrangements such as cartels simply means that they subvert the competition regime where enforcement is attempted (Mateus, 2010). But, a competition agenda has been supported in different countries and we need to understand where competition fits within the changing influence of different interests.

It is evident that, while economic regulations are meant to correct for market failures and natural monopolies (entrenched dominant firms), they also respond to lobbying. The balance of power between different interests in a country thus determines the regulatory arrangements which are part of the wider 'political settlement' (Khan, 2006). In evaluating the regulatory regime, including as it relates to competition, we can distinguish between where rents are conditional on productive investment (an implicit quid pro quo) and where short-term rents are maximised and protected. In the former situation, the elite interests have taken a longer-term view in that they recognise the need for sharing returns and for the growth of public infrastructure and capabilities, as this underpins the long-term sustainability of the economy and hence the value of their stake in it. An evolution towards a more rules-based and less personalised system for allocating access is part of such a trajectory. By comparison, an orientation towards extraction of maximum short-term rents means allowing the unfettered exercise of market power, not disciplined either through regulation or promoting competition, and even while it is evident that there is long-term harm to the economy.

It is perhaps more appropriate to understand these as tendencies whose weight depends on many factors. For example, if a business can relocate with ease, then there is less need to consider the long-term effects. Similarly, if elite interests are able to take rents out of the country without fear that a future regime can take action to recover them, then they will have less of a stake in the future. This is likely where personal relationships can be used by incumbents to block rivals (e.g., through regulations, licence permissions, arbitrary judgments). On the other hand, where buyers are important and have organised interests, they will push for discipline on market power. In the case of the antitrust law in the US, a key constituency promoting its adoption was farmers who were being subject to high input and transport costs due to the power of the trusts. Urban consumers can also be an important pressure group and new entrants are possible sources of support. Research can also play an important role in demonstrating the harm caused by concentrated interests that have been able to undermine competition (see Makhaya and Roberts, 2013).

In assessing the evolution of arrangements governing competition, we consider competition policy and the competition regime to extend beyond the law and mandate of any competition authorities. It includes the links with the regulatory provisions as well as the host of other laws and actions that impact on entry and effective competitive rivalry (das Nair, Mondliwa and Roberts, 2012). Indeed, it is unlikely that competition enforcement by a young competition authority will succeed in disciplining powerful interests. Instead, regional integration, which means greater rivalry from neighbouring countries, might be more effective. Entrants may come from firms in adjacent markets or in an upstream or downstream relationship. Industrial policies may support such entrants. This is where the contribution of the case studies (discussed later) is important. Changing the structure of the economy requires a competition policy which actively opens up participation, including through the enforcement of competition law but also through a wider set of interventions in terms of the regulatory framework, the provision of economic infrastructure, development finance and industrial policy.

Dynamic rivalry and regional integration

As argued above, regional integration can potentially increase both trade and competition, thus enhancing the welfare of the community's citizens. Regional integration brings with it both static and dynamic gains. Static gains from trade under orthodox models, which assume perfect competition, are generally small, with gains from trade creation balanced with gains from trade diversion (Robinson and Thierfelder, 2002; Schiff and Winters, 2003).[5] Generally, a regional integration agreement (RIA) allows free trade among partners to the agreement. That is, import tariffs are reduced to zero for products produced by partner countries.[6] A RIA is said to 'create' trade when the reduction/elimination of import tariffs among RIA partners allows low-cost producers from a partner country to replace production by a high-cost producer within the RIA (Schiff and Winters, 2003). In other words, trade is created when production is reallocated from a high- to a low-cost producer within the RIA, thus allowing for efficiency gains. On the other hand, trade is 'diverted' if reduction/elimination of import tariffs among RIA members allows high-cost producers within the RIA to steal market share from more efficient third-party suppliers who continue to face import tariffs. In this case, trade is diverted from a 'third-party' supplier to a producer within the RIA by virtue of membership of the RIA, and not superior efficiencies.

In practice, however, firms typically possess market power owing to product differentiation and/or scale economies. In this case, the question is whether and how regional integration affects rivalry among firms in the RIA, and how this ultimately impacts welfare. As noted, models of trade factoring in imperfect competition have much larger gains from trade, especially between similar economies. Trade between similar economies often takes the form of trade within the same industries – so-called intra-industry trade. In this case, firms derive market power from the fact that consumers perceive their products to be different (non-homogeneous), implying that each firm faces a downward-sloping demand curve. The question, however, for most RIAs in Africa – e.g., the Southern African Development Community (SADC), the Common Market for Eastern and Southern Africa (Comesa), the West African Economic and Monetary Union – is whether this channel (product differentiation) will yield large enough gains from integration. If countries within the RIA trade according to comparative advantage (typical of developing countries), then product differentiation will have a smaller contribution to gains from integration.[7]

Regional integration can potentially overcome a number of factors negatively affecting the competitiveness of small economies, including a small domestic market size[8] and high concentration.

Firstly, small domestic market size can potentially limit the expansion of domestic firms to reach the MES of production, resulting in failure to realise scale economies. By opening up the regional market to domestic firms, integration potentially relaxes the market size constraint, allowing producers to move down their cost curves and thus enhance competitiveness.

Secondly, small domestic market sizes tend to limit the number of firms that can profitably/optimally operate in the domestic market, and thus tend to cultivate monopolies/oligopolies. High industry concentration reduces firms' incentives to enhance efficiencies, to the detriment of consumers and broader national welfare, particularly when these monopolies operate under tariff and other protectionist measures.[9] Similarly, a small domestic market may limit incumbent firms' incentives to escalate competition by incurring high fixed/sunk costs owing to the small potential returns from such investment (Sutton, 1991, 2006). A RIA can mitigate the inefficiencies associated with the monopolisation of domestic markets by opening up these markets to competition, at least from within the enlarged market. For example, consider three adjacent countries, each with a 'monopoly' producer of cement and applying tariffs to protect their domestic markets. With integration, the tariffs will fall away and the enlarged market will now feature rivalry between three firms, likely resulting in improved x-efficiency and allocative efficiency.[10,11] Thus integration potentially reduces the exercise of monopoly power, promotes competition and enhances welfare.[12] As a corollary, therefore, integration also enhances competitiveness vis-à-vis third-party producers, thus generating long-term gains for the community.

While a RIA will in all likelihood increase competition, the effects on market structure are ambiguous. Market enlargement due to integration could lead to new entry and thus reduction in concentration, provided fixed and/or sunk costs are exogenous. If, however, these costs are endogenous, concentration may actually increase (Sutton, 1991). It is quite plausible that as competition intensifies due to the enlarged market, and especially where products are differentiated, incumbent firms will invest in either quality enhancement, brand image or cost reduction to not only increase their market shares but also to deter entry (Sutton, 1991; Tirole, 1988). If these strategies are successful, a larger market could result in higher industry concentration (but not necessarily less competition).

Realising the potential gains from integration, however, is dependent on a number of factors, including geography, transport costs and exertion of market power – unilateral and/or coordinated. Geography has an important influence on trade. If the population in the RIA is dispersed over a large area, then the natural tendency is to create market regionalisation through small and isolated local markets within the RIA, which favours concentration of industry (Gal, 2001). This will naturally militate against realising the gains from integration. The effects of geography will be exacerbated by weak transport infrastructure and non-competitive logistics sectors. Transport infrastructure and costs are important for trade facilitation. Transport costs can consume away the benefits of tariff reduction, resulting in integration failing to significantly affect trade flows. This suggests that economic and trade infrastructure, particularly transport infrastructure and costs, should be viewed as part of regional integration discussions.

As noted, exerting market power can negate the potential gains from integration. Competition can produce both static gains (allocative efficiency and productive efficiency) and dynamic gains (investment and innovation). Because competition can produce winners and losers, incumbent firms can lobby their governments for protectionist measures, such as regulatory barriers, to defeat competition arising from integration. Domestic distortions such as subsidies and regulations can distort resource allocations within the RIA, thereby negatively affecting trade creation. It is therefore imperative that government industrial policies within the common market area are harmonised, and non-tariff barriers to trade done away with (Peridy and Ghoneim, 2009). National industrial policies can support local entrants, for example by removing regulatory and other entry barriers, and increase competition in the region, but not through undermining integration.

Equally important, governments within the RIA need to harmonise their competition policies, and competition authorities need to standardise their applications of competition policy to create an environment conducive to fair competition. Countries with effective competition policies tend to grow faster than those without because they produce companies that can compete in the local and international markets (Porter, 2002). Recognising the potential dynamic gains through productivity improvements, the objective of competition policy should go beyond the narrow standard of short-term consumer welfare (low prices).

Regional integration, by creating a larger common market, not only benefits incumbent firms within the RIA. A larger market creates opportunities for new entry from within the RIA, and is also likely to attract foreign direct investment. Large third-party suppliers stand to gain from locating production in the RIA and avoiding import tariffs rather than supplying the enlarged market subject to tariffs. At least two benefits come with new entry.

First, new entry intensifies competition within the RIA, thus promoting allocative and productive efficiency, including through its impact on innovation and dynamic effects (the so-called creative destruction) (e.g., Porter, 2002).[13] However, there is also an optimal level of competition, which partly depends on market size (Amsden and Singh, 1994). Many studies have investigated the relationship between competition and innovation (e.g., Aghion, Bloom, Blundell and Howitt, 2005; Aghion, Braun and Fedderke, 2008; Blundell, Griffith and Van Reenan, 1999; Peneder and Woerter, 2013). These studies find an inverted-U relationship between competition and innovation. Vives (2008) provides a theoretical foundation for this relationship. In particular, monopoly/low competition is associated with low innovation, while at the other extreme 'high' competition is also associated with low innovation. This points to the fact that some market power is necessary to induce competitive rivalry, and thus innovation.

Second, and even more important, new entry brings employment opportunities, thus contributing to inclusive growth in the region. Even in models where concentration increases with market enlargement, it turns out that output (and its quality), and thus employment (and its quality), increases with size of the market.

To realise these gains, however, a RIA should do more than just liberalise trade. In particular, infrastructure and trade logistics need to be enhanced, and regulatory and other non-tariff barriers done away with. Countries need to coordinate such investments to ensure maximum economic impact. For example, having a good road network on one side of the border and poor infrastructure on the other side will do little to realise the benefits of trade liberalisation within the RIA. In essence, there is need for broader economic and political cooperation (i.e., deeper integration) in order to fully exploit the benefits of regional integration.

Assessing the record on regional competitive dynamics: Insights from southern and East Africa

Overview and insights from cartels uncovered in South Africa

The regional economic communities (RECs) incorporating countries in southern and eastern Africa each recognise competition as an important part of creating more dynamic regional markets and include competition in their articles. In 2009, SADC member states signed the Declaration on Regional Cooperation in Competition and Consumer Policies. It derives from the SADC Protocol on Trade which requires member states to implement measures to constrain unfair business practices and to foster competition (SADC, 2012). Similarly, the promulgation of the East African Community (EAC) Competition Act in 2006 and the launch of the Comesa Competition Commission in 2013 speak to a growing realisation that the active enforcement of competition law forms part of achieving the broader goals of increased economic participation and development. This also relates to a central theme of this chapter – that anti-competitive conduct can have effects which transcend political borders, and greater cooperation between countries is needed to address those aspects of firm behaviour that undermine common developmental goals.

The adoption of competition law in most REC member states is an acknowledgement that market structure and disciplining the exercise of market power matter for achieving inclusive economic growth. However, most authorities, although active, are severely underresourced and their role poorly understood by decision-making government departments and business and political leaders. In 2016, 17 of the 26 countries forming part of Comesa, the SADC, the Southern African Customs Union (SACU) and the EAC had active competition law regimes (see Bowmans, 2016; GCR, 2013; Gouws, 2013). Despite these challenges, substantial progress has been made across jurisdictions towards greater enforcement of competition law, particularly regarding abuse of dominance cases. Typically, merger control remains the primary activity of many authorities. Less progress has been made in terms of prosecuting cartel conduct, which is perhaps directly linked to the low adoption of leniency programmes and the resource constraints facing authorities. Even less work has gone into understanding and dealing with anticompetitive conduct which has regional dimensions despite the interdependence of most economies across southern and East Africa.

This last aspect is important. The regional scope of anticompetitive conduct is perhaps best demonstrated through examining the record of cartel prosecutions in South Africa. A number of cartels which have been prosecuted by the Competition Commission have affected neighbouring SACU countries in particular (either directly or as a secondary market for South African products) (table 11.1).

Table 11.1 Cartels with cross-border effects prosecuted in South Africa

Cartelised product	Main firms	Countries affected
Scrap metal*	Cape Town Iron and Steel Works, National Scrap Metal, New Reclamation, SA Metal & Machinery Company	Namibia, South Africa
Construction**	Aveng Africa, Basil Read, Group Five, Murray & Roberts, Stefanutti, Wade Walker	Botswana, Burkina Faso, Malawi, South Africa, Zimbabwe
Concrete pipes and culverts***	Aveng (Africa) incl. Aveng (Infraset), Rocla, Swazi Fyfe	Botswana, Mozambique, Namibia, Swaziland, Tanzania, Zambia
Cement†	Lafarge, AfriSam, PPC	Botswana, Lesotho, Namibia, South Africa, Swaziland
Pilings††	Grinaker-LTA (Aveng (Africa)), Esorfranki, Rodio Geotechnics, Dura Soltanche Bachy, Geomechanics, Diabor	Lesotho, South Africa, Swaziland
Steel products†††	Trident Steel (Aveng (Africa)), Macsteel, Highveld	Exports to 'Africa Overland Market', South Africa
Industrial gases∞	Air Products South Africa, Sasol Chemical Industries	Southern African region

Source: Compiled by authors

Notes: *Consent Agreement between Competition Commission and National Scrap Metals (Cape Town) (Pty) Ltd, case no. 51/CR/Aug10.
**Consent Agreements between Competition Commission and Aveng (Africa) Ltd, case no. 2009Feb4279/2009Sep4641; Competition Commission and Murray & Roberts Ltd, case no. 2009May4447; Competition Commission and Stefanutti Stocks Holdings Ltd, case no. 2009Feb4279/2009Sep4641.
***Consent Agreement between Competition Commission and Aveng (Africa) Ltd, case no. 2008Mar3595.
†Consent Agreement between Competition Commission and Lafarge Industries South Africa (Pty) Ltd, case no. 23/CR/Mar12.
††CCSA (2011).
†††Consent Agreement between Competition Agreement and Trident Steel (Pty) Ltd, case no. 114/CR/Dec12.
∞CCSA (2013).

Perhaps the most striking feature of these cartel arrangements is the extent to which they pertained to key industrial products and inputs, including for large infrastructure investment projects. The bottom line is that affected governments and private entities, and taxpayers in particular, have overpaid for a number of important projects that have been affected by anticompetitive arrangements. Recent evidence on the extent of cartel overcharge in South Africa, a measure of the profitability of cartel conduct, suggests that cartel mark-ups are consistent with and in some cases higher than international benchmarks of between 15 and 25% (Khumalo, Mashiane and Roberts, 2014). For example, in concrete pipes the overcharge was estimated to fall in the range of 16.5–28% in Gauteng, and 51–57% in KwaZulu-Natal (Khumalo, Mashiane and Roberts, 2014). In the South African flour cartel, which lasted from 1999 to 2007, mark-ups to independent bakeries were estimated to be in the range of 7–42% (Mncube, 2014).

It is well understood that cartels form in order to maximise the joint profits of their members. The same applies in cartels that operate across the region – through allocating geographic areas to one another and/or agreeing on pricing, they are able to maximise joint profits. To sustain themselves cartels need to block new entrants, such as by making it difficult to access key inputs. In the present context, through allocating country markets, regional cartels appear to have been able to sustain arrangements to prevent further entry and share rents.

In most cases referred to in table 11.1, markets were effectively allocated to different cartelists and prices to be charged were agreed. To our knowledge, there have not been many follow-up investigations in these neighbouring countries, nor have there been claims for damages. This suggests a significant gap in the extent of cooperation between competition authorities as well as in the understanding of the adverse impact of these types of arrangements. Conducting impact assessments on the effects of these regional arrangements and their prosecution would be an important first step in generating support for increased cooperation and allocation of resources towards detecting and prosecuting them. There may be a significant role for RECs in this regard.

A final point regarding cartel conduct in the region is that some of these arrangements, such as in cement, flour and scrap metal, originated from previous interactions between government departments and industry players as part of industry development strategies. For instance, in the scrap metal case, the Department of Trade and Industry in South Africa had a role in encouraging downstream beneficiation and value addition, and in affecting domestic pricing in the metals sector, including facilitating certain interactions between competitors and consumers in the scrap metal industry since 1995.[14] This speaks to the interrelation of government policy and strategies with competition policy, which we discuss as one of the main themes emerging from the recent African Competition Forum (ACF) studies in sugar, cement and poultry industries.

Review of recent studies on regional competitive dynamics

Recent studies do not directly estimate the damage caused by regional arrangements but provide an indication as to the extent of barriers to greater competitive rivalry within the eastern and southern African region. The ACF studies involved research collaboration between competition authorities in six countries (Botswana, Kenya, Namibia, South Africa, Tanzania, Zambia)[15] to understand the regional competitive dynamics in the sugar, cement and poultry sectors. The findings of this pilot research project have highlighted some important cross-cutting themes that affect competition between firms in the region, and patterns of trade and investment. We briefly review the regional structure of each market and draw out the main themes and areas for further research.

Highly concentrated, oligopolistic markets with high structural barriers to entry

The regional industries in sugar, cement and poultry are highly concentrated, reflecting the need to achieve economies of scale in small domestic markets. This is reflective of the fact that both cement and sugar are high-weight, low-value products that are costly to transport. In poultry, economies of scale in production are critical at the grandparent stock and processing/abattoir levels of the market, which is linked, in part, to the high capital outlay required at these levels. This also reflects the pattern of development of the industries in the region, with large multinational firms being present at multiple levels of the value chain.

In cement, many of the same large firms operate and hold controlling interests across the different countries in the study and among smaller independent operators. For instance, in three of the countries, one producer (or group of historically associated producers) accounts for more than 50% of production capacity. In Zambia and Kenya, companies associated with Lafarge through cross-shareholding account for the majority of capacity. In Namibia, recent entrant Ohorongo is effectively the only local producer. Historically in South Africa and the SACU region, three cement firms, Lafarge, Holcim/AfriSam and PPC, have controlled most of the production, including through cross-border cartel arrangements. In Tanzania, the three major firms – Heidelberg (Tanzania Portland Cement), Holcim (Tanga Cement Company) and Lafarge (Mbeya Cement) – are linked to some of the world's largest producers and account for the majority of production. Botswana is largely served by imports from South Africa in addition to small local producers. In the sugar industry, the four countries have highly concentrated markets, with the highest level of concentration by far in Zambia, where multinational firm Zambia Sugar (associated with Illovo Sugar from South Africa, and now owned by Associated British Foods) has a share in excess of 90% of production. In Tanzania, two firms account for 70% of domestic production (not including imports), with the largest being Kilombero (55% owned by Illovo), and Tanganyika Plantation Company, which is owned by Sukari Investments that has interests in Kenya as well. In South Africa, three companies out of six in the industry (Illovo, TSB, Tongaat-Hulett) account for 80% of the market. In this context, Illovo is a regional leader in sugar production with operations in other countries, including Malawi, Mozambique and Swaziland. In Kenya, the four largest producers account for 78% of domestic sugar production although there are more than ten sugar millers in the industry overall.

Finally, the regional poultry industry also consists of a small number of companies operating across all three countries in the study. The main groupings are Astral/Tiger (in South Africa, Botswana, Zambia), Pioneer/Tydstroom/Bokomo/Brink/Irvine's (in South Africa, Botswana, Zambia), Rainbow/Zamchick (in South Africa, Zambia) and Country Bird/Dada/Ross Africa (in South Africa, Botswana, Zambia). Namibia has historically relied on imports. However, Namibia Poultry

Industries is being developed under infant industry protection. In each case, the firms are vertically integrated into various levels of the value chain, including animal feed, primary breeding (including exclusive domain over genetic breeds sourced from international firms), parent stock farms, the production of day-old chicks, growing broilers and processing or abattoirs. It is therefore difficult for independent firms wishing to enter the market and compete at one level of the value chain to do so, given that they often rely on inputs from the vertically integrated multinational firms and on significant capital outlay.

Market structure and poor competitive outcomes reflecting poor policy choices

In each industry under consideration, governments have had a significant role to play in terms of dampening competition in favour of increased investments and infant industry development. While competition policy and industrial policy can be complementary, this requires that the right incentives are given to firms in a manner that encourages effective local entry but stimulates competition as well (Brooks, 2007; Roberts, 2010).

Government policy objectives have been instrumental in shaping the market structure of industries, particularly in cement and sugar. For instance, the cement cartel mentioned above has its roots in industry practices which were condoned by the South African government from as early as the 1920s until 1996. These practices effectively then continued in different forms following the change in legislation regarding these practices. Similarly, the South African sugar industry is widely viewed to operate as a legislated cartel, with the Department of Trade and Industry being party to maintaining the regulatory arrangements that dampen competition by protecting the market from import competition. It is expected that large firms will lobby for regulation which suits their needs in the market, and are more likely to be heard by regulatory and government agencies (Mateus, 2010). While these practices can lead to well-developed industries over time, they also have the effect of dampening competition to the detriment of consumers.

There is therefore a trade-off between the short-term effects of concentration and low levels of competition which harm consumers, and the development of firms through industrial policy strategies. The unfortunate outcome is that in the long run, once firms are established, it is in their interest to protect their position in the market and as such raise strategic barriers to new entry (Mondliwa and Roberts, 2014). The case of the Zambian sugar industry is illustrative.

Zambia Sugar benefited from high levels of investment in capacity in the mid-2000s, encouraged by certain government tax and investment incentives, and protection. Perhaps more than any other firm in Zambia, the company has managed to leverage these incentives to establish a position of significant market power. It is widely accepted that private enterprises, particularly in developing countries, require reasonable and stable rates of profit to sustain their propensity to invest (Singh, 2002). This has been beneficial in terms of the high levels of investment and employment introduced (Zambia now produces more than double the requirements of the local market). However, despite being considered one of the more cost-efficient producers in the region due to investments in new technologies, the prices of sugar in Zambia are relatively high, which has led to recent investigations into excessive pricing against Zambia Sugar. This position of market power is entrenched by a combination of other trade barriers and restrictions put in place by government which prevent foreign firms and imported sugar from competing away the high returns in this market. This is akin to the effect of the brining restrictions in poultry in Zambia, for example, where policies to prevent brined chicken imports mean that import competition is restricted. Due to the scale of investments required in the sugar market, and possibly the high thresholds for firms to qualify for investment incentives, it does not seem that any of the other firms in the market have been able to provide effective competition.

It is clear that the protection of domestic industries is important; indeed, it is this same form of protection which has allowed the South African sugar industry to grow over the years. In Kenya, the government has sought to encourage new entry and provide import protection in sugar. The liberal issuing of licences has led to a market consisting of more than ten millers. However, new entry has not been supported in terms of agricultural policy to develop input markets as well – sugar-cane supplies are extremely poor, resulting in high input costs for millers and high sugar prices which rose even above those in Zambia for several years (Gathiaka and Vilakazi, 2014). This speaks to a miscoordination of policy strategies, which results in harm to consumers and means that entrants cannot become effective domestic and regional competitors.

This is exacerbated by high trade barriers whereby governments control the influx of cheaper sugar to protect domestic producers. Dynamic gains from trade cannot be realised where trade policy conflicts with agricultural and industrial policy objectives. The case of the Tanzanian sugar industry illustrates the fact that managing the price of sugar domestically in the short term is just as important as, and can operate alongside, objectives to invest in the domestic industry. Tanzania has made significant investment in sugar milling and sugar-cane farming capacity and aims to become a net exporter in the next few years. However, the country has also allowed imports, in a controlled manner, into the domestic market to regulate domestic pricing, which has seen the sugar price stabilise in recent years.

The poultry industries in Namibia, Zambia and Botswana follow a similar path in terms of policy to develop the local industry, although each country remains reliant on imports due to limited domestic capacity to produce. There is potential in the industry for firms to gain from cross-border entry and to leverage comparative advantages in key inputs. For instance, the Zambian industry has grown on the back of comparative advantage in a key agricultural input, animal feed. This led, in part, to the entry of Rainbow into the Zambian market through the acquisition of Zamchicks, although this may increase patterns of consolidation in the regional market. Similarly, Country Bird leveraged their access to the Arbor Acres breed to enter South Africa (from their base in Zimbabwe) and compete vigorously. There are therefore gains from trade for firms being able to leverage their advantages in one market into another. Of course, this cannot happen if the same firm is present in each neighbouring market, as demonstrated in the cement case study where Lafarge in Zambia has excess capacity. However, they do not seem to export to countries where they already have a presence. In sugar, Zambia Sugar has excess capacity but there have been limited exports to other countries in the region in which they have a significant presence. This speaks to the role of firms as critical agents in the process of stimulating or restricting greater trade and competition within the region.

Prices reflect low levels of competition and barriers to entry

Competitive outcomes in terms of prices reflect a regional market in which there are clear constraints to greater competition. In each sector, there is evidence of prices which lie above competitive benchmarks. In sugar, although there may be disputes about the factors which constitute costs, prices in both Kenya and Zambia (particularly with a more efficient producer) seem to reflect the constraints imposed by poor choices in terms of industry development policies and policies which have entrenched the market power of incumbent firms, respectively. Estimated ex-factory prices in these countries for 2012 were in the range of 50–100% above world market prices and 30–70% above those in South Africa, which in the context can be considered a reasonable competitive benchmark. Given levels of protectionism and limited competition in the South African market, these differences could be even higher at an ex-factory level. It is important to caution, however, that world market prices in sugar are depressed prices due largely to a legacy of agricultural subsidies in Europe and other large markets.

Cement prices also indicate concerning differences. Notwithstanding the cartel which operated across the whole of SACU until 2009, prices in Zambia and Kenya have been substantially higher than those in South Africa (figure 11.1). This appears to reflect very low levels of competition in these countries, where firms associated with Lafarge have dominated the markets.

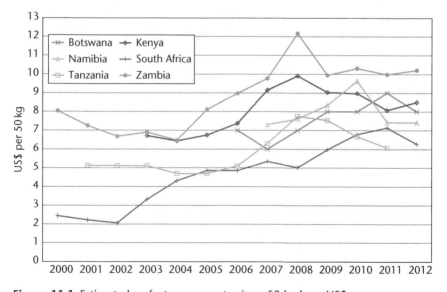

Figure 11.1 Estimated ex-factory cement prices, 50 kg bag, US$

Source: Amunkete et al. (2016)

Levels of effective new entry have remained low in poultry, although there is evidence that where there has been entry, such as by Country Bird in the South African market, there have been benefits in terms of increased competition, as reflected in a significant drop in margins. In the Namibian cement industry, the entry of Ohorongo as a competitor to AfriSam in December 2010 led to a substantial reduction in price in 2011 in nominal currency terms, as well as relative to other countries. In Zambia, the entry of Scirocco Enterprises in 2005 and Zambezi Portland Cement in 2009 saw slight reductions in prices in the following years. However, the positive effects of entry were muted by the fact that these firms entered at very low levels of production capacity to be able to effectively challenge the incumbent, Lafarge Zambia.

Finally, although unrelated to the ACF studies, there is further evidence of the positive effects of new entry in the Zambian and Tanzanian fertiliser industries. Fertiliser markets in the region are largely oligopolistic and dominated by international giants such as Omnia and Yara International. A recent study into competition in the road transportation of fertiliser in Zambia, Malawi and Tanzania shows that new entry into the Zambian fertiliser industry following the uncovering and prosecution of a fertiliser cartel, which lasted from 2007 to 2012, has led to greater price competition. Following the cessation of the cartel, the Export Trading Group, which has grown its share of fertiliser markets in several African countries, brought greater price competition to incumbent cartelists (Nyiombo Investments and Omnia). The growth of the firm in Tanzania has also seen it capture an estimated 20–40% market share, in competition with the dominant incumbent, Yara (Ncube, Roberts and Vilakazi, 2016). Interestingly, in South Africa the same major producers of intermediate fertiliser products, Omnia and Kynoch (then owned by multinational Yara), were found to have engaged in cartel conduct along with Sasol (CCSA, 2010).

These examples highlight the potential for further research into understanding the effects of regional anticompetitive arrangements as well as the impact of entry on domestic and regional markets. Through benchmarking across countries, it becomes possible to quantify the losses and gains to society from competition, or a lack thereof. Importantly, research of this nature can pave the way for motivating, to policy makers and governments in particular, the importance of competition policy as a developmental tool, especially in so far as these arrangements affect key consumer goods and inputs.

Transport and physical barriers to integration

Trade flows are linked to the production and location decisions of firms and the trade policy environment in the region. As discussed, regulatory constraints to trade, including through trade instruments other than tariffs, can sustain the market power of incumbent firms. While the liberalisation of trade through customs unions and the reduction of tariff barriers has increased the scope for greater cross-border trade and competition, a number of constraints remain, such as those relating to rules of origin which require levels of domestic production that underdeveloped countries cannot meet (Edwards and Lawrence, 2010). Furthermore, the experiences in the sugar industry, especially in the cases of Kenya, Tanzania and Zambia, reflect the fact that trade policy affects competitive outcomes in the region in terms of prices and entry. Import quotas are a significant restraint to imports in Kenya, and in Tanzania imports are managed by the state.

In poultry, the available evidence suggests that it costs more to import maize for animal feed from Zambia than from Argentina. Similar concerns were raised by sugar importers in South Africa. This speaks, in part, to constraints in terms of transport infrastructure, the harmonisation of regulations in transportation, as well as delays and costs of transit at border posts. For instance, the study on competition in the transportation of fertiliser in the southern and eastern African regions found that Zambia, as a landlocked state, had improved the levels of competition in its freight sector (and stabilised prices) by improving domestic regulatory measures and increasing efficiency to allow for increased competition in the sector, including from cross-border operators from South Africa and Zimbabwe in particular (Ncube, Roberts and Vilakazi, 2016).

This example illustrates the significance of transportation as an enabler of greater cross-border rivalry. Cross-border competition relies on customers across the region being able to access substitutes in a timely and feasible manner so as to prevent the exercise of market power in a narrow geographic market often delimited by national borders. To take the example of cement, prices in Tanzania are relatively lower than those in neighbouring markets and while the Mbeya Cement (Lafarge) plant is in Tanzania, it is situated just on the border with Zambia, while other plants in Zambia are located further away, nearer to Lusaka. Other things being equal, and absent colonial borders and restrictions, cement produced in this area should serve as a competitive alternative to Zambian cement. However, prices remain vastly different between these areas, which may be due to the fact that Lafarge is also present in Zambia, as well as trade and transport constraints.

These examples illustrate the linkages between trade policy, transportation costs and the strategic location decisions of firms, and the need for further research in this area. Regional integration cannot be achieved where conflicting trade policies across countries, inefficiencies in transportation and the strategic behaviour of firms undermine rivalry between firms across political borders.

Some conclusions and key elements of a research agenda

The competition cases and recent research reviewed above, together with literature on competition and regional integration, highlight a number of key areas for further research.

Firstly, there is strong evidence that anticompetitive arrangements can have a regional dimension. Indeed, cartel arrangements have operated across several countries in key input sectors with high overcharges, which is not unique to the region (see Connor, 2014). There are therefore likely to be significant gains to greater cooperation between competition authorities and further research in detecting these anticompetitive arrangements and quantifying their regional effects. Particular emphasis could be placed on the market behaviour of large multinational firms, including South African players, and their strategic behaviour throughout the region.

Secondly, the research shows that markets in the region are oligopolistic and often dominated by the same large multinational firms operating in small, concentrated markets. These firms have entrenched positions of market power by leveraging close relationships with governments and controlling the location of their production facilities, as well as through 'favourable' trade and physical barriers, such as poor transport networks and regulatory barriers between countries.

Thirdly, strategic and structural barriers have led to poor competitive outcomes in the respective countries and sectors, and in the region more generally, resulting in low levels of new entry as well as limited trade flows. There is therefore scope for new research into the relationships between these different areas of policy and firm conduct towards increasing the potential for greater regional rivalry and integration.

Fourthly, besides understanding regional industrial structures, more studies are needed on industrial and market structures at country and sectoral levels. While there have been several studies on South Africa, for instance, there is still a dearth of studies on the structure and competitiveness of the major industries of most countries in the region, in part because most of the competition authorities in these countries are still young. There is a need for studies that document the nature of competition in these sectors and the welfare costs of anticompetitive arrangements at country and sectoral levels, not least to demonstrate the importance of competitive rivalry for economic development within countries. Such studies could focus on the growth, employment and consumer welfare impacts of anticompetitive conduct by large firms in the respective countries, and would help to strengthen the hand of competition authorities and policy makers.

Finally, the wide acceptance and adoption of competition laws in most countries is a good platform. Quantifying the gains from increased regional rivalry and the losses from anticompetitive arrangements can help to build a case for greater resourcing of competition authorities and RECs to deal with these matters. This will also provide motivation for greater coordination between country policy makers on industrial development and trade policy as they relate to competition. In addition, issues around harmonisation of competition laws and their application across jurisdictions within the RECs is an important area for future research.

Notes

1   For example, North, Wallis and Weingast (2009) highlight the importance of competition in moving to what they characterise as 'open access orders' as opposed to 'limited access orders', but do not analyse the key factors in competitive or uncompetitive outcomes in oligopolistic markets, implicitly assuming that in the absence of artificial barriers to entry markets will approach perfect competition.

2   This is the 'post-Chicago' synthesis.

3   Massimo Motta, lectures.

4   This section draws from Makhaya and Roberts (2014).

5   In perfect competition models, trade is primarily driven by comparative advantage, that is, differences in productivity and/or factor endowments. This trade is also known as inter-industry trade. Orthodox models of regional integration assume perfect competition and homogeneous products. There is hence no rivalry among firms.

6   We abstract here from issues such as 'rules of origin' that may result in tariffs on goods partially produced within the integrated market.

7   Peridy and Ghoneim (2009), in their study of the effects of the Greater Arab Free Trade Area (GAFTA), find small effects from imperfect competition, owing to the fact that most intra-GAFTA trade involves inter-industry trade, with little intra-industry trade. In his study of the growth effects of RIAs, Berthelon (2004) concludes that north–north agreements yield unambiguous and significant positive growth effects while south–south agreements yield ambiguous growth effects, where 'north' is a mnemonic for developed country and 'south' for developing country.

8   It should be noted, however, that a globally competitive industry could develop notwithstanding the small domestic market size. An example is the experience of Nokia in Finland.

9   It is worth pointing out that monopolisation per se is not the evil, but rather the 'lack of contestability'. Lack of competition has negative implications for growth, as it affects incentives to invest, innovate, etc. Indeed, high concentration (monopolisation) could be an endogenous outcome of competition itself (see Sutton, 1991).

10   We say 'likely' for at least two reasons. First, firms could potentially collude and divide the market among themselves, thereby defeating the objective of intensifying competition within the RIA. Second, integration must be completely embraced by the parties and fully implemented. Half-hearted implementation of the RIA provisions may not significantly enhance competition. For example, there is little regional trade in input and final goods markets (e.g., cement, sugar) within the SADC and Comesa RIAs, due at least partly to regulatory barriers and inconsistencies in the support for and enforcement of competition law frameworks.

11   In addition, the enlarged market will now feature differentiated cement products, giving consumers a choice. Consumers will then vote with their purses, forcing a reallocation of production among the three firms (productive efficiency) within the RIA.

12   Integration thus potentially solves one of the major challenges facing competition authorities in small economies – balancing the need to ensure firms are large enough and integrated so as to enjoy economies of scale and ensuring robust rivalry among the firms to ensure allocative and productive efficiency (Gal, 2001).

13   A number of studies find positive growth effects of RIAs. Henrekson, Torstensson and Torstensson (1997) test the growth effects of European integration, namely the European Community (EC) and the European Free Trade Agreement (EFTA). They find that EC/EFTA membership increases growth by about 0.6–0.8 percentage points. Similarly, Berthelon (2004) finds that RIAs largely have positive growth effects.

14   Consent Agreement between Competition Commission and New Reclamation Group, case no. 37/CR/Apr08.

15 The cement study included all six countries; the sugar study looked at Kenya, South Africa, Tanzania and Zambia; and the poultry study assessed the industry in Botswana, Namibia, South Africa and Zambia. See Bagopi et al. (2016); Chisanga et al. (2016); Amunkete et al. (2016).

References

Acemoglu D and J Robinson. 2012. *Why Nations Fail: The Origins of Power, Prosperity, and Poverty*. New York: Crown Business.

Aghion P, N Bloom, R Blundell and P Howitt. 2005. Competition and innovation: An inverted-u relationship. *Quarterly Journal of Economics* 120: 701–728.

Aghion P, M Braun and JW Fedderke. 2008. Competition and productivity growth in South Africa. *Economics of Transition* 16: 741–768.

Amsden A and A Singh. 1994. The optimal degree of competition and dynamic efficiency in Japan and Korea. *European Economic Review* 38: 940–951.

Amunkete T, E Chokwe, G Gabriel, M Humavindu, J Khumalo, T Mbongwe, G Nguruse and BO Nyagol. 2016. Regional cartels and competition in the cement industry across six countries: Botswana, Kenya, Namibia, South Africa, Tanzania and Zambia. In S Roberts (ed.) *Competition in Africa: Insights from Key Industries*, pp. 8–40. Cape Town: HSRC Press.

Bagopi E, E Chokwe, P Halse, J Hausiku, M Humavindu, W Kalapula and S Roberts. 2016. Competition, agro-processing and regional development: The case of the poultry section in South Africa, Botswana, Namibia and Zambia. In S Roberts (ed.) *Competition in Africa: Insights from Key Industries*, pp. 66–101. Cape Town: HSRC Press.

Berthelon M. 2004. *Growth Effects of Regional Integration Agreements*. Central Bank of Chile Working Paper No. 278. http://citeseerx.ist.psu.edu/viewdoc/download?doi=10.1.1.561.7856&rep=rep1&type=pdf.

Blundell R, R Griffith and J van Reenan. 1999. Market share, market value and innovation in a panel of British manufacturing firms. *Review of Economic Studies* 66: 529–554.

Bowmans. 2016. 'An African Firm with a Global Reach' (online document).

Brooks DH. 2007. *Industrial and Competition Policy: Conflict or Complementarity?* Asian Development Bank Institute (ADBI) Research Policy Brief No. 24. http://www.adbi.org/files/rpb24.pdf.

Brusick P and S Evenett. 2008. Should developing countries worry about abuse of dominant power? *Wisconsin Law Review* 2: 269–294.

CCSA (Competition Commission South Africa). 2010. 'Sasol Agrees to Divestiture in the Fertiliser Case'. Media release, 5 July (online document).

CCSA. 2011. 'Competition Commission Refers Pilings Cartel Case to the Competition Tribunal and Settles with Aveng (t/a Steeledale) on Wire Mesh and Rebar Cartels'. Media release, 2 March (online document).

CCSA. 2013. 'Commission Reaches Settlement with Air Products South Africa'. Media release, 28 February (online document).

Chisanga B, J Gathiaka, G Nguruse, S Onyancha and T Vilakazi. 2016. Agricultural development, competition and investment: The case of sugar in Kenya, South Africa, Tanzania and Zambia. In S Roberts (ed.) *Competition in Africa: Insights from Key Industries*, pp. 41–65. Cape Town: HSRC Press.

Connor JM. 2014. 'Price-Fixing Overcharges: Revised 3rd Edition'. February (online document).

Dabbah M. 2010. 'Competition policy, abusive dominance and economic development: Some reflections'. Presented at 37th Annual Conference on International Antitrust Law and Policy, Fordham Competition Law Institute, New York, 24 September.

das Nair R, P Mondliwa and S Roberts. 2012. 'The inter-relationships between regulation and competition enforcement: Regulating for competition? Remedying anti-competitive behaviour through regulation?' Presented at TIPS/Nersa Economic Regulators Conference, Johannesburg, 21–22 August.

Edwards L and RZ Lawrence. 2010. *AGOA Rules: The Intended and Unintended Consequences of Special Fabric Provisions*. National Bureau of Economic Research (NBER) Working Paper No. 16623 (December).

Evans D. 2009. Why different jurisdictions do not (and should not) adopt the same antitrust rules. *Chicago Journal of International Law* 10: 161–188.

Fox E. 2002. What is harm to competition? Exclusionary practices and anticompetitive effect. *Antitrust Law Journal* 70: 372–411.

Fox E. 2003. We protect competition, you protect competitors. *World Competition* 26: 149–165.

Gal M. 2001. Size does matter: The effects of market size on optimal competition policy. *Southern California Law Review* 74: 1437–1478.

Gal M. 2003. *Competition Policy for Small Market Economies*. Boston, MA: Harvard University Press.

Gal M. 2009. Antitrust in a globalised economy: The unique enforcement challenges faced by small and developing jurisdictions. *Fordham International Law Journal* 33: 1–56.

Gathiaka J and T Vilakazi. 2014. 'Regulation, competition and productivity in agriculture: The case of sugar in Kenya benchmarked against South Africa'. Presented at the Second South African Economic Regulators Conference, Johannesburg, March.

GCR (Global Competition Review). 2013. 'Comesa: Overview' (online document).

Gerber D. 2010. *Global Competition: Law, Markets and Globalisation*. Oxford: Oxford University Press.

Geroski P and A Jacquemin. 1984. Dominant firms and their alleged decline. *International Journal of Industrial Organisation* 2: 1–27.

Gouws I-D. 2013. 'African Developments – Mozambique Competition Law' (online document).

Hausmann R, J Hwang and D Rodrik. 2007. What you export matters. *Journal of Economic Growth* 12: 1–25.

Henrekson M, J Torstensson and R Torstensson. 1997. Growth effects of European integration. *European Economic Review* 41: 1537–1557.

Hur JS. 2004. The evolution of competition policy and its impact on economic development in Korea. In P Brusick, AM Alvarez, L Cernat and P Holmes (eds), *Competition, Competitiveness and Development: Lessons from Developing Countries*, pp. 227–249. Geneva: United Nations Conference on Trade and Development.

Khan M. 2006. 'Governance and development'. Paper presented at the Workshop on Governance and Development organised by the World Bank and DFID, Dhaka, 11–12 November.

Khumalo J, J Mashiane and S Roberts. 2014. Harm and overcharge in the South African precast concrete products cartel. *Journal of Competition Law and Economics* 10: 621–646.

Makhaya G, W Mkwananzi and S Roberts. 2012. How should young institutions approach enforcement? Reflections on South Africa's experience. *South African Journal of International Affairs* 19: 43–64.

Makhaya G and S Roberts. 2013. Expectations and outcomes: Considering competition and corporate power in South Africa under democracy. *Review of African Political Economy* 138: 556–571.

Makhaya G and S Roberts. 2014. 'The Changing Strategies of Large Corporations in South Africa under Democracy and the Role of Competition Law'. Centre for Competition, Regulation and Economic Development, University of Johannesburg (online document).

Mateus A. 2010. Competition and development: Towards an institutional foundation for competition enforcement. *World Competition* 33: 275–300.

Mncube L. 2014. The South African wheat flour cartel: Overcharges at the mill. *Journal of Industry, Competition and Trade* 14: 487–509.

Mondliwa P and S Roberts. 2014. 'Review of Economic Regulation of Liquid Fuels and Related Products'. Regulatory Entities Capacity Building Project, Centre for Competition, Regulation and Economic Development, University of Johannesburg (online document).

Ncube P, S Roberts and T Vilakazi. 2016. Regulation and rivalry in transport and supply in the fertilizer industry in Malawi, Tanzania and Zambia. In S Roberts (ed.) *Competition in Africa: Insights from Key Industries*, pp. 102–131. Cape Town: HSRC Press.

North DC, JJ Wallis and B Weingast. 2009. *Violence and Social Orders*. Cambridge: Cambridge University Press.

Page J. 2012. Can Africa industrialise? *Journal of African Economies* 21: ii86–ii125.

Peneder M and M Woerter. 2013. *Competition, R&D and Innovation: Testing the Inverted-U in a Simultaneous System*. Austrian Institute of Economic Research Working Paper No. 488.

Peridy N and A Ghoneim. 2009. Regional integration, imperfect competition and welfare: The experience of the greater Arab free trade area. *Economie Appliquée* 52: 131–156.

Porter M. 2002. 'Competition and Antitrust: A Productivity-Based Approach'. Mimeo (online document).

Rey P and J Tirole. 2006. A primer on foreclosure. In M Armstrong and RH Porter (eds), *Handbook of Industrial Organization* (Vol. 3), pp. 2145–2220. Amsterdam: North Holland.

Roberts S. 2010. Competition policy, competitive rivalry and a developmental state in South Africa. In O Edigheji (ed.), *Constructing a Democratic Developmental State in South Africa: Potentials and Challenges*, pp. 222–237. Cape Town: HSRC Press.

Roberts S. 2013. Competition policy, industrial policy and corporate conduct. In J Lin, J Stiglitz and E Patel (eds), *The Industrial Policy Revolution II: Africa in the 21st Century*, pp. 216–242. Houndmills: Palgrave Macmillan.

Robinson S and K Thierfelder. 2002. Trade liberalization and regional integration: The search for large numbers. *The Australian Journal of Agricultural and Resource Economics* 46: 585–604.

Rodriguez A and A Menon. 2010. *The Limits of Competition Policy: Shortcomings of Antitrust in Developing and Reforming Economies*. The Hague: Kluwer Law International.

Rodrik D. 2007. *Normalizing Industrial Policy*. Commission on Growth and Development Working Paper No. 3. http://siteresources.worldbank.org/EXTPREMNET/Resources/489960-1338997241035/Growth_Commission_Working_Paper_3_Normalizing_Industrial_Policy.pdf.

SADC (Southern African Development Community). 2012. 'Competition Policy' (online document).

Schiff M and LA Winters. 2003. 'Regional Integration and Development'. The International Bank for Reconstruction and Development/The World Bank (online document).

Schmalensee R. 1989. Inter-industry differences of structure and performance. In R Schmalensee and R Willig (eds), *Handbook of Industrial Organization* (Vol. 2), pp. 951–1009. Amsterdam: North Holland.

Singh A. 2002. *Competition and Competition Policy in Emerging Markets: International and Developmental Dimensions*. ESRC Centre for Business Research Working Paper No. 246, University of Cambridge.

Singh A. 2004. *Multi-Lateral Competition Policy and Economic Development*. UNCTAD Series on Issues in Competition Law and Policy. Geneva: United Nations.

Sutton J. 1991. *Sunk Costs and Market Structure*. Cambridge, MA: The MIT Press.

Sutton J. 2004. *Competing in Capabilities: Globalization and Development*. Clarendon Lectures in Economics. Oxford: University of Oxford, Department of Economics.

Sutton J. 2006. 'Market Structure: Theory and Evidence'. Mimeo (online document).

Tirole J. 1988. *The Theory of Industrial Organization*. Cambridge, MA: The MIT Press.

Vickers J. 2005. Abuse of market power. *The Economic Journal* 115: 244–261.

Vickers J. 2007. Competition law and economics: A mid-Atlantic viewpoint. *European Competition Journal* 3: 1–15.

Vives X. 2008. Innovation and competitive pressure. *Journal of Industrial Economics* 56: 419–469.

Whinston M. 2006. *Lectures on Antitrust Economics*. Cambridge, MA: The MIT Press.

Contributors

Brian Chisanga is a research associate at the Indaba Agricultural Policy Research Institute (IAPRI) in Lusaka, Zambia. His research and publications focus on agricultural policy, agricultural marketing and trade for grains, and the welfare of smallholder farmers.

Reena das Nair is a senior researcher at the Centre for Competition, Regulation and Economic Development (CCRED) at the University of Johannesburg, and an economist at Acacia Economics. She has undertaken economic research and provided expert advice in many competition and regulation cases, in several African countries. She has a particular focus on issues related to supermarkets.

Thula Kaira is the founding director of and principal consultant at Optimal Competition and Compliance Solutions based in Lusaka, Zambia. He served as CEO of the Competition Authority in Botswana from 2011 to 2016 and as Executive Director of of the Competition and Consumer Protection Commission of Zambia during the period 2008–2011.

Jonathan Klaaren is professor and former dean of the School of Law at the University of the Witwatersrand in Johannesburg and is also a visiting professor in the Faculty of Humanities with the Wits Institute for Social and Economic Research (WiSER). His current research interests are in the legal profession, economic regulation, public law/human rights, and sociolegal studies in Africa.

Ratshidaho Maphwanya is a principal merger analyst for the Competition Commission of South Africa. His experience spans several economic sectors and industries, and he has worked on a number of the Commission's cases including both merger regulation and investigations into prohibited practices.

Pamela Mondliwa is a researcher at the Centre for Competition, Regulation and Economic Development (CCRED) at the University of Johannesburg and an economist at Acacia Economics. She has published in various journals on the relationship between competition enforcement and economic regulation, and the impact on industrial development.

Gaylor Montmasson-Clair is a senior economist at Trade and Industrial Policy Strategies (TIPS), a South Africa based economic policy think-tank, where he leads work on sustainable growth. He has done extensive research on the transition to a sustainable development pathway from a developing country perspective.

Tapera Muzata is a senior economist at MultiChoice, a broadcast media company, where he provides strategic advice on economics, sector and competition regulation in Africa. He served as a principal economist at the Competition Commission of South Africa and has provided advice to the Competition Tribunal.

Anthea Paelo is a researcher at the Centre for Competition, Regulation and Economic Development (CCRED) at the University of Johannesburg. Her areas of focus include competition economics, regulation, telecommunications, economic development and financial inclusion.

Genna Robb is an economist with Acacia Economics and is a senior research fellow at the Centre for Competition, Regulation and Economic Development (CCRED) at the University of Johannesburg. She served as an economist at the Competition Commission of South Africa and has consulted widely to regulators, government and private companies in South Africa and the region.

Simon Roberts is a professor of economics and executive director of the Centre for Competition, Regulation and Economic Development (CCRED) at the University of Johannesburg. He held the position of chief economist and manager of the Research and Policy Division at the Competition Commission of South Africa from 2006 to 2012. He has published widely in his areas of research, including industrial policy, economic development, competition policy and international trade as well as research and advisory work with, and for, many organisations across southern and eastern Africa.

Witness Simbanegavi is currently the director of research at the African Economic Research Consortium (AERC). He was previously chief director in the Microeconomic Policy and Analysis Unit of the South African National Treasury and has published in leading academic journals such as the *Journal of International Money and Finance* and the *Journal of African Economies*.

Nicholas J. Sitko is assistant professor of International Development in the Department of Agriculture, Food and Resource Economics at Michigan State University. His current research interests focus on land policy and administration, public spending and poverty reduction, and the institutional constraints to food market development in Africa.

Isaac Tausha is a research analytical officer with the Zimbabwe Competition and Tariff Commission. His most recent research has been in the telecommunications sector and the tobacco and beef sectors of agriculture markets.

Imraan Valodia is professor of Economics and dean of the Faculty of Commerce, Law and Management at the University of the Witwatersrand, Johannesburg. His research interests include employment, the informal economy, gender and economic policy, and industrial development. He is a part-time member of the Competition Tribunal and a commissioner on the South African Employment Conditions Commission.

Thando Vilakazi is a senior economist at the Centre for Competition, Regulation and Economic Development (CCRED) at the University of Johannesburg and an economist at Acacia Economics. He has conducted competition law investigations in a range of sectors and provided advisory services to competition authorities, regulators and private enterprises in South Africa and various other African countries.

Tatenda Zengeni is an economist at the Centre for Competition, Regulation and Economic Development (CCRED) at the University of Johannesburg. Prior to joining CCRED Tatenda worked as an economist at the Competition and Tariff Commission in Zimbabwe.

Index

Printed and bound by CPI Group (UK) Ltd, Croydon, CR0 4YY

16/04/2025

14658447-0005